U0008015

貓派狗派 都是台派！Team cat or team dog, we're all team Taiwan!

Good Eye

City Guide
台灣挑剔指南

TAIWAN

Guo Pei-Ling And Her Amazing Friends　**郭佩怜**和她厲害的朋友們———著

CONTENTS
目錄

VOLUME 1 :
NORTHERN TAIWAN
第一輯——北台灣

VOLUME 2 :
CENTRAL TAIWAN
第二輯——中台灣

PREFACE
作者序

Good Eye City Guide: Taiwan is the sequel to *Good Eye City Guide: Taipei*, which came out in the spring of 2017. Thinking back to February 2020 when *Good Eye City Guide: Taiwan* was released, COVID-19 had just started, and global travel restrictions hit the tourism industry hard. I thought the guide might be affected too, but thanks to our wonderful readers, it stayed in demand over the past four years and even got reprinted and updated a few times. I am so grateful for this.

In 2022, when the borders reopened, Taiwan became a hot search term on travel sites like Airbnb, Skyscanner, and Expedia. The island's delicious food, beautiful scenery, and excellent safety record drew the eyes of international travelers. Plus, from 2016 to 2024, under the leadership of former President Tsai Ing-wen and the hard work of the Taiwanese people, Taiwan achieved amazing things. These include impressive pandemic prevention, strong tech capabilities, and becoming the first country in Asia to legalize same-sex marriage (with Taiwanese drag queen Nymphia Wind winning the 16th season of "*RuPaul's Drag Race*" in 2024!).

In addition to the Taiwan you may already know, this guide aims to offer a true Taiwanese perspective, helping you explore the everyday scenes and creativity that make Taiwan so special. The spots and shops featured, from newly opened indie bookstores and secret bars to traditional markets and street vendors, are all places the authors wholeheartedly recommend to friends.

Right now, more than ever, we need support and goodwill from around the world. I believe the charm and warmth of this island will make every traveler a true Friend of Taiwan.

《台灣挑剔指南》是 2017 年春天出版的《台北挑剔指南》的續作。回想起 2020 年 2 月《台灣挑剔指南》出版時，武漢肺炎剛爆發，全球邊境管制讓旅遊業大受打擊。本以為指南也會受到影響，但多虧了讀者們的支持，這本指南在四年間穩定銷售，甚至有機會改版，在此衷心感謝。

2022 年國境開放後，台灣躍升為 Airbnb、Skyscanner 和 Expedia 等旅遊平台的熱門搜尋關鍵字。除了美食、美景和良好的治安吸引了國際旅客的目光外，2016 至 2024 年間，在蔡英文前總統、執政團隊與台灣人民的共同努力下，亮眼的防疫成績、強大的科技實力，以及成為亞洲首個通過同婚的國家（2024 年台灣變裝皇后妮妃雅 Nymphia Wind 在《魯保羅變裝皇后秀》摘下第 16 季冠軍！）等表現，也都讓台灣備受矚目。

除了上述你可能已經認識的台灣外，這本指南希望提供台灣人的視角，讓你深入了解台灣的日常風景與創意，收錄的景點與店家，從新開的獨立書店、祕密酒吧到菜市場與路邊攤，都是作者群們誠心推薦給朋友的地方。

此時此刻，我們比以往更需要來自各界的支持與善意。我相信這座島嶼的魅力與可愛，能讓每位旅人都成為堅實的台派。

Pei-Ling Guo
郭佩怜

INTRODUCTION TO TAIWAN

台灣簡介

馬祖
Matsu

金門
Kinmen

澎湖
Penghu

基隆
Keelung

桃園
Taoyuan

臺北
Taipei

新北
New Taipei

新竹
Hsinchu

苗栗
Miaoli

宜蘭
Yilan

臺中
Taichung

彰化
Changhua

雲林
Yunlin

南投
Nantou

花蓮
Hualien

嘉義
Chiayi

臺南
Tainan

高雄
Kaohsiung

臺東
Taitung

屏東
Pingtung

綠島
Green Island

蘭嶼
Lanyu

來台第一守則 FIRST RULE OF VISITING TAIWAN

台灣是一主權獨立的民主國家，請稱呼我們為台灣人 (Taiwanese)，這會讓你在台灣人心中好感度倍增！

Taiwan is a democratic country with independent sovereignty. To call us Taiwanese will make Taiwanese like you even more.

人口 POPULATION

約 2 千 3 百萬人，人口密度僅次於孟加拉。

Approximately 23,000,000. Population density lower only than Bangladesh.

地理位置 LOCATION

台灣位於東亞，為一在太平洋上的島嶼，與香港、日本及菲律賓相鄰。

Situated in East Asia, Taiwan is a group of islands in the Pacific Ocean, neighboring Hongkong, Japan, and the Philippines.

簽證 VISAS

目前共有 48 個國家的公民入境台灣無需辦理簽證，更多資訊請參考外交部網站 www.boca.gov.tw。

Currently, citizens of 48 countries may come to Taiwan without applying for an entry Visa.

For more information, please visit www.boca.gov.tw

語言 LANGUAGE

台灣華語（與中國普通話口音不同，書寫體則有繁簡之別）、台灣台語、客家語、各原住民族語。

The official language of Taiwan is Mandarin Chinese. Dialects include Taiwanese, Hakkanese, and the various languages of the indigenous tribes. It is worth noting that in Taiwan, Mandarin is spoken with a different accent than that of China; also, in written form, Taiwan uses traditional Chinese characters while China uses simplified characters.

天氣 CLIMATE

台灣全年多雨，夏天相當悶熱；春秋兩季較適合旅行；冬天因無室內暖氣，體感溫度可能比實際溫度更低。台灣經常下雨，隨身攜帶摺疊傘是明智的選擇。

There is no dry season in Taiwan. Summer is hot and humid. Spring and autumn are the best times to travel. There is no indoor heating in most places so it might feel colder than the actual temperature during winter. Keeping a collapsible umbrella in your pack is wise since occasional rain is very likely year-round in Taiwan.

宗教 RELIGION

台灣宗教多元包容，多數信仰佛教、道教與民間信仰，也有基督教、天主教與伊斯蘭教徒。

Taiwan has a diverse religious culture. Buddhism, Taoism, and folk religions make up the majority, while Christianity, Catholicism, and Islam are also prevalent.

歷史 HISTORY

台灣自舊石器時代以來就有人類居住，為南島語系原住民族世居之地。17 世紀開始台灣歷經荷蘭、西班牙、中國與日本統治，命運多舛。二戰後中國發生國共內戰，國民黨撤退來台，以反共為名實施威權統治，台灣進入白色恐怖時代。在黨外人士多年抗爭下，台灣終於在 1986 年成立第二個政黨「民主進黨」，並在 1987 年解嚴，2000 年完成首次政黨輪替，並於 2016 年誕生了台灣第一位女性總統。

更多台灣歷史可參考《臺灣歷史圖說》，或在 YouTube 觀看由「台灣吧」（@TaiwanBar）製作的《動畫臺灣史》。（兩者皆有英文翻譯）

Humans have resided on the island of Taiwan since Palaeolithic times. It is also home to many indigenous Austronesian people. Since the 17th century, Taiwan has undergone colonization by the Netherlands, Spain, China, and Japan. After World War II, the Chinese Civil War between the KMT (the Kuomintang of China) and the Communist Party of China broke out in China. Afterwards, the defeated KMT fled to Taiwan and used an anti-communist stance to start an authoritarian government. Taiwan then entered the so-called White Terror period. Through years of protests and endeavors from numerous activists outside the ruling party, the DPP (Democratic Progressive Party), the second most prominent political party in Taiwan, was founded in 1986, contributing to the lifting of martial law. In the year 2000, the Taiwanese government instituted first party alternation. In 2016, the first woman Taiwanese president was elected.

For more history about Taiwan, please read *A New Illustrated History of Taiwan* by Wan-yao Chou or watch the animation series Taiwan History produced by Taiwan Bar via YouTube @TaiwanBar (both available in English.)

節慶與活動 FESTIVALS AND EVENTS

台灣農曆過年時（國曆 1 或 2 月）多數店家與景點不營業，可避免在此時造訪台灣。其餘活動可參考各縣市基本資訊頁。

You might want to avoid visiting Taiwan during Chinese New Year (January or February) since most businesses and sightseeing spots are closed. For other events, please see the basic information in each chapter.

簡易假期安排建議 RECOMMENDED ITINERARIES FOR SHORT TRIPS

若是時間不多，建議留在台北市區，搭配陽明山踏青、北投泡湯或淡水散步行程即可。若時間充裕，推薦先往花東走，感受台灣大自然與慢活的魅力。若是愛吃鬼，可以直奔台南。

If your time is limited, I recommend staying in Taipei and going for a hike in Yangmingshan, enjoying the hot springs in Beitou, or taking a stroll in Tamsui. If you plan for a longer trip, Hualien and Taitung are recommended for experiencing Taiwan's natural charms and slow-living scene. If you are a food lover, make Tainan your ultimate destination.

TRANSPORTATION
交通

桃園國際機場 TAOYUAN INTERNATIONAL AIRPORT

搭乘機場捷運直搭車約 35 分鐘可到達台北車站。除此之外也可搭高鐵或巴士，再轉乘捷運或計程車到達下榻地點。若在機場搭計程車到台北市區，費用約為新台幣 1,000 左右。

It takes about 35 minutes to travel to Taipei Main Station from the airport by the fast trains of the Taoyuan Metro, also known as the airport express. HSR (High Speed Rail) and shuttle buses also provide excellent transportation from the airport to Taipei City, where travelers can then reach their accommodations via Taipei MRT or taxi. Taxi fare from the airport to Taipei City is about NTD 1,000.

www.taoyuan-airport.com

國內機場 DOMESTIC AIRPORTS

若想到花東、離島旅遊，最舒適便捷的方式為搭乘國內航班，更多資訊可參考 www.taiwan.net.tw/m1.aspx?sNo=0020503

The most comfortable and quickest way to travel to Hualien, Taitung, and the offshore islands is by domestic flight. For more information, please visit

www.taiwan.net.tw/m1.aspx?sNo=0020503

高鐵 HSR (HIGH SPEED RAIL)

在台灣西部旅遊，高鐵是最快速的交通工具，儘管大部分高鐵站離市區都有些距離，但接駁或轉乘都相當方便。

HSR is the most efficient way to travel in western Taiwan. Although most HSR stations are not in city areas, transfer and shuttle services are fairly convenient.

www.thsrc.com.tw

台鐵 TRA (TAIWAN RAILWAYS ADMINISTRATION)

台鐵四通八達、價格實惠，尤其旅行花東，台鐵是多數人的選擇。可上官網查詢時刻與訂票，若不熟悉系統，建議直接至各地火車站購票。

TRA is affordable and ramifies across most of the country. Especially in Hualien and Taitung, TRA is the first choice for most travelers. Check timetables and book tickets via their official website, or if you are not familiar with their online system, just head to any train station to get tickets.

tip.railway.gov.tw

台灣好行 TAIWAN TOURIST SHUTTLE SERVICE

若是自己一人旅行不好包車，也可以參考交通部觀光局主辦的「台灣好行」，有多條從各大交通結點至熱門景點的公車服務，方便自主旅行者規劃行程。

If you are traveling alone and do not feel like hiring a chauffeur, the Taiwan Tourist Shuttle service might be a good option. It operates various routes connecting main transportation hubs to popular sightseeing spots, offering a convenient way for independent travelers to plan their itineraries.

www.taiwantrip.com.tw

大眾運輸 PUBLIC TRANSPORTATION

台灣目前在台北、高雄有捷運可搭乘，其他縣市仍以公車為主，多數城市也有公眾自行車租借系統。建議在車站或便利商店購買可加值的悠遊卡或一卡通，可使用於上述交通工具與便利商店付款。更多資訊可參考本頁最後方網站。

Metro systems are currently available in Taipei and Kaohsiung, while other regions employ city buses as the principal method of public transportation. Public bike rental services are available in most cities. Buying an EasyCard or iPASS at any train station or convenience store is advisable as they are accepted by the above services as well as convenience stores. For more information, please see the websites listed at the end of this page.

YOUBIKE (PUBLIC BIKE RENTAL SERVICE)

在城市漫遊相當推薦租借 YouBike。可使用台灣手機門號加入會員，或直接以信用卡付費，只要至租賃站的 Kiosk (自動服務機) 申辦即可。

I highly recommend renting YouBike when exploring urban areas. You can register for membership using a Taiwanese cell-phone number or by paying via credit card. Tourists can also apply for one-time rentals through the YouBike Kiosk (automated rental machine) located at all rental spots.

計程車 TAXI / UBER

若已是 Uber 使用者，在台灣可繼續使用；台灣計程車車身一律漆為黃色，相當容易辨認，個人建議搭乘台灣大車隊或 Line Go 的車輛。

Uber users can continue to use this service in Taiwan. Taiwanese taxis are all painted yellow and easy to identify; I personally recommend riding with Taiwan Taxi or Line Go.

包車 CHAUFFEUR TAXI SERVICE

若到花東或其他觀光景點旅行，交通可能不好安排，若有預算可考慮包車，更多資訊請參考 P. 19 的旅遊服務推薦，可搜尋適合自己的產品。

It might not be easy to arrange transportation when traveling in Hualien, Taitung, and certain sightseeing spots. If your budget permits, a chauffeur taxi service is a viable option. For more information, please see travel service recommendations on p.19 and look for an option that suits your needs.

其他資訊 OTHER INFORMATION

完整的台灣交通資訊，請參考交通部觀光局網站。

For more information about transportation in Taiwan, please visit the Tourism Bureau's official website:

中文 Chinese: www.taiwan.net.tw/m1.aspx?sNo=0000115

英文 English: eng.taiwan.net.tw/m1.aspx?sNo=0029022

（最重要的）無線網路 (MOST IMPORTANTLY) WI-FI

建議抵達機場後買張有 Wi-Fi 的 SIM 卡，或是租借分享器。

I would suggest that travelers either buy a SIM card with Wi-Fi at the airport or rent a portable Wi-Fi router.

時區 TIME ZONE

GMT+8

貨幣 CURRENCY

新台幣，由於非國際主要貨幣，建議在抵達與離境時兌換新台幣與原國家幣別。

The New Taiwan Dollar (NTD) is not a major international currency; therefore, it is advisable for international travelers to exchange currency upon arrival and departure.

插頭 ELECTRICITY

電壓 110 V, 60 Hz (2 片扁腳的插頭)。

Electrical sockets in Taiwan supply 110 V of electricity at 60 Hz. Sockets are compatible with Type A plugs which have two flat parallel prongs.

水 WATER

不能直接飲用自來水，需另外購入或是自行過濾後煮開。

Tap water isn't directly potable, but is perfectly safe once filtered or boiled. Bottled water is also readily available.

緊急聯絡電話 EMERGENCY NUMBERS

警察局 Police: 110

24 小時免付費旅遊諮詢熱線 24/7 Toll Free Traveling Service Hotline: 0800-011-765

商家營業時間 BUSINESS HOURS

大部分店家除公休日外，全年 10:00 到 20:00 左右皆有營業（更晚也還有夜市與酒吧等，不用擔心找不到東西吃或逛！）

Most shops are open from 10:00 to 20:00, except on scheduled holidays. Bars and night markets are open until quite late, so travelers need not worry about having nowhere to go!

郵寄 POSTAL SERVICE

郵票除了在郵局也能在便利商店購買，郵局營業時間大多為星期一到五的 08:00 到 17:00，信件可自行投入郵筒。

Stamps can be bought in post offices and convenience stores. Post offices operate from 08:00 to 17:00 Monday to Friday. Local and international letters can be thrown into postboxes.

環保 ENVIRONMENTAL AWARENESS

為響應環保，台灣許多店家不主動提供塑膠袋與塑膠吸管，建議可自備購物袋與環保吸管。

In order to promote environmentally friendly shopping in Taiwan, many stores refrain from providing complimentary plastic bags or straws. It is advisable to bring your own shopping bags and reusable straws.

消費 LIVING EXPENSES

以台北為準，其他縣市稍低。

礦泉水 **NTD 25**
早餐（蛋餅 + 小杯紅茶）**NTD 50**
午餐（小吃店）**NTD 100–200**
晚餐（餐廳正餐 + 飲品）**NTD 300–1,000**
住宿（雙人房）**NTD 2,000+**
調酒 **NTD 300**

Using Taipei as the standard, other regions will be slightly cheaper.

Bottled water **NTD 25**
Breakfast (egg omelette and small black tea) **NTD 50**
Lunch (local eatery) **NTD 100–200**
Dinner (meal with drink in restaurants) **NTD 300–1,000**
Accommodations (two-person) **NTD 2,000+**
Cocktail **NTD 300**

小費 TIPPING

台灣沒有小費制度，部分餐廳或店家已將 10% 服務費計入帳單，不須另外給。

There is no tipping in Taiwan. Some restaurants and shops include a 10 percent service charge in the bill.

FOOD
飲食

台灣堪稱美食天堂，早上從廟口小吃、街角的台式早餐店到早午餐，
接著一天有台式與各國料理可供選擇，一路吃到夜市再到深夜食堂，來台灣必須做好變胖的心理準備。

本書因篇幅有限，以下提供更多美食資訊來源：

Taiwan is a heaven for food lovers. From street food in front of temples, Taiwanese-style breakfast eateries on street corners, western-style brunch spots, night markets, to late-night restaurants, all sorts of Taiwanese and foreign cuisine is available to you. Be prepared to gain some weight when traveling here.

Due to space limitations, the following are some tools to aid in your search for Taiwanese delicacies:

書籍 BOOK：Michelin Guide Taipei

米其林台北指南在 2018 年首度發布，2019 年共有 24 間星級餐廳、58 間「必比登推介」餐廳上榜。

Michelin Guide Taipei was released in 2018. A total of 24 restaurants were awarded stars while 58 received Bib Gourmands in 2019.

guide.michelin.com/tw/taipei

網站 WEBSITE：a hungry girl's guide to taipei

台北美食網誌，可依地區和食物類別搜尋，內容十分詳盡，推薦給外國友人。

I highly recommend this detailed and comprehensive food blog that allows you to search for restaurants according to location and type of cuisine.

hungryintaipei.blogspot.tw

食譜 COOKBOOK：The Food of Taiwan

由台美混血的紐約美食作家 Cathy Erway 撰寫，可跟著做一解回國後吃不到台灣美食的苦。

Written by Cathy Erway, a food writer of Taiwanese-American descent based in New York, this cookbook helps you replicate some of the Taiwanese dishes you are sure to miss after you leave Taiwan.

素食 VEGETARIAN OPTIONS

台灣吃素人口眾多，許多人因為宗教或健康因素茹素，因此本來就有眾多素食選擇。從街角麵攤、自助餐到高檔餐廳，甚至葷食餐廳也多半提供素食餐點。更多資訊可參考：

As Taiwan is home to a fair number of vegetarians due to religious or health reasons, there are lots of options for vegetarians, from local eateries and cafeterias to fancy restaurants. Even most non-vegetarian restaurants offer meat-free meals. For more information, please check out:

1. Happy Cow: www.happycow.net
2. Food x Travel The Taiwan Guide to Vegan & Vegetarian Dining (Online PDF published by Tourism Bureau)
3. Vegan Taiwan: vegantaiwan.blogspot.tw
4. Taipei Vegan Map: goo.gl/maps/1wjqCDZLbYL2

報導 MEDIA COVERAGE：
40 of the best Taiwanese foods and drinks

CNN 於 2015 年刊登的文章，獲得廣大迴響，可一次認識台灣美食

Article offering a brief introduction to Taiwanese delicacies published by CNN in 2015, and receiving critical acclaim.

edition.cnn.com/travel/article/40-taiwan-food/index.html

Foodie Instagrams：
@taipeieater, @taipeifoodie, @foodie.taiwan

除了上述三個用心經營的 Instagramer 外，也可用關鍵字搜尋台灣美食。

Besides the three diligent Instagramers mentioned above, you can also use keyword searches.

料理教室 COOKING CLASSES：
Ivy's Kitchen, Cookinn Taiwan

想體驗製作台灣料理，可到這兩家位於台北的料理教室報名課程，網路搜尋名稱都能找到網站。

Interested in learning how to make Taiwanese cuisine? Check out the websites of these two Taipei cooking classrooms and sign up for classes.

酒吧 BARS

多數特色酒吧還是集中在台北，但其他大城市如台中、台南與高雄也有一些好店，更多資訊可參考各縣市酒吧推薦，或是 GQ 的 Bar 專欄、活動「Bar Surfing」的清單與「Thirsty in Taipei」網站。

Not surprisingly, you will find most of Taiwan's unique and eccentric bars in Taipei. However, there are also several great bars located in Taichung, Tainan, and Kaohsiung. For more information, please see the recommended bars listed in each chapter, the GQ Bar column, the list of names in the annual Bar Surfing event, and the Thirsty in Taipei website.

www.gq.com.tw/tag/bar

www.barsurfing.tw/route.html#all-list

www.thirstyintaipei.com

台灣行不能錯過的食物 FOOD YOU SHOULD NOT MISS WHILE TRAVELING IN TAIWAN

水果 FRUIT

台灣水果的高品質與多元性世界少見，嘴巴被養刁的台灣人出國如果吃到不甜的水果還會生氣。跑一趟菜市場、水果店或超市採買，西瓜、香蕉、芒果、蓮霧等都是香甜保證。更多季節水果資訊請參考「農業易遊網」ezgo.ardswc.gov.tw/Fruit/TW/Season_Fruits_All

如果想在回國後回味台灣水果，也推薦購買果乾或果醬，其中推薦獲得世界柑橘類果醬大賽雙金牌肯定的「好食光果醬」(facebook.com/keyajam)。

It's rare to find fruit in such high quality and diversity in any other place in the world as in Taiwan. Some fussy Taiwanese even get mad when they taste the flavorless fruit in other countries. Make a trip to a traditional market, fruit shop, or supermarket and get some watermelons, bananas, mangoes, and wax apples, all of which are sure to be juicy and sweet. For more information about seasonal fruit, please visit Agri Ezgo (ezgo.ardswc.gov.tw/Fruit/TW/Season_Fruits_All)

If you want to continue to savor Taiwanese fruit after leaving Taiwan, I recommend getting some dehydrated fruit products or preserved jams. Among all available brands, I recommend Keya Jam which has recently won two gold prizes in the World's Original Marmalade Awards & Festival. (facebook.com/keyajam)

茶 TEA

若詢問有無推薦的伴手禮時，淡雅的台灣烏龍茶是我心中首選。依產地、品種與製程的不同，烏龍茶也有千變萬化的姿態，更有許多品牌可供選擇，無論是茶包或散裝茶，都能簡單泡出好滋味。更多台灣茶資訊可參考文章〈Taiwan's Top 10 Most Famous Teas〉https://eco-cha.com/blogs/news/taiwans-most-famous-teas

Whenever asked about gift ideas, the mild and elegant Taiwanese oolong tea is always my first choice. Depending on region, cultivar, and production methods, oolong tea can exhibit endless different flavors and forms. Not only available from a variety of brands, oolong tea also comes in a variety of packaging options such as tea bags and loose-leaf tea, either of which is perfect for making a nice, convenient cup of tea. For more information about Taiwanese teas, this article about Taiwan's Top 10 Most Famous Teas at eco-cha.com/blogs/news/taiwans-most-famous-teas is a good resource.

咖啡 COFFEE

台灣人愛喝咖啡超乎想像，從便利商店、連鎖店到世界級咖啡師經營的咖啡館應有盡有。台灣除了自己種咖啡豆外，還有以「From Coffee Bean to Bar」概念研發的咖啡 bar 創新品牌「COFE」值得一試。尋找台灣咖啡廳推薦使用網站「Café Nomad」cafénomad.tw

The Taiwanese passion for coffee goes far beyond what you might expect. You can find coffee sold in convenience stores, chain coffee shops, and cafés operated by world-class baristas. Coffee plants are also cultivated and harvested in Taiwan. Give COFE a try, the innovative coffee bar promoting the idea of "from coffee bean to bar." The Café Nomad website is a recommended resource when searching for cafés in Taiwan: cafénomad.tw/en

手搖飲 BOBA DRINKS

台灣國民飲品「珍珠奶茶」風靡全世界，在日本尤其誇張，各種創意珍珠料理連台灣人都嚇壞了！不過街邊隨處可見的手搖飲店，除了珍奶外還有更多選擇，也可自由選擇糖度與冰塊量，在天氣炎熱的台灣生活，來杯冷涼的手搖飲是生存必需。更多資訊可參考文章〈Boba Explained: A Taxonomy of Taipei's Bubble Tea〉www.eater.com/2019/3/6/18240387/boba-milk-bubble-tea-explained-how-to-order。

Taiwanese bubble milk tea is now a popular trend around the globe, especially in Japan where the Japanese have invented all kinds of foods topped with tapioca balls that even the Taiwanese wouldn't fancy. Visible on almost every street in Taiwan, bubble milk tea shops not only offer the notorious bubble milk tea, also known as pearl milk tea, but also different teas, juices, and other beverages for you to mix and match. Moreover, you can customize the amount of sugar and ice to your liking. A serving of refreshing bubble milk tea in the scorching Taiwanese summer is simply a matter of survival. For more information, the article Boba Explained: A Taxonomy of Taipei's Bubble milk tea is available online at www.eater.com/2019/3/6/18240387/boba-milk-bubble-tea-explained-how-to-order.

酒 ALCOHOL

「乾杯」、「乎乾啦」是台灣人豪爽的典型表現之一，愛喝的你千萬不能錯過台啤金牌、金車威士忌、高粱、小米酒、霧峰農會的「初霧」系列、威石東葡萄酒與各式精釀啤酒如「台虎精釀」與「北台灣啤酒」等好酒，在超商或超市就能找到。

"Ganbei!" in Madarin Chinese and "Hodala!" in the Taiwanese dialect both mean "cheers" or "empty the glass" and are typical demonstrations of the straightforward and generous character of the Taiwanese people. If you enjoy alcoholic drinks, don't miss Taiwan Beer's Gold Medal product, Kavalan's whiskey, Wu-Feng Farmers' Association Distillery's shochu and sake collections, Weightstone's wines, the craft beer from micro-brewers such as Taihu Brewing and North Taiwan Brewing, sorghum liquor, and millet wine—all of which are available in convenience stores and supermarkets.

購物 SHOPPING

果乾、果醬、茶葉、咖啡豆、酒與其他厲害的台灣農產如米、蜂蜜、醬料與乾貨等，可到各地農夫市集、食品雜貨店或誠品選購。

Besides the fruit preserves, jams, teas, coffee beans, and alcohol mentioned above, more awesome Taiwanese products including rice, honey, assorted condiments, and dry ingredients are recommended and available in local farmers' markets, grocery stores, or Eslite Bookstores.

NATURAL ENVIRONMENT
自然生態

四面環海的台灣有著豐富的自然生態，超過 3,000 公尺的山峰就有兩百多座，
只要來一趟就能體驗各式戶外運動，如衝浪、潛水、登山、攀岩等，吸引許多熱愛大自然的外國旅客。
本書雖然是一本風格城市旅遊書，但也希望能盡力提供這方面的資訊，
除了下面介紹的各別網站外，也十分推薦使用「KKday」與「Klook」兩個旅遊體驗預訂平台。

The islands of Taiwan have a diverse natural environment.
It has more than 200 mountains that are over 3,000 meters tall. Various outdoor activities including surfing,
diving, hiking, and rock climbing attract large numbers of nature-loving foreign travelers.

Although this book is mainly focused on arts and culture, I do my best to provide relevant information
regarding outdoor activities. Besides the websites mentioned below, I also recommend checking these two
travel and booking platforms: KKday and Klook.

自行車 CYCLING

捷安特旅行社 Giant Adventure

捷安特是發源自台灣的全球知名自行車品牌，也成立旅行社推
出豐富的自行車遊台灣行程，網站有中、英、日三語，滿足外
國遊客需求。

Giant, a world-famous bicycle brand originating in Taiwan, now
also operates a travel agency providing various cycling tours.
Their website is available in Chinese, English, and Japanese.

www.giantcyclingworld.com/travel

馬修單車 MathewBike

位於台北士林、深受好評的單車店，提供單車出租、單車補給、
旅遊計畫等服務。

Located in Shilin District of Taipei, this acclaimed bike shop
offers bike rental, repair, maintenance, support vehicles for bike
travel, and bike travel planning services.

mathewbike.com/en

登山 HIKING

Taiwan Adventures

提供一日到多日的各式登山行程，推廣台灣美麗的山林文化。

Offering single-day and multi-day hiking tours to promote the
culture of Taiwan's beautiful mountains and forests.

taiwan-adventures.com

藍天遨遊 Blue Skies Adventures

以東北亞第一高峰玉山登山團為重點行程，提供各式戶外活動。

Climbing tour of Jade Mountain, the highest peak in Northeast
Asia, as their spotlight itinerary, also offering other outdoor
activities.

www.blueskiesadventures.com.tw

綜合戶外 OTHER OUTDOOR ACTIVITIES

Taiwan Adventure Outings

提供各式戶外活動，除上述活動外還有溯溪、露營等多元選擇。

Offers various outdoor activities and itineraries including river
tracing, camping and more.

taoutings.com

衝浪 SURFING

Rising Sun Surf Inn

位於北部浪點宜蘭外澳的老字號衝浪旅店，提供教學課程，需
先以 email 預約。

Established surfers' guesthouse situated in one of the prime
surfing spots in northern Taiwan, Wai'ao Beach in Yilan County,
offering coaching classes by advance email request only.

Email: risingsunsurfinn@gmail.com | www.risingsunsurfinn.com

阿飛粉絲團 Afei Fans Club

墾丁、佳樂水一帶的衝浪老店，可線上預約課程，老闆阿飛同
時也是刺青師傅。

Reputable surfing shop for surfers in the Kenting and Jialeshuei
areas. Classes available for online reservation. Host Afei is also
a tattoo artist.

afeisurf@hotmail.com | www.afei.com.tw

潛水 DIVING

台灣潛水 Taiwan Dive Center

希望「將海洋帶入生活」，提供小班教學，高雄、綠島與恆春
都有店。

Operating shops and providing small classes in Kaohsiung,
Green Island, and Hengchun to promote the idea of bringing
the ocean into your life.

www.taiwan-diving.com/home-page

其他資訊網站 OTHER INFORMATION WEBSITES

跟著小飛玩 Follow XiaoFei

由熱愛台灣山林瀑布、野溪溫泉的美國部落客所製作的網站，
提供 GPS 與詳細地圖，也推薦他的 YouTube 頻道。

Website offering GPS information and detailed maps produced
by an American blogger who loves Taiwan's mountains,
forests, and wild hot springs. His YouTube channel is also
recommended.

www.youtube.com/followxiaofei | facebook.com/followxiaofei

台灣原住民早在 17 世紀移入台灣前，就已世代定居於此，無論是居住於平原地帶的平埔族群，或是山林裡的高山族群，皆屬於「南島民族」，目前台灣政府法律認定有 16 族，阿美族、泰雅族、排灣族、布農族、卑南族、魯凱族、賽夏族、雅美族、邵族、鄒族、噶瑪蘭族、太魯閣族、撒奇萊雅族、賽德克族、拉阿魯哇族、卡那卡那富族。

然而回顧歷史，原住民族在幾百年來受到外來統治者的迫害與不公待遇，直到 2016 年，擁有四分之一排灣族血統的前總統蔡英文才代表政府正式向全體原住民族道歉，並設置「原住民族歷史正義與轉型正義委員會」，並推動各項相關法案。

若想認識原住民，或許最簡單的方式是先從聆聽他們的音樂開始，只需要一句，那股野生的力量就能超越語言直擊內心，深刻感受原住民族與土地深刻的連結。其他原住民文化如傳說、工藝、信仰、祭儀以及與大自然共處的哲學等也都讓人著迷，若時間許可，推薦參與部落活動或小旅行親身體驗。

Generations of indigenous peoples have resided on the islands of Taiwan since long before the first foreign ethnic groups began moving here in the 17th century. Both the plains-dwelling and mountain-dwelling indigenous peoples are categorized as Austronesians. Currently, there are 16 principal tribes recognized by the Taiwanese government, including the Amis, Atayal, Paiwan, Bunun, Puyuma, Drekay, Say-Siyat, Tao, Thau, Cou, Kebalan, Truku, Sakizaya, Sediq, Hla'alua, and Kanakanavu tribes.

However, looking back in history, Taiwan's indigenous peoples didn't receive justice for centuries of political persecution and unfair treatment by alien regimes until former president Tsai Ing-wen, who is of one quarter Paiwan descent, delivered a formal apology to the entire indigenous population on behalf of the Taiwanese government in 2016. Meanwhile, the Indigenous Historical Justice and Transitional Justice Committee was founded to promote indigenous-issue-related laws and policies.

If you are interested in Taiwanese indigenous culture, the easiest way to learn more might be to listen to their music. You may quickly feel moved by the wild and primitive power that transcends all languages, allowing you to feel the deep connection between the indigenous people and the land. Other aspects of indigenous culture such as legends, crafts, beliefs, rituals, and a living philosophy that is in harmony with nature, are also fascinating. If time permits, a trip or activity with an indigenous tribe to experience the beauty firsthand is recommended.

更多資訊 MORE INFORMATION

原住民族委員會 Council of Indigenous Peoples
www.apc.gov.tw/portal/index.html?lang=en_US

台灣原住民數位博物館 Digital Museum of Taiwan Indigenous Peoples
www.dmtip.gov.tw/web/en

當代原民媒體 Mata Taiwan
en.matataiwan.com
FB：什麼，你也愛台灣原住民？！ We Love Taiwanese Aborigines

音樂 MUSIC

歌單 Playlist：台灣原住民歌曲 Taiwanese Aboriginal Music
https://reurl.cc/4rbm0D

文章 Article：〈Taiwanese Indigenous Music〉
taiwanbeats.tw/genres/indigenous

推薦電影 MOVIES

《只有大海知道》 *Long Time No Sea*, 2018
《太陽的孩子》 *Wawa No Cidal* (or *Panay*), 2015
《賽德克巴萊》 *Seediq Bale*, 2011

以上可在 Google Play 或 iTunes 上購買收看。
All available on Google Play and iTunes.

部落旅遊 TRIBAL TOURISM

Tribe Asia

提供台灣深度旅遊，包含部落體驗行程安排。

In-depth tour packages exploring Taiwan's natural and cultural diversity.

tribe-asia.com

推薦書籍 READING LIST

台灣部落深度旅遊 北部篇、中南部篇、花東篇

Taiwan's Indigenous Areas: Northern Taiwan, Central and Southern Taiwan, and *Hualien and Taitung*

www.books.com.tw/products/0010639840

CULTURE
文化

若對台灣藝術、設計、建築、音樂、影視等文化創意領域有興趣的朋友，
以下提供一些入口網站，可瀏覽獲得更多相關資訊。

For those who are interested in the cultural and creative fields in Taiwan,
such as arts, design, architecture, music, and movies, below are several web portals offering more information.

新聞與專題 NEWS AND MEDIA COVERAGE

TaiwanPlus

第一個向國際觀眾宣揚台灣的英語影音新聞和節目的官方平台。

Established by the Ministry of Culture Taiwan, it is Taiwan's first platform dedicated to promoting Taiwan to an international audience through English-language video news and programs.

www.taiwanplus.com

台灣光華雜誌 Taiwan Panorama

中、英、日三語月刊，也發行東南亞語雙月刊，了解台灣文化的最佳雜誌。

One of the best monthly magazines to learn about Taiwan. Available in Chinese, English, and Japanese, also published bimonthly in Southeast Asian languages.

www.taiwan-panorama.com/Index.html

關鍵評論網國際版 The News Lens

提供多元觀點的線上媒體，可即時了解台灣時事與文化現況。

Online media covering many topics from different perspectives, allowing readers to keep abreast of current events in Taiwan.

international.thenewslens.com

設計 DESIGN

台灣設計研究院 Taiwan Design Research Institute

國家級設計中心，可獲得最新相關資訊與展覽訊息。

Taiwan's national design center offering the latest in exhibitions and related information.

www.tdc.org.tw/?lang=en

台灣設計展 Taiwan Design Research Institute

每年 8 月由中央與不同地方政府合作辦理，呈現在地設計與產業的現在與未來。

Held every August in collaboration with the central government and various local governments, it showcases the present and future of local design and industry.

www.designexpo.org.tw/en

臺灣文博會 Creative Expo Taiwan

每年 8 月由文化部主辦、設研院執行的年度文創盛事。

Grand annual event held in August for the cultural and creative industry organized by the Ministry of Culture and executed by Taiwan Design Center.

creativeexpo.tw/en

藝術 ARTS

台灣當代藝術資料庫 Taiwan Contemporary Art Archive

認識台灣當代藝術的最佳平台，滿足學術研究或策展需求。

One of the best platforms for learning about Taiwanese contemporary arts, also a good resource for academic and curating purposes.

tcaaarchive.org

藝術進駐網 Arts Residency Network Taiwan

提供台灣駐村單位以及駐村機會資訊。

Providing information about artist-in-residence programs and organizations in Taiwan.

artres.moc.gov.tw/en

表演藝術工具箱 Taiwan Traditional Performing Arts Toolkit

精選戲曲、偶戲、音樂、民俗雜技重要團體與作品。

Introducing a selection of important Chinese opera, puppetry, music, and folk acrobatics groups and works.

toolkit.culture.tw/home/en-us

展覽活動資訊 EXHIBITIONS AND EVENTS

Art Map

串聯台、港與澳的藝術平台，每月發行全台藝文活動摺頁，也可線上閱讀或下載。

Art platform connecting Taiwan, Hong Kong and Macau, issuing a monthly bulletin for up-to-date arts and culture events in Taiwan. Also available online for viewing and download.

www.artmap.xyz

全國藝文活動資訊系統網 National Arts and Culture Info

可查詢全台灣藝文活動資訊，目前僅有中文版。

Website for searching for arts and culture events around Taiwan. Currently only in Chinese.

event.moc.gov.tw

文化快遞 (台北) Culture Express (Taipei)

台北市藝文資訊刊物，並有英、日語摺頁可在藝文場館、捷運站等地索取。

Pamphlet offering arts and culture information in Taipei available in all MRT stations and cultural venues. English and Japanese versions also available in bulletin form.

cultureexpress.taipei/English

電影 MOVIES

電影工具箱 Taiwan Cinema Toolkit

精選介紹台灣 160 部電影作品，涵括台語片、新電影運動與國際得獎片。

Introducing 160 important Taiwanese films including films in the Taiwanese dialect, films from the Taiwan New Cinema movement, and international-award-winning films.

toolkit.culture.tw/home/en-us

金馬影展 Golden Horse Film Festival

台灣、華人電影圈最重要的獎項與影展。

The most important award and film festival for the Taiwanese and Chinese film-making industry.

www.goldenhorse.org.tw

金馬奇幻影展 Golden Horse Fantastic Film Festival

由金馬影委團隊於 2010 年創辦，以「奇幻」為主題，選片沒有極限，影單出現各種 B 級片、Cult 片都不奇怪。

In 2010, the Golden Horse Film Festival Committee started this fantastic film festival. The sky's the limit. This festival includes B movies, cult favorites.

www.ghfff.org.tw

出版與書展 PUBLISHING AND BOOK FAIRS

文學工具箱 Taiwan Literature Toolkit

系統性介紹台灣文學史、重要作家與代表作品。

Systematically introducing the history of Taiwanese literature, important writers, and their best works.

toolkit.culture.tw/home/en-us

台北國際書展 Taipei International Book Exhibition

每年 1 月或 2 月舉辦的國際書展，可一次掌握台灣出版動態。

Annual international book fair held in January or February revealing the latest from the publishing industry.

www.tibe.org.tw/en

草率季 Taipei Art Book Fair

台北最有趣的大型藝術書刊市集，喜歡獨立出版的人不能錯過。

Unique and eccentric art book fair in Taipei. A must-see for people who like independent publications.

facebook.com/taipeiartbookfair

音樂 MUSIC

Taiwan Beats

幫助台灣流行音樂面向全球的新媒體，網站有中英日版。

New media connecting Taiwanese pop music to the world. Available in Chinese, English, and Japanese.

taiwanbeats.tw

貢寮海洋音樂祭 Hohaiyan Rock Festival

每年夏天在新北福隆海水浴場舉辦的老字號音樂盛會。

Large, well-established music event held each summer at Fulong Beach in New Taipei City.

facebook.com/hohaiyan

台灣聲音地圖計畫 Taiwan Soundmap Project

從聲音認識台灣，結合 google map 定位整合而成的聲音資料庫。

Sound map database integrated with Google Maps allowing you to discover Taiwan through sound.

soundandtaiwan.com

建築 ARCHITECTURE

Taiwanese Architecture

國外建築網站，可從頁面上 Google Maps 點選有興趣的建築獲取相關資訊。

International architecture website offering information about architecture in Taiwan by searching Google Maps on their webpage.

www.archdaily.com/country/taiwan

村落之聲 Village Taipei

台北都市再生基地與相關資訊平台，推薦給對都市議題有興趣的朋友。

Information platform about urban revival sites in Taipei, for friends who are interested in urban issues.

www.urstaipei.net/en

台灣城市探險 Taiwan Urban Exploration

集結到台灣各地廢墟或遺址探險的紀錄，看見更多台灣樣貌。

Records of explorations of ruins and abandoned sites, allowing you to discover a different side of Taiwan.

spectralcodex.com/collections/taiwan-urban-exploration

LITERATURE

文學

倘徉翻頁之間的島嶼時光——複寫一面書單裡的台灣風景
Wander the islands through the written word,
replicating a piece of the Taiwanese landscape between the pages of books

5 個主題，10 種角度，無數次讚嘆，每本書都值得細細品嚐。
Five topics, ten perspectives, and countless rounds of applause.
Every book is worthy of attentive reading.

by 陳育律 Hank Chen

一、穿梭在今昔 Between the past and the present

1 黃崇凱 / 文藝春秋

2 周芬伶 / 花東婦好

小說跳脫時間軸的限制，遊走亦虛亦實、古今交融的場域。《文藝春秋》以舉重若輕的姿態，縱覽百年來的近代文化發展，《花東婦好》以波瀾壯闊的女性書寫，帶來國境之南的歷史回眸。

1 Huang Chong-Kai / *The Contents of the Times*

2 Chou Fen-ling / *Fuhao, a Lady in Eastern Taiwan*

Two novels casting off the limitation of a regular timeline, lingering between reality and fiction, the past and the present. *The Contents of the Times* effortlessly overviews the serious topic of Taiwan's cultural development over the past century. *Fuhao, a Lady in Eastern Taiwan* is a magnificent women's tale presenting a retrospective history of southern Taiwan.

二、島上的孩子 Children of the island

3 陳思宏 / 去過敏的三種方法

4 楊富閔 / 花甲男孩

成長是人人必經之路，難免帶著酸苦滋味。在村鎮裡長大的孩子，常比城裡人看得更細膩。《去過敏的三種方法》裡的彰化永靖，或者《花甲男孩》中的台南大內，都是最真實的台灣風土。

3 Kevin Shih-Hung Chen / *Three Ways to Combat Allergies*

4 Yang Fu-min / *A Boy Named Flora A*

To walk the bittersweet path of growing up is inevitable for everyone. Those who grow up in the countryside often have more sensitive eyes than those who grow up in the city. Yongjing Township of Changhua County as portrayed in *Three Ways to Combat Allergies*, and Danei District in Tainan City as the setting of *A Boy Named Flora A* provide two of the most authentic scenes of rural Taiwan.

三、漂流與落地 Drifting and rooting

5 蘇偉貞 / 租書店的女兒

6 吳鈞堯 / 熱地圖

戰事留下了特殊的地景，《租書店的女兒》裡的眷村、《熱地圖》裡的戰地金門，既日常又非日常。大時代的動盪、新時代的變化，一層疊加一層，具體而微地展現於家族與個人的生命史。

5 Su Wei-chen / *The Memories of Books*

6 Wu Chun-yao / *Hot Maps*

The veteran's village in *The Memories of Books*, and the Kinmen battlefields in *Hot Maps* present landscapes both ordinary and extraordinary, as inherited from wartime history. Beneath the turning wheel of time, the turmoil of the changing era builds up layer by layer, revealing sophisticated chronicles of families and individuals.

四、向山海走去 Toward the mountains and the sea

7 亞榮隆・撒可努 / 山豬・飛鼠・撒可努

8 夏曼・藍波安 / 冷海情深

台灣的自然美景多樣，無論《山豬・飛鼠・撒可努》的山林，或《冷海情深》的蔚藍太平洋，都那麼令人神往。走出都市文明，且聽最早定居這塊土地上的人，用自己祖先的聲腔娓娓道來。

7 Sakinu Yalonglong (or Ahronglong Sakinu) / *The Sage Hunter*

8 Syaman Rapongan / *Cold Sea, Deep Feeling*

Taiwan encompasses a beautiful and diverse natural environment. Either the jungles in *The Sage Hunter* or the azure ocean in *Cold Sea, Deep Feeling* may be the subject of yearning. Forsake urban civilization and listen to the first group of people to reside on this land telling their stories in the voices of their ancestors.

五、在移動之間 Shifting within

9 顧玉玲 / 我們：移動與勞動的生命記事

10 張貴興 / 沙龍祖母

位處東亞的重要節點，台灣宛如航道上的一艘大船，更是許多來來去去的人，暫時或者最終選擇的留下來的家。認識完整的台灣，少不了《我們》中當代移工或《沙龍祖母》的東南亞華僑。

9 Ku Yu-ling / *Our Stories: Migration and Labour in Taiwan*

10 Chang Guei-sing / *Grandma's Photo Studio Shoot*

Located at an important convergence point in East Asia, Taiwan is not only like a large ship on a grand transportation channel but also a home, whether temporary or final, for many migrants. To learn about Taiwan in a more comprehensive way, the migrant laborers in *Our Stories* and the overseas Chinese from Southeast Asia in *Grandma's Photo Studio Shoot* are entities not to be neglected.

TECHNOLOGY
科技

台灣，這座引領全球製造業的隱形冠軍之島，正悄悄在進行一場從蘋果到特斯拉的硬體復興，以及從傳統產業到「新創之島」的品牌再造與變革。這裡的供應鏈牽動著全球的手機製造及行動通訊，現在也掌握半導體、電池生產、AI 等電動車和自駕車關鍵零組件及技術的發展。

過去兩三年，我們看到愈來愈多國際人才及新創團隊到台灣落地，這個有華人地區唯一的民主政府、雄厚的科技與設計人才、以及美好生活的地方。不管是民間力量主導的「Anchor Taiwan」、「AppWorks」，或是國發會主辦的「台灣新創競技場」、經濟部主導的「林口新創圈」、科技部規劃的「台灣科技新創基地」等單位，都一點一滴為台灣和世界連結努力。(文 / 邱懷萱)

Taiwan has been an invisible champion leading the world's hardware and software innovation. It's transforming from being the supply chain for Apple to Tesla, from traditional manufacturing to being the key of enabling frontier technologies such as AI, 5G, autonomous driving and blockchain. Quietly, a hardware renaissance is taking place, as the latest innovation requires deep hardware and software integration, which is Taiwan's specialty. There is also a force to inject modern entrepreneurship into its solid traditional industries, rebranding itself to be an "Startup Island."

Over the past several years, increasing numbers of international professionals and groups have been relocating to Taiwan, the only democracy in the Chinese-speaking world. Taiwan boasts robust technology heritage, a deep talent pool, and incredible quality of life. There are several initiatives around connecting the world with Taiwan through entrepreneurship, including non-governmental softlanding platform Anchor Taiwan, accelerator AppWorks, Taiwan Startup Stadium funded by the National Development Council, Startup Terrace led by the Ministry of Economic Affairs, and Taiwan Tech Arena initiated by the Ministry of Science and Technology, to name a few. (by Elisa Chiu)

新創盛事 POPULAR STARTUP EVENTS

Computex Taipei (6 月 | June)

1981 年創立的台北國際電腦展，可一次獲得最新、最豐富的產業資訊。

International computer expo in Taipei established in 1981 for sharing the latest and most comprehensive industry news.

www.computextaipei.com.tw/en_US/index.html

InnoVEX (6 月 | June)

與國際電腦展同步舉行的亞洲指標新創展會。

Asia's leading startup expo held simultaneously with Computex Taipei.

innovex.com.tw

Meet Taipei 創新創業嘉年華 (11 月 | November)

由台灣科技媒體《數位時代》舉辦，集結完整創業資源與鏈結。

Organized by Taiwanese technology media magazine *Business Next*, integrating startup resources and networks.

meettaipei.tw

民間單位 NON-GOVERNMENT ORGANIZATIONS

Anchor Taiwan

國際人才落地對接平台，連結產業文化與新創和投資社群。

Softlanding platform for international professionals and startups with entrepreneurial programs, tech communities and investor networks.

anchortaiwan.com | facebook.com/anchortaiwan.group

之初創投 AppWorks

台灣知名創業加速器，著重 AI、區塊鏈及大東南亞區的連結。

Famous Taiwanese startup accelerator, focusing on AI, blockchain, and network technologies in the greater Southeast Asia region.

appworks.tw

政府單位 GOVERNMENT ORGANIZATIONS

台灣新創競技場 Taiwan Startup Stadium (TSS)

輔導具有潛力的台灣科技創業公司連結國際市場的創業家聚落。

Startup community coaching potential technology startup companies in how to link with the overseas market.

www.startupstadium.tw

林口新創圈 Startup Terrace

世大運選手村場域活化，歡迎國際加速器及新創團隊進駐。

Welcoming international accelerators and startups to revitalize the former athletes village of the 2017 Summer Universiade.

www.startupterrace.tw/en

台灣科技新創基地 Taiwan Tech Arena (TTA)

進駐台北小巨蛋內，串聯技術、資金並與國際交流的平台。

Platform in the Taipei Arena connecting technology, venture capitalists, and the international community.

taiwanarena.tech

來台灣旅遊若有預算，尤其是計畫造訪交通較不便利的地區，可考慮參加旅行社的套裝或客製行程，或參加定點式的體驗活動，讓旅途更為順暢。以下推薦幾個旅遊相關網站或 APP（皆有英文版）：

If your budget permits, especially when planning to visit remote areas, fixed or customized tours as provided by travel agencies might be something to consider. Sometimes even participating in a single tour activity at a certain spot can make your entire journey a lot easier. Below are several recommended travel websites and apps available in English:

旅行社 TRAVEL AGENCIES

MyTaiwanTour

主力接待外國旅客訪台，經營的旅遊誌也有許多實用資訊。

Offering guided tours for travelers from abroad, providing useful information through their online journal.

www.mytaiwantour.com | taiwan-scene.com

Round Taiwan Round

提供套裝與客製化行程，推出的「Tripool」接駁服務讓旅遊更方便。

Providing fixed and customized tours and Tripool shuttle service to make your trip easier.

www.rtaiwanr.com | www.tripool.app

Topology

協助外國觀光客客製化台灣旅遊服務的旅行社。

Travel agency providing customized travel services for foreign tourists.

topologytravel.com

導覽 GUIDED TOURS

Like it Formosa

提供台北、大溪、台南與高雄的免費導覽，也能客製行程。

Free-of-charge guided tours in Taipei, Daxi, Tainan, and Kaohsiung, also provide customized planning service.

www.likeitformosa.com/tour

島內散步 Walk in Taiwan

提供台灣各式主題或客製化中英日導覽服務。

Customized thematic guided tours, available in Chinese, English or Japanese.

walkin.tw

旅遊體驗平台 TRAVEL E-COMMERCE PLATFORM

台灣兩大旅遊體驗預訂平台，可訂購門票、交通、體驗活動等。

Two of the primary platforms for booking activities, event tickets, and transportation.

Klook www.klook.com/zh-TW
KKday www.kkday.com/zh-tw

旅遊資訊 TRAVEL INFORMATION

HereNow

線上城市導覽媒體，目前台灣有台北與高雄兩個城市。

Online city guide media currently available for Taipei and Kaohsiung.

www.herenow.city

Taiwan Everything

台灣旅遊與生活線上媒體並發行雙月刊《Travel in Taiwan》。

Online media about lifestyle and travel in Taiwan, also publishing the bimonthly magazine Travel in Taiwan.

www.taiwaneverything.cc | Magazine: issuu.com/travelintaiwan

訂房與住宿 ACCOMMODATIONS AND BOOKINGS

Dear b&b

台灣第一個專為旅人設計精選的旅宿指南，網站有中英日語言。

Online guide introducing selected guesthouses for travelers in Taiwan, available in Chinese, English, and Japanese.

dearbnb.com

9floor

台灣最有質感的共生公寓，若預計在台北待超過一個月，可以申請住宿。

Beautiful co-living apartment in Taipei, open for rental applications of a month or longer.

9floor.co

YouTubers

最近也有許多介紹台灣生活的國外 YouTuber，可以觀看他們的影片更認識台灣。

Videos created by expats who have been sharing their lives in Taiwan on YouTube may be a good way to learn about Taiwan.

酷的夢 Ku's dream（法國｜France）
莫彩曦 Hailey（美國｜US）
Iku 老師 Ikulaoshi（日本｜Japan）
韓勾ㄟ金針菇 Korean Enoki Mushroom（韓國｜Korea）
不要鬧工作室 Stop Kidding Studio（各國｜Multiple Countries）

雨港之都，
不是海港味，就是雨水味

Photo credit : kenner116

基隆
KEELUNG

THE RAINY SEAPORT CAPITAL OF TAIWAN

———————— Yun-Han Kao 高韻涵

"You're from Keelung? It rains so much there!" is the classic comment Keelung locals get from outsiders.

Due to its topography and seasonal winds, Keelung is indeed rainy year-round and locals all know better than to leave the house without an umbrella. See if you're lucky enough to have a sunny day during your visit!

Keelung was developed into an important hub for transportation and trade because of its convenient location and its easy access to the ocean. Not only was Keelung the first city in Taiwan to have an operating railway line, it was also the first to boast a bay bridge. Trading saw Keelung through a golden era; after its prosperity, Keelung was left with products of portal culture such as imported goods, coffee shops, taverns, and chikuwa (Grilled fish paste rolls). Currently, most people who reside in Keelung spend about 30-40 minutes to commute to Taipei for work, which is not nearly as long as it sounds. On the other hand, this quick commute also seems to make Keelung locals forget their roots.

In recent years, the Keelung City Government has put a lot of their resources into revitalizing the city. Interesting shops and organizations are starting to establish their presence in Keelung and many local youths have returned to their roots to integrate Keelung's rich history, culture, and art into present day living. Check out Chaojing Bay Festival and Zhengbin Art Festival, two wonderful festivals that inspire locals and visitors alike to return to their true roots.

「你是基隆人呀？基隆很常下雨耶！」

身為基隆人最常聽到外地人這樣反應。受地形和季風影響，基隆四季多雨，只要是基隆人，包包裡一定都有把傘。如果來這裡旅行碰上大晴天，那你一定是非常幸運的人！

基隆因水利、地理位置之便，很早就被開發為交通重要樞紐，不僅有台灣第一條鐵路，也有第一座跨海大橋。港口貿易更讓基隆走過輝煌時代，舶來品委託行、咖啡廳、酒家、炭烤魚漿「吉古拉」等，皆是港都文化留下的產物。隨著時代變遷，今日許多基隆人通勤於台北、基隆之間，常有朋友聽到我說要「回基隆」時，都以為要坐很久的車，其實搭客運 30 至 40 分鐘就到了！但這樣方便的距離，也讓基隆人忘了自己是基隆人。

近年來基隆市政府開始活化地方，許多有趣店家進駐，還有深耕家鄉的青年團隊與串聯基隆歷史、生活與藝術的有趣活動，例如「基隆潮境海灣節」與「正濱港灣共創藝術節」等，讓人相當期待基隆未來的發展。我想，離真的「回基隆」的那天也不遠了吧！

From Taipei it takes about 40 minutes via TRA shuttle train or Tze-chiang Limited Express to arrive at Keelung. You can also take various intercity buses that typically take around 30-40 minutes. In Keelung I recommend walking, taking the bus, or riding shared taxis, which is in and of itself a unique local experience.

台北搭乘搭台鐵「區間車」、「自強號」到基隆站約 40 分鐘。亦可在台北各地搭乘客運抵達基隆，約需 30-40 分鐘車程。在市區適合徒步、搭公車，或是體驗基隆獨有的「撿客」（與陌生人共乘計程車）。

RECOMMENDATIONS
推薦

◤ READING LIST 旅遊書籍

KEELUNG STROLL：《雨都漫步：跟著雨傘人回家旅行》
Local teams share must-see landscapes and favorite walking routes.
在地團隊分享不可錯過的地景與私房散步路線
⌐ books.com.tw/products/0010821218

THE AROMA OF KEELUNG《基隆的氣味》
A Keelung daughter and her husband's travel guide written from the perspective of travel and history
基隆女兒與女婿的邀請，用旅遊文學與文史作家的角度旅行基隆
⌐ books.com.tw/products/0010689142

◤ LOCAL PUBLICATIONS 在地刊物

KEELUNG WAY
A brand-new, high-quality quarterly published by the Keelung City Cultural Affairs Bureau
基隆文化局發行的全新質感季刊
⌐ www.klccab.gov.tw/EBook/QuarterlyCultural

KEELUNG RAIN《雞籠霧雨》
A local publication created by local youths; while it's no longer in print, it is still available online
由在地青年編纂的地方刊物，雖已停止更新，但過往文章可在網路閱讀
⌐ vocus.cc/keelungoldstory/home

◤ GUIDED TOURS 導覽

KEELUNG FOR A WALK 雨都漫步
A well-received guided tour in both Chinese and English led by local youths; download their walking map on their website
由在地年輕人帶領，深受好評的中英文導覽團隊，網站有散步地圖可以下載
⌐ keelung-for-a-walk.com

◤ TRAVEL WEBSITES 旅遊網站

TRAVEL KEELUNG 基隆旅遊網
Keelung's official travel website, available in various languages
基隆旅遊官方網站，有多國外語資訊
⌐ tour.klcg.gov.tw

BACK TO KEELUNG 回基隆
A Facebook page dedicated to sharing the stories, discoveries, and thoughts of youths who have returned to their hometown
優質臉書專頁，分享在地青年的回鄉反思與發現
⌐ facebook.com/backtoKL

KEELUNG YOUTH FRONT 基隆青年陣線
Founded by a group of youths who work with community development and cultural movements, Keelung Youth Front hosts a wide variety of events such as Khóo Tsú-song Festival
由從事社造、文化運動之青年所組成，時常舉辦各式活動如「梓桑文化祭」
⌐ facebook.com/KeelungYouthFront

◤ ANNUAL EVENTS 年度活動

KEELUNG CHAOJING BAY FETIVAL (JUNE AND JULY)
基隆潮境海灣節 (6月-7月)
A cultural and music festival themed around the ocean that makes locals proud
以基隆人引以為傲的海洋生活態度打造的藝文、音樂節慶
⌐ chaojingbay.com.tw

ZHENGBIN ART FESTIVAL (JULY AND AUGUST)
正濱港灣共創藝術節 (7月-8月)
Founded by the Xing Bin Mountain team, this art festival encourages collaboration and exchange between local residents and resident artists
由星濱山團隊推動，激起在地居民與藝術家的新火花
⌐ facebook.com/zhengbinart

Photo credit：寺人孟子

Photo credit：bryansjs

Photo credit：Erica Liu

Photo credit：bryansjs

Photo credit：yenlife007

A BAIMEWENG FORT 白米甕砲台

The beauty of this fort, which served as a gun emplacement for three hundred years, has been beautifully preserved

雖已不見300多年前的砲台，美麗海景依舊如昔

⌂ 基隆市中山區光華路37號
No.37, Guanghua Road, Keelung city

B ZHENGBING FISHING PORT 正濱漁港

The once-prosperous fishing port was left in decline and has now been revitalized by locals through art and collaboration

日治時期繁榮後沒落，經由在地團隊以藝術共創重新活絡

⌂ 基隆市中正區中正路與正濱路交街處
Chungchen Road and Chengbin road intersection, Keelung City

C AGENNA SHIPYARD RELICS 阿根納造船廠

Come appreciate the Keelung sunset in this century-old shipyard

來超過百年歷史的造船廠遺址看基隆夕陽

⌂ 基隆市中正區正濱路116巷75號
No.75, 116 Lane, Chengbin Road, Zhongzheng Dist., Keelung city

D HEPING ISLAND PARK 和平島公園

A national treasure of a park that spans land and sea

擁有天然海水池與國家級地質景觀的祕境公園

⌂ 基隆市中正區平一路360號 ｜+886-2-2463-5452
No. 360, Ping 1st Rd., Zhongzheng Dist., Keelung City
08:00-19:00 (November-April 08:00-18:00)

E CHAOJING PARK 潮境公園

An outdoor museum located in an ecologically rich intertidal zone

潮間帶生態豐富的戶外美術館，散步觀海的好去處

⌂ 基隆市中正區北寧路369巷61號
No. 61, Ln. 369, Beining Rd., Zhongzheng Dist., Keelung City

F WANGYOUGU 望幽谷〔忘憂谷〕

A nature trail where you'll forget all your troubles

有種使人「忘」卻所有煩「憂」的魔力步道

⌂ 基隆市中正區八斗街右轉八斗子海濱公園
Badou St., Zhongzheng Dist., Keelung City
GPS座標：N25°08'42.3″ E 121°47'55.2″

Photo credit：Space Moor

Photo credit：基隆市文化局

Photo credit：Tzaba

Photo credit：元山・美學 EONS

A SEA TO SEE BOOKAFÉ 見書店

An independent bookstore/café/select goods shop that also hosts lectures and concerts

以海洋為主，身兼選品、咖啡店，不時舉辦講座或音樂會

基隆市仁愛區仁二路236號 | +886-2-2428-1159
No. 236, Ren 2nd Rd., Ren'ai Dist., Keelung City
Mon.-Fri. 11:00-22:00, Sat. 09:00-00:00, Sun. 09:00-22:00

B HOUSE K 岞書屋

"岞" signifies a mountain retreat. Discover Keelung's secret, high-quality bookstore beside Keelung Tower

「岞」為山上的空間之意，基隆塔旁的祕密質感書店

基隆市中正區信二路284-1號 | +886-2-2424-2351
No. 284-1, Xin 2nd Rd, Zhongzheng District, Keelung City
Fri.-Sat. 10:00 – 22:00, Sun. 10:00 – 18:00

C 1937 EONS 元山・美學 EONS

A sophisticated art gallery hidden near Ren'ai Market

隱身在仁愛市場旁的質感藝廊

基隆市仁愛區愛二路21號 | facebook.com/1937EONS
No. 21, Ai 2nd Rd., Ren'ai Dist., Keelung City
Fri.-Sun. 12:00-18:00

D SPACE MOOR 永畫海濱美術館

A creative art hub built by a local team, located next to the Zhengbin Fishing Harbor

由在地團隊打造，正濱漁港旁的藝術創意基地

基隆市中正區中正路539號 | +886-2-2463-6930
No. 539, Zhongzheng Rd., Zhongzheng Dist., Keelung City
13:00-18:00

E TZABA 喳吧工作室

Converted from an old garage, Tzaba sells and offers DIY workshops for making leather items

車庫改建的空間，選購、體驗DIY皮件的好去處

基隆市中正區義一路154號 | +886-921-802-146
No. 154, Yi 1st Rd., Zhongzheng Dist., Keelung City
Thur.-Sat. 14:00-18:00 | Workshop: linktr.ee/TzaBa

F ALLEY DESIGN STUDIO 飾不飾獨創設計工作室

An eco-friendly jewelry line that uses repurposed and recycled materials

用金工製作複合媒材與塑料再生飾品，藉機喚起環保意識

基隆市中正區義二路124號 | +886-989-456-690
No. 124, Yi 2nd Rd., Zhongzheng Dist., Keelung City
11:30-18:30 (Closed on Sundays)

Photo credit 行旅女子

A GRILLED CHIKUWA 手工炭烤吉古拉
Fish paste rolls grilled over charcoal, a unique local delicacy
魚漿厚實口感與炭烤香味，只有基隆才有的好味道

📍 基隆市中正區正濱路27號 | +886-910-251-920
No. 27, Zhengbin Rd., Zhongzheng Dist., Keelung City
07:00-11:00 (Closed on Mon. and Tue.)

B PORK LIVER, INTESTINE, AND SEAFOOD 豬肝腸海鮮店
Try this traditional Keelung dish of pork and pork liver
基隆在地傳統古早味小吃，豬肉與豬肝的絕妙搭配

📍 基隆市仁愛區孝三路65巷7號
No. 7, Ln. 65, Xiao 3rd Rd., Ren'ai Dist., Keelung City
08:00-20:00 (Closed on Mon. and Thur.)
+886-2-2428-3630

C XIASAN ROAD RICE SAUSAGE 孝三路大腸圈
Try one of Keelung's most iconic staples: traditional steamed glutinous rice sausage paired with assorted meats
古法蒸煮糯米腸搭配黑白切，基隆小吃的代表之一！

📍 基隆市仁愛區孝三路99巷3號 | +886-932-258-621
No. 3, Ln. 99, Xiao 3rd Rd., Ren'ai Dist., Keelung City
10:00-18:00 (Closed on Mondays)

D MOMMY LIAO'S BUBBLE MILK TEA 廖媽媽珍珠奶茶專賣鋪
A must-try in Keelung, their homemade tapioca balls are sheer perfection
來到基隆必喝的珍珠奶茶，手工珍珠Q勁十足

📍 基隆市仁愛區孝三路84號2樓
2F., No. 84, Xiao 3rd Rd., Ren'ai Dist., Keelung City | 11:00-21:30
+886-2-2423-0398

E LONG LEG NOODLE 長腳麵食
For those who love noodles, this is a must-visit place to enjoy the simple and flavorful local taste
熱愛乾麵的人不容錯過，簡單的在地鹹香滋味

📍 基隆市仁愛區孝三路99巷1號 | +886-989-717-019
No. 1, Lane 99, Xiaosan Rd., Ren'ai Dist., Keelung City
07:00-15:00 (Clsoed on Thur. and Sun.)

F A-BEN LIVE SEAFOOD 阿本活海鮮
A restaurant serving freshly-caught seafood, try their signature pickled cabbage
自家漁船捕撈新鮮魚貨的熱炒店，招待泡菜不簡單

📍 基隆市中正區和一路2巷1-42號 | +886-2-2462-1766
No. 1-42, Ln. 2, He 1st Rd., Zhongzheng Dist., Keelung City
10:00-20:30

Photo credit：圖們咖啡

Photo credit：FLOW CAFE

Photo credit：萬祝號

A TUMAN CAFÉ 圖們咖啡

A unique coffee shop located near Keelung Fishing Port, serving coffee made from their own roasted beans
基隆正濱漁港旁的個性咖啡館，使用自家烘培豆子

基隆市中正區中正路551號 | +886-2-2462-8727
No. 551, Zhongzheng Rd., Zhongzheng Dist., Keelung City
11:00-18:00 (Closed on Thursdays)

B FLOW CAFE

A coffee shop combining floral arrangement workshop and desserts, located near Keelung Train Station
基隆火車站旁，結合花藝與甜點的咖啡館

基隆市仁愛區忠二路68號2F | facebook.com/flowcafetw
2F, No. 68, Zhong 2nd Rd., Ren'ai Dist., Keelung City
13:00-18:30 (Closed on Wed. and Thur.)

C WANCHU COFFEE 萬祝號

Experience the shipbuilding culture of Keelung at a unique coffee shop reborn from a fishing tackle store
感受基隆造船文化，由鋼索釣具行重生的質感咖啡廳

基隆市中正區中正路560號 | +886-2-2428-2680
No. 560 Zhongzheng Rd., Zhongzheng Dist., Keelung City
11:00-19:00

D SPANGLE INN 粼島旅宿

An artistic lodging sits by Zhengbin Fishing Port
坐落在正濱漁港旁的藝術旅宿

基隆市中正區正濱路34號
No. 34, Zhengbin Rd., Zhongzheng Dist., Keelung City
www.spangleinn.com
+886-918-834-549

E KEEBE HOTEL 集好.旅店

A lodging tucked away in Miaokou Night Market with its name "KEEBE" taken from the word meaning "flavor" in Taiwanese
KEEBE 取自台語「氣味」的發音，隱身於廟口夜市中的旅館

基隆市仁愛區仁二路215號 | +886-2-2420-1166
No. 215, Ren 2nd Rd., Ren'ai Dist., Keelung City

F LIGHT INN 輕旅

With an extremely convenient location, this inn is perfect for backpackers
市區絕佳位置，以愛基隆的心開設的背包客棧

基隆市仁愛區愛三路87號6樓之1 | +886-2-2426-0799
6F.-1, No. 87, Ai 3rd Rd., Ren'ai Dist., Keelung City
facebook.com/lightinnkeelung

CITY CENTER ROUTE

市區路線

KEELUNG STATION
AND DOWNTOWN

基隆火車站與市區周邊

A 12-HOUR GOURMET TRIP THAT WILL CHALLENGE BOTH YOUR PHYSICAL STRENGTH AND ABILITY TO EAT!
12 小時！挑戰體力與肚皮的美食之旅！

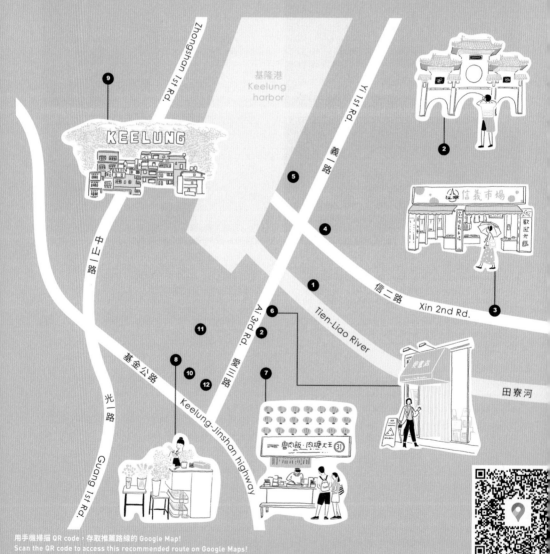

基隆港
Keelung
harbor

KEELUNG

Zhongshan 1st Rd.

Yi 1st Rd.

義一路

中正路

Ai 3rd Rd.

愛三路

信二路 Xin 2nd Rd.

Tien-Liao River

基金公路

光一路

Guang 1st Rd.

Keelung-Jinshan highway

田寮河

魯肉飯・肉焿大王 (31)

用手機掃描 QR code，存取推薦路線的 Google Map！
Scan the QR code to access this recommended route on Google Maps!

1) 08:00   Have breakfast at Zhou's Scallion Pancake or 171 Breakfast

2) 09:00   Hike the trail in Zhongzheng Park for a bird's-eye view of Keelung

3) 11:00   Enjoy a post-hike stroll in Xinyi Market and get some food

4) 13:00   Walk down Yi 2nd Road, locally known as Keelung's Ginza

5) 14:30   Enjoy some afternoon tea by the port at Loka Café

6) 16:00   Visit Sea to See Bookafé or stroll through E-SQUARE

7) 17:00   Go to Miaokou Night Market for dinner

8) 18:30   Go shopping at the Keelung Consignment Commercial District

9) 20:00   Enjoy a night-time view at the Huzishan Keelung Landmark

10) 22:00   Indulge in a nightcap at Zhe Shi Izakaya Restaurant

11) 02:00   If you're still awake at this ungodly hour, visit Kanziding Fish Market

12) 03:00   Get some breakfast/late-night snack at Zhutian Fresh Fish

1) 08:00   早餐去「周家蔥油餅」或「171 早餐」

2) 09:00   爬「中正公園」鳥瞰基隆港

3) 11:00   運動完去「信義市場」邊逛邊吃

4) 13:00   拜訪舊街風情「基隆銀座」：義二路

5) 14:30   來個港邊下午茶「Loka Café」

6) 16:00   前往「見書店」或逛逛「東岸商場 E-SQUARE」

7) 17:00   基隆味「廟口夜市」不容錯過！

8) 18:30   吃飽悠悠散步「基隆委託行商圈」

9) 20:00   搭車去「Keelung 地標」看夜景

10) 22:00   夜景薰陶後去「擇食居酒屋」小酌一下

11) 02:00   還有體力的話，拜訪全台最早的魚市場「崁仔頂」

12) 03:00   不知是早餐還是消夜，去「朱添鮮魚號」吃海鮮

08:00
ZHOU'S SCALLION PANCAKE
1. 周家蔥油餅

Enjoy some crispy-on-the-outside and chewy-on-the-inside scallion pancakes with eggs at Zhou's Scallion Pancake and don't forget to order their signature soy milk! If it's a Western breakfast that you crave, try 171 Breakfast — I highly recommend their scrumptious and filling grilled sandwiches that come with sliced cabbage, cucumber, cheese, and steak.

到「周家蔥油餅」嚐嚐外酥內軟的蔥油餅加蛋，搭配帶點微焦香的豆漿！如果想吃西式早餐，「171 早餐」的現烤三明治是基隆高 CP 值代表，每款現烤三明治都有滿滿的高麗菜絲和小黃瓜絲，推薦起士牛肉蛋現烤三明治！一口咬下去大滿足～

09:00
ZHONGZHENG PARK
2. 中正公園

The three-tiered Zhongzheng Park has been central to the childhood memories of many locals for generations. The first level of the park houses the Keelung Martyrs' Shrine and the children's playground; the second level houses the Zhupu Altar, the ceremonial site for Ghosts' Festival; and the third level enshrines the Statue of Great Goddess Kwan-yin, upon which the whole of Keelung port can be seen. If you're lucky you might even see cruise liners moored at the port.

中正公園是許多基隆人的童年遊樂場，從入口走到制高點共有三層，第一層為基隆忠烈祠、兒童遊樂場，第二層為中元普渡祭典的主場所——主普壇，第三層則是基隆地標——大觀音像，在這裡可以鳥瞰整個基隆港，幸運的話可以看到郵輪停靠。

11:00
XINYI MARKET
3. 信義市場

Whether it's fresh produce, daily supplies, clothes, or second-hand goods you're looking for, Xinyi Market has it all! I recommend getting a bite to eat in the market at Jia Hong Rice Noodle Soup, Shandong Wang's Shengjian Bao, or Marlin Vermicelli. There are also several options outside the market, including Lailai Rice Cake Soup, Wang Long Lamb Noodles, Lin's Trotter Soup, and Zheng Pai Curry.

從蔬果生鮮、日用品、服飾到二手貨，這裡應有盡有！市場內還有「家弘米粉湯」、「山東王家水煎包」、「旗魚麵線羹」等隱藏美食！市場外也有「來來粿仔湯」、「旺龍館羊肉麵」、「林家原汁豬腳」、「正牌咖哩飯」等選擇可以大飽口福。

13:00
YI 2ND ROAD COMMERCIAL DISTRICT

4. 義二路周圍商圈

During the Japanese colonial period, Yi 2nd Road became a flourishing commercial district selling primarily imported goods due to its proximity to the port. Independent Bookstore, the very first bookstore to sell Traditional Chinese volumes in Taiwan, was born on this road. After the trading business died down in Keelung, a lot of old shops had to close their doors. Fortunately, new blood has poured into this area with the establishment of shops such as Alley Design Studio and Tzaba, a leather goods shop.

日治時期義二路因鄰近港口，進口許多舶來品，成為當時最熱鬧的商圈，台灣第一家販售繁體中文書籍的書店「自立書店」也在此誕生。雖然商圈沒落後有許多老字號熄燈，但近年有新血像是「飾不飾獨創設計工作室」、「Tzaba 喳吧」手做皮件工作室等進駐，值得一遊。

14:30
LOKA CAFÉ

5. LOKA 咖啡

Taking its name from the word loka, meaning long-legged in Taiwanese, Loka is a café in an apartment building mezzanine. Through the windows on three sides, one can take in the cruise ships by the harbor. In addition to its good coffee and tasty drinks, there are limited daily desserts for you to choose from.

有著一雙長腳的老闆開的咖啡店，取名為長腳的台語發音「Loka」，位在基隆港邊舊式公寓的神祕夾層裡，透過三角窗可以遠眺港邊郵輪停靠，除了有好喝的咖啡飲品外，還有每日限量甜點，每次來都有不同選擇喔！

16:00
E-SQUARE
AND
SEA TO SEE BOOKAFÉ

6. 東岸商場 與 見書店

Located in the city center, E-SQUARE is not only a commercial district but also a circular bus station where various bus routes pass through. It also has a rooftop playground with a great view of the city. Sea to See Bookafé, located on the first floor, is a wonderful independent bookstore that is themed around the ocean and its beauty. Come peruse stories about the city and its ocean.

「東岸商場 E-SQUARE」位於基隆市中心，是商場也是公車的循環站，在這裡可以搭乘不同路線的公車前往各景點，特別的是頂樓有海洋風的操場，可以邊慢跑邊看基隆港美景。一樓有間充滿海洋意象的獨立書店「見書店」，可以坐下來尋覓關於海洋、基隆的故事。

☐

17:00
MIAOKOU NIGHT MARKET
7. 廟口夜市

Come visit one of Taiwan's most famous night markets! Every local has a list of their favorites; mine include tempura, bite-sized sausages, minced pork rice, pork nugget soup, pao pao ice, and last, but certainly not least, roasted sandwiches (from the stall in front of Three Brother's Tofu Pudding). Here's another secret tip: after most stalls close down for the night, midnight snack stalls start opening up, so you'll never grow hungry.

台灣最著名的夜市之一，每個基隆人都有自己的口袋清單。天婦羅、一口吃香腸、滷肉飯、肉羹湯、泡泡冰是必吃美食，位在「三兄弟豆花」前的炭烤三明治更是基隆人的最愛。偷偷說：夜市打烊後還有消夜場攤位陸續開店，半夜餓了可以再回來哦！

☐

18:30
KEELUNG CONSIGNMENT
COMMERCIAL DISTRICT
8. 基隆委託行商圈

Take a walk around the Keelung Consignment Commercial District, a place where men and women shopped at foreign boutiques during the time of Martial Law in Taiwan. After decades of decline, the district has recently been revitalized with the presence of new commercial spaces such as Cycling Life Café de MaruCorner.

吃飽到曾經風光一時的委託行附近逛逛，在戒嚴時期，這裡是仕紳淑女來尋找國外精品的好去處。近年來沒落的商圈漸漸開始有在地青年前來開設風格店家，像是「丸角自轉生活咖啡」等，讓委託行一帶又逐漸受到年輕人的關注。

☐

20:00
HUZISHAN KEELUNG LANDMARK
9. 虎仔山「Keelung 地標」

Hail a cab and head to Huzi Mountain on the west bank of the wharf. Enjoy the silent night music of insects as you make your meandering way up the mountain. Sit in front of the Keelung Landmark and take in all of Keelung, its port, and its sprawling city view. Then, end your night with romance.

接著搭乘計程車前往碼頭西岸的虎仔山，通過蜿蜒的停車場道路緩緩上山，寂靜的夜晚只剩蟲鳴的聲音，坐在閃亮的「Keelung 地標」前，俯瞰基隆港口和車水馬龍的市區夜景，心情也逐漸平靜下來，有種說不出的浪漫。

22:00
ZE SHI IZAKAYA RESTAURANT

10. 擇食居酒屋

Keep this romantic evening going with a nightcap. Return to the city and head to Ze Shi Izakaya Restaurant to let your troubles melt away with draft beer and good food made from high quality ingredients.

想延續浪漫氛圍，這時候最適合小酌一下。回到市區，闖入夜晚的菜市場巷弄中，有家日式氛圍的深夜食堂「擇食居酒屋」躲在裡頭。來杯生啤酒、吃吃新鮮食材製作的美味料理，就讓所有煩惱在這裡被療癒。

02:00
KANZIDING FISH MARKET

11. 崁仔頂

Kanziding Fish Market, Taiwan's largest fresh fish wholesale market, is well worth staying up into the wee hours of the night. During the Japanese colonial period, Kanziding—meaning at the top of the stone steps in Taiwanese—was known as Xuchuan Canal, the canal where fishing boats passed through, fishermen used to carry their loads by hand and climb up the stone steps to arrive at the market where professional auctioneers auction off the day's best catches. There is no better way to experience the true authenticity and grit of Keelung than witnessing the rituals of this fish market.

撐到此時就是為了拜訪北台灣最大的生鮮魚貨批發漁市！「崁仔頂」是石階上的意思，以前這裡是旭川運河，可以通行漁船，魚貨卸下必須爬上石階送上漁行，最新鮮的魚貨再透過拍賣員「糶手」的喊價賣出。要感受最生猛道地的基隆，這裡不容錯過。

03:00
ZHUTIAN FRESH FISH

12. 朱添鮮魚號

Kaniding Fish Market is the perfect spot for satisfying late-night cravings. If cooking freshly purchased seafood at home is not an option, go to Zhutian Fresh Fish for the freshest sashimi. Their menu changes daily as they only serve the day's best catches. Tell the owner the number of people dining, your budget, and preferences and they will customize a menu for you. Come end your Keelung trip with a warm bowl of white miso soup and a plate of fresh sashimi!

崁仔頂魚市場周圍有許多深夜美食，若不方便採買魚貨又想品嚐的朋友，可以到「朱添鮮魚號」品嚐新鮮現切的生魚片，魚種依當日採買為主，可以與老闆說明人數、預算和想吃的部位客製化點餐，以鮮甜的生魚片搭配白味增湯，為基隆旅行劃下完美的句號吧！

GHOST FESTIVAL

雞籠百年宗教盛事──熱鬧整個農曆七月的「中元祭」

Photo credit：panda

SPECIAL FEATURE
KEELUNG 基隆特輯
SPECIAL FEATURE

In the seventh lunar month, also known as the Ghost Month, one can see the elaborately decorated Zhupu Altar (main salvation altar) shining on the hillside to the east of Keelung Harbor. The night before the Zhongyuan Festival (on the 15th day of the seventh lunar month), the Procession of Water Lantern takes place downtown. As the Dintao performing troupes of the local major clans parade through the streets packed with lantern floats and crowds in midtown, the highlight would be releasing burning water lanterns around midnight. People would gather at the fishing port of Oceanview Alley, yelling "Fa-o, wang-o" to pray for prosperity and wellbeing for their families and Keelung.

The origin of the grand ceremony in Keelung can be traced back to the Zhang Quan Battle in the Qing Dynasty when the immigrants from the Quanzhou or Zhangzhou regions in China often fought over the land ownership. After one gruesome battle resulting in serious casualties, community leaders decided to bridge the rift between feuding parties and hold rituals to deliver Laodagong, the souls died from the strife. A temple was built in their remembrance that later became the Laodagong Temple. They also set the rules that, incorporating the original Zhongyuan Festival, each local clans would take turns to organize the Pudu Ceremony to appease hungry spirits, as well as hold Dintao performance competition to enhance the harmony between communities. Therefore, since 1855, the clan in charge of that year's Zhupu would try every means to make the ceremony perfect to avoid disgracing their clan. During Japanese colonial period, the first permanent Zhupu Altar was built in Keelung Takasago Park. Unfortunately, during World War II, it was severely damaged by the bombing of the U.S. Army. The city government then built a new altar on the hilltop in Zhongzheng Park, which became the central venue of the festival. If you are interested in Taiwan's religious culture, do visit the most lively Keelung Mid-Summer Ghost Festival and witness the power of faith that brings the whole city together. (by Imobert Ho)

每年到了俗稱鬼月的農曆 7 月，就能看見精心布置的「主普壇」在基隆港東側的山丘上閃閃發亮。到了中元節（農曆 7 月 15）前夕，市區還會為了「放水燈遊行」進行交通管制，各宗姓的陣頭在街上比拚，燈車、花車與人潮擠爆市區，午夜更迎來「放水燈」重頭戲，大家在「望海巷」港邊大聲喊著「發喔，旺喔」，祈求家族與基隆運勢興旺、平安。

在基隆，中元節之所以會演變成這樣的大型祭典，可追溯至清代的「漳泉械鬥」，由中國來的漳泉移民，在基隆落腳後隨著地盤的擴張開始發生衝突。在一場死傷慘重的大規模械鬥後，雙方長老為了消弭漳泉界線，決定將往生者集中祭祀稱為「老大公」，也就是基隆「老大公廟」的原型；更決議在每年中元節，結合原有的普渡孤魂野鬼的習俗，不分漳泉，由各姓氏輪流舉辦普渡活動，同時也舉辦陣頭競賽，希促進族群間和平相處。因此從咸豐 5 年（1855）開始，每年輪值主普的姓氏，都會想盡辦法讓當年普渡盡善盡美，才不會砸了自己姓氏的招牌；日治時期更在基隆高砂公園內興建首座永久性的主普壇，可惜戰後受美軍轟炸與火災之故嚴重毀損，市政府遂改在中正公園山頂興建新的主普壇，成為今日祭典的核心場地。若對台灣的宗教文化有興趣，千萬別錯過北台灣最熱鬧的基隆中元祭，親身感受讓整個城市動起來的信仰的力量。（文／何昱泓）

KEELUNG MID-SUMMER GHOST FESTIVAL
基隆中元祭

www.rs-event.com.tw/2019kmsgf

A HARBOR CITY IN TRANSITION THROUGH REGIONAL REVITALIZATION

SOCIAL INNOVATION

基隆地方創生現場，看見不一樣的港都風貌

The trend of regional revitalization has arisen in Taiwan in recent years. Both the government and nongovernmental groups have initiated programs that stimulate and change the local communities around Taiwan. Keelung, the harbor city in the north, is no exception, as many interesting groups have taken action to revive local communities. Keelung Old House is one of the Keelung Government's programs that provides an online platform to connect the vacant old houses with people proposing new ideas and document the stories of renovating old houses. Also a governmental program, the Shanhai Workshop based at Taiping Elementary School by Keelung Harbor, annually inviting local and foreign architects, artists, and residents to creatively organize activities from transforming the community environment to holding markets on the hillside. All of these efforts would make one feel the change of Keelung.

Among many active local nongovernmental groups, Zhengbin Art (p.21) was founded by a team of local youths with arts and cultural backgrounds. Based at Zhengbin Fishing Harbor for a long time, they have discovered issues of local development with the involvement of residents. The team organized the first Zhenbin Art Festival in 2018 and established Zhenbin Creative School in 2019, having a variety of activities that opened up the possibilities of the harbor area. And KeeLung For A Walk (p.21) and Keilang Camino are the groups devoted to promoting local tours and cultural experiences. With their in-depth guided tours, they hope to bring more people to explore and learn more about Keelung.

Once the most prosperous and modern city in northern Taiwan, although Keelung has gradually lost its role in leading trends, there are people all working towards reviving Keelung at the fishing harbor, on the hill, at the consignment shops and many other sites. With one visit, you can feel the city's booming energy.

近幾年全台興起一股「地方創生」的浪潮，無論是由官方或民間發起的計畫，都為各地帶來了新的刺激與改變，港都基隆自然也不例外，許多有趣的團隊紛紛出現。像是基隆市政府主辦的「基隆老屋偵探社」，透過網路平台媒合閒置老屋與空間需求者，並記錄老屋再生故事；同樣由市府舉辦的「山海工作營」，以基隆港邊的太平國小為基地，每年號召國內外建築師、藝術家與在地居民共同參與，激盪創意，小至社區環境改造，大至在山坡上舉辦熱鬧的市集活動，都讓人感覺基隆正在蛻變中。

除了官方活動外，民間也有許多活躍的在地組織，像是由多位青年創立的「星濱山團隊」(p.21)，長期在正濱漁港蹲點，與居民共同探索地方發展課題。2018 年星濱山團隊舉辦了首屆「正濱港灣共創藝術節」，更在 2019 年底成立「星濱海港學校」，規劃各式活動體驗，為漁港帶來更多可能性。其他像是致力於導覽與文化推廣的「雨都漫步」(p.21)與「雞籠卡米諾」，都希望能帶領更多人走踏基隆，透過深入淺出的解說，讓大家更認識這個地方。

曾經是北台灣最繁華摩登的基隆港都，雖然隨著時代變遷漸漸失去引領潮流的地位，但在漁港邊、山丘上、委託行內及各個角落，都有人正為基隆努力著。只要來一趟，就能真切感受到這股熱力。

KEELUNG OLD HOUSE 基隆老屋偵探社
facebook.com/Keelungoldhouse

KEILANG CAMINO 雞籠卡米諾
facebook.com/keilangcamino

台北 TAIPEI

台灣旅遊起點 亞洲最舒服的城市

Photo credit : Evan Lin

THE STARTING POINT FOR TRAVELING IN TAIWAN, THE MOST STRESS-FREE CITY IN ASIA

To all the travelers who are visiting Taipei for the first time, welcome! As the capital city of Taiwan, Taipei is an ever-changing city with countless fresh happenings and places to explore. It's a safe and free city embracing diverse cultures and convenient transportation, and no doubt the best place to start your journey in Taiwan.

For sure, the Taipei 101 observatory is a must-visit, however, the view looking out over the city from the top of Xiangshan (Elephant Mountain) just before sunset is even more stunning. Don't miss the world-famous Din Tai Fung restaurant, but also make time to try out other distinctive restaurants and local street food throughout the city. Eslite bookstore is a great platform to learn more about Taiwan's creative arts, design, and cultural scenes, yet only if you visit the independent shops down in alleyways will you see the true energy and style of Taipei.

With the passion to introduce the wonderfulness of Taipei to the world, the bilingual (Chinese and English) *Good Eye City Guide: Taipei* was published in the spring of 2017, selecting 300 worth-visiting shops and recommending 12 walking routes in the hopes that, with the book in hand, travelers can easily complete their adventures. In the Taipei section of *Good Eye City Guide: Taiwan*, a wider selection of shops has been added. However, for a more comprehensive guide to Taipei, please refer to *Good Eye City Guide: Taipei*. Last but not least, let's take a fun little quiz to find out the best route for your day!

Quiz link——
game.goodeye.guide

Web App and Order online——
portaly.cc/goodeye

對於第一次來到這個城市的旅人，想先跟你說聲歡迎光臨！台北做為台灣的首都，時時刻刻都在變化中，永遠都有新鮮事等待探索，這個文化多元、交通便利又自由安全的城市，作為認識台灣的起點是最適合不過了。

是的，台北 101 一定要上去一次，但黃昏時在對面的象山上看台北更是美麗；鼎泰豐不容錯過，不過台北還有更多有態度的餐廳與在地小吃；誠品是首次接觸台灣藝文與設計創意的絕佳平台，接著還得要鑽進巷弄踏訪更多有趣店家，才能真正看到台北的風格與能量。

因為想把台北所有的美好分享給大家，2017 年春天出版的中英雙語的《台北挑剔指南》，收錄了 300 家優質好店並規劃了 12 條散步路線，讓讀者能夠按圖索驥，輕鬆地在台北冒險。因此在《台灣挑剔指南》中，台北部分僅補充了更多風格店家。若要完整體驗台北，請務必搭配《台北挑剔指南》一起服用！

最後來玩個小遊戲，看看今天想怎麼逛台北吧！

遊戲連結——
game.goodeye.guide

Web App 與線上訂購——
portaly.cc/goodeye

It takes about 35 minutes from Taoyuan International Airport to Taipei Main Station by the fast trains of the Taoyuan Metro known as the airport express. The public transportation services in Taipei are highly accessible. EasyCard can be used when taking the metro, riding buses, and renting YouBike. For taxi service, Taiwan Taxi Company is recommended. Uber is also available throughout the city.

Taipei Metro: metro.taipei

搭乘機場捷運直搭車約 35 分鐘可到達台北車站。台北市區交通便利，用悠遊卡可搭乘捷運、公車與租借公共自行車 YouBike。若要搭乘計程車可選擇台灣大車隊，另 Uber 也可在台北使用。

台北捷運：metro.taipei

RECOMMENDATIONS
推薦

◤ READING LIST 旅遊書籍

TAIPEI, TO-SIA: HOW TO TRAVEL LIKE A LOCAL 《台北多謝：陪你旅行當道地的台霸郎》
Explore Taipei's Hidden Gems with Local Experts (Bilingual: Madarin Chinese and English)
跟著道地台北人逛台北私房景點（中英雙語）
⌐ books.com.tw/products/0010891275

CITIX60 TAIPEI：60 CREATIVES SHOW YOU THE BEST OF THE CITY 《CITIX60：台北》
Secret spots recommended by 60 Taipei's creatives
集結60位台北創意人推薦的私房景點
⌐ CN version：books.com.tw/products/0010758684
⌐ ENG version：books.com.tw/products/F014016060

TAIPEI CITY WALK: DON'T JUST PASS BY, EXPERIENCE IT 《台北城市散步：走過，不路過》
Get to know Taipei from various in-depth topics including social and historical perspectives
從各種主題和社會議題深度認識台北
⌐ books.com.tw/products/0010756875

TAIPEI：THE MICHELIN GUIDE 《台北米其林指南》
Worth keeping as a reference whether or not you have a Michelin star bucket list
無論是否想摘星，都相當值得參考
⌐ books.com.tw/products/0010818085

◤ GUIDED TOURS 導覽

WALK IN TAIWAN 島內散步
The top brand for guides of Taiwan's cities with in-depth itineraries from various perspectives
台灣城市導覽第一品牌，從各種角度規劃深度行程
⌐ Web: walkin.tw | facebook.com/walkin.tw

◤ TRAVEL WEBSITES 旅遊網站

TRAVEL TAIPEI 台北旅遊網
Official Taipei travel website. Available in multiple language versions containing the latest information
官方旅遊網站，有多國語言與最新資訊
⌐ travel.taipei

HereNow TAIPEI
Taipei city guide operated by a Japanese cultural media group offering a great selection of shops
日本藝文媒體經營的台北城市指南，選店極佳
⌐ herenow.city/zh-tw/taipei

◤ LOCAL PUBLICATIONS 在地刊物

TAIPEI PICTORIAL AND TAIPEI 《台北畫刊》與《TAIPEI》
Nice culture and tourism magazines published by the Department of Information and Tourism of the Taipei City Government. Available free of charge at all MRT stations
觀傳局出版的質感文化觀光刊物，可在捷運各站索取
⌐ e-book：books.taipei/index

◤ ANNUAL EVENTS 年度活動

NUIT BLANCHE 白晝之夜 (OCTOBER｜10 月)
Nighttime adventure in the city to discover the vibrant arts and culture energy of Taipei
在夜晚探險台北，看見城市的藝文能量與活力
⌐ facebook.com/NuitBlancheTPE

TAIWAN LGBT+ PRIDE 臺灣同志遊行 (OCTOBER｜10 月)
Biggest LGBT+ pride parade in Asia. Come celebrate being yourself together!
亞洲最大同志遊行，一起來慶祝你是你自己！
⌐ facebook.com/Taiwan.LGBT.Pride

A AMA MUSEUM 阿嬤家 - 和平與女性人權館

The first women's and human rights education site to open in Taiwan, primary about the history of Taiwan's wartime comfort women

第一座以慰安婦史料為核心的女性人權教育基地

台北市大同區迪化街一段256號 | 10:00–17:00 (Closed Mon. and Tue.)
No. 256, Sec. 1, Dihua St., Datong Dist., Taipei City

B SIN HONG CHOON TRADE CO. 新芳春行特展

Century-old tea factory. Guided tours provided on weekend afternoons

百年古蹟製茶廠，週末下午有固定導覽

台北市大同區民生西路309號 | +886-2-2550-4141
No. 309, Minsheng W. Rd., Datong Dist., Taipei City
10:00–19:00, Saturday: 10:00–21:00 (Closed on Mondays)

C SUN SUN MUSEUM 森 3

Multi-functioned experimental space combining visual arts, fashion, and art curation

結合視覺、時尚、展策的複合實驗空間

台北市中山區龍江路45巷18號1樓
1F, No. 18, Ln. 45, Longjiang Rd., Zhongshan Dist., Taipei City
facebook.com/sunsunmuseum | 10:00–19:00 (Closed on Mondays)

D MOOM BOOKSHOP

Independent bookstore with a selection of arts and photography books from Taiwan and abroad

以國內外藝術、攝影相關書籍為主的獨立書店

台北市大安區忠孝東路三段251巷8弄16號
No.16, Ally.8, Lane 251, Sec.3, Zhonxiao E Rd., Daan Dist., Taipei City
facebook.com/moom.bookshop | Tue.-Sun. 12:00-20:00, Sat. 12:00-21:00

E ILLUMINATION BOOKS 浮光書店

Petite independent art bookstore hidden on a second floor in an alleyway

藏身巷弄二樓的小型藝文獨立書店

台北市大同區赤峰街47巷16號2樓
2F, 16, Lane 47, Chifeng St., Datong Dist., Taipei City
facebook.com/IlluminationBooks | 12:00-22:00

F BASISBOOKS 基地書店

The first comic bookstore devoted to Taiwanese comics and related merchandise

第一間以台灣原創漫畫、相關商品展售為題的圖文書店

台北市大同區華陰街36-38號
No. 36-38, Huayin St., Datong Dist., Taipei City
facebook.com/basisbooks.tw | 10:00-20:00 (Closed on Mondays)

Photo credit：Craig Ferguson

Photo credit：Kamaro'an House

Photo credit：Kris Kang

A LAI HAO TAIWAN GIFT SHOP 來好
Selection of the best gifts made in Taiwan
羅蒐與自製台灣最佳伴手禮

台北市大安區永康街6巷11號 | +886-2-3322-6136
No. 11, Ln. 6, Yongkang St., Da'an Dist., Taipei City
facebook.com/taiwanlaihao
10:00-21:30

B A LETTERPRESS 一間印刷行
Selling a portable DIY letterpress kit designed by
themselves and promoting handmade papers
販售自行研發的「隨身活版印刷機」也推廣手工造紙

台北市大同區太原路97巷12號 | facebook.com/aletterpress.tw
No. 12, Ln. 97, Taiyuan Rd., Datong Dist., Taipei City
09:30-18:00 (Closed Sun. Mon. and THur.)

C 裏 URA.219
Discover a stylish space that blends a historic house, fashion
brands, vintage plants, and delightful coffee and tea
結合老宅、服裝品牌、古物植栽與咖啡茶飲的質感空間

台北市大同區迪化街一段219號
No. 219, Section 1, Dihua Street, Datong District, Taipei City
11:00-19:00 (Closed on Mon. & Tue.) | FB: Ura.219

D LETTERPRESS TEA HOUSE 無事生活
Space with tea ceremonies, flower arrangement, and
letterpress. Experiential classes for foreigners available
結合茶道、花藝與活版印刷，提供海外人士體驗課程

台北市信義區吳興街461號 | facebook.com/letterpress.teahouse
No. 461, Wuxing St., Xinyi Dist., Taipei City
14:00-19:00 (Closed Mon. to Wed.)

E KAMARO'AN HOUSE
Bringing the breeze of the Pacific Ocean to Taipei, visit
Kamaro'an to discover their exquisite craftsmanship and design
將太平洋的風帶進台北，來此尋找 Kamaro'an 的工藝設計

台北市大安區新生南路三段11巷2號 | +886-2-2356-3616
No. 2, Ln. 11, Sec. 3, Xinsheng South Rd., Da'an Dist., Taipei City
15:00-18:00, Weekends 13:00-18:00 (Closed on Mon. and Tue.)

F WANDERLAND HIRUNOMI 萬華世界下午酒場
All-day drinking allowed! Enjoy local market food with your
drinks and experience the vibrant Wanhua style from morning
全日飲酒許可！可外帶旁邊市場美食享用，早上就能體驗萬華Style

台北市萬華區三水街70號 | FB: WANderLAND.HIRUNOMI
No.70 , Sanshui Street, Wanhua District, Taipei City
10:00-18:00, Fri. and Sat. 10:00-23:00 (Closed on Mondays)

Photo credit : Yu Chocolatier

A LOGY

Michelin 1-Star restaurant led by a Japanese chef. My first choice among restaurants of similar quality

由日本大廚領軍的米其林一星餐廳，同等級首推

台北市大安區安和路一段109巷6號 | logy.tw
No. 6, Ln. 109, Sec. 1, Anhe Rd., Da'an Dist., Taipei City
17:30–19:30, 20:00–22:30 (Closed Mon. and Tue.)

B TAÏRROIR 態芮

Michelin 1-Star French cuisine infused with Taiwanese flavors

吃得出台灣味的法式米其林一星料理

台北市中山區樂群三路299號6F
6F., No. 299, Lequn 3rd Rd., Zhongshan Dist., Taipei City
12:00–14:30，18:00–22:30 (Closed on Tuesdays)
Online reservation : inline.app/booking/tairroir/tairroir

C YAMASAN 山男

Modern izakaya serving Taiwanese- and Japanese-infused cuisine

提供融合台日風味料理的現代居酒屋

台北市大安區光復南路260巷34號 | +886-2-2778-0978
No. 34, Ln. 260, Guangfu S. Rd., Da'an Dist., Taipei City
18:00–23:00

D YU CHOCOLATIER 畬室 法式巧克力甜點創作

Must-try for chocolate lovers. Other sweets are also scrumptious

巧克力愛好者不能錯過，其他甜點也精緻好吃

台北市大安區仁愛路四段112巷3弄10號
No. 10, Aly. 3, Ln. 112, Sec. 4, Ren'ai Rd., Da'an Dist., Taipei City
12:00–20:00 (Closed on Wed.) | facebook.com/yuchocolatier

E LIQUIDE AMBRÉ 琥泊

Stylish stationery store hidden on a second floor, offering four tea sections per day

隱身風格文具店二樓，每日提供四個場次茶席

台北市大安區樂利路72巷15號2樓
2F., No. 15, Ln. 72, Leli Rd., Da'an Dist., Taipei City
12:00–19:00 (Closed on Mon.) | reurl.cc/vnaW5k

F SIMPLE KAFFE

World champion coffee's flagship shop, offering desserts made with passion

世界冠軍咖啡旗艦店，甜點也用心製作

台北市中正區忠孝東路二段27號
No. 27, Sec. 2, Zhongxiao E. Rd., Zhongzheng Dist., Taipei City
10:00–17:00 | facebook.com/SimpleKaffa

Photo credit: PAWNSHOP

A PUN

Personal favorite hidden in an alleyway, serving high-quality food and cocktails

藏在防火巷的心頭好，調酒和餐點都在水準之上

📍 台北市大安區信義路四段378巷5號 | +886-2-2700-5000
No. 5, Ln. 378, Sec. 4, Xinyi Rd., Da'an Dist., Taipei City
Mon.-Thur. 20:00-02:00, Fri.-Sat. 20:00-03:00

B STAFF ONLY CLUB

Mystical members-only retro bar, offering travel passes for foreign travelers

會員限定的神祕復古酒吧，提供國外旅客Travel Passes

📍 台北市中正區水源路1-10號 | www.staffonlyclub.com
No. 1-10, Shuiyuan Rd., Zhongzheng Dist., Taipei City
Mon.-Thur. 19:00-01:00, Fri.-Sat. 19:00-02:00 | +886- 2-2362-8682

C PAWNSHOP

For those who love music and nightlife, the legendary underground club KORNER is back

台北傳奇地下夜店KORNER回來了，給愛音樂與夜晚的你

📍 台北市大安區信義路四段279號B1
B1, No.279, Sec.4 Xinyi Road, Daan District, Taipei City
Fri. and Sat. 22:00-05:00 | facebook.com/pawnshop279

D KIMPTON DA AN HOTEL 金普頓大安酒店

Design hotel at a great location. Their restaurant, The Tavernist, is also recommended

位置絕佳的設計旅館，也推薦餐酒館The Tavernist

📍 台北市大安區仁愛路四段27巷25號
No. 25, Ln. 27, Sec. 4, Ren'ai Rd., Da'an Dist., Taipei City
+886-2-2173-7999 | facebook.com/KimptonDaanHotel

E THE DOOR INN 門草行旅

White-themed guesthouse located in Dadaocheng area

座落於台北大稻埕的純白旅宿

📍 台北市大同區安西街23號
No. 23, Anxi St., Datong Dist., Taipei City
facebook.com/thedoorinn
+886-911-248-080

F 9FLOOR 玖樓共生空間

Shared-apartment community with the best design in Taipei, offering rental periods of one month or more

台北最有質感的公寓社群，最短租期一個月

📍 台北市萬華區和平西路三段66號
No. 66, Sec. 3, Heping W. Rd., Wanhua Dist., Taipei City
9floor.co

DEMOCRACY AND LGBT+ RIGHTS IN TAIWAN

持續進步中的台灣

Photo credit：Manl

Walking through Taiwan's democracy and social movements

Whenever asked about Taiwan's political situation, I always proudly say that Taiwan is the most democratic country in the Chinese-speaking world. Our democratic freedom did not come at a small price and our progress in the complicated realm of international politics is still precarious. This tenacious land has welcomed its third party alternation and produced the first female president in our history. Activists from the past are now entering the parliament; young people are starting to retrace the histories before their time and are paying attention to and even participating in political activities.

Places tourists now visit might very well have played important roles in the fight for democracy in the past. Wisteria Tea House, a popular spot for foreigners, was an important meeting house for political dissidents in the 70s. The plaza in front of the ever-bustling Longshan Temple was where democracy fighter Zheng Nan-Rong launched the 519 Green Movement. This social movement pressured the government into lifting the martial law, returning Taiwan's freedom that we continue to enjoy today. Treasure Hill Artist Village was once a military dependents' village that faced demolition until residents of the village, faculty members and students of National Taiwan University, and non-governmental organizations joined efforts to save the village. Treasure Hill was then eventually transformed into the city's first village-based historical relic. Liberty Square, a tranquil place for a nightly stroll, has been where countless Taiwanese people have made themselves heard by demonstrations in silence and in protest.

走過台灣民主與社會運動

每當被問到台灣的政治狀況時,我總是很驕傲地說台灣是華語世界裡最民主的國家,儘管台灣的民主自由得來不易,目前也在複雜難解的國際政治現實中搖晃前進,但是這塊堅韌的土地在 2016 年迎來了歷史上第三次的政黨輪替,有了第一位女性總統,曾經的社運健將進入國會,更多年輕人開始回溯在自己生命記憶以外的歷史,關注甚至親身投入政治活動。

走在台北,如今的觀光勝地,可能都有一段追求民主或是抗爭的過去。外國朋友喜愛去的「紫藤廬茶館」,在 70 年代是黨外人士的聚所;人潮鼎沸的「龍山寺」,在取消戒嚴的前一年,民主鬥士鄭南榕先生在龍山寺前發起了「519綠色運動」,間接促成政府解嚴,台灣才享有今日各種自由;由眷村改建成藝術村的「寶藏巖」,當時台北市政府打算強制拆除,在居民與部分台大師生、NGO 團體的抗爭下,最終保留部分,並成為台北市第一處以聚落形態被保留的市定古蹟;夜晚散步舒適宜人的「自由廣場」,幾十年來無數台灣人為了不同理念在此靜坐、抗議,勇敢為自己與理想發聲。

This is a travel book themed around design, lifestyle, and culture, but it is also a silent protest against the underestimation of the lovely city of Taipei. It is a diplomatic exercise that aims to better introduce Taiwan as a country to those outside its borders. Then, our foreign friends can fall in love with this place and become our steadfast allies. Due to the length of the book, I can only take a very general approach to this grand subject; for this I feel deeply apologetic to those who have made a great sacrifice and effort in the past. Listed below are a few books and websites that shed light on this topic:

ON THE ROAD TO FREEDOM: A BACKPACKER'S GUIDE TO TAIWAN'S STRUGGLE FOR DEMOCRACY
⌐ www.books.com.tw/products/0010618713

THINKING-TAIWAN
⌐ www.thinkingtaiwan.com

Taiwan's LGBT+ scene

Taiwan has often been donned the most LGBT+-friendly country in Asia by the foreign media. While Taiwan's LGBT+ parties are not quite as flamboyant as those held in Bangkok, our propagation for LGBT+ rights has always been ahead of its time. Taiwan is the first country in Asia to allow gay marriage after a landmark ruling by the island's constitutional court in May, 2017.

Taiwan's LGBT+ culture has been booming since the 90s. Literary classics, such as Pai Hsien Yung's *Crystal Boys* and Qiu Miao Jin's *Dying Testament in Montmartre*, were translated into numerous languages, serving as important mediums of promoting Taiwan's LGBT+ culture to the world. Since its inauguration in 2003, the annual Taiwan LGBT+ Pride Parade has developed into the largest LGBT+ pride parade in Asia. The parade advocates civil partnership rights and equality without discrimination. It also strives to connect with disadvantaged people at every social level and continues to explore and expand the spectrum of the LGBT+ community.

For young Taiwanese people, LGBT+ rights is undoubtedly a familiar issue. LGBT+ people and culture have become more common than ever in the mainstream media. Even cafés as well as art and cultural spaces in large cities often show their support by displaying rainbow stickers and flags. To gain a more profound understanding of Taiwan's LGBT+ culture and revolutionary history, one ought to visit 228 Memorial Park and Red House or visit Gin Gin Books and Fem Books to read up on the latest LGBT+ art and cultural news. (by Chai)

LEZ'S MEETING
⌐ www.lezsmeeting.com

TAIWAN TONGZHI HOTLINE ASSOCIATION
⌐ hotline.org.tw

其實這本以設計、生活與文化為主題的旅遊書,也是一個無聲的抗議,覺得台北這個可愛的城市太被低估;它也是一個外交運動,希望讓更多國內外的朋友更深入地認識台灣這個國家,愛上這個地方,成為我們最溫柔堅定的盟友。礙於篇幅僅能非常粗淺的介紹這個宏大主題,深感對不起民主鬥士與社運前輩們的奉獻與努力,以下推薦幾本書籍與網站,供有興趣了解的朋友們參考:

書籍:《自由背包客:台灣民主景點小旅行》
⌐ www.books.com.tw/products/0010618713

網站:想想台灣
⌐ www.thinkingtaiwan.com

台灣 LGBT+ 現場

台灣曾多次被外媒稱做為「亞洲最友善同志的國家」,光看同志派對這方面台灣或許不及曼谷豔麗,然而在權益倡導上,台灣一直走在最前線,2017 年 5 月台灣大法官更釋憲保障同性伴侶也應享有結婚的權益,成為亞洲第一個承認同性婚姻的國家。

台灣的同志文化,從 90 年代開始蓬勃發展,經典文學著作如白先勇《孽子》與邱妙津《蒙馬特遺書》更相繼被翻譯至多國語言,成為台灣同志藝文向世界發展的重要媒介。而 2003 年首次舉辦,一年一度的「台灣同志遊行」(Taiwan LGBT+ Pride),也已成為亞洲最大規模的同志遊行,核心議題強調伴侶權、反歧視、與連結各個階層的性弱勢,不斷探索並擴張同志族群的多元光譜。

對於台灣新世代的年輕人來說,同志議題絕對不會是陌生的詞彙,除了主流媒體上越來越常見的同志曝光率之外,各大城市的咖啡廳與藝文空間,亦不難發現店家張貼象徵「同志友善」的彩虹貼紙或彩虹旗。若想更深入了解台灣的同志文化與歷史,不妨至「二二八和平公園」與「紅樓廣場」走走,或者探訪「晶晶書庫」與「女書店」增補最新的同志藝文消息。如果想要更深入了解台灣 LGBT+,可逛逛下面幾個網站。(文/柴)

LEZS 女人國
⌐ www.lezsmeeting.com
台灣同志諮詢熱線協會
⌐ hotline.org.tw

山海之間，台北之外，我們是新北市

新北
NEW
TAIPEI

THIS IS NEW TAIPEI BETWEEN THE SEA AND MOUNTAINS

Surrounding Taipei, close to the mountains and facing the sea, New Taipei City is the most populous region in Taiwan with its 29 districts and abundance of nature and culture. With each district having its own characteristics, the city is next to impossible to generalize. The most popular among them are the Shulin and Tamsui areas, which are easy to reach via Taipei MRT. Also, the picturesque mountain towns of Jiufen and Jinguashih in the district of Ruifang, with their rich history of gold mining. Lastly, Yehliu Geopark in Wanli district, known for its Queen's Head rock formation.

New Taipei has recently mustered numerous local organizations and projects. One of which is the Bank of Culture in the district of Pingxi. The Bank of Culture designs ecological, paper-made lanterns in hopes of reducing waste while preserving the local traditions. Also JustPinglin, created by a youthful team, which introduces its visitors to the Pinglin tea village through food culture and short tours.

The first Burmese immigrants arriving in Taiwan set foot in the district of Zhonghe. As a result, the following generations together with the local Taiwanese have set up a new publication, Minglar Par. It recounts the story of Burmese in Taiwan. Following suit, the Xizhi Street Museum in Xizhi district also appeared. It is run by young people who print local publications and start up community spaces.

Although some people think that New Taipei City is a mere periphery of Taipei, the city actually has a more diverse personality and scene than its capital counterpart—that is, if you are willing to step out of the Celestial Kingdom of the Taipei's high and mighty!

環繞著台北、近山臨海的新北市，總共有 29 個行政區，是台灣人口最多的縣市，豐富的自然人文景觀，讓其難以被一概而論，每個區域都有各自的特色。像是與台北捷運連通而最容易抵達的紅樹林與淡水一帶、有著金礦歷史與山城美景的九份與金瓜石（瑞芳區）、因「女王頭」奇景聞名的「野柳地質公園」（萬里區）等，都是遊客絡繹不絕的地方。

近期新北市也有許多地方團隊或相關計畫值得關注，如「文化銀行」研發出紙製環保天燈，希望在保存平溪傳統的同時也減低垃圾量；由年輕團隊創立的「坪感覺」，則透過美食與小旅行讓遊客更認識茶鄉坪林。

台灣第一批緬甸移民落腳的中和，也出現了由新一代華僑與在地人組成的新媒體「緬甸街」，述說緬台故事；連多被認為是單純住宅區的汐止，也出現了青年組織「返腳咖」，出版地方刊物並開設社區交流空間。

儘管有人認為新北市為台北的附屬地帶，但它其實有著比首都更為多元的個性與風貌，只要踏出天龍國，立刻就能感受到！

Taipei Metropolitan Area MRT and bus network are conveniently inseparable, providing access to great locations in Taiwan. In the city districts, for cyclists you can use the app YouBike to hire bicycles. The app WeMo facilitates scooter rental, though you will need a valid international driving license.

Taiwan Railways: www.railway.gov.tw
Taiwan Tourist Shuttle Bureau: www.taiwantrip.com.tw

雙北的捷運、公車網絡緊密便捷,搭乘客運、台灣好行與台鐵可達知名景點。市區內也可租借 YouBike 與共享機車 WeMo Scooter(需在 app 上傳護照與國際駕照)。

台鐵: www.railway.gov.tw
台灣好行: www.taiwantrip.com.tw

RECOMMENDATIONS
推薦

◤ READING LIST 旅遊書籍

NEW TAIPEI STYLE《新北風格私旅:樂遊繽紛活力城》
New Taipei City government's ten walking routes in New Taipei City
新北市府策畫,帶你走10條新北散步路線
⌐ books.com.tw/products/0010650050

NEW TAIPEI STORY《新北好本事 生活微旅行 不一樣的新北行旅 不停歇的新意文創》
Familiarize yourself with New Taipei through personal inteviews and recounts with locals
由各地職人故事深度認識新北
⌐ books.com.tw/products/0010694127

NEW TAIPEI'S HIKING TRAILS《新北登山小旅行:64條山海步道輕鬆行》
The most detailed map of New Taipei's hiking trails and information for those who love nature
給喜愛自然的朋友,最詳盡的新北登山步道地圖與資訊
⌐ books.com.tw/products/0010672773

◤ LOCAL PUBLICATIONS 在地刊物

MINGALAR PAR《緬甸街》
Learn more about the Burmese culture on Huaxin Street in the district of Zhonghe. The magazine is in Chinese and Burmese
中緬雙語,從中和華新街深入理解緬甸文化
⌐ facebook.com/MingalarparTaipei | www.mp-taipei.com

NEW TAIPEI CITY ART《新北市藝遊》
The monthly art and culture magazine published by the city government. There is also the *New Taipei City Cultural*
市府出版的藝文活動月刊,另有《新北市文化季刊》
⌐ e-book : www.culture.ntpc.gov.tw

THE CAN《甘樂誌》
Starting off from Sanxia District, the farmers and workers who cultivate Taiwan share their recounts
「甘樂文創」從三峽出發,忠實記錄耕耘台灣的人事物
⌐ www.thecan.com.tw

◤ TRAVEL WEBSITES 旅遊網站

NEW TAIPEI TOURISM 新北市觀光旅遊網
An official travel website for comprehensive information on culture, sightseeing and festivals
官方旅遊網站,可獲得文化、觀光、節慶完整資訊
⌐ Web : tour.ntpc.gov.tw | facebook.com/ntctour

NEW TAIPEI ART AND CULTURE NEWS
文青不在家,往新北的路上
A real-time medium for New Taipei's art and culture news
新北藝文資訊的即時資訊站
⌐ facebook.com/e7summer

◤ GUIDED TOURS 導覽

CAN'S FUN 甘樂文創一遊
A variety of tour experiences in Sanxia District provided by CAN. Reservation required
由三峽團隊甘樂文創所經營的多種體驗遊程,需預約
⌐ www.thecan.com.tw/tour

◤ ANNUAL EVENTS 年度活動

HOHAIYAN ROCK FESTIVAL (AUGUST)
新北市貢寮國際海洋音樂祭 [8月]
Already a well-established Taiwanese music festival and a platform for many Taiwanese bands
台灣老字號音樂祭活動,許多台灣樂團發跡於此
⌐ facebook.com/hohaiyan

PINGXI LANTERN FESTIVAL (THE 15TH DAY OF THE 1ST LUNAR MONTH)
平溪天燈節 [每年農曆正月15日]
Pingxi District's celebratory lantern festival that sees lanterns rise in a spectacle to behold
平溪元宵慶祝活動,天燈冉冉上升,場面壯觀
⌐ ylccb.gov.tw

Photo credit：新北市政府觀光旅遊局

Photo credit：國家人權博物館

Photo credit：新北市美術館

A TAMSUI-KAVALAN TRAILS 淡蘭古道

Hike on the 19th century historic trails that connect Taipei to Yilan 來19世紀連接台北宜蘭的古道散步

⌐ facebook.com/walkTKT
Book:《淡蘭古道 [北路]》*Tamsui-Kavalan Trails Northern Trails*
books.com.tw/products/0010820387
Web: tour.ntpc.gov.tw/zh-tw/Tour/List?wnd_id=40&type=134

B NATIONAL HUMAN RIGHTS MUSEUM
國家人權博物館 白色恐怖景美紀念園區

Come to grips with what is history and human rights at the prison yard for the victims of white terror
在曾是白色恐怖受難者的監禁場域重新理解歷史與人權

⌐ 新北市新店區復興路131號 | 09:00-17:00 (Closed on Mondays)
No. 131, Fuxing Rd., Xindian Dist., New Taipei | www.nhrm.gov.tw

C NEW TAIPEI CITY ART MUSEUM 新北市美術館

A new art landmark in New Taipei City, inspired by the concept of "a modern art museum amidst the reed beds"
新北藝術地標，以「蘆葦叢中的現代美術館」為設計發想

⌐ 新北市鶯歌區館前路300號 | +886-2-2679-6088
No. 300, Guanqian Road, Yingge District, New Taipei City
10:00-17:00 (Closed on Mondays)

D BRILLIANT TIME: SOUTHEAST THEME BOOKSTORE
燦爛書店：東南亞主題書店

Southeast Asian bookstore that lends books instead of selling them. Related activities are frequently organized
一間只借不賣的東南亞文化書店，時常舉辦相關活動

⌐ 新北市中和區興南路一段135巷1號 | Fri.-Sun. 14:00-21:00
1, Ln. 135, Sec.1, Xinnan Rd., Zhonghe Dist., New Taipei | FB: btbookstw

E SMALL SMALL BOOKSHOP 小小書房

Independent bookshop at Dingxi MRT Station that focuses on humanities. See website for lectures and events
頂溪站的人文獨立書店，講座活動可上網站查詢

⌐ 新北市永和區文化路192巷4弄2-1號
No. 2-1, Aly. 4, Lane 192, Wenhua Rd., Yonghe Dist., New Taipei
smallbooks.com.tw | 13:30-22:00

F GUTTA BOOKS & COFFEE 無論如河

An independent bookstore on the Tamsui riverbank that focuses on healing and arts
淡水河畔以療癒身心、藝術為主題的獨立書店

⌐ 新北市淡水區中正路5巷26號2樓
2F, No. 26, Lane 5, Zhongzheng Rd., Tamsui Dist., New Taipei
13:00-21:00 | facebook.com/guttabooks

A Q.B. DAYS 靠北過日子

A Café that serves also good food near the sea. It is more convenient to visit on weekdays

在海邊提供好食物的咖啡店，平日去更舒服

新北市金山區海興路174號 | facebook.com/qbdays
174, Haixing Rd., Jinshan Dist., New Taipei | +886-2-2408-2332
11:00-19:00 (Closed on Wednesdays)

B STONEWALL CAFÉ 石牆仔內咖啡館

Pastoral coffee shop in a century-old courtyard offering traditional lunch and dinner

百年三合院裡的田園咖啡店，提供中式午晚餐

新北市淡水區忠寮里大埤頭3號 | +886-2-2621-0252
No. 3, Dapitou, Tamsui Dist., New Taipei City
11:00-19:00 (Closed on Mon. and Tue.)

C CHLIV NEW TAIPEI JIUFEN

World Latte Art Championship winning café in Jiufen mountain town

隱身九份山城的世界拉花冠軍咖啡

新北市瑞芳區輕便路59-1號
No. 59-1, Qingbian Rd., Ruifang Dist., New Taipei City
10:00-18:00 | +886-2-2406-2308

D SOMEWHERE OUT THERE 山凹

A hidden gem coffee shop nestled in Sandiaoling, where you can enjoy coffee, desserts, and the serene mountain views

隱身在三貂嶺的質感咖啡廳，享受咖啡、甜點與寧靜山景

新北市瑞芳區魚寮路110號 | facebook.com/somewhereouthere110
No. 110, Yuliao Road, Ruifang District, New Taipei City
預約制 By appointment only.

E SUGARHOLIC 嗜甜

Bakery with affordable and delicious cakes near Tamkang University

淡江大學旁平價美味的溫馨蛋糕店

新北市淡水區北新路184巷142弄23號
No. 23, Aly. 142, Ln. 184, Beixin Rd., Tamsui Dist., New Taipei
13:00-21:00 | facebook.com/sugarholic.tw

F JOUONS ENSEMBLE PÂTISSERIE 稻町森法式甜點舖

A renowned specialist for French desserts. There are only a few seats inside—take away is possible

板橋法式甜點專賣名店，店內位子較少可外帶食用

新北市板橋區貴興路86號 | +886-2-2958-8806
No. 86, Guixing Rd., Banqiao Dist., New Taipei City
13:00-19:00 (Closed on Tuesdays)

Photo credit : 青青餐廳

Photo credit : 名流水岸

Photo credit :

A JUSTPINGLIN 坪感覺

A diner based on healing. It has Pinglin's afternoon tea and sales of agricultural produce

療癒系餐廳，有坪林下午茶並販售小農作物

新北市坪林區坪林街12號 | facebook.com/justpinglin12
No. 12, Pinglin, Pinglin Dist., New Taipei City
11:00-17:00 ,weekends 11:00-19:00 (Closed on Mon. to Wed.)

B ELITE CUISINE 名流水岸

Indulge in a mindful retreat for your body and mind with a no-menu vegetarian restaurant by the riverside in Wulai

在烏來河岸邊的無菜單蔬食料理，來沉澱身心吧

新北市石碇區碇格路二段2號 | +886-933-615-950
No. 2, Sec. 2, Dingge Rd., Shiding Dist., New Taipei City
11:30-14:30, 17:30-21:00 (Closed on Mon. and Tue.)

C MOON PAVILION 望月樓

Come savor the flavors of modern Cantonese cuisine, innovative dim sum, and stunning skyline vistas

來此享用新派粵菜、造型港點與高空美景

新北市板橋區新站路16號百揚大樓48F | +886-2-7705-9703
48F, Baiyang Building, 16 XinZhan Rd., Banqiao Dist., New Taipei
11:30-14:30, 18:00-21:30

D TCHIN TCHIN RESTAURANT 青青餐廳

Founded by renowned Taiwanese chef A-Fa, dedicated to promoting Taiwanese culinary culture

由台菜名師阿發師創立，致力於推動台菜文化

新北市土城區中央路三段6號 | +886-2-2267-1127
No. 6, Sec. 3, Zhongzheng Rd., Tucheng Dist., New Taipei City
1:00-14:00, 17:00-21:00

E LIU BIJU 六必居潮州沙粥鍋

A heaven for those who love casserole and crabs. Be sure to make a reservation

愛吃熱粥與蟹膏人的天堂，務必先預約

新北市板橋區中山路一段160-3號 | +886-2-2952-8827
No. 160-3, Sec. 1, Sanmin Rd., Banqiao Dist., New Taipei City
11:30-13:30, 17:30-21:30, weekends 11:20-22:00

F TASTE OF YUNNAN 雲南口味

Come to the Myanmar Street to taste the authentic Burmese cuisine

來緬甸街品嚐道地的滇緬料理

新北市中和區華新街48號 | +886-2-8943-4119
No. 48, Huaxin St., Zhonghe Dist., New Taipei City
Fri.-Sun. 07:00-13:00

Photo credit：Stella Tsai

A VOLANDO URAI SPRING SPA & RESORT 馥蘭朵烏來

A hot spring hotel along the Nanshi River in Wulai District
烏來南勢溪畔的溫泉藝文酒店

⌐ 新北市烏來區新烏路五段176號
No. 176, Sec. 5, Xinwu Rd., Wulai Dist., New Taipei City
facebook.com/taiwan.volando
+886-2-2661-6555

B THREE ZHI VILLA 三芝洋房招待所

A beautiful villa in Sanzhi District's Zhi Bai Yi Village that
serves only one group at a time
一天只招待一組客人，在三芝芝柏藝村裡的老屋民宿

⌐ 新北市三芝區迎旭街13號
No. 13, Yingxu St., Sanzhi Dist., New Taipei City
+886-926-000-596 | facebook.com/threezhivilla

C MUDAN MOUNTAIN RIVER 牡丹小山溪

A hidden hot spring retreat in Mudan Village, offering
breathtaking mountain views and rejuvenating herbal baths
隱身在牡丹小鎮裡的祕密湯屋，享受深山美景與藥浴

⌐ 新北市雙溪區牡丹里 | instagram.com/mudan_montain_river
Mudan Village, Shuangxi District, New Taipei City
私訊 Instagram 預約 | DM on Instagram for reservations

D ADAGIO JINGUASHI 緩慢金瓜石

Come to Adagio Jinguashi to experience the local slow
travel, restful lifestyle, and slow food
來緩慢金瓜石慢遊、慢活、慢食

⌐ 新北市瑞芳區山尖路93之1號 | +886-971-566-188
No. 93-1, Shanjian Road, Ruifang Dist., New Taipei City
facebook.com/adagio.travel

E OWL STAY-JIUFEN 九份山居

A hostel full of youthful vitality in which one can attend
night tours and catch the sunrise in the morning
青年旅宿獨有的活力，可參加夜間導覽，早起看日出

⌐ 新北市瑞芳區基山街247號
No. 247, Jishan St., Ruifang Dist., New Taipei City
+886-2558-5050 | owlstay.travel/room

F XINGFU SHANXING 幸福山行

A romantic mountain house made of glass along the Jing
Tong Old Street
想要點浪漫，可以來菁桐老街旁的山居玻璃屋

⌐ 新北市平溪區靜安路二段274巷10號
No. 10, Ln. 274, Sec. 2, Jing'an Rd., Pingxi Dist., New Taipei
+886-2-2495-2728

THE OLD STREET ROUTE
老街路線

AROUND JIUFEN
and JINGUASHIH

九份、金瓜石周邊

ENJOY A CUP OF TEA AND IMAGINE THE GOLDEN YEARS 喝杯茶，遙望黃金歲月

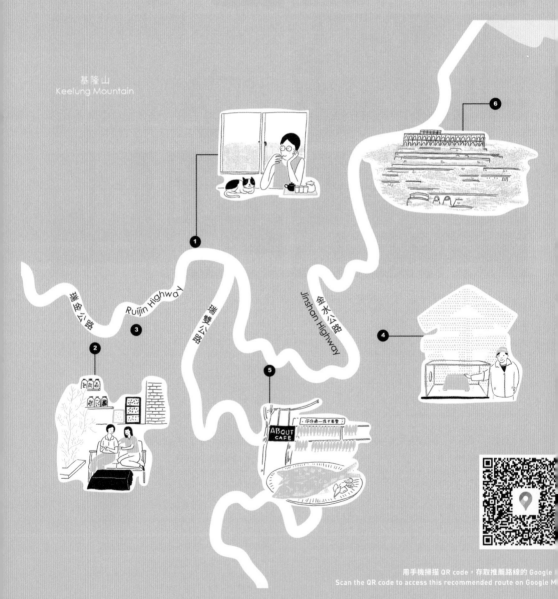

基隆山
Keelung Mountain

貂金公路

Ruijin Highway

瑞雙公路

金水公路
Jinshan Highway

ABOUT CAFE

1) 10:00   Catch the morning bus to Jiufen Old Street and mingle with the crowd

2) 12:30   Have a cup of herbal tea at the Wild Herbs Gallery to catch your breath

3) 14:00   Overlooking the sea, unwind at the Jiufen Teahouse

4) 16:00   Proceed to Jinguashih and learn about the mountain town's gold panning history in the New Taipei City Gold Museum

5) 18:00   Tuck away to dine at one of the mountain town's great restaurants

6) 19:30   See the Remains of the 13 Levels lit in amber

---

1) 10:00   一早先搭公車,來「九份老街」體驗一下跟觀光客人擠人

2) 12:30   在「野事草店」喝杯青草茶喘口氣

3) 14:00   來九份茶館悠閒泡茶,遠眺海景

4) 16:00   前往金瓜石,在「黃金博物館」認識山城淘金歷史

5) 18:00   在藏身在山城中的餐廳好好吃頓晚餐

6) 19:30   看琥珀色燈光照亮「水湳洞選煉廠遺址」

Reminders:

· It rains a lot in Jiufen, so remember to pack rain gear!

· There are insane amounts of people during holidays and weekends, so visiting on weekdays is strongly recommended.

· Staying overnight lets one marvel at the beauty of the mountain town's morning, twilight and night. Those not planning to stay the night ought to pay attention to the departure time of the afternoon and evening buses.

小提醒:

· 九份多雨,記得攜帶雨具!

· 假日人潮洶湧,強烈建議平日前往。

· 若能在此住一天,可一次看見山城的日出、黃昏與夜晚美景,若無過夜也要注意回程公車時間。

10:00
JIUFEN OLD STREET

1. 九份老街

The fascinating mountain town of Jiufen has always been welcoming to international travelers. Take the Keelung bus number 1062 from the Zhongxiao Fuxing metro station (exit 1) that will arrive to the Old Street. Try Alan Caoziguo, Ah Gan Taro Balls or other well—known snacks along the way. Finally, feel the charm of the old Taiwan at the Shengping Theater which was featured in the film director Hou Hsiao-Hsien's drama *A City of Sadness*.

有著迷人風景的山城九份，一直深受國際旅客歡迎。從台北市忠孝復興站 (1號出口) 搭1062基隆客運就可以直達老街，沿路可試試「阿蘭草仔粿」、「阿柑姨芋圓」等知名小吃，最後到侯孝賢導演《悲情城市》取景的「昇平戲院」，感受台灣舊時氛圍。

12:30
WILD HERBS GALLERY
AND
CHIUFEN STUDIO

2. 野事草店 與 九份文史工作室

A farmhouse brunch shop Hi, Ryou Caf'e used to operate on Pucheng Street in Taipei but was relocated to Jiaofen where it now collects local plants and stories for herbal teas and chicken cakes. Chiufen Studio next door is a fruit of Mr. Luo's hard labor, as he operates the space much like a community library, leading people to see the history of Jiaofen (group tours can be reserved).

本來在台北浦城街經營小農早午餐店的「日愣」，結束營業後來到了九份開設「野事草店」，採集當地植物與故事元素放入青草茶與雞蛋糕中。隔壁的「九份文史工作室」是由長期在地耕耘的羅濟昆老師所經營的空間，像是社區圖書館般的存在，帶領大家看見九份歷史人文 (可團體預約導覽)。

14:00
TEA AND POTTERY APPRECIATION

3. 喝茶賞陶

Only a fool would come to Jiaofen and not have a rest in one of its tea-houses. Savor the virgin leaves at Jiufen Teahouse whilst appreciating the pottery works of Mr. Hong. When in need of a lunch to go along with your tea, head over to A-MEI Tea House or Siidcha. Those who wish to avoid the crowds can seek Jiufen's tranquility in the company of some food and tea farther ahead at Shuyao.

來到九份如果沒有在茶樓泡壺茶，好像就少了那麼一味。來「九份茶坊」品茗，看看洪志勝老師的陶藝作品吧！若想用午膳，可到有茶也有供餐的「阿妹茶樓」與「吾穀茶糧」。不喜歡人群的朋友，可以到遠一點的「树橎」，在茶食之中找回九份的寧靜。

THE OLD STREET ROUTE
老街路線

16:00
NEW TAIPEI CITY GOLD MUSEUM
4. 黃金博物館

Continue to what was once the largest gold mining area in Asia, Jinguashih. The old mining office was renovated into the New Taipei City Gold Museum, which hosts a gold bar that weighs 220 kilograms. To experience the mine's old working conditions, one can buy the entrance ticket at the Benshan Wukeng, at the back of the park. Following the trail leads to Jinguashi Shrine where one can behold the golden sunset of the gold mountain town.

繼續前往曾是亞洲最大金礦產區的金瓜石，由昔日的採礦辦公室改建而成的「黃金博物館」還收藏了重達 220 公斤的大金塊！在園區後方的「本山五坑」可購買門票進入體驗舊時礦工工作場景，沿著登山步道可抵達「金瓜石神社遺址」，在金黃色的夕陽中遠眺黃金山城美景。

18:00
DINNER
5. 晚餐

On weekdays, you can dine at Take a Walk Diner run by Take a Walk Café where the meal is a fixed set of the owner's special home-style cooking. On holidays, one can venture into Shibuyan and have a go at their signature dish of preserved salted threadfin with maofan rice. Its owner also runs the About Cafe_pasta in Jinguashih, serving Italian pasta and coffee. If you have a car, consider visiting the slightly farther Huí Huí gastropub (reservations required). Nearby, you'll find the charming independent bookstore Feishudian.

平日來晚餐可以到由「散散步咖啡旅宿」經營的「迷迷路食堂」，吃老闆特製的家常定食料理。若在假日前往可以到「食不厭」吃招牌午仔魚一夜干與貓飯，老闆在金瓜石也經營「寬哥的關於咖啡」，提供自製義大利麵與單品咖啡。若有交通工具也推薦到稍遠一些的餐酒館「迴回」（需事先預訂），一旁有迷人的獨立書店「非書店」。

19:30
REMAINS OF THE 13 LEVELS
6. 水湳洞選煉廠遺址

After dinner, carry on to what was once an ore refining site during the Japanese occupation era, Remains of the 13 Levels. It was gradually abandoned due to a decline in production. In autumn 2019, the unit in charge at the Taiwan Power Company invited Zhou Lian, an internationally renowned light artist, to revamp the ruins into a light art installation and to return the once luminous mountain town to some of its former splendor. The beautiful amber-colored ruins can be seen lit every evening between 18:00 – 21:00.

吃飽前往「水湳洞選煉廠遺址」，這裡曾是日治時期的選礦煉製場，在礦業沒落後逐漸荒廢，直到 2019 年中秋，主管單位台電公司邀請國際照明大師周鍊為遺址設計燈光藝術，重新點亮了曾經輝煌的山城。現在每日晚間六點到九點都能欣賞閃爍著琥珀色的美麗遺址。

BANQIAO, YINGGE AND SANXIA DISTRICTS

板橋、鶯歌與三峽周邊

WANDER THE GARDENS OF A TRADITIONAL MANSION, STROLL THE STREETS OF A POTTERY TOWN

逛大戶人家，看陶藝之美

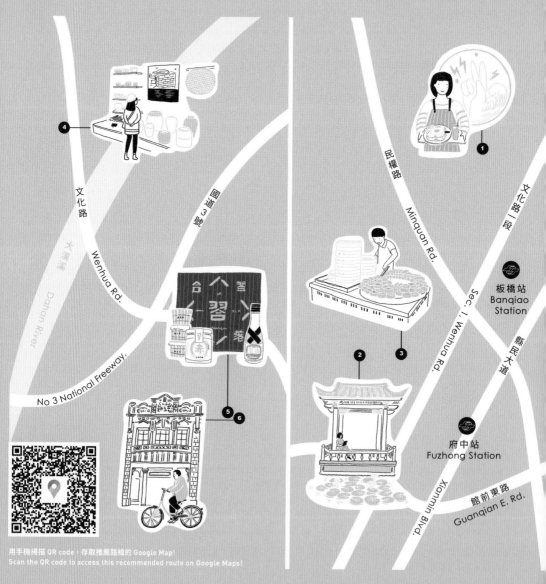

文化路

大漢溪
Dahan River

Wenhua Rd.

國道３號

No 3 National Freeway

民權路

Minquan Rd.

文化路一段

Sec. 1 Wenhua Rd.

板橋站
Banqiao Station

縣民大道
Xianmin Blvd.

府中站
Fuzhong Station

館前東路
Guanqian E. Rd.

用手機掃描 QR code，存取推薦路線的 Google Map！
Scan the QR code to access this recommended route on Google Maps!

1)	09:00	Have breakfast at Hoochuu in Banqiao, in the administrative center of New Taipei City
2)	10:00	Walk to Ci-Hui Temple in seek of blessings and see The Lin Family Mansion and Garden from the Qing dynasty
3)	11:00	Pick up a few delicious consumables from the nearby market and proceed to Yingge District
4)	13:00	Learn the tricks to making pottery at the New Taipei City Yingge Ceramics Museum and shop on the Old Street for ceramics
5)	16:00	Transfer to Sanxia District and see its creativity and vitality in CAN
6)	18:00	Finish the day of leisure with a dinner on the Sanxia Old Street

1)	09:00	一早先到新北行政中心板橋，在「好初二二」吃早餐
2)	10:00	散步到「慈惠宮」求平安符，再到「林本源園邸」看清代豪宅
3)	11:00	在附近吃點市場美食墊墊胃，接著前往鶯歌
4)	13:00	到「鶯歌陶瓷博物館」認識陶瓷工藝，在老街添購杯壺碗盤
5)	16:00	轉往三峽，在「甘樂文創」看見地方創意與活力
6)	18:00	在三峽老街晚餐，結束悠閒的一日

Reminders:

Yingge District tends to be busy during holidays with some of the shops closed on weekdays. For those wishing to avoid the crowds, going on weekdays is of greater convenience.

小提醒：

鶯歌假日較為熱鬧，有些店家平日不營業。但若想避免人潮，平日前往比較舒服。

09:00
HOOCHUU BREAKFAST RESTAURANT

1. 好初二二

Arrive early in Banqiao, the administrative center of New Taipei City, which is actually known to have many brunch and sweets shops on a par with Taipei. Apart from its delicious food, Hoochuu is interesting for their themed activities which they hold every other Sunday, and if you visit around the Christmas season, its staff are dressed to impress. As the weather gets colder, they start to sell much liked soups, so remember to be early for the queue.

早上來到新北市政府所在地板橋，這一帶其實有許多不輸台北市的早午餐店與甜點店，但「好初」除了餐點美味還相當有趣，每個月第二個禮拜日店家都會舉行主題日活動，每年聖誕節店員更是精心打扮。個人喜歡天冷時推出的湯品，記得早點去排隊！

10:00
CI-HUI TEMPLE
AND
THE LIN FAMILY MANSION AND GARDEN

2. 板橋慈惠宮 與 林本源園邸

After done eating, visit The Lin Family Mansion and Garden and see the Qing dynasty structures. There is a tour every morning at 10:00 to which one can sign up in advance. After the tour is over, you may pay your respects to the goddess Mazu at the Ci-Hui Temple. If traveling with children, Banqiao 435 Art Zone is recommended for its large grass field.

吃飽到俗稱「板橋林家花園」的「林本源園邸」看清代林園建築，每日 10:00 有固定導覽，可以提前抵達登記參加。逛完可到板橋「慈惠宮」拜媽祖，求個平安符。若是帶小朋友一同旅行，也推薦有著大草皮的「板橋 435 藝文特區」。

11:00
LUNCH

3. 午餐

Huangshi Market close to The Lin Family Mansion and Garden has many local eateries, such as the Minyuan on Beimenjie Street with its tasty noodles and different kinds of shortcake. Other recommendations include Gongkou Street's Banqiao thick soup with shrimp and Kaochi fried squid (remember to order the assortment of Yuguo rice, radish cake and sticky-rice sausage).

林家花園附近的黃石市場一帶有許多在地小吃，像是北門街上的「明園江浙點心」，麵點美味外，各式酥餅也不可錯過。其他還推薦宮口街上的「簡秋香油飯」、「板橋蝦仁焿」和「高記生炒魷魚」（記得點盤綜合芋粿、蘿蔔糕和糯米腸！）。

13:00
YINGGE CERAMICS MUSEUM
4. 鶯歌陶瓷博物館

Take a train to the little ceramics town of Yingge. Once familiar with the New Taipei City Yingge Ceramics Museum's history of ceramics and the contemporary ceramic art, carry on and take a stroll on the Yingge Old Street which many of the ceramic vendors gather. Many of the old school kiln yards, such as The Shu's Pottery and Tai-Hwa Pottery, have set up a sightseeing workshop or a flagship store on the Old Street. There are plenty of different stores to visit and compare so don't judge everything by your first shop.

搭火車前往陶瓷小鎮鶯歌，先在「鶯歌陶瓷博物館」看製陶歷史與當代陶藝創作，再到各式陶器店家聚集的鶯歌老街逛逛。老牌窯廠像是「新旺集瓷」與「臺華窯」等也在老街設有觀光工廠或旗艦店。小心別在第一家就失手，可以多逛多比較！

16:00
CAN
5. 甘樂文創

Continue by taking a taxi to Sanxia District, which was once heavy with indigo dyers, and which is Taiwan's number one when it comes to green tea producers. It is recommended to first pop in at the shop CAN. Established by locals, it provides tasty Sanxia treats and knowledge about the district. CAN also provides tours and DIY courses on crafting tea and indigo dye. Reservations can be made on their official website at: www.thecan.com.tw

接著搭計程車前往三峽，這裡曾是藍染重鎮，也是台灣綠茶產地之一。建議先到由在地人創辦的「甘樂文創」，從這裡提供的三峽好食、好物快速認識三峽。甘樂也提供製茶、藍染 DIY 等多項體驗課程與導覽，可先上官網預約：www.thecan.com.tw

18:00
SANXIA OLD STREET
6. 三峽老街

Come the evening, walk along the Sanxia Old Street and behold the incense stands and carvings of the exquisite Qingshui temple. Solitary travelers can have a crack at Hodao diner's battered pork chop set, though groups will enjoy a table at the authentic Taiwanese fried food restaurant Shilaichen, *rechao* style. To top it off, visit the Fumeishuan Bakery and buy the Sanxia brand pastries which are crispy on the outside and soft on the inside, and which have different flavors, both hot and cold.

晚上逛逛三峽老街，先參觀香火鼎盛、雕飾精美的清水祖師爺廟。若是一人出遊可到「厚道飲食店」嗑香酥排骨飯；若一群人可前往「喜徕珍古井餐廳」點桌台式家常熱炒。吃飽記得前往「福美軒餅舖」買外酥內軟的三峽名產「金牛角」，熱吃冷吃都有不同風味。

A ROMANTIC RAIL LINE
OF HISTORICAL COAL MINNING FAME

PINGXI LINE

平溪線鐵道：因煤礦而生的浪漫支線

Photo credit：kob

SPECIAL FEATURE
NEW TAIPEI
新北煤樣

Branching off at Ruifang, the railway trip of the Pingxi Line starts from Sandiaoling. As the train passes by one long-forgotten village after another: Dahua, Shifen, Wanggu, Lingjiao, Pingxi, and Jingtong, it's like exploring the history of Taiwan's coal industry. As the train slowly runs into the beautiful forest, one may stop at the less traveled Dahua station first. Right by the station, Yu Lu Café, hidden in a single-story house, is like an old friend waiting for your visit. After having a cup of heartwarming coffee, the next stop is the most bustling town on the Pingxi branch line—Shifen, where one may stroll through the old streets and waterfall-viewing suspension bridge. And at the New Pingxi Coal Mine Museum transformed from a former coal mine, one can ride Taiwan's first electric locomotive, lovingly called the one-eyed monk, and experience the life of a coal miner.

Next coming to Pingxi, a town renowned for its sky lanterns that can be released here legally, one wouldn't want to miss the chance to enjoy this special cultural experience. Developed by the Bank of Culture and Yiqiao Traditional Sky Lantern Studio's craftsman Lin Guohe, the eco-friendly sky lanterns send not only the wishes written on the lanterns but also the hope of environmental protection up into the sky. Then arriving at Houdong, an important coal mine in the past, now earns a big name for its cat village where one can take a pleasant walk with the companion of cats. On your way back, rest a bit at Café Hytte in Sandiaoling. Reinvented from a nearly deserted house, the unpretentious coffee shop provides a getaway spot for those who in search of tranquility and imparts a sense of nostalgia. (by Chia-Fang Li)

Transportation: Transferring to Pingxi Line at Ruifang Station of Taiwan Railways, one can purchase One Day Pass for Pingxi Line (NTD 80 and with lovely illustration) on the platform, or just swipe in and out of stations with the EasyCard (NTD 15 per ride between stations on the line).

火車從瑞芳彎入，在三貂嶺開始了平溪支線的旅行，唸著一個又一個遺落在森山的村落：大華、十分、望古、嶺腳、平溪、菁桐，串聯起來就是一部台灣的礦業史。跳上慢駛的火車，搖搖晃晃進入美麗的山林，先在人煙稀少的「大華車站」下車，藏在平房裡的「與路」，像老朋友那般靜候。在一杯溫暖的咖啡之後，往下一站繼續前進，來到平溪線上最熱鬧的「十分站」，有老街風光、懷舊吊橋，還有「新平溪煤礦博物館」把老礦區化為展場，這裡可搭乘暱稱「獨眼小僧」的台灣最早電氣化火車頭，追溯從前人入山採礦的生活記憶。

再來到台灣可合法施放天燈的「平溪站」，自然不可錯過這項有趣的文化體驗。由「文化銀行」與「藝巧傳統天燈工藝社」的藝師林國和推動的「環保天燈」，不只是把心想願望寄託，更把友善環境的希望升空。接著抵達「猴硐站」，這裡曾是重要的礦區，如今卻成了聲名大噪的「貓村」，可體驗有貓咪相伴的散步旅行。回程時，可在「三貂嶺站」的咖啡店稍作歇息。低調經營的廢墟咖啡「Café Hytte」，選擇在人煙罕至的山野開店，給予人們避世求靜之處，感受平溪線上的歲月之美。（文／李佳芳）

交通： 由台鐵「瑞芳站」轉搭平溪支線，可在月台購買「平溪線一日券」（新台幣80元，有可愛插畫的車票可留做紀念。）也能直接刷悠遊卡上車（各站單程全票一律15元。）

YU LU CAFÉ
與路咖啡

新北市平溪區六分13號 | facebook.com/yulucafe
No. 13, Liufen, Pingxi Dist., New Taipei City
12:00-18:00 (Closed on Thursdays and Fridays)

YIQIAO TRADITIONAL SKY LANTERN STUDIO
藝巧傳統天燈工藝社

新北市平溪區十分街129號 | +886-2-2495-8829
No. 129, Shifen St., Pingxi Dist., New Taipei City
08:00-18:00 (Closed on Mondays)

TEMPLES

求財運？來新北就對了！

edit · ChungFun Wen

Taiwanese are crazy about "baibai" (praying for blessings) as there are more than 10,000 registered temples around Taiwan. Among them, several are allegedly work with remarkable miracles. If you'd like to appeal for riches, visit New Taipei City and go to the Earth God and Tiger God for their blessings.

Zhonghe: Hongludi Nanshan Fude Temple

Sits on Nanshijiao Mountain, Nanshan Fude Temple was originally a small temple built for the Earth God by the tea farmers who first settled here. As the God's blessing was regarded efficacious, it had drawn many worshippers who financed to extend it into the grand building of today. On the way to the Temple, one can see the imposing statue of Earth God standing midway up the hill from afar. Next to the statue is the God of Fortune Temple, where one can exchange "chienmu" (an NTD 1 coin blessed by the God of Fortune). It is believed that keeping the coin in your wallet would bring in more money. Then ascending by the stone steps to the main hall, one can enjoy a panorama of the city on the adjoining platform, while the amazing night view is especially recommended. (As the long flights of stone steps could be challenging, it is recommended to arrange transportation by vehicle to the main hall. Or one can take a shuttle bus arranged by the temple during the Lunar New Year holidays or on the birthday of the Earth God.)

Shiding: Fuhu Temple (Temple of Tiger God)

Huyegong (Tiger God), or respectfully called the General Xiantan, is a deified figure of the mount of gods and thus usually the offerings to Tiger God are placed below the shrine tables. Tiger God is also the guardian spirit of children, while nowadays many people would also turn to him for a blessing for their pets. According to the folklore, Tiger God would help bring in money, therefore worshippers would offer eggs—his favorite food—while praying for riches. When purchasing joss paper at Shiding's Fuhu Temple, one would get a cute sachet shaped like Tiger God as a gift. The sachets are in black, white, yellow, red, and green, representing five types of fortune. At the beginning of each Lunar New Year, the color of that year's sachet would be decided by Tiger God, so if you'd like to collect all the colors, come visit Taiwan every year for five consecutive years!

台灣人熱愛拜拜，光是全台有登記的廟宇數量就超過一萬座，其中有不少特別靈驗的廟宇，若想求財，不妨來趟新北，讓土地公與虎爺公保佑你財運亨通！

中和：烘爐地南山福德宮

「南山福德宮」最早是來此開墾的茶農所興建的小廟，因相傳靈驗，吸引許多虔誠信眾，並集資擴建成今日規模。前往福德宮的路上，遠遠就能看見矗立在半山腰的巨大土地公像，旁邊就是「財神殿」，可以來求「錢母」，放在皮夾中可吸引錢財進來。順著旁邊的登山石階往上走約半小時，就能抵達「正殿」，旁邊則是能將台北盡收眼底的觀景台，相當推薦來此欣賞夜景。（石階對體力不好的人來說會有些吃力，建議驅車前往正殿，或選在春節及土地公誕辰期間拜訪，可搭乘廟方安排的接駁車。）

石碇：伏虎宮（虎爺公廟）

虎爺公，尊稱下壇將軍，為諸神坐騎，一般多供於神桌下，是小孩子的守護神，現代人也會請虎爺收寵物為「契子」保平安。根據傳說虎爺會幫忙咬錢，因此也有許多人會帶著虎爺愛吃的雞蛋向虎爺求財。在虎爺公廟只要購買金紙，皆會附贈一個可愛的虎爺香包，共有黑、白、黃、紅、綠五色，各有其象徵意義。每年農曆年初時，虎爺會開示決定該年香包的顏色，如果想五色都搜集，得連續五年都來台灣玩囉！

HONGLUDI NANSHAN FUDE TEMPLE
烘爐地南山福德宮

⌐ 新北市中和區興南路二段399巷160-1號
No.160-1, Ln. 399, Sec. 2, Xingnan Rd., Zhonghe Dist.,
New Taipei City | 24小時開放 Open 24 hrs

FUHU TEMPLE 伏虎宮

⌐ 新北市石碇區潭邊里外按5之2號
No. 5-2, Wai'an, Tanbian Village, Shiding Dist., New
Taipei City | 07:00-19:00

最受年輕人歡迎的宜居城市

桃園
TAOYUAN

A LIVABLE CITY WELL-LOVED BY YOUNG PEOPLE

When you travel to Taiwan from abroad, you might assume you'll be arriving in Taipei because of the TPE written on your flight ticket. Instead, the first Taiwanese city you encounter is Taoyuan which, though not likely to be listed in your travel itinerary, is surprisingly one of the best cities in Taiwan to live in.

Young families choosing to avoid the sky-high real estate costs in Taipei often settle here, and are an important part of the population in Taoyuan, helping to make it the youngest city by average age in all of Taiwan.

Furthermore, the Taoyuan City Government has been very active in building the city's image by remodeling the office and the name cards of the Department of Public Information. They even commissioned Aaron Nieh, a famous Taiwanese graphic designer, to design the city magazine, *Taoyuan Story*, which presents readers with a fresh new look for a government publication.

As one of Taiwan's principal industrial cities, Taoyuan has attracted nearly 110,000 migrant workers from Southeast Asia, which has shaped the city's diverse and modern culture. Restaurants opened by new immigrants and foreign workers and offering exotic delicacies around both the Taoyuan and Zhongli Train Stations are places worth taking a trip to see, and to taste.

In recent years, Taoyuan has become a new home to numerous stylish shops, and a few arts and cultural events, such as the Taoyuan Land Art Festival and the Daxidaxi festival that combined folk religion and contemporary creativity. Unexpectedly dynamic and engaging, next time you're passing through the airport, take a detour and explore more of Taoyuan!

各位來到台灣的朋友們，雖然機票上目的地寫著 TPE 可能會讓你以為即將抵達台北，不過其實你首先踏上的，是一個名叫桃園的城市。

這裡也許不是大家旅遊的首選地，不過卻相當適合生活，許多負擔不起台北高房價的年輕家庭選擇在此安身立命，是台灣平均年齡最年輕的地方。

同樣地，桃園市政府也相當有活力，像是新聞處的辦公室和名片應該是各縣市政府中最有設計感的，市府出版的《桃園誌》也請來台灣知名設計師聶永真重新打造簡潔風格，為公家刊物帶來不常見的美感。

除此之外，身為台灣工業重鎮之一的桃園，也吸引了近 11 萬名的東南亞移工前來工作打拚，並漸漸在桃園形塑出多元的文化樣貌，尤其桃園與中壢火車站附近有許多新住民或外籍移工開設的美食餐館，相當值得去探險品嚐。

近年桃園也有不少風格店家出現，更固定舉辦地景藝術節、結合宗教與當代創意的「大溪大禧」慶典等活動，讓桃園變得更加活潑有趣，下次別再只去機場啦，一起去桃園逛逛吧！

Departing from Taipei Station on the HSR, it takes about 20 minutes to get to the Qingpu area of Zhongli District. To reach Taoyuan City, it takes about 40 minutes either by TRA or by bus from the main bus station. When traveling within Taoyuan, city buses and YouBike are available. However, renting a scooter provides you more mobility.

台北往桃園可搭乘高鐵，約 20 分鐘抵達中壢區青埔；若要到桃園市區，建議選擇台鐵或是由台北轉運站搭乘客運前往，約 40 分鐘內可抵達。市區內有公車與公共自行車 YouBike 可租借。若要更方便移動，建議租機車代步。

RECOMMENDATIONS
推薦

READING LIST 旅遊書籍

THE PLACE: TAOYUAN《本地 THE PLACE 01：桃園》
One of the best in-depth travel guides about Taoyuan's culture, customs, and people
從文化、習俗、人物等多角度切入，目前最棒的桃園深度旅遊書

⌐ books.com.tw/products/0010820628

TAOYUAN WALKING GUIDE《走讀桃園指南》
An in-depth Taoyuan walking guide co-created by local teachers, students, and historians
由在地師生與文史工作者共創的桃園走讀指南，城市歷史與人文

⌐ www.books.com.tw/products/0010989399

TAOYUAN STORY: CITY ISSUE 桃園誌專刊《城市誌》
Selected content from *Taoyuan Story* published by the city government, with detailed information introducing sightseeing spots
由桃園市政府集結《桃園誌》旅遊內容而成，詳細介紹各區景點

⌐ ebook.tycg.gov.tw/book/content.php?id=392

LOCAL PUBLICATIONS 在地刊物

TAOYUAN STORY《桃園誌》
Diligently produced local monthly magazine published by the city government. Online version available
桃園市政府發行的在地月刊，編輯用心，可線上閱讀

⌐ e-book：ebook.tycg.gov.tw/book/list.php?type=11

A BOOK OF DAXI《一本大溪》
Best reading material to discover the town of Daxi, published by Wood Art Ecomuseum
大溪木藝生態博物館出版，認識大溪的最好讀物

⌐ e-book：ebook.tycg.gov.tw/book/list.php?type=21

TRAVEL WEBSITES 旅遊網站

TAOYUAN TRAVEL 桃園觀光導覽網
Official Taoyuan travel website. Multiple language versions available
桃園旅遊官方網站，有多國外語資訊

⌐ travel.tycg.gov.tw

TAOYUANOTHER
Social media platforms sharing shops, spots, and events worth visiting
即時分享桃園好點好店與活動的粉絲專頁

⌐ facebook.com/taoyuanother｜IG：taoyuanother

GUIDED TOURS 導覽

TAOYUAN OLD TOWN NIGHT TOUR 桃園舊城夜導覽
Led by Siang Kháu Lū Cultural Kitchen, offering rice cuisine classes. Booking in advance for both tours and cooking classes required
由雙口呂文化廚房帶領，也舉辦米食廚藝課（需預約）

⌐ facebook.com/siangkhaulu｜siangkhaulu.com/tours-in-taoyuan

TRAVEL ZHONGLI 旅壢
Short trips in Zhongli organized by Taoyuan Art and Culture Front
由桃園藝文陣線成立的品牌，透過小旅行帶大家認識中壢

⌐ facebook.com/TravelJhongli

ANNUAL EVENTS 年度活動

TAOYUAN LAND ART FESTIVAL (SEPTEMBER)
桃園地景藝術節 (9月)
Discover arts in every corner of Taoyuan, expanding your vision of the environment
讓藝術進入桃園各區，打開對環境的想像

⌐ facebook.com/TaoyuanLandArt

Photo credit：Kris Kang

Photo credit：馬祖新村眷村文創園區

Photo credit：橫山書法藝術館

Photo credit：雙口呂

Photo credit：大溪木藝生態博物館

A TAOYUAN 77 ART ZONE 桃園 77 藝文町

Cultural park conversion of old Japanese police dormitories, holding frequent exhibitions and bazaars
日式警察宿舍群改造的文創園區，時常舉辦展覽與市集

⌂ 桃園市桃園區中正路77巷5號 | facebook.com/Taoyuan.77CityPlay
No. 5, Ln. 77, Zhongzheng Rd., Taoyuan Dist., Taoyuan City
11:00–22:00 (Closed on Mondays)

B HENGSHAN CALLIGRAPHY ART CENTER 橫山書法藝術館

An exquisite art museum that combines the elements of ink pond and inkstone table, promoting the art of calligraphy
建築融合「墨池」與「硯台」，推廣書藝的絕美美術館

⌂ 桃園市大園區大仁路100號 | +886-3-287-6176
No. 100, Daren Road, Dayuan District, Taoyuan City
09:30–17:00 (Closed on Tuesdays)

C SIANG KHÁU LŪ 雙口呂

A traditional courtyard house for making and enjoying rice cakes while learning about festive traditions
三合院中做粿、吃粿，也品嚐粿的節慶故事

⌂ 桃園市大溪區南興路一段277號 | siangkhaulu.com
No. 277, Section 1, Nanxing Road, Daxi District, Taoyuan City
預約制 By appointment only | facebook.com/siangkhaulu

D MATSU NEW VILLAGE CULTURAL AND CREATIVE PARK
馬祖新村眷村文創園區

A preserved base for military dependents' village culture, hosting regular cultural and creative market events
眷村文化保存基地，定期舉辦文創市集活動

⌂ 桃園市中壢區龍吉二街155號 | 09:00-21:00 (Closed on Mondays)
155, Longji 2nd St., Zhongli Dist., Taoyuan City | FB: ArtMatsuVillage

E ZONE ART 众藝術

Experimental site primarily dedicated to contemporary visual arts
以視覺藝術為主的當代藝術實驗場域

⌂ 桃園市桃園區中埔六街196巷22號 | facebook.com/ZATaoyuan
No. 22, Ln. 196, Zhongpu 6th St., Taoyuan Dist., Taoyuan City
12:00–18:00 (Closed on Mon. and Tue.)

F DAXI WOOD ART ECOMUSEUM 大溪木藝生態博物館

A museum complex dedicated to promoting the art of woodworking and the culture of Daxi
推廣木藝與大溪文化的博物館群

⌂ 桃園市大溪區中正路68號 | +886-3-388-8600
No. 68, Zhongzheng Road, Daxi District, Taoyuan City
FB: DaxiWoodartEcomuseum | 09:30-17:00 (Closed on Mondays)

Photo credit：啡蒔

Photo credit：只是光影 獨立咖啡廊

Photo credit：奮死唱片行

A MEET BOOKS 天井逅書

Elegant bookstore hidden in an old house down on Daxi Old Street

隱身在大溪老街古宅中的氣質書店

桃園市大溪區中山路12號 | facebook.com/meetbooks
No. 12, Zhongshan Rd., Daxi Dist., Taoyuan City
10:00–17:00 (Closed Mondays and Tuesdays)

B LIFESTYLE BOOKSTORE 晴耕雨讀小書院

Bookstore with a yard, sunshine, and it's own unique lifestyle

一家有草地、有陽光的生活風格書店

桃園市龍潭區福龍路二段169巷181弄30衖90號
No. 90, Aly. 181, Ln. 169, Sec. 2, Fulong Rd., Longtan Dist., Taoyuan
facebook.com/lifestylebookstore
10:00–18:00 (Closed on Mon. and Tue.)

C LANG HUAN BOOKSTORE 瑯嬛書屋

A gender-themed bookstore that regularly organizes lectures and events

性別主題書店，不定期舉辦各式講座與活動

桃園市中壢區榮民路165巷6號 | facebook.com/l.h.bookstore
No. 6, Lane 165, Rongmin Road, Zhongli District, Taoyuan City
14:00–21:00, Sat. 11:00–21:00, Sun. 11:00–18:00 (Closed on Tue. and Wed.)

D VERSE CAFE BY MINORCODE 啡蒔

Enjoy coffee, delicious Western cuisine, and curated lifestyle products, with occasional brand pop-up events

結合咖啡、美味西餐與生活選品，不定時有品牌客座活動

桃園市桃園區同德十一街45號 | +886-3-347-0077
No. 45, Tongde 11th St., Taoyuan Dist., Taoyuan City
10:30–17:30 (Closed on Thur. and Fri.)

E THE LIGHT DANCE WITH SHADOW INDIE CAFE & ART
只是光影 獨立咖啡廊

A cultural café that hosts various exhibitions and events

舉辦各式展覽與活動的老牌藝文咖啡館

桃園市桃園區新民街43巷10之1號 | facebook.com/riverdays
No. 10-1, Lane 43, Xinmin Street, Taoyuan District, Taoyuan City
14:00–19:00 (Clsoed on Tue. and Wed.) | +886-3-335-0368

F GROUPIES RECORDS 奮死唱片行

Nostalgic record store in Zhongli offering both mainstream and indie music

中壢老派唱片行，主流、獨立音樂都能在此找到

桃園市中壢區中平路30號3樓 | facebook.com/GroupiesRecords
3F., No. 30, Zhongping Rd., Zhongli Dist., Taoyuan City
15:30–22:00, weekends 15:00–22:00

Photo credit : Cake King

A CORK BISTRO 軟木塞義法小館

Ample portions of creative Italian-French food. The chicken broth of the day is my favorite

分量創意俱足的義法餐館，喜愛每日雞高湯

桃園市龍潭區中豐路上林段295號 | +886-3-470-2885
No. 295, Sec. Shanglin, Zhongfeng Rd., Longtan Dist., Taoyuan City
11:30–15:00, 17:00–21:30 (Closed on Tuesdays) | FB: corkbistro.tw

B ZHONG-ZHEN MARKET 忠貞市場

Enjoy Yunnanese/Burmese delicacies such as migan–flat rice noodles–at Dahuzi or Wuming

來「大鬍子米干」或「忠貞誠」吃滇緬美食

桃園市中壢區龍平路110號
No. 110, Longping Rd., Zhongli Dist., Taoyuan City
06:00–14:00 (Closed on Mondays)

C YOU-ZHUAN HOTPOT 佑專沙茶石頭火鍋店

An old hot pot restaurant in Taoyuan offers "shacha hot pot" and "stone hot pot"

桃園老牌火鍋店，有沙茶火鍋與石頭火鍋可選擇

桃園市桃園區中山路446之1號 | +886-3-333-6897
No. 446-1, Zhongshan Rd., Taoyuan Dist., Taoyuan City
16:00–22:00 (Closed on Tuesdays)

D CAKE KING 佳樂精緻蛋糕專賣店

Their aromatic and sweet Taiwanese take on Boston cream pie topped with milk powder is soft and incomparable

撒上奶粉、香甜軟綿的波士頓派宇宙無敵！

桃園市桃園區民生路124號 | facebook.com/lovecakeking
No. 124, Minsheng Rd., Taoyuan Dist., Taoyuan City | 08:30-21:30

E TAMA TAMA 慢食堂

A sweet-tooth's favorite, offering various hot and cold sweets, grilled dango, and mochi

甜點控報到，各式自製冷熱甜品和烤糰子與麻糬

桃園市桃園區鎮三街52號 | facebook.com/tamaice
No. 52, Zhen 3rd St., Taoyuan Dist., Taoyuan City
11:00–18:00 (Closed on Mondays)

F PEANUT HOUSE 張豐盛 花生之家

Try their signature peanut-sesame soft ice cream and then grab some peanut butter to go

來吃招牌花生芝麻霜淇淋，再外帶花生醬回家

桃園市中壢區中正路349號 | +886-3-492-0606
No. 349, Zhongzheng Rd., Zhongli Dist., Taoyuan City
09:00–21:00, weekends 09:00–18:00 (Closed on Mondays)

Photo credit：河童

Photo credit：谷點咖啡民宿

Photo credit：The Westin Tashee Resort

A THERE CAFÉ&LIVE HOUSE
Established music performance space in Taoyuan
桃園老字號的音樂表演空間

桃園市桃園區復興路454號
No. 454, Fuxing Rd., Taoyuan Dist., Taoyuan City
facebook.com/ThERELiveHouse
表演活動請洽臉書 | For performance events, please check FB page.

B KAPPA 河童
A restaurant and bar that serves delicious curry, tasty cocktails, coffee, and offers an all-day dining experience
有咖哩、好喝調酒和咖啡和全日餐酒館

桃園市中壢區青峰路一段49號 | +886-3-287-2878
No. 49, Section 1, Qingfeng Road, Zhongli District, Taoyuan City
12:00–15:00, 17:30–01:00

C VESPER CIGAR BAR 偉朋雪茄館
Owner with extensive whiskey and cigar knowledge. Cocktails also available
老闆有豐富威士忌與雪茄知識，也可來杯調酒

桃園市桃園區同安街176號 | +886-3-358-7646
No. 176, Tong'an St., Taoyuan Dist., Taoyuan City
19:00-02:00, Fri. and Sat. 19:00-03:00

D BEFORE B&B 烏樹林BEFORE
Stylish B&B doubles as a bookstore and a craft beer house
結合書店與精釀啤酒的質感民宿

桃園市龍潭區龍平路115巷138弄76號
No. 76, Aly. 138, Ln. 115, Longping Rd., Longtan Dist., Taoyuan City
facebook.com/wususlinB4

E GOOD DIAN COFFEE HOUSE 谷點咖啡民宿
One-night accommodations with two meals. Peaceful life surrounded by Lala Mountain
一泊二食，被拉拉山包圍的愜意生活

桃園市復興區華陵里巴陵8鄰30號
No. 30, Baleng, Fuxing Dist., Taoyuan City
www.goodian.com.tw

F THE WESTIN TASHEE RESORT 桃園大溪笠復威斯汀度假酒店
Close to Ta Shee Golf & Country Club and within a 10-minute drive to the Daxi Old Street
鄰近大溪高爾夫球場，10分鐘車程也能抵達大溪老街

桃園市大溪區日新路166號 | +886-3-272-5777
No. 166, Rixin Rd., Daxi Dist., Taoyuan City 335, Taiwan
facebook.com/WestinTashee

TAOYUAN
TRAIN STATION AREA

桃園火車站周邊

A LEISURELY STROLL IN TAOYUAN 悠閒走逛桃園

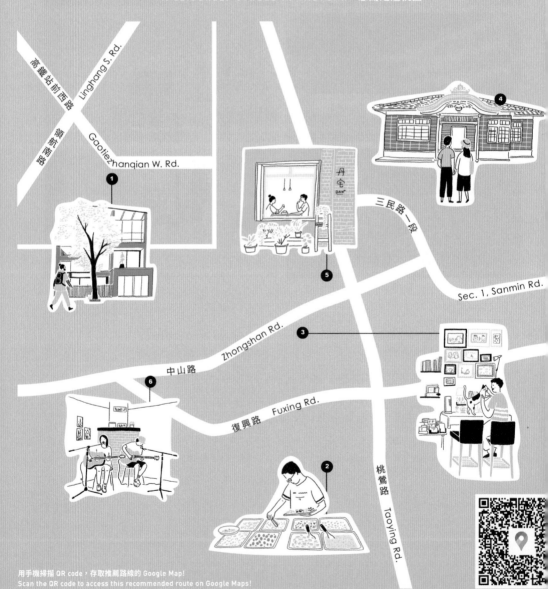

用手機掃描 QR code，存取推薦路線的 Google Map!
Scan the QR code to access this recommended route on Google Maps!

1)	10:00	Arrive at Taoyuan by the HSR and grab a taxi to A. Heritage (Xi Yuan Art Gallery)
2)	12:00	Transfer to the rear train station to enjoy Southeast Asian cuisine
3)	14:30	Stop for a rest at The Light Dance with Shadow Indie Café and check out some shops in the neighborhood
4)	16:00	Stroll around Taoyuan's Martyrs' Shrine, a former Japanese Shinto shrine
5)	18:00	Enjoy dinner at a restaurant in an old house or any number of other restaurants in the Zhongzheng Arts District
6)	19:30	Have some drinks and watch a live performance at ThERE CAFÉ & LIVE HOUSE

1)	10:00	從高鐵青埔站下車前往「霥園美術館」
2)	12:00	轉乘到後火車站享用東南亞美食
3)	14:30	在藝文咖啡廳「只是光影」小憩，接著逛逛附近小店
4)	16:00	到舊時為日本神社的「桃園忠烈祠暨神社文化園區」散步
5)	18:00	在老屋餐廳或藝文特區附近的店家享用晚餐
6)	19:30	吃飽去「ThERE 音樂展演空間」看表演或小酌一杯

Reminders:

A. Heritage requires reservations and welcomes visitors exclusively on Saturdays. We suggest scheduling your Taoyuan adventure for a Saturday to explore this cultural gem. On other days, consider visiting Taiwan's premier aquarium, "Xpark." It's the perfect spot to marvel at charming marine life and refresh your spirit!

小提醒：

霥園美術館採全預約制，目前只開放禮拜六預約參觀，因此建議安排週六造訪桃園。週六以外的時間，也推薦至「Xpark 都會型水生公園」，看看可愛的海洋生物們療癒身心！

10:00
A. HERITAGE

1. 襲園美術館

Designed by architect Abraham Lee, A. Heritage is a bright fair-faced concrete building displaying the creations and the lifestyle ideals of the artists-in-residence. Lectures, workshops, and other activities are sporadically held here. Reservation two days prior to the visit is required. Furthermore, the Taoyuan Museum of Fine Arts, set to open in 2026, is also located in the Qingpu area, and should definitely be added to your itinerary.

從高鐵青埔站下車走路 15 分鐘即可抵達建築師李靜敏親手打造的「襲園美術館」(需 2 日前預約),這是一座以清水模為主體的明亮建築,展示著藝術家們的創作和理想生活的樣貌,並不定時舉辦講座、工作坊等活動。而預計 2026 年完工的「桃園市立美術館」也同在青埔區,屆時來桃園可一同參觀。

12:00
SOUTHEAST ASIAN CUISINE

2. 享用東南亞料理

The large numbers of Southeast Asian migrant workers who have come to work in Taoyuan have enriched the city with a vibrant tapestry of cultures and delicious cuisine. Along Dalin Road and Yenping Road near the Taoyuan Train Station, you can find a variety of authentic Indonesian and Vietnamese restaurants and snacks that are simply delectable! After a satisfying meal, don't forget to visit the Southeast Asian cultural bookstore "SEAMi" on Dalin Road. Here, they occasionally host various lectures and markets related to Southeast Asian culture.

來桃園工作的眾多東南亞移工,為桃園帶來了豐富多元的文化與美食,桃園後火車站的「大林路」與「延平路」上有許多道地的印尼、越南東南亞餐廳與小吃,都相當美味!吃飽別忘了到大林路上的東南亞文化書店「望見書間」逛逛,這裡不定時舉辦各式相關講座與市集。

14:30
THE LIGHT DANCE
WITH SHADOW INDIE CAFÉ

3. 「只是光影」獨立咖啡廳

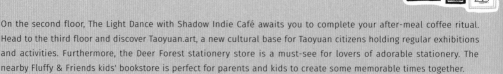

On the second floor, The Light Dance with Shadow Indie Café awaits you to complete your after-meal coffee ritual. Head to the third floor and discover Taoyuan.art, a new cultural base for Taoyuan citizens holding regular exhibitions and activities. Furthermore, the Deer Forest stationery store is a must-see for lovers of adorable stationery. The nearby Fluffy & Friends kids' bookstore is perfect for parents and kids to create some memorable times together.

吃飽到藏在 2 樓的「只是光影」喝杯咖啡,3 樓還有「藝文小地方」,定期舉辦展覽與各式活動,成為桃園市的民間文化基地。喜歡文具的朋友,可以到同在新民老街上的「小鹿文具所」逛逛;若是親子旅遊,附近還有可愛的童書店「毛怪和朋友們」!

16:00
TAOYUAN'S MARTYRS' SHRINE
4. 桃園忠烈祠暨神社文化園區

If you are interested in Japanese culture and heritage, Taoyuan's Martyrs' Shrine is one of the most well-maintained, large-scale martyrs' shrines in Taiwan and is a must-see. Once a Japanese Shintoism shrine during the Japanese colonial period, the nationalist government transformed this site into a hall for the worship of martyrs who fought against the Japanese army. Hiking along the stone steps up to the hill and walking through the torii–a traditional Japanese gate–you now enter the territory of kami, where Japanese and Taiwanese cultures intertwine.

對日式古蹟與文化有興趣的朋友，台灣少數保存完整、頗具規模的桃園忠烈祠不容錯過。曾供奉日本神道教神靈的神社在國民政府來台後，改為祭祀抗日烈士的忠烈祠，沿著石階登上山丘，跨入鳥居，代表來到神的領域，也來到台日歷史文化交會之處。

18:00
DINNER TIME
5. 晚餐時間

Visit The Chos situated in an old house for pasta, quesadilla, fried chicken and a glass of their signature cocktail (or tasty desserts for non-drinkers) for dinner. If you feel like an adventure in Taiwanese flavor, just head to the Zhongzheng Arts District and try Nanping Goose Shop's sliced goose, noodle soup, and various side dishes. Beloved by locals, the Vietnamese Delicacies in the same corner is also recommended.

晚餐可到由老屋改造而成的「粗蒔」享用義大利麵、墨西哥烤餡餅或炸雞，並來杯店家特調（若不想喝酒，甜點也好吃！）。如果想吃點台灣味，可以到藝文特區一帶的「南平鵝肉專賣店」切盤鵝肉配湯麵小菜，也推薦旁邊深受在地人喜愛的「越南美食」。

19:30
TIPSY TIME AFTER DINNER
6. 小酌一杯

Spend your evening enjoying live music at ThERE CAFÉ & LIVE HOUSE. Remember to check the performance schedule via their Facebook page before making the trip. If you can't make it to a live performance, it is a delightful place to simply have some drinks or beer. Vesper Cigar Bar, recommended by my drinker friend, is another good place to enjoy whiskey and cocktails.

晚上到桃園的「ThERE 音樂表演空間」看現場演出吧，記得先上臉書粉絲頁查詢活動，若剛好沒遇上表演，也能在此喝杯飲料或啤酒。想小酌一杯也可以到經過酒鬼朋友認證的「偉朋雪茄館」，喝杯威士忌或調酒。

DAXI
地方創生在大溪

Photo credit : Kris

Daxi is more than its famous dried bean curd and the old quarter packed with tourists. In recent years, more and more young people have returned to their hometown and try to interpret Daxi through their perspectives, breathing a new life into this century-old town in Taoyuan.

The rebirth of old houses

Sinnan 12 on Zhongshan Road is one of the best examples of young returnees creating new local businesses. The building with a Baroque-style archway that was popular during Japanese colonial period was the former residence of Dr. Fu Zujian. A group of youths spent over a year on the renovation while preserving its three courtyards. The space has been divided into a cultural and creative shop, performance venue, restaurant, independent bookshop, and lodging, presenting the century-old house's history to the public.

Stepping out of Sinnan 12, across the road sits the Lantia Teahouse, the residence of the late Qing Dynasty's governmental official Lu Yingyang. A few years ago, the nearly dilapidated mansion was bought and restored by eight architects who love old houses. Now the building's front half serves as an exhibition space, while the back is a teahouse. For those who love woodcarving arts, the exquisite wooden carvings between beams and pillars are a must-see.

說到大溪,可不是只有名產豆干而已。除了觀光客絡繹不絕的大溪老街,近年有許多年輕人選擇回到家鄉,嘗試以不同的角度詮釋他／她們所認識的大溪,也為這座百年老城注入一股全新的活力泉源。

老屋新生

位在中山路上的「新南 12 文創實驗商行」,就是青年返鄉的最佳例子之一,外觀承襲日治時期風靡一時的巴洛克式牌樓建築,這裡曾經是大溪醫師傅祖鑑的居所,現在由年輕團隊進駐,歷經一年多的修繕,保留原本三進三落的結構,並將空間劃分為文創商品與展演、餐廳、獨立書坊及民宿等區域,也讓百年老屋的歷史底蘊再次被看見。

走出新南 12 文創實驗商行,斜對面即是清末大溪秀才呂鷹揚的故居「蘭室」,原本近乎荒廢的建築在幾年前被八位熱愛老屋的建築師共同買下且致力修繕,目前屋內前半部為展覽空間,後半部為茶坊,若喜愛木雕的朋友千萬不可錯過梁柱間精美的木雕細節。

Strolling along Denglong Road into Daxi's old quarter, one would find Back Street Office Café sit in the alley next to Furen Temple. This heartwarming space with abundant wood elements stands out the bustling old town. The shop owner came from Taichung and built bonds with Taoyuan due to projects of renovating old houses. As he won the neighbors' hearts with sincerity, the small café has become the place for the locals to gather and exchange conversations. Also, because of Daxi's clean water resources, Back Street is the first shop that brews coffee with well water in Taiwan, the refreshing sweetness of its coffee is worth tasting.

The Celebration for Guan Gong's Birthday in a new era

In recent years, Daxi Puji Temple Celebration for the Birthday of Holy Emperor Guan, a traditional ceremony incorporating performing arts has drawn not only the attention of the younger generation but also numerous tourists. Since 1917, each year Daxi holds a grand celebration on Guan Gong's birthday (the 24th day of the sixth lunar month) to commemorate his blessing. Before the celebration, Daxi residents would join Shetao (local clubs of different trades) and practice folk-art performances in order to express their respect to Guan Gong in the deity processions on his birthday. Young people who are away from home would also return to join the festivities, and thus it is deemed as important as the Lunar New Year celebration for Daxi locals.

In addition to the traditional religious rituals, Daxi locals worked with Puji Temple and other groups to invite arts and cultural creators to participate. Moreover, the festival was turned into an attraction through integration with events like music and theatre performances, markets, and photography exhibitions. For example, one of the performances in 2019 was the collaboration of the national treasure performing group Chen Xihuang Traditional Puppet Troupe and the indie Taiwanese rock band Sorry Youth, demonstrating the amazing energy of creativity. As the traditional meets the modern, the town now embraces a wealth of new possibilities. If you'd like to see a different Daxi, come visit the town during this period and experience the exceptional festive mood. (by Vivian Yang)

沿著登龍路漫步進入大溪老街,「草店尾事務所」就落腳在福仁宮旁的小巷子,木質調的溫暖空間是喧鬧老街中的獨特存在。出身台中的店主因老屋改造工作而與桃園結緣,以外地青年的誠意打動街區,如今小小的咖啡店已然是街坊鄰居自然群聚、閒話家常的所在。也因為大溪乾淨的水質,使得這裡成為全台灣首家使用井水沖煮咖啡的店家,清甜的滋味值得一嚐。

新世代的關公聖誕慶典

除了店家之外,近年因結合藝文表演重回年輕一代焦點的「大溪普濟堂關聖帝君聖誕慶典」,也為大溪帶來許多觀光人潮。大溪自1917年以來,為了感念關聖帝君的庇佑,每年都會在關公誕辰日(農曆6月24日)舉辦盛大的慶祝活動。大溪人還依不同職業別組成「社頭」(社團),在活動前練習各種陣頭技藝,只為了在當天的遶境儀式中,展現對關公的崇高敬意。不僅在地人有志一同,遠在他鄉的孩子們也會趁著這天回鄉共襄盛舉,也讓慶典有了「大溪人第二個過年」的稱呼。

聖誕慶典除了傳統祭祀活動外,也在大溪當地居民、普濟堂與相關單位攜手努力下,邀請各方藝文創作者們參與,近年更透過音樂、市集、攝影展、劇場等形式,讓慶典更為精彩。比如2019年其中一場演出,找來國寶級布袋戲團「陳錫煌傳統掌中劇團」以及獨立台語搖滾樂團「拍謝少年」跨界合作,展現驚人創作能量,整座城市因著「傳統」與「現代」的交織而有了嶄新的可能。如果想看見不一樣的大溪,不妨趁著這段期間造訪,感受一下熱鬧沸騰的節慶氛圍。(文/楊孟珣)

BACK STREET OFFICE CAFÉ 草店尾事務所

桃園市大溪區草店尾1巷1號
No. 1, Ln. 1, Caodianwei, Daxi Dist., Taoyuan City
13:00-19:00 (Closed on Wednesdays)
facebook.com/bscafe.ltd

SINNAN 12 新南 12 文創實驗商行

桃園市大溪區中山路12號
No. 12, Zhongshan Rd., Daxi Dist., Taoyuan City
11:00-17:00 (Closed on Mon. and Tue.)
facebook.com/sinnan12

台灣少數還願意生孩子的城市
（由此可見它的好）

新竹
HSINCHU

ONE OF FEW TAIWANESE CITIES WITH GROWING FAMILIES (MUST BE A GOOD PLACE TO LIVE)

Photo credit : James Lin

The first time I went to Hsinchu was probably in college while visiting old classmates who attended National Tsing Hua University and National Chiao Tung University, two schools renowned for their engineering and science programs. To be honest, apart from being able to name three of Hsinchu's specialties—pork balls, rice noodles, and the Science Park—my knowledge of Hsinchu was very limited. When it came to good food, I even thought Hsinchu was a desert (I hereby apologize to all Hsinchu locals).

Fortunately, I have come to befriend several wonderful people who hail from Hsinchu and so have been properly reintroduced to Hsinchu in all its glory. More than being known as Taiwan's Silicon Valley and boasting Taiwan's highest birthrate*, Hsinchu truly is a happening city where interesting spaces and activities abound.

If you are a novice to Hsinchu, I would suggest starting your visit in the old city district (currently the North District), which is centered around Hsinchu City God Temple. There's no better way to see the city than meandering through the lanes and alleys and discovering old residences, local eateries, and new shops. The old city district is also the base of several organizations who are working to revitalize Hsinchu, such as CitiLens, a local publication studio known for their magazine, *Pork Ball Soup*, and Jiang Shan Yi Gai Suo, an arts and cultural space.

I also recommend visiting Chupei City in Hsinchu County. This up-and-coming area has been absorbing much of Hsinchu growing population and has attracted many independent bookstores, shops, and restaurants.

第一次造訪新竹，應該是大學時到以理工科系聞名的「清華大學」與「交通大學」找高中同學敘舊。老實說自己對新竹的了解相當貧乏，除了名產貢丸、米粉以及新竹科學園區外，可說是一無所知，甚至還覺得新竹是美食沙漠（在此跟新竹人道歉）。

還好，這幾年結交了幾位出身此地的有為青年，慢慢地跟著他們重新認識了新竹（也終於吃到了在地美食），發現原來這裡不只有科技新貴和新生兒*，還有更多有趣的空間與活動正在發生。

第一次來新竹不妨從鐵道以西、以城隍廟為中心的舊城區（新竹市北區）開始逛起，這裡的巷弄藏著許多老屋、道地小吃與新興小店。舊城也是年輕團隊振興新竹文化的基地，如出版在地刊物《貢丸湯》的「見域工作室」以及藝文展演空間「江山藝改所」都在此落地生根。

另外位於新竹縣的竹北市近年來吸引了許多在竹科工作的人口遷入，不少獨立書店與餐廳也隨之進駐，成為下個讓人期待的新竹生活場域。

*Taiwan has the world's lowest birthrate yet Hsinchu has the highest birthrate in the country!

* 在生育率全球倒數第一的台灣，新竹市是出生率最高的城市！

TRANSPORTATION 交通

It takes roughly half an hour to arrive at Hsinchu Station from Taipei via the high speed rail. Another 20 minutes will get you from the station to the city center where a wide variety of transportation is available, including: buses, YouBikes (which also run on EasyCard), and Uber.

台北搭乘高鐵至新竹站約半個小時，再到市區約需 20 分鐘。市區移動可搭乘公車或騎乘 YouBike（可使用悠遊卡），Uber 數量也充足。

RECOMMENDATIONS 推薦

◤ READING LIST 旅遊書籍

EXPERIENCE HSINCHU《走進無牆美術館：獨一無二的新竹國際導覽，體驗1,428 平方公里生活的美好和價值》
A comprehensive guide to the 13 townships of Hsinchu County from the perspective of an art curator
以藝術策展的眼光完整介紹新竹縣 13 鄉鎮的美

⌐ books.com.tw/products/0010772854

PROMENADE WITH FOOD《風城味兒：除了貢丸、米粉，新竹還有許多其他》
A collection of in-depth articles on Hsinchu's food, customs, and culture
深入描寫新竹美食、風土與人文味的飲食文集

⌐ books.com.tw/products/0010776695

◤ LOCAL PUBLICATIONS 在地刊物

PORK BALL SOUP《貢丸湯》
A quarterly magazine about Hsinchu, compiled by local youths
由新竹在地青年編集，認識風城的最佳季刊

⌐ citilens.cc | 各大書店皆有販售 Available at major bookstores

IN HSINCHU《IN新竹》
Each issue features an in-depth introduction on an industry, providing a professional perspective to learn more about Hsinchu
每期選定一個產業專題深入介紹，從職人角度認識新竹

⌐ 各大書店皆有販售 Available at major bookstores

◤ ILLUSTRATED MAPS 地圖

BIRD'S-EYE VIEW OF HSINCHU《新竹鳥瞰圖》
Take a bird's-eye view of Hsinchu's historical sites
從鳥瞰圖認識新竹古建築

⌐ 購買可洽詢 muyemapper@gmail.com
⌐ To purchase, please contact muyemapper@gmail.com

◤ TRAVEL WEBSITES 旅遊網站

HSINCHU CITY TRAVEL 新竹市觀光旅遊網
Hsinchu City's official travel guide website, offering great information in many travel categories
新竹市政府官方網站，有多元主題分類

⌐ tourism.hccg.org.tw

HAKKA HSINCHU 好客竹縣
The official travel website for Hsinchu County
新竹縣旅遊官方網站

⌐ travel.hsinchu.gov.tw

◤ GUIDED TOURS 導覽

HSINCHU RAILWAY STATION VISITOR INFORMATION CENTER: TOUR OLD HSINCHU CITY
新竹市火車站旅遊服務中心：舊城小旅行
A Chinese and English guided tour around old Hsinchu city from 10:00-11:00 am on weekends; sign up in advance via Facebook
每週六上午10:00-11:00舉行中英文舊城導覽，活動需事先於臉書報名

⌐ facebook.com/Hsinchu.Railway.Station

HSIN-STORY EXPLORATION ROUTE 新竹城事探索路線
A guided weekend walking tour organized by CitiLens; please sign up and pay on their website
由見域工作室規劃的舊城散步路線，需先於網站報名繳費

⌐ www.citilens.cc/pages/citi-tour

◤ ANNUAL EVENTS 年度活動

CHUCHANG ZHONGYUAN CITY GOD FESTIVAL (DURING THE SEVENTH MONTH OF THE LUNAR CALENDAR)
竹塹中元城隍祭〔農曆 7 月〕
Come confess your sins to the City God and pray for his pardon and blessing during the benjia ceremony!
自認有罪的人可以來「夯枷」請求城隍爺除罪！

⌐ www.weiling.org.tw

Photo credit：KRIS KANG

Photo credit：新竹市政府

Photo credit：將軍村

A HSINCHU CITY GOD TEMPLE 新竹都城隍廟

Taiwan's largest temple enshrining the highest ranking God

全台最大、「官階」最高的城隍神祇

新竹市北區中山路75號
No. 75, Zhongshan Rd., North Dist., Hsinchu City
+886-3-522-3666

B HSINCHU ZOO 新竹市立動物園

The oldest (and most beautiful) zoo that has been redesigned with an animal-friendly concept

以動物友善概念重新改建、現存最老（也最美）的動物園

新竹市東區食品路66號 | +886-3-522-2194
No. 66, Shihpin Road, East District, Hsinchu City
09:00–17:00 (Closed on Mondays)

C GENERAL VILLAGE 將軍村

Revitalized military dependents' village with shops and periodic markets and exhibitions

由眷村聚落活化，現有商家進駐，不定時舉辦市集展覽

新竹市東區金城一路69號 | +886-917-531-462
No. 69, Jincheng 1st Road, East District, Hsinchu City
10:00–18:00 (Closed on Mondays)

D HSIN CHIHPING FORMER RESIDENCE 辛志平校長故居

The former principal's residence of Hsinchu High School, now transformed into a restaurant and cultural space

歷任新竹中學校長宿舍，現為餐廳與藝文空間

新竹市東區東門街32號 | +886-3-522-0351
No. 32, Dongmen Street, East District, Hsinchu City
09:00–17:00, 18:00–22:00 (Closed on Mondays)

E OR BOOK STORE 或者書店

An independent bookstore in the New Tile House Hakka Cultural District

新瓦屋客家文化保存區內的氣質獨立書店

新竹縣竹北市文興路一段123號 | +886-3-550-5069
No. 123, Sec. 1, Wenxing Rd., Zhubei City, Hsinchu County
10:00–18:00 (Closed on Tue. and Wed.)

F ROSE COLORED BOOKSTORE 玫瑰色二手書店

A heartwarming used bookstore transformed from an old house in Hsinchu

新竹老屋改造的溫暖二手書店

新竹市北區集賢街19號 | +886-3-523-0331
No. 19, Jixian St., North Dist., Hsinchu City
12:00–21:00 (Closed on Thursdays)

Photo credit : Kris KANG

Photo credit : 新村小商號

Photo credit : 敲敲金工

A JIANG SHAN YI GAI SUO 江山藝改所

A unique space offering books, coffee, contemporary art exhibitions, and accommodation

有書、咖啡和當代藝術的展演與住宿空間

新竹市東區興達街1號 | +886-3-526-6456
No. 1, Xingda St., East Dist., Hsinchu City
14:30-22:00 (Closed on Wednesdays and Weekends)

B SPRING POOL GLASS STUDIO + THE POOL 春室

A design café and glass art studio located in Hsinchu Park, which also holds occasional glass workshops

在新竹公園裡的設計咖啡廳與玻璃工藝博物館

新竹市東區東大路一段2號 | +886-3-561-1039
No. 2, Section 1, Dongda Road, East District, Hsinchu City
10:00-17:30 (Closed on Mondays)

C OR CRAFT LIFE 或者工藝櫥窗

A comfy space integrating handicrafts and exhibitions, bringing craft products into our daily life

結合工藝選品與展覽的舒適空間，讓工藝進入日常生活

新竹市北區中央路75號 | facebook.com/OrCraftLife
No. 75, Zhongyang Rd., North Dist., Hsinchu City
10:30-18:30 (Closed on Tue. and Wed.)

D HIGHLIGHT STATIONARY 嗨賴文具工作室

A stationery store that also serves coffee

可以坐下來喝杯咖啡的文具選品店

新竹市北區江山街26-2號
No. 26-2, Jiangshan St., North Dist., Hsinchu City
14:00-21:00 (Closed on Tue. and Wed.)
+886-965-663-231

E NEW VILLAGE GROCERY 新村小商號

Promoting plastic reduction, the store offers related grocery and produce from small organic farmers

推廣減塑生活，販售相關雜貨與有機小農作物

新竹市北區集賢街54號 | +886-936-036-871
No. 54, Jixian St., North Dist., Hsinchu City
Fri.-Sun. 14:00-20:00 (Closed from Mon. to Thur.)

F CHOCCY METAL CAFÉ 敲敲金工

The first coffee shop that offers metalworking classes in Hsinchu

新竹第一間金工教學咖啡店

新竹市北區大同路140號 | facebook.com/choccymetal
No. 140, Datong Rd., North Dist., Hsinchu City
11:00-19:00

A PICCOLA ENOTECA 彼刻義式餐酒館

The best Italian food in Hsinchu
在新竹想吃西餐就來這裡

⌐ 新竹縣竹北市成功二街102號
No. 102, Chenggong 2nd St., Zhubei City, Hsinchu County
11:30-14:00, 18:00-22:00 (Closed on Sun. and Mon.)
+886-3-668-8313

B HOHMARKET 厚食聚落

An environmentally friendly marketplace that also sells produce, pastry, meals and coffee
有食材、烘焙、咖啡、廚房的綠色聚落

⌐ 新竹縣竹北市光明六路東二段95-5號 | +886-3-550-6289
95-5, Dong Sec. 2, Guangming 6th Rd., Zhubei City, Hsinchu County
10:00-18:00 (Closed on Mondays)

C YAN PING FOOD MARKET 延平大飯店

A local late-night favorite for supper
新竹在地鐵皮屋消夜場 (不是飯店喔)

⌐ 新竹市北區延平路一段「10元商店」旁 | +886-3-522-1026
Sec. 1, Yanping Rd., North Dist., Hsinchu City
17:00-00:00 (Closed on Mondays)

D CHU LE FOOD VILLAGE 竹樂食堂

A menuless restaurant serving Taiwanese cuisine that has been blessed by the former mayor
前市長也推薦的無菜單台菜餐館

⌐ 新竹市北區西大路690號 | +886-3-534-0996
No. 690, Xida Rd., North Dist., Hsinchu City
11:30-14:00, 17:30-21:00

E BMT LIFE AND NATURE 半畝院子

A tranquil tea house and restaurant
都市中最舒心的閑靜茶館與廚房

⌐ 新竹縣竹北市光明六路東二段381號
381, Dong Sec. 2, Guangming 6th Rd., Zhubei City, Hsinchu County
12:00-17:00 (Clsoed on Mon. to Wed.)
+886-3-668-5700

F SAMBAR CAFÉ 台灣水鹿咖啡館

Indigenous cultural café, famous for their latte art
有著圖騰拉花的原住民文化咖啡館

⌐ 新竹市北區大同路202號 | +886-3-525-1913
No. 202, Datong Rd., North Dist., Hsinchu City
09:00-17:00 (Closed on Mondays)

Photo credit：或者風旅

Photo credit：Tender Cocktail Bar

Photo credit：Bar Reviver

A EAST MARKET 1001 東市 1001

A super-relaxed bar inside the Dongmen market
來菜市場內的酒吧最輕鬆自在

📍 新竹市東區東門市場 1001 攤
Stand 1001, Dongmen Market, East Dist., Hsinchu City
+886-926-905-759
17:00-02:00

B TENDER COCKTAIL BAR

A passionate bar combining music and cocktails, themed
around Taiwan's independent music scene
結合音樂與調酒，以台灣獨立音樂為主題的個性酒吧

📍 新竹市北區經國路一段542號2樓 | +886-3-533-5003
2F, No. 542, Section 1, Jingguo Road, North Dist., Hsinchu City
20:00-02:00, weekends 20:00-03:00 | instagram: tender_542

C BAR REVIVER

A hidden bar on the second floor of a ramen shop, aiming
to rejuvenate people through their cocktail creations
隱身在拉麵店2樓的小酒館，希望藉由調酒讓人恢復元氣

📍 新竹市東區勝利路102號2F | +886-3-527-8787
2F, No. 102, Shengli Road, East Dist., Hsinchu City
20:00-03:30 (Closed on Tuesdays) | facebook.com/BarReviver2017

D OR INN 或者風旅

Positioning itself as a friend to travelers in Hsinchu,
allowing them to experience the beauty of the city
以旅人在新竹的好友自居，讓旅人感受新竹美好

📍 新竹市北區大同路175號 | +886-3-522-0505
No. 175, Datong Road, North Dist., Hsinchu City
facebook.com/orinn.hsinchu

E SOUTHGATE HOSTEL 城南新事

A comfortable backpacker hostel above Jiang Shan Yi Gai
Suo
江山藝改所樓上的舒適背包客棧

📍 新竹市東區興達街1號
No. 1, Xingda St., East Dist., Hsinchu City
facebook.com/southgatehostel

F HOTEL INDIGO HSINCHU SCIENCE PARK

A brand new design-forward hotel in Hsinchu
新竹新開幕的當代設計旅館

📍 新竹市東區公道五路二段111號 | +886-3-516-9308
No. 111, Sec. 2, Gongdao 5th Rd., East Dist., Hsinchu City
www.hotelindigohsp.com

OLD CITY ROUTE

舊城路線

HSINCHU RAILWAY STATION
AND CITY GOD TEMPLE AREA

新竹火車站與城隍廟周邊

TAKE A TOUR AROUND OLD HSINCHU!　走一圈新竹舊城！

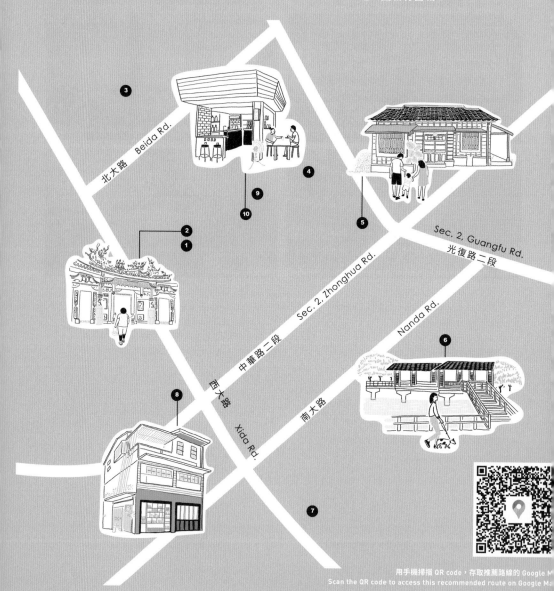

北大路　Beida Rd.

Sec. 2, Guangfu Rd.
光復路二段

Sec. 2, Zhonghua Rd.

中華路二段

Nanda Rd.

西大路

Xida Rd.

南大路

用手機掃描 QR code，存取推薦路線的 Google M
Scan the QR code to access this recommended route on Google Ma

1) **09:30** Have a local breakfast at Central Market or West Gate Market

2) **10:30** Visit City God Temple and pay your respects to the City God himself!

3) **11:00** Take a look at local shops, the puppetry museum, and Chinese medicine apothecaries

4) **12:30** Enjoy lunch in the Qin Shui Park area.

5) **14:00** Stroll to Headmaster Xin Zhi Ping's Former Residence and Hsinchu Railway Art Village

6) **15:30** YouBike or walk to Hsinchu Park where cherry blossoms are in full bloom in springtime

7) **16:30** Head to Chulian Market for ba-wan and fish balls, and try out local mugwort soap

8) **17:30** Go to Jiang Shan Yi Gai Suo, a café/cultural space in a historical setting

9) **18:30** Have dinner around East Gate Market

10) **20:00** Time for a night cap or some late-night live music

---

1) **09:30** 早餐就到「中央市場」或「西門市場」吃在地小吃

2) **10:30** 到「都城隍廟」跟城隍爺打聲招呼！

3) **11:00** 逛逛小店、偶戲館和中藥行

4) **12:30** 在「親水公園」附近享用午餐

5) **14:00** 漫步到「辛志平校長故居」和「新竹鐵道藝術村」

6) **15:30** 騎 YouBike 或走路到「新竹公園」，春天有絢爛盛開的櫻花

7) **16:30** 往「竹蓮市場」吃肉圓、魚丸，再買塊艾草肥皂

8) **17:30** 到老屋新生的藝文咖啡店「江山藝改所」逛逛

9) **18:30** 在「東門市場」或附近餐廳吃晚餐

10) **20:00** 去酒吧小酌或聽聽表演

*In collaboration with Citilens Studio | 企劃協力：見域工作室

09:30
CENTRAL MARKET
1. 中央市場

Conveniently located next to the City God Temple, Central Market is famous for local eatery foods that will make for a wonderful breakfast—try Ah-Jin's Glutinous Rice Dumplings, Osmanthus Roll-Up, and Chuqian Lin's Sticky Rice (also try their taro rice cake). Continue your morning feast at West Gate Market; try Ximen Rice Noodle Soup, Temple Duck and Rice, and finish your breakfast with some dessert at Hui Xin's Shaved Ice.

早上先到城隍廟旁品嚐老新竹人的在地小吃,從「中央市場」的「阿金糯米餃」、「桂花潤餅」和「竹塹林記油飯」 (芋粿巧也好吃)一路吃到「西門市場」的「西市米粉湯」(大麵糊必吃)和「廟口鴨香飯」,想吃甜湯附近也有「慧 心冰店」。

10:30
HSINCHU CITY GOD TEMPLE
2. 新竹都城隍廟

Founded over two centuries ago, Hsinchu City God Temple is one of Hsinchu's three main temples. If you happen to be here during the seventh month of the lunar calendar, you'll find yourself amidst the Chuchang Zhongyuan City God Festival. This longstanding tradition is inaugurated each year by the day one benjia ceremony and leads into the Ghost Festival on the 15th day.

吃飽來參拜已有兩百多年歷史、新竹三大廟之一的「新竹都城隍廟」,若在農曆 7 月造訪新竹,還有機會參與歷史悠 久的竹塹中元城隍祭,其中初一的「夯枷」以及 7 月 15 日中元節的「城隍爺遶境賑孤」是其中的重頭戲。

11:00
NORTH GATE MAIN STREET
3. 北門大街

Follow the historical Beimen Street and make your way to Guo Da Glove Puppetry Museum for a riveting glove puppetry performance. Then visit Hong-An Apothecary, a traditional Chinese medicine shop that has been operated for over a century by the four generations of the same family. Here, you will be able to experience the once popular local custom of drawing divination prescription sticks. In the summer, you can also custom-make mosquito repellent packs. Last but not least, visit Chang He Temple and pay your respects to Mazu.

沿著北門大街一邊欣賞舊時建築,一邊散步到「國達民俗偶戲文物館」看布袋戲偶,接著在以傳承四代的百年中藥行 「鴻安堂」體驗抽藥籤的民俗文化(夏天還可以自製防蚊包),最後抵達「長和宮」參拜媽祖。

12:30
RED LEAF RESTAURANT
4. 紅葉餐飲

Follow Beida Road to Qinshui Park and you'll find plenty of great lunch options in the area. If you're dining alone, I recommend the Japanese set meal restaurants Pomelo or Jing Jia by the Hsinchu Moat. For those willing to walk a bit further, "TAIVII Gastropub" offers delicious Taiwanese cuisine in a Japanese heritage building. In your post-lunch stupor, don't forget to go to Fu Yuan Peanut Butter for an unexpected Hsinchu specialty.

沿著北大路走抵達親水公園一帶享用午餐，推薦護城河畔的日式定食餐廳「柚子」或「井家」，或是再走一點路到「TAIVII 餐酒館」，在日式古蹟裡享用美味台菜。吃飽別忘了到附近扛幾罐新竹名產「福源花生醬」回家。

14:00
HEADMASTER XIN ZHI PING'S FORMER RESIDENCE
5. 辛志平校長故居

Take a post-lunch stroll to Headmaster Xin Zhi Ping's Former Residence. Built during the Japanese colonial period as a dormitory, the elegant space is now open for tours and also offers tea ceremonies. Head over to Hsinchu Railway Art Village, Taiwan's only arts and cultural space adjacent to the railroad. Allow your thoughts to wander as you watch trains speed by on an old loading platform.

餐後散步至由日治宿舍活化新生的「辛志平校長故居」，可以只參觀優雅的老宅也可坐下沏壺好茶。旁邊的「新竹鐵道藝術村」是全台唯一鄰近鐵路的藝文空間，天氣好的時候不妨坐在原本的貨車月台看火車駛過，讓思緒放空。

15:30
HSINCHU PARK
6. 新竹公園

Visit the newly revitalized Hsinchu Park whose expansive grounds include gorgeously preserved Japanese gardens, the Hsinchu Confucian Temple, as well as the new and improved Hsinchu Municipal Zoo. Next to the park is the Glass Museum of Hsinchu City where cherry blossoms will be in full bloom during springtime.

來到剛完成再生計畫的「新竹公園」走走，廣大的園區保留了日式風格的麗池園林，園內還有改造重生的「新竹市立動物園」、「新竹孔廟」等景點。一旁的「新竹市立玻璃工藝博物館」前，春天時更有絢爛盛開的櫻花，美不勝收。

☐
16:30
CHULIAN MARKET
7. 竹蓮市場

Visit another one of Hsinchu's three main temples—Chulian Temple, where you can pray to Guanyin. Then go to Chulian Ba-wan for deep fried dough, filled with pork marinated in red yeast and spring onions; also try their short rib soup. Shi Family Fish Balls is another local favorite that you have to sample.

Makeup lovers have to check out Wan Chu Cosmetics, a local establishment that's nearly a century old. The owner, whose glowing complexion is a testimony to the quality of their products, is an expert at recommending the appropriate products for every skin type. Apart from their classic face powder, I also recommend trying their homemade mugwort soap.

到同樣是新竹三大廟的「竹蓮寺」參拜觀音，接著去附近的「竹蓮肉圓」品嚐包著紅糟肉和青蔥的油炸肉圓和骨仔肉湯，「石家魚丸」也深受在地人喜愛。

女性同胞千萬別錯過旁邊已有將近百年歷史的「丸竹化妝品」，保養得宜、相當有個性的老闆娘會根據個人膚質推薦適合的產品，除了經典的香粉外也可以帶塊丸竹自製的天然艾草皂。

☐
17:30
JIANG SHAN YI GAI SUO
8. 江山藝改所

Jiang Shan Yi Gai Suo is a double entendre of the phrase "easier to move mountains and alter streams than to change one's nature." The organization works to promote contemporary arts and social welfare by taking on the forms of a café, an independent bookstore, a performance space, and a hostel. The multifunctional space is also a venue for lectures and events and has become a stronghold for Hsinchu's efforts to revitalize the city's arts and culture. I also highly recommend In the Shadow of Gleam, a café in a revitalized old residence.

「江山藝改所」取「江山易改，本性難移」的諧音命名。在這裡，推廣當代藝術文化與關注社會議題是本性，而難以界定的江山場域則同時擁有咖啡店、獨立書店、展演空間和民宿等多重功能。除了時常舉辦各式講座與活動外，餐飲也用心不馬虎，是新竹重要的新興藝文基地。附近同樣由老屋改建的咖啡廳「暗室微光」也相當推薦。

18:30
DONGMEN EAST GATE MARKET
9. 東門市場

For dinner I recommend Rong's Hakka Rice Balls (their sesame paste noodles are also delicious). Having recently undergone a revitalization project, East Gate Market has been restored to its former glory as a hub of the finest local eateries. Right outside the market is Under the Canopy's fried chicken, Yu Xiang's fish cake, and Duck Xu's stir-fried congealed blood. In the market we have delicious Thai food, Taiwanese kebabs, and Xiang Chu Food Hall—famous for their creative twist on the traditional oyster vermicelli soup; they add fried chicken to the dish.

After dinner you can either visit the Dongmen Youth Startup Hub on the third floor or have a traditional popsicle at 814 Datung Ice Shop. I also recommend heading to OR House, a place transformed from a department store during the Japanese ruled period. There, you can browse curated shops, visit exhibitions, or leisurely enjoy a cocktail!

晚餐時分可選擇「榮記客家湯圓」（麻醬麵也好吃），也可前往近來因活化再造重新熱絡起來的「東門市場」，外頭有「戲棚下」炸雞店、「漁香」甜不辣和「鴨肉許」的炒鴨血，場內有「享來初」加入鹹酥雞的創意麵線、泰國菜和台式串燒等各式料理。

吃飽不妨上 3 樓的「青年基地」逛逛進駐的工作室，或到「814 大同冰店」再吃一枝古早味冰棒。吃完後，推薦前往由日治時期的百貨公司改造而成的「或者新州屋」，逛選品店、看展覽，或者悠哉地喝一杯調酒！

20:00
EAST MARKET 1001
10. 東市 1001

If you're not in a hurry to leave after dinner, why not have a drink at East Market 1001, a chill and friendly bar that allows you to enjoy food from other eateries (the stall across from the bar is an eatery run by the owner's family; I highly recommend their assorted braised foods plate!).

P.S. Keep an eye out for evening events at Jiang Shan Yi Gai Suo.

吃完晚餐別急著離開東門市場，推薦到一樓的「東市 1001」酒吧小酌一杯，在這裡喝酒就像在家裡一樣輕鬆，還可以外帶其他攤的食物（對面攤是老闆家中經營的小吃店，推薦滷味拼盤！）

P.S. 也可看看「江山藝改所」是否有晚間活動。

RICE NOODLES

三分日曬、七分風乾————九降風吹拂下的新竹米粉

Photo credit：Ian Chen

SPECIAL FEATURE
HSINCHU
新竹特輯
SPECIAL FEATURE

The cold and dry northeast seasonal winds—locally known as September winds—has shaped Hsinchu in many ways, including creating Hsinchu's famous rice noodles. There are two main ways to make rice noodles, one is boiling and the other is steaming. Boiling was the traditional method and produced thicker and denser noodles that took longer to cook and required soaking beforehand. During the Japanese colonial period, the new technique of steaming rice noodles was introduced, which produced a more delicate texture and is now what Hsinchu rice noodles are known for.

According to local oldtimers, rice noodles originated from Nanshi in Hsinchu, a fan-shaped terrain through which the plentiful Keya River runs. In this region, strong winds blow all year round, which is essential for manufacturing rice noodles. At the height of Hsinchu's rice noodle manufacturing industry, there were more than a hundred rice noodle factories.

In the early days, rice noodles were dried solely by wind and sun. After Mid-Autumn Festival and up until Tomb Sweeping Day is when the cold and dry northeast seasonal winds blow, taking away moisture from rice noodles and helping them dry properly. Noodles produced during this season are of the best quality and keep for a long time. The old saying "three parts sun-dried and seven parts wind-blown" sums it all up.

Another old saying "Good wood is not used to build pigpens and a fair maiden ought not be married to a rice noodle maker." reflects how tough the rice noodle making business is. Rice noodle makers rise well before sunrise to start the arduous process of grinding the rice paste, pressing the rice sheets, steaming the noodles, and laying them out to dry under the sun. At the crack of dawn, manufacturers will drive their trucks full of rice noodles to the riverside and lay them out on ground to dry. Moisture is the enemy of rice noodles and sudden rain could be ruinous, which is why it is crucial to keep a keen watch on the weather! (by Citilens Studio)

乾冷而強勁的東北季風——「九降風」，造就了新竹的風土物產，米粉就是其中之一。新竹米粉主要分為兩類：用水煮的水粉，以及用蒸的炊粉。過去在「米粉寮」地區，大家以製作水粉為主，水粉較粗、口感較扎實，不過料理前需要花較長時間將一片片乾米粉泡軟。日治時期引入了炊粉技術，口感較細軟，算是新竹特產！

老新竹人口中的「米粉寮」，位在新竹市的南勢里，這裡臨近水源豐沛的客雅溪，又因為由西北向東南如畚箕狀開啟的地形，不分冬夏，風勢都受地形影響而增強，成為製作米粉的絕佳條件。極盛時期，曾有 100 間以上的米粉工廠。

早期，米粉乾燥全靠風吹日曬，家家戶戶都練就了一身不需要看氣象報導，就能知曉天氣變化的好本事。每年中秋節過後，一直到隔年清明節前，乾冷的東北季風盛行，拂去多餘的水分，此時生產的米粉，做出來的米粉品質最好、不易變質。「三分日曬，七分風乾」，一語道盡新竹米粉好吃的關鍵。

米粉寮流行著一句古老的俗諺：「好材不做豬寮梁，阿娘不嫁米粉寮。」說的就是從事米粉業的辛酸血淚：為了爭取到多一些日曬時間，天還沒亮就要開始一系列瑣碎且繁重的工作，包含磨米漿、壓米粉、將米粉送入蒸箱蒸熟、扒米粉等，一刻都不得放鬆。天微微亮，各家駛著鐵牛車，載著一落落的米粉，到溪邊空曠處曝曬米粉。米粉怕潮濕，若有突如其來的降雨便會將心血毀於一旦，必須時刻注意天氣，一刻都不得閒呢！（文／見域工作室）

PORK BALLS

吃一口風城味——新竹貢丸好吃的祕訣

Pork balls are made all over Taiwan but only Hsinchu has made it a local symbol. Times may changes and preferences may differ but Hsinchu never fails to produce the most scrumptious and toothsome pork balls.

Premium Hsinchu pork balls are made from the shank, which is the most exercised muscle on a pig and the leanest meat. In order to produced juicy and toothsome pork balls, the meat must be pounded repeatedly (which is where it got its name gong wan) into a pulp and squeezed by hand into uniform balls before it is boiled. Each step is done with great care and expertise.

Masters of the pork ball making craft produce such scrumptious and toothsome pork balls that Hsinchu has become known for it. However, the process is highly labor-intensive and even the most experienced masters can only produce 15-25 kg worth of meatballs in a day if they want to maintain quality and uniformity.

To increase production and save time, Hsinchu pork ball experts collaborated with manufacturers to develop pork ball machines that are currently used by most major producers. Modern pork ball making has been streamlined into a production line of mincing, paste-making, shaping, boiling, cooling, and packaging. This seemingly simple process still requires a high level of experience and skill. Not to mention quality control, which entails making sure the meat is always fresh and that lean to fat ratio is perfect.

The quality of the meat, the ingredients added to the paste, and the length of time the paste is stirred are all key factors to making the perfect pork ball. As the stronghold of Taiwan's best pork balls, Hsinchu offers a wide variety of vendors and the intense competition ensures that none will disappoint. So make sure to order a bowl of pork ball soup wherever you go! (by Citilens Studio)

*In Taiwanese "gong" means to pound and "wan" means ball.

雖然全台各地都有貢丸,卻只有「新竹貢丸」成為地方的代名詞。時代變遷,做法上多少有調整,不變的是新竹貢丸依然又香又富有彈性。

新竹貢丸首選豬隻的後腿肉來製作。後腿是豬隻最常活動的部位,肉質緊緻,油脂分布少,韌性很強。在過去,要做出肉汁鮮美又口感爽脆的貢丸,豬肉得先經過貢丸師傅反覆捶打做成肉漿,再以手工用虎口將肉漿一顆顆擠出為貢丸,最後放入熱水定型,每個流程都不能馬虎。這樣的拋打過程,也是「摃(貢)丸」名稱的由來。

在老師傅的巧手下,手工製作的貢丸充滿肉香、口感彈牙,因而聲名大噪。然而,手工製作限制了產量,即使是很熟練的師傅,一天頂多生產出 30 斤到 50 斤,品質也很難完全一致。

因此,新竹的貢丸師傅們和廠商合力研發機具,成為今日各大工廠看到的機械化生產線。現代貢丸製作的生產線,大致上分為幾個步驟:絞肉、打漿、塑型、定型、冷卻、包裝。看似不算太複雜的生產流程,卻需要一定的經驗和技術,評估每天豬肉油脂的分布狀況和新鮮度,調整機器。

一顆貢丸好不好吃,取決於選用的肉品以及打漿時加入的原料及打漿時間。為什麼呢?在這個以貢丸聞名的城市,幾乎每家有品牌的貢丸,都會嚴選使用的肉品及調料,只要偷工減料,口感就會輸人一大截。因此在新竹的小吃攤點碗貢丸湯,總是不會讓人失望。(文/見域工作室)

* 摃(貢)的發音為台語敲打的意思。

來苗栗，慢一點

苗栗
MIAOLI

SLOW DOWN IN MIAOLI

Photo credit：曾成訓

The most enjoyable, stress-free way to get around in Miaoli is either by scooter or by car so that you can explore the natural treasures offered by the mountains and the sea. If you take Provincial Highway 1, you may want to start your journey from such coastal townships as Houlong, Tongxiao, and Yuanli to appreciate the boundless ocean views. Then make a turn onto Provincial Highway 3, also known as the Inner-Mountain Highway or Hakka Romantic Avenue, and drive along the Central Mountain Range and into the Hakka villages in the mountains.

Keep heading toward the township of Sanyi where golden blooming canola fields bathe in the warm sun during spring and summer. Hiking upward on the winding mountain road, you will find surging waterfalls echoing through the valleys, which are the Valley of the Gods Waterfalls formed by erosion from the Fengmei River of Nanzhuang Township, as well as the Kuhua Pond Waterfall surrounded by lofty rocks. Look up–the towering coniferous forest in front of you used to be the sacred territory for the indigenous Saisiyat people. Stretching your arms towards the sky, the ethereal aura of Mother Nature and the universe itself all seems within your grasp.

Despite the fact that Miaoli is hardly ever a traveler's first choice, as it is not so flourishing as other big cities in Taiwan, none-the-less, as the elderly locals say, any undeveloped place is a good place. The yet-to-be-urbanized parts of Miaoli allow you to perceive developing scenes of quotidian life, as well as impressive and skillful craftmanship and aesthetics. Among all the charming little towns, the townships of Nanzhuang and Sanyi have even been recognized as Slow Cities by Cittaslow International of Italy. Come experience the slow life near mountains and sea in Miaoli and get to know the sincere side of Taiwan. (by Ting-Huang Hsuan)

來苗栗旅遊，最好的方式是騎機車或開車，才能夠輕鬆自在地探索大自然給予苗栗的山海瑰寶。若行駛台1線，可以從有著一望無際海景的後龍、通霄和苑裡等海線鄉鎮，再彎入與中央山脈緊鄰綿延、俗稱「內山公路」的浪漫台3線，進入山區的客家村落。

從三義往前行，春夏能看見暖陽灑落大地，閃耀著黃澄澄光芒的美麗油菜花田，再沿著山路小徑蜿蜒上去，奔騰瀑布聲迴盪溪谷，是南庄風美溪沖刷出的神仙谷和巨石林立的苦花潭瀑布。抬起頭望向高聳入天的針葉林，這裡曾是賽夏族的神聖領地，往上伸出雙手彷彿就能觸摸到天地氤氳。

儘管苗栗不是一般旅客旅遊的首選，也不若幾個大都市繁華，但就像老一輩苗栗人所說的，沒被開發的地方，都是好地方。尚未都市化的苗栗，更能看出常民生活發展出來的軌跡，也有許多令人驚嘆的工藝美學，其中南庄與三義更是義大利國際慢城組織認證的慢城。來苗栗慢遊吧！在山海之間，看見台灣最樸實可愛的樣子。（文／黃宣庭）

TRANSPORTATION
交通

It takes about 45 minutes to get from Taipei to Miaoli Station via the HSR. Once there, a transfer to the TRA will get you to the downtown area, which only takes about 10 minutes. When traveling in the downtown area, city buses and YouBike are available, including Easy Card services. However, renting a scooter might be even more convenient.

台北搭乘高鐵至苗栗站約 45 分鐘，再到市區可轉乘火車，僅需 10 分鐘車程。市區移動可搭乘公車或騎乘 YouBike（可使用悠遊卡），租借機車移動可能會更方便。

RECOMMENDATIONS
推薦

◣ TRAVEL WEBSITES 旅遊網站

MIAOLI CULTURAL TOURISM 苗栗文化觀光旅遊網
Official Miaoli travel website. Follow the Facebook page for the latest news
苗栗官方旅遊網站，臉書專頁可追蹤最新活動訊息

⌐ Web : miaolitravel.net | facebook.com/TourMiaoli

CREATIVE MIAOLI 文化創意新苗栗
Instantaneous first-hand arts and cultural information about Miaoli
來此獲得第一手苗栗藝文活動資訊

⌐ facebook.com/creativemiaoli

◣ READING LIST 推薦書籍

WONDERFUL SHORT TRIPS IN MIAOLI: LOCAL FOOD ✕ NOSTALGIC OLD STREETS ✕ SECRET SPOTS
《苗栗美好小旅行：在地美食✕懷舊老街✕私房景點》
Rare Miaoli travel guide with comprehensive introductions
少數完整介紹苗栗的旅遊書

⌐ books.com.tw/products/0010739307

◣ LOCAL PUBLICATIONS 在地刊物

CHIM CONG《尋庄》
Nanzhuang's local magazine, founded in 2014. Order via the webpage link below
2014年發刊的南庄地方刊物，可在以下網址購買

⌐ www.facebook.com/find.village2014

HI HOME《掀海風》
Yuanli's independent magazine inspired by local environmental/political activities. Order at the website link below
因地方運動而生的苑裡獨立刊物，可在以下面網址購買

⌐ www.hihomeway.com/products/sayhihome-no1

◣ GUIDED TOURS 導覽

YUANLI HI HOME 苑裡掀海風
Independent bookstore in Yuanli providing in-depth short-trip planning service. Send request messages via the Facebook page below
苑裡獨立書店，提供深度小旅行規劃，可私訊臉書粉絲頁詢問

⌐ facebook.com/taketheseawind

MIAOLI TOURIST SHUTTLE ROUTES 台灣好行苗栗
Government operated tourist shuttle service. Nanzhuang route currently available. For bus stop locations, check out the website link below
官方經營的觀光巴士，目前有南庄線，停靠點可參考網站

⌐ www.taiwantrip.com.tw/line/5?x=2&y=1

◣ ANNUAL EVENTS 年度活動

THE BAISHATUN MAZU PILGRIMAGE (BETWEEN LUNAR JANUARY AND APRIL) 白沙屯媽祖進香 (農曆1月-4月間)
The longest Mazu foot pilgrimage in Taiwan
台灣徒步距離最長的媽祖進香遶境活動

⌐ www.baishatun.com.tw

MIAOLI OCEAN FESTIVAL (JULY-AUGUST)
苗栗海洋觀光季 (7月-8月)
Summer festival combining elements from Miaoli's fishing harbors, environmental protection activities, music performances, and fireworks
結合苗栗漁港、生態保育與音樂煙火的夏日慶典

⌐ www.miaoli.gov.tw

MIAOLI ARTS FESTIVAL (SEPTEMBER-DECEMBER)
貓裏表演藝術節 (9月-12月)
Founded in 2017, hosting diverse performances including music concerts and theatrical presentations
2017年創辦，有音樂會、劇場等多元形式演出

⌐ facebook.com/Miaoliartsfestival

A THE WAY WE WISH 日榮本屋

A local independent bookstore where one can enjoy reading over a drink

苗栗地方獨立書店，可點杯飲料坐在店內好好看書

苗栗縣苗栗市中山路129號
No. 129, Zhongshan Rd., Miaoli City, Miaoli County
13:00–18:00 (Closed on Mon. and Tue.)

B HUATAOYAO 華陶窯

Beautiful park with landscaped gardens and pottery art, offering pottery classes, meals and park tours

有植物與陶藝的美好天地，可玩陶、用餐、賞園，需先預約

苗栗縣苑裡鎮南勢里2鄰31號 | facebook.com/hwataoyao
No. 31, Neighborhood 2, Nanshi, Yuanli Township, Miaoli County
09:30–16:30 (Closed on Mondays, reservation is required.)

C LUZHUNAN 蘆竹湳古厝

Explore this interesting 300-year-old house for food and good fun!

來300年古厝走踏，有吃、有玩、有趣！

苗栗縣頭份市蘆竹南15鄰191號 | facebook.com/luzhunan
No. 191, Neighborhood 15, Luzhu, Toufen City, Miaoli County
08:00–17:00 (Closed on Tuesdays)

D QIANSHAN GREEN 淺山綠

A plant-themed bookstore located in the countryside, hosting various lectures and events from time to time

開在鄉間的植物主題書店，不定時舉辦各式講座活動

苗栗縣裡鎮南勢七鄰93號 | facebook.com/PlantsCreateLife
No. 93, Nanshi 7th Neighborhood, Yuanli Township, Miaoli County
10:30–18:30 (Closed on Mon. to Thur.)

E CHOOART VILLA 樹也

Reconnect with nature and soak in hot springs embraced by trees

回歸自然，在樹木的擁抱中泡湯

苗栗縣三義鄉龍騰村5鄰外庄27-1號
No. 27-1, Waizhuang, 5th Neighborhood, Longteng Village, Sanyi Township, Miaoli County | www.chooart.com.tw

F ONSEN PAPAWAQU 泰安觀止溫泉會館

Enjoy outdoor and indoor hot springs in primitive mountain jungles

來原始山林泡美人湯吧，有湯屋與露天風呂可選擇

苗栗縣泰安鄉錦水村圓墩58號
No. 58, Yuandun, Tai'an Township, Miaoli County
facebook.com/OnsenPapawaqa

Photo credit：KAORI Dining

Photo credit：Kris Kang

A   CHUAN LONG DOU FU FANG 穿龍老屋豆腐坊
Delicious tofu, douhua, and soymilk made with sun-dried
sea bittern
海水日曬鹽鹵的美味豆腐、豆花與豆漿

苗栗縣公館鄉福基村120號 | facebook.com/ChuanLongDouFuFang
No. 120, Fuji, Gongguan Township, Miaoli County
08:30-13:00, Weekends 08:30-16:00 (Closed on Mon.)

B   LAO-JIA RICE DINING HALL 老家米食堂
Learn about Hakka rice culture by tasting Hakka flat rice
noodles and deep-fried tangyuan
來此品嚐客家粄條與糯米炸湯圓，認識客家米食文化

苗栗縣南庄鄉大同路25-1號 | +886-3-782-2882
No. 25-1, Datong Rd., Nanzhuang Township, Miaoli County
11:00-18:00 (Closed Wednesdays and Thursdays)

C   THREE 叁代堂
Hakka cuisine handed down through three generations.
Sauces and Hakka side dishes available for sale
傳承三代的客家美食，也販售醬料與客家小點

苗栗縣三義鄉水美街283-1號 | +886-3-787-5070
No. 283-1, Shuimei, Sanyi Township, Miaoli County
11:30-15:00, 17:30-20:30 (Closed on Tuesdays)

D   KAORI DINING
Casual fine dining establishment created by local young
chefs embracing their hometown's culinary culture
返鄉青年結合在地飲食文化開設的 Casual fine dining

苗栗縣頭份市上庄路30號 | facebook.com/kaori.dining
需事先預約 Pre-reservation is required.
No. 30, Shangzhuang Road, Toufen City, Miaoli County

E   PERGRAM COFFEE 沛克咖啡店
Stylish café in Miaoli offering in-house roasted beans and
specialty coffee
苗栗的質感自烘咖啡廳，也販售精品咖啡豆

苗栗縣苗栗市中山路108號 | facebook.com/pergramcoffee
No. 108, Zhongshan Rd., Miaoli City, Miaoli County
11:00-19:00 (Closed on Mondays)

F   THE SPOT COFFEE COMPANY 新興大旅社（老地方咖啡）
Enjoy a hand-brewed coffee at a local historic inn and
soak in the nostalgic atmosphere
來在地老旅社享用手沖咖啡，感受往日風情

苗栗縣苗栗市建國街3號 | +886-3-726-0133
No. 3, Jianguo St., Miaoli City, Miaoli County
10:00-22:00

MIAOLI TRAIN STATION AREA
AND YUANLI

苗栗火車站周圍與苑裡

SLOW DAY-TRIP IN MIAOLI　來苗栗輕鬆慢遊一日

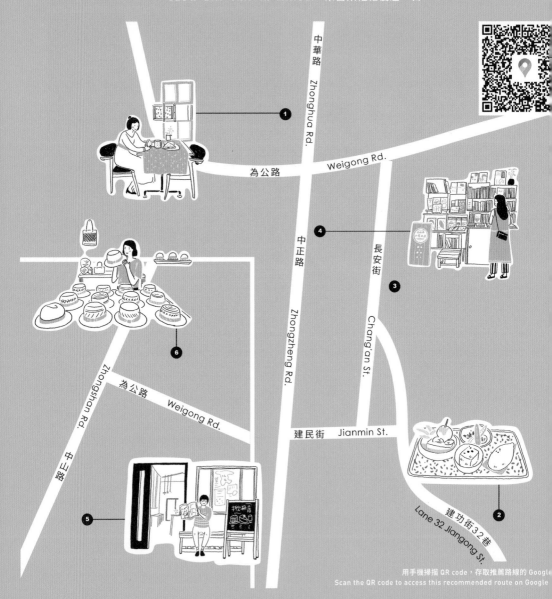

中華路 Zhonghua Rd.

為公路　Weigong Rd.

中正路

長安街

Chang'an St.

Zhongzheng Rd.

建民街　Jianmin St.

Zhongshan Rd.

為公路　Weigong Rd.

路正中

建功街 32 巷

Lane 32 Jiangong St.

用手機掃描 QR code，存取推薦路線的 Google
Scan the QR code to access this recommended route on Google

1)	09:30	Explore the local markets, and enjoy a delicious breakfast
2)	10:30	Visit nearby Yuqing Temple and Railway Village
3)	12:00	Try out local street food or the menuless lunch of The Heart Feast
4)	13:30	Spend some time with books or have a cup of coffee at The Way We Wish bookstore
5)	15:30	Head to Xian-Ce-Dian bookstore in Yuanli township and explore coastal Miaoli
6)	16:30	Learn about rush-weaving culture at Sunnyrush and discover the small town of Yuanli

1)	09:30	來到北苗、南苗市場逛逛、吃點早餐
2)	10:30	逛逛市場附近的「玉清宮」與「鐵道一村」
3)	12:00	中午吃在地小吃或是「二分之三咖哩專門店」
4)	13:30	吃飽到「日榮本屋」看書或是喝杯咖啡
5)	15:30	前往苑裡「掀冊店」，認識海線苗栗
6)	16:30	到「藺子」探索藺草編織文化與苑裡小鎮

Reminders:

From Miaoli to Yuanli, you can take a direct bus on route 5814; if you choose to travel by Taiwan Railways commuter train, you will need to transfer at Zhunan Station, with both methods taking about an hour. If you drive or take a taxi, the journey will take approximately 40 minutes.

小提醒：

從苗栗到苑裡，可以搭乘 5814 路公車直達；如果選擇台鐵區間車，則需在竹南車站轉車，兩種方式的車程都約為一小時。如果自行駕車或搭乘計程車，約 40 分鐘可抵達。

09:30
BEIMIAO AND NANMAIO MARKET
1. 北苗市場 與 南苗市場

Located next to Miaoli Train Station, Beimiao Market is home to a variety of local products and Hakka cuisine. I recommend trying the delicious and chewy A-Po Fenyuan on the first floor. As for the larger Nanmiao Market, the busiest areas are Rice Market Street and Bo-ai Street, where you can find many popular local snacks. In the morning, why not try a bowl of stir-fried noodles with pig's blood soup at Nammiao There Sisters' Breakfast!

位於苗栗火車站旁的「北苗市場」，藏著許多在地物產與客家美食，推薦到一樓吃碗香甜有嚼勁的「阿婆粉圓」。而規模較大的「南苗市場」，以米市街、博愛街最為熱鬧，附近有許多深受在地人喜愛的小吃，早上不妨到「南苗三姐妹早餐」吃碗炒麵配豬血湯！

10:30
YUQING TEMPLE AND MIAOLI TRAIN PARK
2. 玉清宮 與 苗栗火車頭園區

Yuqing Temple is one of the most reputable Guandi temples in Miaoli, where banglong (throwing fireworks to dancing dragons), the famous Miaoli lantern festival activity, is held yearly. Next, take a walk at the recently-transformed creative site, Miaoli Train Park, that sporadically holds markets and events and explore some local shops. Check out the schedule at their website before making the trip.

玉清宮是苗栗香火鼎盛的關帝廟，每年元宵著名的「（火旁）龍」（用鞭炮炸舞龍）的活動就在此為祥龍點睛。接著再到近期成為苗栗創意據點的「苗栗火車頭園區」散步，除了有小店進駐，這裡也不定期舉辦市集與活動，可先上網查詢再安排行程。

12:00
LOCAL STREET FOOD AND CURRY
3. 在地小吃 與咖哩

For lunch, you can enjoy the chewy and flavorful Chestnut Sticky Rice nearby, or visit Alanjie's Eatery for their famous crystal dumplings (open until 12:30 PM, so be mindful of the time). I also recommend the Two-thirds Curry House near the train station—be sure to try the hamburger steak curry!

午餐可以在附近吃Q彈夠味的「栗香糯米飯」或是來「阿蘭姊小吃店」吃著名的水晶餃（營業時間到12:30，要注意時間）。另外也推薦火車站附近的「二分之三咖哩專門店」，務必試試漢堡排咖哩！

13:30
THE WAY WE WISH
4. 日榮本屋

Spend a part of your afternoon with books at the emerging multifunctional independent bookstore, The Way We Wish, where occasional lectures are held. If you happen to crave some coffee, The Spot Coffee Company which was converted from an old hotel, Pergram Coffee with their decent coffee and dessert offerings. You can also keep an eye out for interesting events at the nearby Lao-Jia Arts and Cultural Living Space, which opens occasionally.

吃飽到苗栗新興的複合式書店「日榮本屋」看看書，這裡不定期舉辦講座。若想來杯咖啡，推薦由旅社改造的「新興大旅社」、咖啡甜點都美味的「沛克咖啡店」。可留意附近不定時開放的「老家藝文生活空間」（FB: soulxfamily）有什麼有趣活動！

15:30
THE XIAN-CE-DIAN BOOKSTORE
5. 掀冊店

Take a train to the small coastal town of Yuanli and visit the Xian-Ce-Dian bookstore, a hub of arts, culture, and local Yuanli living. The bookstore was founded by a group of young environmental activists who relocated back to their hometown. Besides publishing the local magazine *Hi Home*, they also sporadically hold lectures and events and provide drinks, meals, and local farmers' products.

接著搭火車到海線小鎮苑裡，首站來到苑裡藝文與生活中心「掀冊店」，這裡由一群一起參與環保運動的返鄉青年共同創立，除了曾出版地方刊物《掀海風》外，店裡也提供飲品餐點，不定時舉辦講座活動，並展售在地小農產品。

16:30
SUNNYRUSH
6. 藺子

Local rush-weaving culture was once a source of glorious pride for Yuanli. Check out the traditional hat and mat shops on the old street, then pay a visit to Sunnyrush, founded by young startups and devoted to preserving the traditional craft, to learn about this culture and buy a rush hat souvenir. If you get hungry before leaving Yuanli, you can enjoy some refreshing tofu pudding at Good Soyfoods' or have a meal at the Western-style private kitchen The Afterglow. It's a great way to end your relaxed day in Miaoli.

來苑裡不能錯過曾經輝煌一時的苑裡藺編工藝，在老街散步，逛逛傳統帽蓆行，再到由年輕人創立、希望守護傳承這門工藝的「藺子」認識藺草文化，順便帶頂草帽回家。若肚子餓離開苑裡前可到「原豆粹食」享用冰涼的豆花，或前往西式私廚料理「沐暉苑食」用餐，結束今日的苗栗慢遊。

INDIGO DYEING, RUSH WEAVING AND WOOD SCULPTURE

藍染、藺草與木雕

Photo credit｜台灣...

With impressive arts and crafts hidden within, the simple towns of Miaoli are treasure hunting spots for weaving, indigo dyeing, and wood sculpture lovers from around the world. If time permits, I highly recommend you take an arts and crafts tour and discover Miaoli from the perspective of daily-life aesthetics.

Indigo Dyeing: Zhuo Ye Cottage

Following Hakka culture across the strait to Taiwan, indigo dyeing has been applied to make Hakka blue shirts for its bug-repellant and skin-purifying effects arising from the natural scent carried by indigo plants, and became an important symbol of Hakka culture. In fact, Sanyi Township was not traditionally a main manufacturer, but the foggy weather provides a perfect environment for indigo plants to grow, allowing the couple Zheng Mei-Shu and Zhuo Ming-Bang to establish Zhuo Ye Cottage for their indigo dyeing revival efforts.

When entering the park, my pace naturally slowed. Designs and details made with recycled and eco-friendly materials could be found in every corner. Organic vegetables were on offer in the dining hall surrounded by waters and mountains. Because of its slow and steady pace, Zhuo Ye Cottage was able to build up a coexisting environment for production, life, and ecology, which makes it a must-see to experience both indigo dyeing and slow living.

純樸的苗栗藏著閃閃發光的工藝寶藏，吸引了國內外對編織、藍染與木雕有興趣的人前來挖寶。若有時間，誠摯推薦大家來趟工藝之旅，從日常美學的角度深度認識苗栗。

藍染：卓也小屋

藍染隨著客家文化渡海來台，藍草提煉出的青靛染料與其天然香氣帶來的護膚防蟲功效，被運用在客家藍衫，成為客家文化的重要代表；三義雖然不是傳統藍染重鎮，卻有著藍草生長所需的種植環境，讓霧濛濛的三義恰好成為「卓也小屋」創辦人卓銘榜、鄭美淑夫婦復育藍染的最佳選擇。

走進園區，心自然而然地就會慢下來，隨處可見回收資源與環保建材打造的小細節，還能在青山綠水環繞的餐廳享用有機蔬菜。因為慢，卓也反而打造出「生產、生活、生態」萬物共榮的生態環境。若想體驗藍染DIY與在地慢活，建議走一趟卓也小屋。

Rush weaving: Taiwan Yuan-li Handiwork Association

Harvested from local water fields of expansive green, the triangular-stalk rush turns yellow under the warm sun. A mild rush scent permeates the sun drying area. Bunches of warm golden rushes and piles of mats woven by local ladies are symbols of this simple town of Yuanli where people once devoted their whole heart to the culture of growing, harvesting, and creating hand-made rush crafts. Once the third major produce of Taiwan and the most important source of income for Yuanli, rush is no doubt a shared memory for all local residents. However, the craft has declined during the industrialization of the area which occurred after the nationalist government took over Taiwan post Japanese colonial era. Fortunately, local residents have proactively established Rush Yuan-li Handiwork Association to hand down the century-old craft, allowing the town to preserve the techniques of senior masters and to support the creativity of returning young artists. After experiencing the weaving techniques, take a walk on the old street and feel the classic nostalgia of Yuanli.

Wood sculpture: Buddhist statues in Tongxiao and art sculptures in Sanyi

During the Japanese colonial period, Sanyi produced a large amount of camphor oil. A local happened to use an abandoned piece of camphor tree as decoration and attracted Japanese people's attention. The golden era of Sanyi wood sculpture therefore began, and over one hundred sculpture studios spreaded across the town. Prominent sculpture masters like Li Jin-Chuan and Ju Ming were both nourished in the neighboring Tongxiao Township. Over time, Sanyi and Tongxiao differentiated their target markets which the former focuses more on art sculptures while the latter changed its specialty to Buddhist statues. Pay a visit to Sanyi Wood Sculpture Museum and its neighborhood, and bathe in the refreshing wood scents. If you are interested in learning more about wood sculpture, as long as you dare to ask, craftsmen and artists here would all be happy to share their knowledge. (by Ting-Huang Hsuan)

藺草：台灣藺草學會

一片片綠油油的藺草水田，三角藺草採收下來後被暖陽照得由青轉黃，淡淡自然的清香瀰漫在行完日光浴的曬草區，一把把溫暖的金黃色澤，還有阿姨們靈活巧手編織的藺蓆，簡樸的苑裡小鎮一直堅持著純手工種植、收割與編織的藺草文化。藺草曾經是台灣第三大農作物，也是鎮上最重要的經濟來源，在台灣光復後隨工業化發展逐漸式微。只要提起藺草，絕對是苑裡人共同的回憶，好在地方居民自主組織起「台灣藺草學會」，才讓百年藺編工藝得以傳承與重生。鎮上保留下許多師傅講究的手藝和迴游青年創建的風貌，體驗完藺編後漫步在老街上，好好地感受一下苑裡的老派經典。

木雕：通霄佛雕、三義藝雕

三義在日治時期盛產樟腦油，因有人撿拾廢棄樟木雕成擺飾後深受日人喜愛，開啟了三義木雕的黃金年代，全盛時期有上百家木雕業者，鄰鎮通霄也孕育出許多雕刻大師如李金川與朱銘等人。後期兩地也漸漸做出市場區隔，三義的木雕多藝術創作，通霄地區則改雕神佛。來三義可以到「三義木雕博物館」與附近逛逛，這裡隨處皆是木頭獨有的清香，只要開口，師傅們都會真誠熱切地向你解講來由。（文 / 黃宣庭）

ZHUO YE COTTAGE 卓也小屋
苗栗縣三義鄉雙潭村13鄰崩山下1-5號
No. 1-5, Bengshanxia, Sanyi Township, Miaoli County
facebook.com/joyesanyi

Photo credit: 台灣藺草學會

TAIWAN YUAN-LI HANDIWORK ASSOCIATION 台灣藺草學會
苗栗縣苑裡鎮山腳里14鄰378號
378, Neighborhood 14, Shanjiau, Yuanli Township, Miaoli County
facebook.com/trianglarlin

SANYI WOOD SCULPTURE MUSEUM 三義木雕博物館
苗栗縣三義鄉廣聲新城88號
No. 88, Guangsheng Xincheng, Sanyi Township, Miaoli County
facebook.com/SWSMuseum

大家都說我有台中腔 (胡說！)

Photo credit：Daniel???

台中
TAICHUNG

THEY SAY I HAVE A
TAICHUNG ACCENT...
NONSENSE!

Taichung is Taiwan's second largest metropolis. The two Chinese characters in Taichung—*tai* (台) for taiwan and *chung* (中) or middle—translates to the middle of Taiwan. Staying true to its name, Taichung's personality and development seem to be guided by a philosophy of following the middle-of-the-road. It does not strive to be the most bustling city nor does it boast the most gorgeous scenery; rather, Taichung marches to the beat of its own drum, offering an irreplaceable sense of ease and comfort. It is no wonder that an increasing number of locals have chosen to remain in the comforting bosom of their hometown and that outsiders, attracted by the city's undeniable charm, move to the city; the resulting increase in population has begun to transform the once quiet city of Taichung.

Whenever I roam the streets of Taichung on my trusty moped, I never cease to discover new and fascinating establishments such as stores, restaurants, and hostels. These organizations tend to pop up in areas such as the center of the city, known as the Central and Western Districts of Taichung; in the burgeoning Park Lane by CMP; and in Taichung's 7th Redevelopment Zone, which houses the National Taichung Theater. At the outer rim of the city, in areas like Qingshui and Wufeng townships, newly founded independent bookstores and café have been adding fresh color to the local charm.

After you've exhausted Taipei, Hualien, Taitung, Tainan, and Kaohsiung, why not head over to Taichung and wind down in our charming city? The weather is so balmy that we really don't mind being last on your list of destinations.

台中，台灣的第二大都會區。「中」在中文是「中間」的意思，因此台中意指台灣中部。不知是否是名字的關係，台中的個性與發展也頗有中庸之道，它可能不是台灣最繁華、最好吃或風景最美的地方，但它依著自己的步調與那無可取代的舒適感，讓越來越多台中人選擇留在故鄉，甚至吸引不少外地人來此定居，使得原本平靜的城市風景也漸漸起了變化。

每次回台中騎著摩托車閒逛時，總能在各處發現新開的店家、餐廳或民宿等有趣空間*，這些地方多數出現在市中心，如「中區」、「西區」或是這幾年蓬勃發展的「勤美商圈」與有著國家歌劇院的「七期重劃區」；在外圍的各區如清水、霧峰等，也慢慢出現有特色的獨立書店、咖啡廳等風格先遣部隊，為地方增添嶄新活力。

如果去玩台北、花東、台南和高雄之後不知道要去哪裡的話，不如就來台中走跳放空吧！我們不介意大家把台中排在行程後面啦，反正這裡天氣很好，什麼都很大，生活也是那麼舒服自在。

*Taichung has so many interesting shops that it's impossible to include them all in our guide. We've shared many great spots and stores along the routes, so be sure not to miss them!

* 台中有許多有趣的店家，難以在店家介紹中全部收錄。還有許多好點 / 好店鋪在散步路線中分享，請勿錯過！

TRANSPORTATION
交通

It takes roughly an hour to arrive at Taichung's Wurih Station from Taipei via the high speed rail. Another 15 to 20 minutes will get you from the high speed rail station to the city center where a wide variety of transportation is available, including: buses, YouBikes (which also run on EasyCard), and Uber.

台北搭乘高鐵至台中烏日站約一個小時，轉乘接駁車或計程車到市區約需 15 到 20 分鐘。市區移動可搭乘公車或騎乘 YouBike（可使用悠遊卡），Uber 數量也充足。

RECOMMENDATIONS
推薦

▊◤ READING LIST 旅遊書籍

THE ALLEY LIFE IN TAICHUNG《台中巷弄日和：IG 注目店家、老眷村、獨立書店，走踏滿載夢想的文創之城！》
A comprehensive guide to Taichung with delightful illustrations and pictures
風格可愛，完整介紹台中的旅遊書
⌐ books.com.tw/products/0010762225

MY TAICHUNG DIARY《手繪台中日和：快與慢、晴與雨、南與北的中間生活》
A sentimental guide to Taichung with delicate hand-drawn illustrations
以細膩手繪插圖與情感書寫台中
⌐ books.com.tw/products/ 0010773946

SAVORING TAICHUNG《細味臺中》
A must-read book on Taichung's food culture
台中飲食文化深度好書
⌐ books.com.tw/products/0010637577

▊◤ LOCAL PUBLICATIONS 在地刊物

PAPER FOR TAICHUNG《溫度》
A local paper written and compiled by local youths, available for free online and at select locations
由在地青年編纂的地方刊物，可免費在寄放點索取，也可線上閱讀
⌐ facebook.com/TaiwanYouthFoundation
⌐ e-book：issuu.com/takeyouflying

DA-DUN PAPER《大墩報》
Hand-illustrated maps of Taichung with a total of ten maps, each with a different theme. Available for NTD 50 per map at the Downtown Renaissance Association
台中主題手繪地圖，總共十刊，中城文化再生協會有販售（一刊50元）
⌐ facebook.com/GoodotVillage

▊◤ TRAVEL WEBSITES 旅遊網站

TAICHUNG TRAVEL NET 臺中觀光旅遊網
Taichung's official travel website, full of useful information and available in several languages
台中市旅遊官方網站，有多國外語資訊
⌐ travel.taichung.gov.tw/en-us

▊◤ GUIDED TOURS 導覽

TC TIME WALK 台中時空漫步
Guided walking or bike tours led by local youths, available in English
由在地年輕人帶領，深受好評的英文步行、單車導覽團隊
⌐ tctimewalk.com

COME AND SEE TAICHUNG 看見台中城
These unique guided tours are led by elderly locals or displaced residents of Taichung; they are sure to show you Taichung from a different perspective. Only available in Chinese
由街友帶路的城市導覽（僅中文）
⌐ facebook.com/seetaichungcity

▊◤ ANNUAL EVENTS 年度活動

THE GRAND NINE-DAYS-AND-EIGHT-NIGHTS PARADE OF DA JIA MAZU (DURING MARCH OF THE LUNAR CALENDAR)
大甲媽祖9天8夜遶境（農曆3月）
Hailed by Discovery Channel as one of the world's three largest religious activities
被探索頻道列為世界三大宗教活動盛事
⌐ dajiamazu.org.tw

TAICHUNG JAZZ FESTIVAL 臺中爵士音樂節 (OCT. | 10月)
The largest Jazz festival in Taiwan for 10 consecutive days!
連續10天不間斷的全台最大爵士盛宴！
⌐ facebook.com/taichungJAZZfestival

Photo credit：林峻永〔臺中國家歌劇院提供〕

A NATIONAL TAICHUNG THEATER 臺中國家歌劇院

Known as Toyo Ito's most challenging architectural feat
號稱全球最難蓋的伊東豊雄建築作品

台中市西屯區惠來路二段101號
No. 101, Sec. 2, Huilai Rd., Xitun Dist., Taichung City
11:30-21:00 (Friday and weekends 11:30-22:00)
+886-4-2251-1777

B NATIONAL TAIWAN MUSEUM OF FINE ARTS
國立台灣美術館

Asia's largest and most important art museum
亞洲占地最大、重要的國家級美術場館

台中市西區五權西路一段2號 | +886-4-2372-3552
No. 2, Sec. 1, Wuquan W. Rd., West Dist., Taichung City
09:00-17:00, weekends 9:00-18:00 (Closed on Mondays)

C IBS 菩薩寺

A modern-style Buddhist temple, the curated shop, Vimal
House, also holds exhibitions occasionally
風格現代的佛寺，藝文選品空間維摩舍不定期舉辦展覽

台中市大里區永隆路147號 | +886-4-2407-9920
No. 147, Yonglong Rd., Dali Dist., Taichung City
13:00-18:00, weekends 09:00-18:00 (Closed on Mon. and Tue.)

D BAKKI HANDMADE

Independent publications, homemade cakes, and more
有著獨立刊物、手作蛋糕和更多可能的祕密空間

台中市西區五權西六街136巷6-1號
No. 6-1, Ln. 136, Wuquan W. 6th St., West Dist., Taichung City
13:00-18:00 (Closed on Mon. and Tue.)
facebook.com/BakkiHandmade

E BIEN BOOKS 邊譜

A bookhouse full of cultural ambience is the new location
of Tunghai Book Studio
老字號東海書苑新據點，充滿人文氣息的獨棟書屋

台中市西屯區台灣大道三段408號 | facebook.com/bienbooks
No. 408, Sec. 3, Taiwan Blvd., Xitun Dist., Taichung City
12:00-23:00 (Closed on Tuesdays)

F ZHONGXIN MARKET 忠信市場

A creative hub from a traditional market, with many
interesting shops. Also, visit the similar Model Market
市場再生的創意聚落，類似空間還有模範市場也值得造訪

忠信：台中市五權西路一段67號 | 模範：台中市模範市場一巷50號
Zhonxin: No. 67, Sec. 1, Wuquan W. Rd., West Dist., Taichung City
Model: No. 50, Mofan Market 1st Alley, West Dist., Taichung City

Photo credit：留白計畫

Photo credit：ZOODY

Photo credit：家務室

Photo credit：分子藥局

A CAMEZA

For lovers of photography and vintage camera gear
給喜歡攝影與老件的你

⌐ 台中市西區五權西五街20巷7號
No. 7, Ln. 20, Wuquan W. 4th St., West Dist., Taichung City
13:00-19:00 (Closed on Mondays)
+886-4-2378-6090

B BLANK PLAN 留白計畫

A four-story cultural space that combines tea art, wine
tasting, curation, and various possibilities
結合茶藝、品酒、策展與各式可能的4層樓藝文空間

⌐ 台中市西區五權西四街45號 | facebook.com/blankplan.tw
No. 45, Wuquan West 4th Street, West District, Taichung City
14:00-18:30

C HOME WORK 家務室

Environmentally friendly daily goods store
友善環境的生活雜貨屋

⌐ 台中市南區頂橋三巷24-1號 (學田有藝2F)
24-1, Dingqiao 3rd Ln., South Dist., Taichung (2nd floor of XueTian Café)
13:00-17:30, weekends 11:00-17:30 (Closed on Mon. and Tue.)
eco-homework.com | +886-4-2407-0792

D AT_SOLIDART BOOKS & GALLERY 實心裡 生活什物店

Comfortable and high quality stationery and goods store
舒服有質感的文具與生活小物店

⌐ 台中市南屯區大容東街10巷12號
No. 12, Ln. 10, Darong E. St., Nantun Dist., Taichung City
13:30-18:30, Saturday 12:00-19:00 (Closed on Sun., Mon. and Tue.)
+886-4-2325-8108

E ZOODY

A local and highly stylish footwear brand
源自台中的個性鞋履品牌

⌐ 台中市西區公益路68號1F
1F., No. 68, Gongyi Rd., West Dist., Taichung City
+886-4-2328 1000 #1190
www.zoody.tw

F MOLECURE 分子藥局

Taiwan's poshest pharmacy that also serves pour-over
coffee
台灣最時髦的藥局，提供手沖咖啡

⌐ 台中市西屯區惠來路二段236-1號 | +886-4-2251-5065
No. 236-1, Sec. 2, Huilai Rd., Xitun Dist., Taichung City
10:00-21:00

Photo credit: 澀

Photo credit: Coffee Stopover

A 上下游 NEWS&MARKET

An independent media/local produce space

獨立媒體與台灣農產選物店

⌐ 台中市西區五權西二街100號

No. 100, Wuquan W. 2nd St., West Dist., Taichung City

10:30-19:00 (Closed on Sundays)

+886-4-2378-3835

B PETIT ÉTÉ 小夏天

Vietnamese food so delicious it sparks joy. Please check the available slots for reservation on its Facebook page

2樓洋房裡的越南幸福料理，採提前預約制

⌐ 台中市中區自由路二段28-2號 | +886-4-2221-1282

No. 28-2, Section 2, Ziyou Road, Central District, Taichung City

11:30-18:00 (Closed on Wed. and Thur.) | facebook.com/petitete13

C SUR- 澀

A Michelin-starred restaurant led by a young chef team

年輕廚師團隊帶領的米其林一星餐廳，需訂位

⌐ 台中市中區中山路29號3F | Closed on Mon. and Tue.

3F, No. 29, Zhongshan Rd., Central Dist., Taichung City

每月1號 12:00 開放訂位 Reservations open monthly on the 1st at 12:00

inline.app/booking/taichung/surcuisinetw

D YIZHONG FENG-REN ICE 一中豐仁冰

Salty and sweet plum with shaved ice, runner beans, and ice cream float

鹹梅子冰、花豆與汽水冰淇淋的絕妙滋味

⌐ 台中市北區育才街3巷4-6號 | +886-4-2223-0522

No. 4-6, Ln. 3, Yucai St., North Dist., Taichung City

10:00-22:30

E WU WEI TSAO TANG TEAHOUSE 無為草堂

A tranquil tea house to forget all your worldly troubles

遺世獨立的閑靜茶館

⌐ 台中市南屯區公益路二段106號

No. 106, Sec. 2, Gongyi Rd., Nantun Dist., Taichung City

+886-4-2329-6707

10:30-21:30

F COFFEE STOPOVER BLACK

A coffee connoisseur's heaven where you can choose your own roast, the basement is home to Genki Records

咖啡控控天堂，可自選烘焙度。地下室是元氣唱片行

⌐ 台中市西區福龍街7號 | +886-4-2208-0580

No. 7, Fulong St., West Dist., Taichung City, Taiwan

14:00-19:00 (Closed on Sun. and Mon.)

Photo credit : Tipsy Room

Photo credit : Vender

A SOUND LIVE HOUSE 迴響音樂藝文展演空間
Live music, bar and art exhibition space
酒吧、音樂展演與藝文展覽空間

⌐ 台中市中區中山路108號
No. 108, Chung Shan Rd., Central Dist., Taichung City
18:00-01:00 (Closed on Mondays and Tuesdays)
+886-4-2451-1989

B TIPSY ROOM 西渴室
A rare British-style, no-menu, laid-back bar in Taichung
台中少數英倫風格的無酒單自在酒吧

⌐ 台中市西區向上路一段260號 | 18:00-02:00
No. 260, Section 1, Xiangshang Road, West District, Taichung City
+886-905-301-098

C VENDER
A creative secret bar hidden behind a vending machine,
also serving Singaporean and Malaysian cuisine
隱藏在販賣機後面的創意祕密酒吧，也提供星馬料理

⌐ 台中市西區五權西四街118號 | +886-4-2372-5875
No. 118, Wuquan West 4th St, West District, Taichung City
18:00-02:00, Fri. and Sat. 18:00-03:00

D THE PLACE TAICHUNG 大毅老爺行旅
A brand new gallery-inspired hotel
新開幕的藝廊概念飯店

⌐ 台中市西區英才路601號
No. 601, Yingcai Rd., West Dist., Taichung City
+886-4-2376-6732

E RYOKOUSHANOMORI 旅人之森生活旅行案內所
Offers Taichung's best stay experience, don't forget to
check out their adorable first floor boutique
台中城市體驗首選，一樓有(會失心瘋的)可愛選品店

⌐ 台中市北區英士路66巷20號
No. 20, Ln. 66, Yingshi Rd., North Dist., Taichung City
joying23@gmail.com

F SOF HOTEL 植光花園酒店
A historical hotel with a gorgeous courtyard
有著美麗天井的歷史建築旅館

⌐ 台中市中區光復路52號
No. 52, Guangfu Rd., Central Dist., Taichung City
+886-4-2223-0880

CITY CENTER ROUTE

城中路線

TAICHUNG RAILWAY STATION
AND OLD DOWNTOWN

台中火車站周邊與舊市區

BE A TAICHUNG'S OLD-TIMER FOR ONE DAY! 來當一天老台中人！

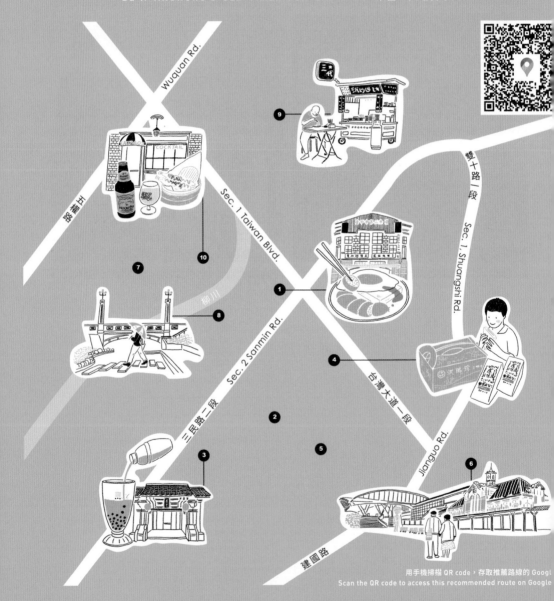

用手機掃描 QR code，存取推薦路線的 Googl
Scan the QR code to access this recommended route on Googl

1)	09:30	Have breakfast at the Second Market, try meat buns, the classic trio (turnip cake, eggs, and sticky rice sausage), and black tea
2)	10:30	Take a stroll and visit historical sites from the Japanese colonial period: Taichung Prefecture Hall Park and Taichung Shiyakusho
3)	12:00	Enjoy a fabulous lunch followed by dessert at Chun Shui Tang Cultural Tea House (at the original or Central District location)
4)	13:30	Time to shop for local goods and souvenirs
5)	14:30	Stroll alongside Lyu Chuan and pop into some book stores and shops
6)	16:00	Explore the Taichung Railway Station and the surrounding area
7)	18:00	Have a gourmet dinner at Shoal or grab a quick bite to eat at Zhongxiao Night Market located behind the station
8)	19:30	Take a post-dinner stroll alongside Liuchuan Canal
9)	20:30	Get ready for round two in Zhonghua Night Market
10)	21:30	Get yourself a nightcap or massage

1)	09:30	來「第二市場」吃早餐，肉包、「三樣」和紅茶！
2)	10:30	散步到日式古蹟「臺中州廳」與「臺中市役所」
3)	12:00	在「春水堂」創始店或中區老店午餐，飯後還有甜點名店
4)	13:30	台中名產與伴手禮血拚時間
5)	14:30	漫步綠川，順道逛逛書店與小店
6)	16:00	在台中車站附近探險，車站建築也值得一看
7)	18:00	到「魚麗」吃晚餐吧！或在車站後頭的「忠孝夜市」就近解決
8)	19:30	閒逛到柳川走走，消化一下準備下個行程
9)	20:30	是的，讓我們再戰一回中華夜市
10)	21:30	小酌一杯（或去按摩）

09:30
SECOND MARKET
1. 第二市場

Established during the Japanese colonial period, Second Market is a local hub of delicious eateries that are well-loved by locals and tourists alike. My personal favorites include Wang's (famed for their san-yang, a breakfast trio consisting of turnip cake, sticky rice sausage, and egg), Yan's (get the meat buns and wonton soup), Li Hai Minced Pork Rice, and last but not least, Old Lai's black tea. In the summer, Lin's Traditional Eatery serves white jute soup, a Taichung specialty that is a must-try for visitors.

日治時期興建的第二市場，有許多深受本地人與觀光客喜愛的美味小吃，個人推薦「王記」（菜頭粿、糯米腸加蛋稱為「三樣」）、「顏記」肉包（記得點餛飩湯）、「李海魯肉飯」，最後別忘了買杯「老賴」紅茶。市場內的「林記古早味」，夏天時會賣帶有一點點苦味的台中特產「麻薏湯」，可以試試！

記得先去老店「長崎蛋糕」預訂蜂蜜蛋糕，在指定時間去提領。

10:30
JAPANESE STYLE ARCHITECTURE
2. 日式官廳建築

Take a post-breakfast stroll and visit two marvelous Japanese style governmental buildings, Taichung Prefecture Hall Park and Taichung Shiyakusho. The former is in the process of being transformed into an art museum; the latter has been converted to a space for restaurants and galleries. Nearby, visit the revitalized Taiwan Confucianism Examination Shed for coffee and exhibitions, or explore the National Comics Museum which is great for kids.

散步到兩棟華麗的日式官廳建築「臺中州廳」與「臺中市役所」，前者未來將規劃為美術館，後者已活化成為餐飲與藝廊空間；附近還有結合咖啡與展覽的古蹟再生空間「臺灣府儒考棚」以及適合帶小朋友去的「國家漫畫博物館」。

12:00
THE ORIGINAL CHUN SHUI TANG
3.「春水堂」創始店

If you're a fan of bubble milk tea, you must pay homage at Chun Shui Tang, the alleged founding place of bubble milk tea. Have lunch while you're there (the Kung Fu noodles with stewed egg is my usual order). Lunch options in the area also include Qin Yuan Chun, a local fixture for authentic Jiangsu cuisine, and Fan's Chin Chih Yuan, a restaurant famed for their pork chop rice. For dessert, try Xin Fa Tang's honey bean shaved ice and Don-don taro balls.

如果愛喝珍珠奶茶，中午就到號稱「世界珍珠奶茶發源地」的「春水堂」創始店吃頓午餐朝聖一下吧（我都點功夫麵加滷蛋）！這一帶午餐選擇還有老字號的江浙菜「沁園春」與「范記金之園草袋飯」（排骨飯）。午後甜點有蜜豆冰大王「幸發亭」和來自大坑的「東東芋圓」可選擇。

13:30
TAICHUNG SPECIALTIES
4. 台中名產

Suncake —a flaky pastry with a gooey, malty fillin—is basically synonymous with Taichung. Naturally, every Taichung family has their own preferred suncake vendor; mine is Amin division-old Sun Tong Food (for lemon cake my family prefers Sun Booth). While you're on this block, you have to go to Hung Rui Chen (try their famous ham sandwich and Taiwanese macaron)and Chen Yun Pao Chun, a century-old pastry shop that originated in Fongyuan.

說到有著香甜麥芽內餡的台中名產「太陽餅」，每個台中家庭都有自己偏好的店，我們家喜歡「阿明師老店」（檸檬餅則會買25號的「太陽堂老店」）。這個街區還有必買的「洪瑞珍」火腿三明治、「榮記餅店」的（台式馬卡龍「小西點」也好吃），以及來自豐原的百年餅鋪「陳允寶泉」。

14:30
SHIN SEI GREEN WATERWAY
5. 綠川水岸廊道

Follow Zhongshan Road, formerly known as Shin Sei Bridge Pass, and you'll arrive at Taichung's latest attraction, Shin Sei Green Waterway—Taiwan's first trademark-registered waterway. The adorable logo, featuring a stylized rendition of the waterway, has been widely applied to the area and can be seen on railings, manholes, and various merchandise. The city has completely revitalized this historically significant canal, turning it into a popular attraction. In 2012, Dawn Cake Corporation renovated a dilapidated Japanese style building that used to be a ophthalmology clinic, transforming it into a sweet shop that is both retro and fantastical. Miyahara Ice Cream not only became a huge tourist attraction, it also encouraged community-based and design-oriented organizations—chiefly, Happen Social Design and Downtown Renaissance Association—to establish a presence in the city's Central District.

I also recommend visiting Fourth Credit Union, another great project by Dawn Cake Corporation, the bookstore/café Fleet Street, and HAUSINC 1035, a coffee shop revitalized from a century-old eye clinic. Additionally, check out the creative hub Fusion Space 1962, which used to be a cosmetics factory. Personally, I love the Tu Pang restaurant on the first floor and the Anathapindika Bookstore on the third floor.

沿著舊稱「新盛橋通」的中山路往前走，會抵達經過整治成為台中最新景點的「新盛綠川水岸廊道」，這是台灣第一條有註冊商標的河川（設計得非常可愛），商標被運用在周邊的欄杆、人孔蓋甚至商品上，全新的綠川風景讓復甦中的中區更加熱鬧。2012年「日出」團隊改造了廢棄多時的日式建築「宮原眼科」，以復古魔幻的甜品空間之姿再度登場，吸引了大批觀光客前往，加上關心社會設計與文化的團隊如「好伴」、「中城再生文化協會」相繼進駐，逐漸將中區帶回市民關注焦點。

這邊還推薦同是「日出」出品的「第四信用合作社」、書店兼咖啡店「Fleet Street」、百年眼科醫館再生的「HAUSINC 1035」咖啡館，以及前身為化妝品工廠的創意聚落「復興工廠」，個人偏愛1樓的「地坊餐廳」以及3樓的「給孤獨者書店」。

16:00
TAICHUNG RAILWAY STATION
6. 台中車站

In days past, Taichung Railway Station and the adjoining First Plaza were considered Taichung's busiest and most popular commercial spaces. However, as other commercial districts began to develop and prosper, the popularity of the area dwindled. After more than a decade of commercial stagnation, migrant workers from Southeast Asia have reinvigorated the plaza, opening up various businesses and making it a regular weekend gathering place. The plaza was officially renamed ASEAN Square in 2016. Since Taichung Railway Station was confirmed to undergo the Taiwan Railway Administration Elavatization project, several cultural preservation organizations have fought to preserve the station's historical belltower and Western-influenced facades while new improvements were underway. Now, the station is a place where historical elements meet contemporary conveniences and a platform for multicultural exchange.

台中車站與旁邊的「第一廣場」早期可說是台中最繁華的街區，隨著其他商圈逐漸發展，顯得老舊的車站一帶逐漸沒落。在十幾年的停擺後，來自東南亞的移工們慢慢承接起這棟大樓，在此經營各種商家，賦予它新生命與活力，成為移工們假日休閒的去處，第一廣場也在2016年改名為「東協廣場」。而台中車站確定高架化後，在文資團體的爭取下，以保留有著美麗鐘塔洋樓的舊站體方式興建新站，如今車站周遭已煥然一新，來此不妨感受一下其多元的文化與新舊建築交錯的魅力。

18:00
SHOAL, A CULTURAL DINING SPACE
7. 魚麗人文共同廚房

Shoal is a menuless restaurant famed for serving traditional and often labor-intensive dishes. With their two chefs who come from backgrounds in journalism, you can be sure that your meal will be accompanied by good conversation and a detailed history behind each served dish. In 2013, Shoal's owners were faced with public scrutiny due to their actions of bringing vegetarian meals to Zheng Xing Ze—a man on death row who was later acquitted —in order to show support for whom they believed to be an unjustly accused man. Through their cooking, the owners were able to stand firm in their moral beliefs through a difficult period of social pressure and succeeded in expressing their conviction in humanity and justice in a gentle yet resolute fashion. (It is necessary to make reservations if you would like to dine at Shoal. If that is not available to you, Zhongxiao Night Market behind the station is a great option for sampling a wide variety of eatery delights.)

晚餐搭車前往富有人情味、以傳統功夫菜聞名的無菜單餐館「魚麗」，兩位新聞背景出身的主廚會在「桌邊說菜」，讓人更了解每一道菜背後的故事。2013年開始，魚麗以送素菜便當行動支持死囚鄭性澤，這則冤案後遭平反，但在當時的輿論壓力下，魚麗仍透過料理溫柔堅定地表達關懷。在這裡，每一道菜都用心製作，所以才撫慰人心。（魚麗需事先訂位，若遊客求方便也可以在車站後方的忠孝夜市大啖夜市美食。）

19:30
YANAGAWA WATERWAY

8. 柳川水岸步道

Take a post-dinner stroll alongside Liuchuan Riverside Walk. Taichung's irrigation department and civilian organizations worked together to properly redesign and manage local canals and rivers that had become run-down. After years of collaborative effort, these waterways are once again functional parts of the city.

吃完晚餐到整治過的柳川水岸步道散散步，在台中水利局與民間單位合作下，過往幾條被水泥加蓋的重要河川，經過水利治理與設計，再度進入台中人的生活日常。

20:30
ZHONGHUA NIGHT MARKET

9. 中華夜市

Visit Zhonghua Night Market for some of Taichung's oldest and most beloved eateries. The market is located on Zhonghua Road which runs parallel to Liuchuan Riverside Walk. Having grown up in the area, I was practically raised on the food from these eateries, many of which are owned by my old neighbors. My first choice is Three Generation Stir-fried Noodles; this combination of delectable noodles, fried in lard and paired with stewed pork soup, is simply unbeatable. You also have to try New Taiching Ba-Wan, Zhonghua Mochi King, Zhonghua Road Wide Noodle Soup (a Taichung specialty), and Tantzu Stinky Tofu.

與柳川平行的中華路上有著充滿老字號小吃攤的中華夜市，我因為老家就在這一帶，可說是從小吃到大，許多攤販甚至還是鄰居。個人首推「三代炒麵」，用豬油拌炒的油潤麵條與肉羹湯是絕配！其他如「新台中肉圓」、「中華麻糬大王」、「中華路大麵羹」（台中特產）與「潭子臭豆腐」等，都是推薦的老味道。

21:30
GET A DRINK OR A MASSAGE

10. 小酌一杯（或去按摩）

Sao-Bao Bar & Kitchen—located next to Sunrise Movie Theater (which, you will be happy to know, allows outside food)—serves Taiwanese pork buns and beer in a fun and delightful ambience. If you're craving something sweet, try some baked toast from A-dou Bo's frozen taro and Malulian's taro balls. Finally, end your action-packed day with a blissful massage session at Young Song Spa.

在（可以帶夜市小吃進去的）日新戲院旁，有著結合刈包與啤酒的酒吧「騷包」，氣氛輕鬆愉快。如果想吃點甜的，附近推薦「阿斗伯冷凍芋」（烤吐司別錯過）或是有著最好吃芋圓的「瑪露連」；若是嫌今日行程太操勞，趕快到「春不荖足湯養生館」徹底放鬆一下，結束美好一日。

SCIENCE MUSEUM
AND ART MUSEUM AREA
科學博物館與美術館周邊

A CULTURAL AND ARTISTIC ROUTE   由綠意串起的人文藝術軸線

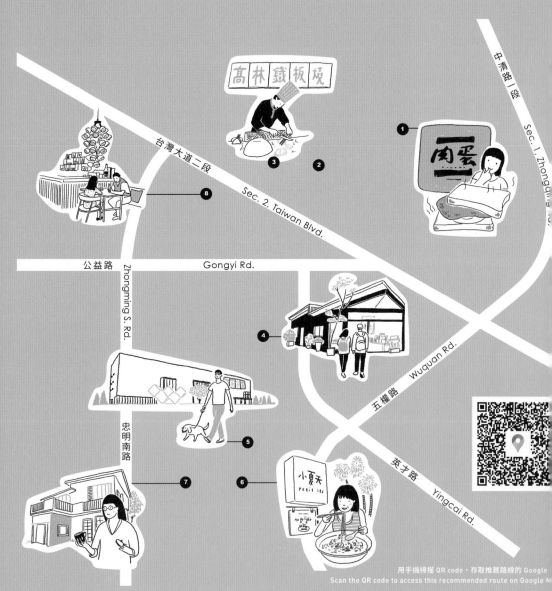

1) 09:30 Start your day off right at Pork Egg Toast

2) 10:30 Visit the National Museum of Natural Science or Sixth Market

3) 12:00 Take your pick of teppanyaki at Kaolin Teppanyaki, hamburgers, soups, or vegetarian cuisine

4) 13:30 Visit a cultural and creative community and its shops

5) 15:30 Continue shopping at boutiques or head over to the National Taiwan Museum of Fine Arts and Zhongxing Market

6) 18:00 For dinner, you can choose from traditional Chinese cuisine or an upgraded version of beef noodles

7) 19:30 Have a post-dinner browse around local shops

8) 21:00 Come have a cup of coffe or a glass of cocktails

1) 09:30 用「肉蛋吐司」開啟今日

2) 10:30 到「國立自然科學博物館」或「第六市場」逛逛

3) 12:00 鐵板燒老店「高林」、漢堡、湯品或蔬食料理任君挑選

4) 13:30 逛舊時宿舍改造的文創聚落與附近小店

5) 15:30 繼續逛選品店或是前往「國立台灣美術館」與「忠信市場」

6) 18:00 晚餐可選中式料理或是升級版牛肉麵

7) 19:30 到小店逛逛消化腸胃

8) 21:00 喝杯咖啡，或來杯調酒吧

09:30
PORK EGG TOAST
1. 肉蛋吐司

Starting out as a food cart in 1985, Pork Egg Toast—which appropriately enough, comprises of a slice of sizzling pork and a fried egg, sandwiched between two slices of fresh white toast—is now a local fixture. This staple breakfast has sustained many a student and has become a tourist favorite. Don't be alarmed by the hungry mob; I know for a fact that this breakfast place is highly efficient. Go ahead and order their signature pork egg toast as well as their salad toast, egg pancake, and iced milk tea.

1985 年由攤車開始經營的「肉蛋吐司」，靠著兩片鮮甜的白吐司夾著香煎豬肉片與荷包蛋的美好滋味，陪伴許多台中孩子長大，更是觀光客最愛的台中早餐之一。雖然人潮眾多，但店家出餐速度快，推薦招牌肉蛋吐司、招牌沙拉吐司、蛋餅搭配冰奶茶！

10:30
NATIONAL MUSEUM OF NATURAL SCIENCE
2. 國立自然科學博物館

It would be safe to say that the National Museum of Natural Science is a field-trip stop that every Taichung child has made. (Look for my favorite exhibit, the roaring Tyrannosaurus.)After visiting the museum, don't forget to swing around back to stroll through the largest botanical garden in Taiwan. If nature and science are not your cup of tea (which is the case with me), visit the Sixth Market on the third floor of the Park Lane Shopping Center, where there is good shopping and delicious local eatery food.

到科博館校外教學應該是每個台中人小時候的回憶（每次去一定要去找那隻會吼叫的暴龍），後頭還有全台最大的植物園。若對自然科學比較沒有興趣（沒關係我也是），也可造訪位於金典綠園道 3 樓的「第六市場」，在舒適的環境裡逛逛各式攤販，品嘗新鮮美味的在地小吃。

12:00
LUNCH TIME
3. 午餐時間

It would not be a real visit to Taiwan if you didn't try Taiwan's famous one meat and two vegetables teppanyaki. If you go to the long-established and well-loved Kaolin Teppanyaki, make sure to also order the pan-fried banana or taro drizzled with honey for an unforgettable dessert. Additionally, I highly recommend the gourmet burger restaurant, Farm Burger, and Veggie Wonderland, an Italian vegetarian restaurant.

來台灣一定要吃一次「一肉兩菜」的台式鐵板燒，老字號的「高林」選多了飯後甜點煎香蕉或芋頭，淋上蜂蜜的滋味難忘！其他還有有著多家分店的手作漢堡店「田樂」和蔬食義大利餐廳「野菜共合国」也相當推薦。

13:30
VISIT TAICHUNG'S MOST PROSPEROUS COMMERCIAL AREA

4. 走訪台中最熱鬧的區域之一

1. Eslite Park Lane and CMP Block Museum of Arts

Since its inauguration in 2008, Eslite Park Lane has brought new vitality to the West District and catalyzed commercial and cultural development. In 2019, CMP Block Museum of Arts and prestigious Japanese architect Kengo Kuma will embark on a collaborative journey to transform the museum space. All in all, this area is the perfect place for a post-lunch digestive stroll.

2. PARK2

PARK2 is the latest creative lifestyle hub by the CMP GROUP. This two-story, 2,000 square meter space brings together numerous distinctive brands, including cafes, restaurants, and bars. Weekends feature outdoor DJ performances and various market activities, making it a must-see spot for both its offerings and ambiance. It's the trendiest and most relaxed gathering place in Taichung recently. If you're looking for a drink in the evening, I recommend Draft Land for their Cocktails On Tap, and Petit Petit Bar & Coffee which also offers delicious food. (instagram: park2_cmp)

3. Lanes and alleys of Zhongxing Street

The lanes and alleys of Zhongxing Street are full of interesting shops. Visit Washida Home Store, a boutique shop from Tainan, then walk to Green Ray Project, a collective housed in a former dormitory for municipal workers. This area is a hub for unique shops and dining establishments, including Green Ray+marüte, a gallery space known for its collaborative exhibitions with Japanese artists, and the independent bookstore BOOK MARÜTE. If you're feeling peckish, have a gourmet donut at Haritts Donuts and Coffee or try some rich and creamy douhua—made from scratch using Taiwanese soy beans—and shaved ice desserts at TW Soy Milk Shaved Ice Shop.

1. 勤美誠品與勤美術館

2008 年開幕的勤美誠品，在當時著實為台中帶來了一股新活力，並快速帶動周邊發展，除了應運而生的店家，連綠園道上也開始多了各式活動，假日總是吸引眾多人潮前往；旁邊的勤美術館也在 2019 年與日本建築大師隈研吾合作改建，令人期待，吃飽飯後不妨先前往這兩個地方散步消化。

2. 草悟廣場

PARK2 草悟廣場是勤美集團最新打造的新型態公園，占地 2,000 平方公尺的 2 層樓建築匯集了咖啡、餐廳、酒吧等眾多特色品牌，週末還有戶外 DJ 表演和各式市集活動，軟硬體都相當有看頭，是台中近期時髦又放鬆的風格聚會場所。晚上想在此喝一杯的話推薦供應 Cocktails On Tap 的「Draft Land」以及餐點也好吃的「Petit Petit Bar & Coffee」。

3. 中興街巷弄

接著逛逛中興街附近的小店，如從台南來的選品店「Washida Home Store」，並漫步到由舊時自來水宿舍改造而成的創意聚落「綠光計畫」，這一帶聚集了許多有趣的店家與餐飲店，像是與日本香山獨立書店「BOOK MARÜTE」合作的藝廊空間「綠光 +marüte」，時常舉辦日本藝術家展覽，值得前往。如果嘴饞這裡有來自東京的手工甜甜圈名店「Haritts donuts&coffee」以及「美軍豆乳冰」，夏天不妨來吃使用台灣黃豆做成的濃郁豆花和各式冰品。

☐
15:30
UNIQUE SHOPS
5a. 來逛更多風格小店

I highly recommend checking out ARTQPIE, a reading space founded by couple Arqi and Janeni who also publish independent publications that are well worth collecting. Also high on my list of recommendations are TPL Stationery (a multifunctional cultural space), Little Seed Collection (a children's boutique), and Cut&paste Select Shop (a stylish fashion boutique).

Forestmosa, the shop of fragrance products and Taiwan's handicrafts founded by Lavender Cottage is located inside, as well as Shenji 368 Entrepreneurial Village, where market events are often held on weekend. For those who like almonds, 30 Almonds offers almond tea with various flavors; and for dessert fiends, the patisserie CJSJ started by a Michelin pastry chef is a must-visit. For tea lovers, be sure to visit Zhao Zhao Tea Lounge.

繼續往下走首推由個性夫妻檔 Arqi 和 Janeni 成立的閱讀空間「本冊圖書館」（其獨立出版的刊物值得收藏）。其他小店還有「茶筆巷文具生活空間」、親子選物店「Little Seed Collection」以及個性服裝選品店「減貼選物」等。

接著到同由舊宿舍改造而成的新興聚落「審計新村」，裡面有由「薰衣草森林」開設的香氛與台灣工藝選品店「森林島嶼」，還有時常在週末舉辦市集活動的「審計 368 新創聚落」。喜歡杏仁的朋友這裡有「三時杏仁茶房」，甜點控千萬不能錯過由法國米其林甜點廚師開設的法式甜點店「CJSJ」，愛喝茶的朋友請前往「兆兆茶苑」。

☐
15:30
NATIONAL TAIWAN MUSEUM
OF FINE ARTS
5b. 國立台灣美術館

This national museum holds some of the most seminal pieces of Taiwanese art, including painter Tan Ting-pho's (Chen Cheng Bo) *Chiayi Park*. Apart from its impressive permanent collection, the museum also hosts a wide range of design fairs and special exhibitions as well as the Taiwan Biennial. Across from the museum is Zhongxin Market, a unique alternative cultural and art space in which galleries, shops, and residences merge and blend into one fascinating entity.

國家級的「國立台灣美術館」收藏了許多台灣重要藝術家作品，如畫家陳澄波的〈嘉義遊園地〉，除了常設展與特展外，也舉辦台灣美術雙年展。在其對面的「忠信市場」是獨具個性的藝文替代空間，市場裡藝廊、店家與住家的日常界線模糊，但也讓這裡更為有趣迷人。

18:00
GUBAMI
6. 升級版牛肉麵

For dinner, head to Wuquan West 3rd Street, which is lined with numerous restaurants. If you're in a group, I recommend trying Pin Hong Qiao, a Chinese restaurant where almost every dish is worth trying. Another option is Gubami, a high-end beef noodle shop created by Asia's Best Female Chef, Chen Lanshu. After indulging in the upgraded version of Taiwanese beef noodle, don't forget to head upstairs to the hidden gem Goût Bar for a drink.

晚餐就到各大餐廳林立的五權西三街覓食吧，人多的話推薦中餐廳「品虹橋」，幾乎每道菜都可圈可點，請安心點餐！其他也有由亞洲最佳女主廚陳嵐舒打造的高檔牛肉麵店「Gubami」，吃完升級版的台灣牛肉麵後，別忘了上樓到祕密酒吧「好吧 Goût Bar」喝一杯。

19:30
BROWSE THE SHOPS
7. 逛逛小店

Take a post-dinner browse at high-end clothing stores Zasso and CameZa, a select shop that carries miscellaneous goods and second-hand cameras. Another interesting local fixture is a produce market on "Park Lane" that was established by independent media News & Market. Their freshly ground peanut butter is simply unforgettable. The market closes at 7 pm so plan ahead to make it in time.

吃飽可以到有著高品質織品的服裝選品店「草也」和結合生活雜貨與二手相機的選品店「CameZa」逛逛。另外關注土地議題的獨立媒體「上下游」也在綠園道上開設了農產市集，現磨花生醬一吃難忘（營業至晚間 7 點，有興趣需提早前往）。

21:00
END YOUR DAY
WITH COFFEE OR COCKTAILS
8. 咖啡 或 調酒

End you day at Art aNew - Gallery & Café or LEFT, a restaurant by day and bar by night. On Fridays and Saturdays, Forro Café is a wonderful place to unwind and listen to some live music. Other excellent cafés that are only open during daytime include KOPHY, Solidbean, and Retro Mojo Coffee.

搭車前往集合藝廊、咖啡館和小酒吧的「Art aNew - Gallery & Café」或是餐酒館「左派」小喝一杯，週五、週六也可以到氣氛輕鬆的「Forro Café」聆聽現場表演。（這一帶有不少優秀的咖啡廳如「KOPHY」、「Solidbean」與「Retro Mojo Coffee」等，晚間無營業，有興趣可安排白天造訪。）

A YOUNG MAN'S MAZU PILGRIMAGE

少年的媽祖遶境之旅

從台中大甲到嘉義新港，9 天 8 夜、107 間廟、330 公里的旅程

You may have imagined that somewhere in the world can be found a journey similar to what is mentioned in *The Alchemist*: When you want something, all the universe conspires in helping you to achieve it. So long as you have the wish to walk with Mazu, everyone you meet along the way will help you complete this journey.

Since early times, the Jenn Lann Temple in Dajia holds a yearly activity on the evening of the Lantern Festival. By casting wooden divination blocks, the start time and route of the Mazu pilgrimage is determined. The route is largely fixed, allowing believers to arrange their own participation, whether they plan to follow on foot, by bicycle, or by scooter or car. For those who are unable to participate in the whole pilgrimage, the release of the pilgrimage route allows people to make their own way to join Mazu in traversing at least a part of the journey.

During the pilgrimage, everyone you meet along the way greets you with a broad smile, encouraging you to keep it up as you are almost there! Every neighborhood and town along the route sets out decorative lanterns and banners, dancing and singing in order to welcome your arrival. Every rest station tent is full of volunteers preparing food and tea for your enjoyment free of charge. If you are unable to continue due to fatigue or injury, volunteer medical aid will help you with a massage or to patch up your injury. Many believers participating in the pilgrimage by car customize their vehicles and drive slowly along with the parade, allowing you to rest in their cars when the hot daytime sun becomes unbearable, or driving you to the next rest station at the end of the day when you are too tired to continue on foot. Along this road of devotion and virtue, everyone is willing to help you in completing the journey and reaching your destination.

你可曾想像過世界上有一趟旅程，好像牧羊少年奇幻之旅裡寫到的——「當你真心渴望某樣東西時，整個宇宙都會聯合起來幫助你完成」。只要，你許下跟著媽祖走上一程的心願，路上所有的人都等著幫助你完成這趟旅程。

自古以來，大甲鎮瀾宮會在每年元宵節的晚上，以擲筊方式來決定媽祖遶境起駕的日期與路線。大致固定的進香路線讓信眾們得以依據自己的腳程安排，選擇徒步、鐵馬或騎車、開車的方式隨行，而公開遶境日期則讓無法全程參與的信徒，都能自行估算時間與路程，陪媽祖走上一段。

遶境的途中，路上所有的人都笑容滿面地向你打招呼，告訴你快到了，加油！路線所經的鄰里鄉鎮無不張燈結綵、載歌載舞歡迎你的到來，每個休息站的布棚底下都有義工煮飯烹茶讓你免費享用，走不動了、受傷了有志工義診幫你推拿包紮，許多開車的信徒還自行改裝遶境專用的貨車，隨著遶境步行隊伍緩緩地開著，白天充當信徒們遮陽下小憩的所在，夜裡則將體力無法負荷的信徒們載往下一個休息站。在這條虔誠善念的路，所有人都在幫助你持續走下去，完成這趟旅程。

Blessings offered in food not words

Back in 2011, on the evening before setting out on my first Dajia Mazu pilgrimage, my elders kept saying the most interesting things. They insisted that I shouldn't think of the pilgrimage as a difficult task which can help me lose weight. Rather, if I succeed in not gaining weight, that is reason enough to count my blessings!

I still recall that we set out at 11:05 am that day, and by 12:19 we were eating sesame flatbread with youtiao and soymilk provided by the Yuhuang Temple in Shalu. Over the next nine days, we never felt hungry once. Following Mazu to offer sincere prayers at every temple rest stop, there was always a snack to be had. Every one of the believers we met along the way seemed most concerned that we hadn't gotten enough to eat. Nobody worries that you might eat too much. The spring rolls in Zhanghua's Yong'an Temple, the taro sago at the Qiedongwang Temple, the oily rice and herbal tea from the Beichen Temple of Caifengan, the taro cake from the Funing Temple in Yuanlin Township, the rice noodles and wood-fired douhua from Huayan Monastery in Beidou Township, the organic guava from Sanqian Temple in Xizhou village, the black nightshade congee from Wuji Temple in Yuanchang village, the thick rice noodles from Futian Temple in the town of Xiluo, the fenguo dumplings from Wende Temple in Huatan Village… the list goes on! The Mazu believers may be shy in verbalizing blessings, but only because they've put all of their energy into preparing such authentic snacks for the enjoyment of Mazu's pilgrims.

One host of a temple along the way put it very well when he said, We prepare these snacks to create positive connections with all of Mazu's virtuous pilgrims. It doesn't matter how much you eat, we provide these vegetarian snacks to offer peace and contentment, to wish you all peace and smooth sailing along your pilgrimage. As such, we ate some of their peace-imparting blessings, and created lots of positive connections every day. To travel 330 kilometers over nine days isn't all that difficult a distance to cover for most people. All you really need is the right intention. On the evening that Mazu was to return to Her imperial home, I made a special effort to hurry back to the town to welcome Her. As I waited for Her return in a spot where people had done so for more than 20 years, the feeling was one of remarkable calm.

The sound of firecrackers shook the heavens as usual, while good friends and family came and went, exchanging cordial greetings with one another. Whenever their curiosity prompted them to ask about whether or not anything of interest came to pass on this journey, or as with every year, the most beloved question of holy signs came up in conversation, I could only answer with a smile, It's really amazing, I don't even know where to begin. Everyone should join this pilgrimage parade at least once in their lifetime.

Something which I always bore in mind without ever speaking it aloud is that, at the moment on this journey when everyone regarded me as if I was their own child, providing me with the kindest blessings and assistance, it was then that I experienced the most sacred of signs in my entire life. (by Giang Giang)

說不出口的祝福，請你多吃一點。

2011 年第一次參加大甲媽祖遶境的前夕，前輩們打趣地說不要想說遶境很辛苦可以減肥健身，不要變胖就謝天謝地了。

還記得那天出城的時候是 11 點 05 分，12 點 19 分我們就在沙鹿的玉皇殿吃起廟方供應的美味豆漿與燒餅油條了。接下來的 9 天我們都沒有餓過，一路上隨著媽祖到每一間駐駕的廟宇，誠心地拜拜、然後упот用點心，一路上所有的信徒只怕你吃不飽，不怕你吃多，彰化永安宮的春捲、茄荖王廟的芋頭西米露、彩鳳庵北辰宮的油飯與青草茶、員林鎮福寧宮的芋粿、北斗鎮華巖寺的柴燒豆花與河粉、溪州鄉三千宮的有機芭樂、元長鄉無極聖殿的龍葵粥、西螺福天宮的現做米苔目、花壇鄉文德宮的粉粿等，媽祖信徒們羞於出口的祝福，全部放在這些誠心準備的點心裡，請你享用。

途中一位廟祝說得精采，他說：「各位媽祖遶境的善信大德，我們準備點心來與你們結善緣，吃多吃少沒關係，這些素菜是提供給大家吃平安、吃心意的，祝福你們遶境一路平安順利。」於是我們就在吃一點保平安的信念之下，每天都結很多善緣、吃好幾份平安。9 天 330 公里的路程對多數人來說，並非十分艱難的距離，你所需要的，就只是一份心意。媽祖回鑾的那個晚上，我特地趕路提前回到鎮上準備迎接祂，我站在 20 幾年來每年都等待著祂的位置，感覺特別的平靜。

鎮內鞭炮依舊震天炸響地彼此較勁，親戚朋友在門前來來去去的寒暄問暖，每當他們好奇地詢問這趟旅程之中是否發生許多軼聞趣事，或問起往年我們最愛閒聊的媽祖遶境神蹟等等，我都只能回報他們一個微笑說：實在太棒了，我不知道該從何說起，人生一定要走上這一回。

而我放在心底始終沒說口的是，當一路上每個人都將你視如己出，給予你最善良祝福與協助，這一刻，已經是我生命裡最神聖的神蹟了。(文 / 薑薑)

THE GRAND NINE-DAYS-AND-EIGHT-NIGHTS PARADE OF DA JIA MAZU (DURING MARCH OF THE LUNAR CALENDAR)
大甲媽祖9天8夜遶境（農曆3月）

⌐ dajiamazu.org.tw

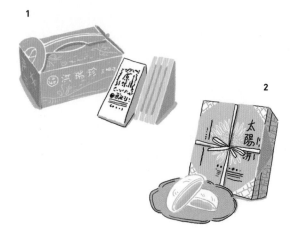

台中推薦伴手禮

Listed below are Taichung's specialty goods that you must bring home, even if your suitcase is about to burst:

以下是行李爆炸也要扛回家的台中名產推薦：

1 Hung Rui Chen Ham Sandwich
洪瑞珍火腿三明治

How they make a simple combo of toast, egg, and ham so delicious is still beyond me.

還是搞不懂只是吐司夾火腿和蛋皮為什麼可以那麼好吃！

台中市中區中山路125-2號
No. 125-2, Zhongshan Rd., Central Dist., Taichung City
Mon.-sat. 09:00-22:00, Sun. 10:00-22:00
+886-4-2226-8127

---

2 Suncake 太陽餅

Taichung's most famous specialty pastry, suncake is a flaky pastry with a sweet and sticky malt filling. My personal recommendation is "Amin's Suncake." (Yes, I do have a membership card but, no, I can't let you use it!)

台中最有名的特產，由酥皮包裹著綿密麥芽內餡，我們家喜歡「阿明師老店」（我有會員卡但不能給你 sorry，怕老闆生氣）。

台中市中區自由路二段11號
No. 11, Sec. 2, Ziyou Rd., Central Dist.,Taichung City
08:30-22:30
+886-4-2227-4007

3 Weightstone 威石東葡萄酒

Unique wine made from a special variety of grapes known as Taichung No. 3 (or Musann grape).

台中三號（木杉葡萄）釀出的台灣風味葡萄酒。

weightstone.tw

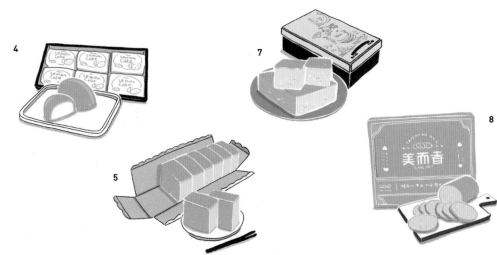

4 Lemon Cake 檸檬餅

Delicate lemon sponge cake wrapped in a golden pastry shell; my personal favorite vendor is Sun Booth.

金黃外層包裹綿密海綿蛋糕的檸檬餅，要買「太陽堂老店」的（吃習慣了）。

⌐ 台中市中區自由路二段25號
No. 25, Sec. 2, Ziyou Rd., Central Dist., Taichung City
08:00-22:00
+886-4-2220-0012

5 Banshin Castellana Cake
坂神本舖長崎蛋糕

Only available through on-site reservation and pick-up (be sure to look up their pick-up schedule). The best part of the cake is where the sweet sponge cake is stuck to the parchment paper.

只能現場預訂與領取（還得依照店家指定的時間），黏在底部紙上的綿密蛋糕底最好吃。

⌐ 台中市中區台灣大道一段388號
No. 388, Sec. 1, Taiwan Blvd., Central Dist., Taichung City
09:00-19:00 (Closed on Mondays)
+886-4-2222-6506

6 Wu-Feng Sake 初霧燒肘

From Wu-Feng Farmer's Association Distillery, this sake is great for both drinking and brewing plum wine.

霧峰農會出品，單喝或用來釀（梅）酒都非常棒！

⌐ 台中市霧峰區中正路345號
No. 345, Zhongzheng Rd., Wufeng Dist., Taichung
+886-4-2339-9191
Mon.-Fri. 08:00-17:00, weekend 09:00-17:00
www.twwfsake.com

7 Dawn Cake 日出乳酪蛋糕

Cake that looks as good as it tastes (with gorgeous packaging that makes for the perfect gift). There are multiple Dawn Cake locations, for more information please visit their website.

少數兼具美觀與美味的糕餅店（包裝精美，送禮有面子），有多家分店，營業資訊請參考官方網站。

⌐ dawncake.com.tw

8 Taichung Ham 美而香台中哈姆

A Taiwanese style sweet and savory ham that you can't miss.

不能錯過的台式香甜火腿滋味。

⌐ 台中市西區五廊街98-5號
No. 98-5, Wulang St., West Dist., Taichung City
Mon.-sat. 09:00-18:00, Sun. 13:00-18:00
+886-4-2372-5854

9 Dong Quan Chili Sauce & Da Yue Aged Vinegar
東泉辣椒醬、大越老醋

Taichung essentials that you'll find in every household.

老台中人家中必備的那幾味。

⌐ 台中市中區台灣大道一段581號
No. 581, Sec. 1, Taiwan Blvd.,
Central Dist.,Taichung City
08:30-18:00 (Closed on weekends)
+886-4-2222-3377

9

最早的辣台派*台灣人 從這裡來

photo credit : sfmine7?

彰化
CHANG
HUA
TAIWAN'S FIERCEST PEOPLE

—————— Han-Hao Chang 張翰豪

As a local Changhuanese, people often ask me: what is Changhua known for? For a long time, my answer was ba-wan and the famous Lukang Town. Wanting to learn more, I delved into the history of Changhua and discovered the city's rich and fascinating stories. While Taiwan was under Japanese colonial rule, Changhua was infamous for its revolts and uprisings, so much so that the Japanese parliament described it as an origin of infectious thought.

Changhua is also known for its many temples—which historically served as gathering places for leftists and activists—as well as its unique local delicacies: ba-wan, mao-shu noodle, and braised pork with rice. These hearty and budget-friendly staples have served generations of Changhuanese and have been featured in the writings of authors such as Lai He and Yang Shou Yu to depict the life of the city's locals. In the past, the people of Changhua played an instrumental part in political revolutions and literary movements. Changhuanese, such as musician Lim Giong and poet Wu Sheng, are continuing to shape their community by engaging with the people and enriching Changhua through the art of words and music.

The media recently revealed that Changhua's Yuanlin Township has the highest number of multimillionaires and luxury vehicles in the country and has also become the center of development in southern Changhua. It should come as no surprise that the area is also home to a number of lovely cafés and restaurants that are worth checking out. New and interesting stores are also popping up all over northern Changhua (where Changua City and the famous Lukang Township are located)so you'll have plenty to explore and discover!

身為彰化人常被問：「你們彰化有什麼？」除了肉圓與鹿港小鎮，我還真說不出什麼名堂。然而重新攤開史冊，才發現這是座被低估的城市，彰化在日治時期可是被日本議會稱為「思想惡化之地」、勇於反抗殖民威權的叛逆城市！

這裡的廟宇曾是左派人士的集會所在；彰化美食三寶：肉圓、貓鼠麵與爌肉飯，在當時已是餵飽知青的國民銅板美食，更被作家賴和、楊守愚等人寫進記載庶民生活的小說裡。彰化人參與了革命，寫小說引領台灣新文學運動；現在還有林強創作走在尖端的電子音樂、溪州詩人吳晟一家持續用文學與音樂關懷土地與農業。

對比彰化在城市行銷上的低調，前陣子員林鎮被媒體披露為全台億萬富翁與雙 B 轎車密度最高的地方，更開了許多愜意的咖啡館與餐館，連帶成為南彰化的發展核心；而位於北彰的彰化市與鹿港近期也有許多有趣店家出現。「你們彰化有什麼？」，我的答案是：「來了你就知道。」

* Pro-Taiwan rapper Dwagie saluted former President Tsai Ing-wen and her efforts in fighting for Taiwan's sovereignty by calling her a "spicy Taiwanese lady." In a later statement, former President Tsai called upon Taiwanese people to "be fierce for your country because we are Taiwanese and are spicy when we need to be."

* 饒舌歌手大支以「辣台妹」致敬維護台灣主權的前總統蔡英文，後蔡前總統稱：「若台灣有需要時，我們都是辣台派，該辣就辣。」

TRANSPORTATION
交通

It takes about an hour to arrive at Taichung's New Wujih Station from Taipei via the High Speed Rail and an additional 15-minute transfer via local train to get to downtown Changhua. Alternatively, you could also take the slow train or bus from Taipei to Changhua; both options take around three hours. In Changhua, your best mode of transportation is by foot, YouBike, or scooter (rentals are available around the train station).

台北搭高鐵至台中彰化站車程約 1 小時，轉乘區間車至市區約 15 分鐘。若搭乘台鐵或客運至彰化約 3 小時左右。在市區適合徒步、騎乘 YouBike 或摩托車（火車站附近可租借）。

RECOMMENDATIONS
推薦

◤ READING LIST 旅遊書籍

CHANGHUA FOOD DIARIES《彰化小食記》〔增修版〕
Explore Changhua with this drool-inducing food guide
按圖索驥吃美食，是遊樂享受，更是學問
⌐ books.com.tw/products/0010719279

XIAOXI STREET《小西巷》
Get a glimpse of Changhua's past through family histories
用一部家族史窺探彰化的前世今生
⌐ books.com.tw/products/0010763350

◤ GUIDED TOURS 導覽

LUKO CHANGHUA TRAVEL LIBRARY 旅庫。彰化
An in-depth and well-organized tour of Changhua that is focused on local temples, eateries, railroads, and ecology
針對廟宇、小吃、鐵道、生態等主題規劃深度導覽
⌐ facebook.com/changhua.travel.library

◤ ANNUAL EVENTS 年度活動

WANGGONG MIDSUMMER MUSIC FESTIVAL (JULY)
王功漁火節 (7月)
Come enjoy beer, seafood, and music at Changhua's hottest summer event!
彰化年度夏季盛事，來喝啤酒啖海鮮，吹風聽音樂！
⌐facebook.com/WangGongYuHuoJie

TIENCHUNG MARATHON (NOVEMBER)
田中馬拉松 (11月)
Participate in Taiwan's most enthusiastic marathon event and have the whole town cheer you on
台灣最熱情！全鎮居民都出來幫你加油的馬拉松
⌐ facebook.com/520marathon

◤ TRAVEL WEBSITES 旅遊網站

TRAVEL IN CHANGHUA 彰化旅遊資訊網
Chanhua's official travel website, offering great information in many travel categories
彰化市政府官方網站，有多元主題分類
⌐ tourism.chcg.gov.tw

◤ LOCAL PUBLICATIONS 在地刊物

TSIONG HUÀ LÁNG《烔話郎》
In addition to publications, its website also has abundant information about Changhua
除紙本刊物外，網站也有豐富資訊，串聯許多年輕在地店家，掌握地方最新動態
⌐ facebook.com/changhuarun
⌐ whitepost.co

CHANGHUA WAY《彰化味》
A seasonal publication that features villages and towns and records local stories
地方誌季刊，走訪各大鄉鎮，記錄在地故事
⌐ www.facebook.com/CHANGHUAWAY2020

THE KIDS FROM LUKANG《今秋誌》
A three-year publication recording the experiences of young adults returning to their homes in Lukang, available for purchase on Facebook
鹿港囝仔製作的返鄉紀實3年刊，可在臉書專頁購買
⌐ facebook.com/tkfl.tw

YUANLIN STORY《員林紀事》
A local lifestyle magazine documenting the big and small events of Yuanlin
記錄員林大小事的在地生活誌
⌐ https://www.facebook.com/linlinlocallife

Photo credit：Ting Liu

Photo credit：彰化縣政府

Photo credit：南方書店

Photo credit：台豐高爾夫球場

A   SUSUBOOKS

A picture book-themed bookstore that hosts occasional small exhibitions and hands-on workshops
繪本主題書店，不定期舉辦小型展覽與手作坊

⌂ 彰化縣社頭鄉社斗路一段353號2F
2F, No. 353, Sec. 1, Shedou Rd., Shetou Township, Changhua County
13:00-18:00

B   NANFANG BOOKSTORE 南方書店

A longstanding and welcoming traditional bookstore in Changhua
彰化最資深、平易近人的地方老派書店

⌂ 彰化縣彰化市三民路9-1號 | +886-4-722-2672
No. 9-1, Sanmin Road, Changhua City, Changhua County
09:30-18:00

C   TAI FONG GOLF COURSE 台豐高爾夫球場

The new Changhua landmark designed by Portuguese architect Álvaro Siza. Sign up for an architectural tour
建築大師阿爾瓦羅西薩設計，可報名參加建築巡旅

⌂ 彰化縣大村鄉學府路77號 | +886-4-852-0101
No. 77, Xuefu Rd., Dacun Township, Changhua County
06:00-18:00 | www.taifonggolf.com.tw/tour

D   GUASHAN SQUARE 卦山村

A local artisan hub where you can enjoy a cup of coffee and participate in various workshops
在地職人聚落，來喝杯咖啡、參加各式工作坊

⌂ 彰化縣彰化市卦山路8-1號2F | instagram: @chgsquare
2F., No. 8-1, Guashan Rd., Changhua City, Changhua County
10:00-18:00, Fri.-Sat. 10:00-20:00 (Closed on Mon.)

E   LAI HO MEMORIAL 賴和紀念館

A collections of documents and manuscripts from Lai Ho, the Father of Modern Taiwanese Literature
收藏「台灣文學之父」賴和的文獻、手稿等珍貴資料

⌂ 彰化縣彰化市中正路一段242號4F | facebook.com/laiho528
4F., No. 242, Sec. 1, Zhongzheng Rd., Changhua City
10:00-17:00 (Closed on Sun. and Mon.) | +886-4-724-1664

F   LUKANG LUNGSHAN TEMPLE 鹿港龍山寺

Built during Ming-Qing Dynasty transition, Lunshang Temple is beautifully preserved and nationally known as the temple of folk art
建於明末清初，保存完好，被譽為民間藝術殿堂

⌂ 彰化縣鹿港鎮龍山街100號 | +886-4-777-2472
No. 100, Longshan St., Lukang Township, Changhua County

Photo credit：鹿港永樂酒店

Photo credit：豪所在

Photo credit：東皐歇咪

Photo credit：十儿ˋ小市集

A AIYA BUNGUM 愛治文具房

Named after the owner's grandmother, this stationery store can be a dangerous place for stationery-fanatics

以奶奶為名，文具迷在此容易失心瘋

⌐ 彰化縣彰化市長安街76巷7-2號
No. 7-2, Ln. 76, Chang'an St., Changhua City, Changhua County
12:30-19:00, weekend 12:00-20:00 (Closed on Mon. & Tue.)

B HAO ATELIER 豪所在

A curated shop specializing in socks and a creative hub for various activities, with Hao Coffee located next door

織襪選品店與創意活動聚所，旁邊還有豪咖啡

⌐ 彰化縣社頭鄉社斗路一段353號
No. 353, Sec. 1, Shedou Rd., Shetou Township, Changhua County
12:00-20:00 (Closed on Wed. and Thur.)

C JU DESIGN STUDIO 十儿ˋ小市集

A collective shop featuring handmade creations and serving snacks and drinks

集結多位手作創作者的作品展售，店裡也提供點心飲品

⌐ 彰化市長安街76巷7-2號2F | facebook.com/ju.design.studio
2F, No. 7-2, Lane 76, Chang'an Street, Changhua City
12:00-20:00 (Closed on Mon. and Tue.)

D UNION HOUSE LUKANG 鹿港永樂酒店

Boutique accommodation near Longshan Temple in Lugang, offering breakfast with local delicacies

鹿港龍山寺旁的質感住宿，早餐提供在地美食

⌐ 彰化縣鹿港鎮三民路152號
152, Sanmin Road, Lugang Township, Changhua County
www.unionhouse.com.tw

E TANG-KO HIOH-MÎ 東皐歇咪

A cultural hub in Lugang where you can experience the local lifestyle and indulge in the team's canteen and bar

體驗鹿港生活文化的好起點，團隊還經營食堂與酒吧

⌐ 彰化縣鹿港鎮復興路318號
No. 318, Fuxing Road, Lugang Township, Changhua County
www.facebook.com/tkhm.lukanghomestay

F H. 1967

A clean and comfy lodging transformed from an old house in downtown Changhua

位於彰化市區，乾淨舒適的老屋空間

⌐ 彰化縣彰化市太平街22號 | +886-4-712-5885
No.22, Taiping Street, Changhua City, Changhua County
facebook.com/H-1967-2207912916118472

A A-ZHEN BUNS 阿振肉包

A century-old shop for tasty buns with a meaty filling

柔嫩外皮裡包裹著紮實內餡與百年鹿港故事

彰化縣鹿港鎮中山路71號
No. 71, Zhongshan Rd., Lukang Township, Changhua County
+886-4-777-2754
09:00-19:00

B A-TIAN CLAM NOODLE 阿添蛤仔麵

Succulent clam meat and fresh broth, don't forget to order some chicken rolls

享用飽滿蛤蜊與香甜湯底，別忘配一份雞卷

彰化縣彰化市民族路455號 | +886-4-726-4655
No. 455, Minzu Rd., Changhua City, Changhua County
10:30-19:30 (Closed on Thur.)

C SHANG DING ZAN SMOKE-FREE BBQ 尚鼎讚無煙燒烤

A clean and healthy approach to BBQ

乾淨且講究健康的燒烤方式深受喜愛

彰化縣彰化市永安街308號 | +886-932-539-969
No. 308, Yong'an St., Changhua City, Changhua County
17:00-23:30 (Closed on Tue.)

D HANBIN CRYSTAL DUMPLING 漢彬水晶餃

Always handmade, always satisfying

手工堅持，無論寒暑喝一碗綜合湯都很滿足

彰化縣鹿港鎮民族路189號
No. 189, Minzu Rd., Lukang Township, Changhua County
+886-934-252-761
07:00-13:00

E A-SAN BA-WAN 阿三肉圓

Owned by the same family for four generations, their translucent wrapper made from sweet potato starch is much loved by locals and tourists alike

傳承四代，地瓜粉做成的Q彈外皮深受當地人與遊客喜愛

彰化縣彰化市三民路242號 | 10:30-19:00 (Closed on Mondays)
No. 242, Sanmin Rd., Changhua City, Changhua County

F SHAN HANG RICE CAKE 杉行碗粿

Mushroom and pork rice cake with a bowl of assorted soup is a local favorite

內行要點一香菇豬肉碗粿加一碗綜合湯

彰化縣彰化市成功路312號 | +886-4-726-0380
No. 312, Chenggong Rd., Changhua City, Changhua County
06:30-18:00

FOOD AND COFFEE
食物與咖啡

Photo credit: 右舍咖啡

A L'TOIT RESTAURANT 厝頂法式料理

A French restaurant, every dish from appetizer to dessert is a piece of art

從前菜到甜點，每一道都是藝術品的法式餐廳

彰化縣員林市員東路二段390號 | +886-4-836-4253
No. 390, Sec. 2, Yuandong Rd., Yuanlin City, Changhua County
18:30-21:30

B STABLE FLY 穩定飛行模式

Uber stylish vintage café, also try the Ming Ming Bakery on the second floor

超酷古著咖啡館，也推薦2樓的「明明Bakery」

彰化縣彰化市永樂街44巷2號 | +886-4-722-0663
No. 2, Ln. 44, Yongle St., Changhua City, Changhua County
12:00-22:00 (Closed on Tuesdays)

C WHITE POST CAFÉ & STUDIO 白色方塊咖啡 & 工作室

Promoting arts and culture in Changhua

在潔白的空間裡推廣藝文與彰化

彰化縣彰化市公園路一段50號 | +886-4-720-2209
No. 50, Sec. 1, Gongyuan Rd., Changhua City, Changhua County
12:00-21:00, weekends 12:00-18:00 (Closed on Fri.)

D VICINOCAFE 右舍咖啡

A classic fruit-themed coffee shop in Yuanlin with captivating window views

有著迷人窗景的員林經典水果系咖啡店

彰化縣員林市萬年路三段67號 | +886-4-836-4864
No. 67, Wannian Rd., Sec. 3, Yuanlin City, Changhua County
08:00-15:00

E SUBI COFFEE & BAKERY

A gorgeous bakery that serves my favorite cakes

有美麗窗花的老屋甜點店，最愛常溫蛋糕

彰化縣員林市中山路二段131巷28號
28, Ln. 131, Sec. 2, Zhongshan Rd., Yuanlin City, Changhua County
12:00-18:30 (Closed on Wed.)
+886-4-837-2312

F NO.9 WORKSHOP 酒號工作室

Custom-made cocktails and an easy-going vibe, feel free to bring your own food

依照客人習慣調酒，可以自帶外食的輕鬆酒吧

彰化縣彰化市成功路55號 | +886-910-308-597
No. 55, Chenggong Rd., Changhua City, Changhua County
19:30-01:30

CITY CENTER ROUTE
城中路線

CHANGHUA STATION AREA
AND BAGUA MOUNTAIN

彰化火車站周邊與八卦山

EXPERIENCE THE BEST OF CHANGHUA IN ONE DAY 讓你一日就懂彰化市

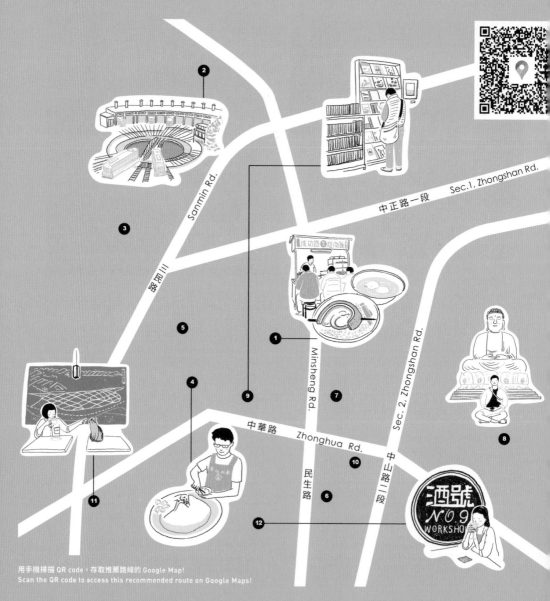

Sanmin Rd.

中正路一段　Sec.1, Zhongshan Rd.

Minsheng Rd.

Sec. 2, Zhongshan Rd.

中華路　Zhonghua Rd.

民生路

中山路二段

用手機掃描 QR code，存取推薦路線的 Google Map!
Scan the QR code to access this recommended route on Google Maps!

1)	09:00	That's right... braised pork with rice for breakfast!
2)	10:00	Visit Changhua Roundhouse, a must-see for railway fanatics
3)	11:00	Walk around the station and experience Changhua's rich history and modern development
4)	12:00	A foodie's pilgrimage... one of everything please!
5)	14:00	Understand Changhua's history by visiting the Xiaoxi Street
6)	15:00	Explore bookstores that help preserve local history
7)	16:00	Have some afternoon tea and buy some souvenirs
8)	17:00	Visit the Changhua Confucius Temple and surrounding area
9)	18:00	Enjoy a sunset city view atop Bagua Mountain
10)	19:00	Have dinner at the foot of Bagua Mountain
11)	20:00	Spend the evening in a cafe
12)	21:00	How about braised pork rice and cocktails for a late-night snack?

1)	09:00	不用懷疑,早餐就吃爌肉飯
2)	10:00	讓鐵道迷痴狂的「台鐵扇形車庫」
3)	11:00	從老到新,火車站周邊歷史文化力大爆發
4)	12:00	市區小吃巡禮,甜的鹹的全都來一份
5)	14:00	兜轉小西街,探索彰化的身世
6)	15:00	逛逛藏身城區裡的文化守護者
7)	16:00	來杯下午茶,帶點伴手禮
8)	17:00	探訪彰化古蹟「彰化孔廟」與周邊
9)	18:00	「八卦山」看夕陽與彰化市景
10)	19:00	在八卦山腳下吃晚餐
11)	20:00	晚上繼續泡咖啡館吧
12)	21:00	消夜用爌肉飯配調酒,如何?

09:00
A-QUAN BRAISED PORK RICE

1. 阿泉爌肉飯

Braised Pork Rice is a true Changhua staple—locals have it for breakfast, lunch, and dinner—and everyone has their favorite restaurant. So, let go of your diet and cholesterol concerns and join in! My personal favorite has to be A-Quan Braised Pork Rice, which is conveniently located in the station area. They also serve delicious soups and trimmings.

除了肉圓彰化人更愛吃爌肉飯，每個人都有自己偏愛的店家，從早餐到消夜，不管哪餐吃都不違和。放下熱量與膽固醇的包袱，入境隨俗用一碗爌肉飯開啟彰化之旅吧。個人推薦在火車站附近的「阿泉爌肉飯」，記得搭配小菜和湯品。

10:00
CHANGHUA ROUNDHOUSE

2. 台鐵扇形車庫

Changhua Train Station is where the railway mountain line converges with the ocean line. This fan-shaped station is also Taiwan's only living historical relic, a historic site which is still fully functional and in use. The Roundhouse is also known as the train engine motel because the concentric railways allow trains from various lines to come in and receive maintenance after lengthy journeys.

彰化火車站是台灣西部鐵道「山海線」的交會點，這裡的扇形車庫是全台唯一還在使用的百年活古蹟，其移動轉盤設計與被稱為「火車頭旅館」的車頭存放空間，皆為鐵路迷爭相目睹風采的設備。

11:00
TRAIN STATION
AND
ITS SURROUNDINGS

3. 火車站周邊

Nan Fang Bookstore is Changua's oldest bookstore and where generations of Changhua children spent their childhood. The recently renovated Wang Zhang Fa Store is also a great place to visit if you fancy Baroque aesthetics and architecture.

彰化最老的書店「南方書店」是許多彰化小孩的回憶；另外巴洛克百年老厝「王長發商號」也在近期改建開放，可來此小憩並欣賞巴洛克風格的建築立面。

12:00
CHANGHUA EATS

4. 彰化小食

For lunch, go to Changhua Vegetarian for wide noodles with bean curd and soup. I also recommend Zheng Changhua Ba-wan for a proper ba-wan. While in Changhua, you have to try mao-shu noodles, which translates into cat mouse noodles. Thankfully, these noodles have absolutely nothing to do with either. Cat and mouse noodles are usually comprised of noodles with shrimp balls, mushrooms balls, chicken rolls, and a rich broth. After lunch, go to Tong Zhong Rice Ball Dessert or Frozen Taro Soup for some delicious dessert.

中午到「彰化素食」吃大麵條配豆皮與豆包湯，也推薦有Q彈外皮與紮實餡料的「正彰化肉圓」；彰化特有小吃「貓鼠麵」無關貓與鼠，但一定有蝦丸、香菇丸、雞捲與濃郁湯頭。飯後可到「銅鐘圓仔湯」與「冷凍芋仔湯」吃點甜品。

14:00
XIAOXI STREET

5. 小西街

Stroll through Xiaoxi Street and look at all the fascinating household window displays to get a glimpse into daily Changhua life. The hotel-turned Red Leaf Café has testifies to the prosperous past of Changhua, while the stationery store Aiya Bungum owned by two young sisters, where you'll find an eclectic selection of books, clothing, and stationery. This enchanting blend of old and new elements breathes new life into the historic streets.

漫步「小西街」巷弄，細看常民住宅的窗花雕飾；「紅葉大旅社」見證了彰化熙來攘往的過往歷史；年輕女孩開設的文具店「愛治文具房」，裡頭有選書、特色服飾及精緻文具。新舊元素融合，讓老街有了新氣象。

15:00
SPRING AND AUTUMN ART SUPPLY
AND
DA YUAN BAKERY

6. 春秋美術社 與 大元餅行

Next, let's explore the traditional landscapes of Changhua. The owner of Spring and Autumn Art Supply is a lantern master who has been practicing the art of lantern-making for over six decades. His son has now taken over the family business and will continue to pass on this ancient artform. Don't miss the famous mochis at Da Yuan Bakery, known for their delightful sweet and savory fillings. Try the salty meat mochi for a unique and delicious experience!

接著來尋找傳統彰化風景，「春秋美術社」的老師傅投身手工燈籠製作逾一甲子，現在由兒子接手，傳承古老文化。再散步到城隍廟巷內的「大元餅行」，有著Q彈外皮與綿密甜鹹內餡的「麻糬」是必帶伴手禮，個人最推鹹肉口味！

CITY CENTER ROUTE

城中路線

☐

16:00
STABLE FLY
7. 穩定飛行模式

Have an afternoon coffee at Stable Fly, a bakery-turned café with French windows that lead into a spacious courtyard. I recommend trying the coriander coffee! The second to fourth floors are also home to many interesting brands and shops. Stable Fly regularly hosts various markets, exhibitions, and pop-up events, bringing a fresh new look to the declining Yongle Commercial District.

前身為糕餅行的咖啡館「穩定飛行模式」，保留了舊時天井格局，1樓搭配大面落地窗，午後在此喝杯咖啡非常愜意（推薦試試香菜咖啡！）；2到4樓也都有許多有趣品牌及店家進駐。這裡不時也舉辦各式市集、空間展覽和快閃活動，為已逐漸沒落的永樂商圈帶來嶄新風貌。

☐

17:00
CHANGHUA CONFUCIUS TEMPLE
AND
CHANGHUA PAPAYA MILK KING
8. 彰化孔廟 與 彰化木瓜牛乳大王

Changhua Confucius Temple is a Grade 1 historical site and a must-see while you're in Taiwan. Take note of the traditional courtyard-home structure which often serves as a symbol for institutions dedicated to the development of cultural education. After visiting the temple, walk across the street and grab a papaya milk at Changhua Papaya Milk King. If you're here in the summer, order some cold desserts and a plate of fresh fruit to fend off the sweltering heat...take a papaya milk to go!

逛逛一級古蹟「彰化孔廟」，保留四進三院的傳統格局，是台灣中部文教發展的象徵；接著到對面的「彰化木瓜牛乳大王」買杯自然甜的木瓜牛奶，爬八卦山時帶著喝，盛夏也可坐下來吃點冰品與新鮮切盤水果消消暑氣。

☐

18:00
BAGUA MOUNTAIN
9. 八卦山

Despite its history of being a strategic military stronghold, Bagua Mountain is now the perfect place to appreciate the sunset or to go for a light hike. At the summit of the mountain sits the Eight Trigram Mountains Buddha Landscape, a calming sight that can be seen from almost anywhere in the city. Afterwards, go to White Post Café and Studio for coffee and, oftentimes, arts and cultural exhibitions.

曾經是軍事戰略要址，現在是欣賞日落與散步絕佳地點的「八卦山」，山頂有著無論在市區哪個角落都能看到的「八卦山大佛」，令人安心。下山後可到「白色方塊咖啡＆工作室」喝杯咖啡，這裡也時常舉辦藝文展覽，值得造訪。

19:00
HEI ROU NOODLES
10. 黑肉麵

Hei Rou Noodles, named after the owner's nickname which means black meat, is famous for their danzai noodles and pork chop rice. The pork chops are first fried then braised and taste heavenly. Clam noodles—a unique but lesser-known Changhua specialty—are soup noodles loaded with fresh clam meat that locals usually pair with chicken rolls.

「黑肉麵」的黑肉其實是老闆的外號，這裡有名的除了切仔麵，更受在地老饕推崇的是排骨飯，排骨先炸過再滷，味道與嚼勁都恰到好處；蛤仔麵是被低估的彰化小吃，新鮮湯頭配上一整碗肥嫩蛤仔肉，吃起來很滿足，最好再配一份雞卷，彰化人都這樣吃！

20:00
CAFÉ TIME
11. 泡咖啡店

The Planet Café, owned by two female entrepreneurs, not only serves coffee and meals but also host lectures on gender, political, and environmental issues. Trip Coffee is a great place for travelers because they offer great traveling tips. I also highly recommend getting some coffee and dessert at Yan Café, located in the Youngle Street Commercial District.

兩個女生打造的「The planet 星球咖啡」，除了咖啡與輕食，更精彩的是不定期舉辦的性別、政治、環保等議題講座；「旅咖啡」則是各地旅人最溫暖的燈塔，在這裡可以獲得最道地的旅行建議；另外永樂街商圈內的老屋咖啡店「咖啡烟」，咖啡與甜點都很棒。

21:00
FISH MARKET BRAISED PORK RICE
AND
NO.9 WORKSHOP
12. 魚市場爌肉飯 與 酒號工作室

NO.9 Workshop is the perfect hang-out spot for night owls. The friendly owner is known to create unique cocktails for customers according to their personality and preferences. Another bonus is that you are allowed to bring outside food to enjoy with your drinks. I recommend ordering take-out from Fish Market Braised Pork Rice and having a cocktail or beer to wash down the food.

「酒號工作室 NO.9 Workshop」適合夜貓子流連，健談的老闆會根據客人的個性、喜好量身打造酒款，還可以自帶小吃外食，相當有人情味。在這 24 小時都能吃到爌肉飯的城市，酒號工作室歡迎你帶一碗飄油香的魚市場爌肉飯來這大口吃肉，大口喝酒。

CHANGHUA
彰化特輯

SPECIAL FEATURE

CHANGHUANESE WHO HAVE HELPED SHAPE TAIWAN

一起認識，
這幾位影響台灣文化的彰化人

Compared to Taipei and Kaohsiung, Changhua is not nearly as heavily featured in the media. Nevertheless, it holds a unique place in my heart because I find that the people possess a strength that is unobtrusive but determined. This is a place where people believe that it is the power of soft yet unwavering persistence that will ultimately change and shape the world. From the perspective of literary and musical development, there are some key Changhuanese that you need to know.

對比北高兩市，彰化不是媒體寵兒，沒有炒新聞的人物搏版面，在曝光度上相形失色。但我總覺得這是個「曖曖內含光」的地方，人們守本分，但又有些叛逆，他們以創作溫柔地推翻不公的世界。從台灣的文學與音樂發展來看，有幾位彰化人你應該要認識。

LET TAIWANESE PEOPLE TELL THEIR STORY IN THEIR OWN LANGUAGE
—
LAI HO

讓台灣人
用自己的語言說故事
—— 賴和

SLAUGHTER WITH WORDS AND AWAKEN WITH TRUTH
—
LI ANG

用文字殺豬，
台灣女人的覺醒
—— 李昂

WORLD RENOWNED TAIWANESE ELECTRONIC MUSICIAN
—
LIM GIONG

台灣製造
世界級的電子音樂
—— 林強

A GENTLE FORCE OF PROTECTION
—
WU SHENG, WU ZHI NING WU YIN NING

守護島嶼的溫柔力量
—— 吳晟、吳志寧、吳音寧

Hailed as the Father of Modern Taiwanese Literature, Lai Ho was a doctor, author, and political activist. After obtaining his medical degree from Taihoku Imperial University (currently National Taiwan University), Lai began to practice medicine alongside Japanese doctors. Outraged by the vast discrepancy in compensation between Japanese and Taiwanese doctors, he returned to his hometown in Changhua and founded the Lai Ho Hospital. He also joined the Taiwan Culture Association, dedicated himself to social movements, and edited the *Taiwan People News*. Lai was a tireless advocate for Taiwanese to use their own language to tell their stories. He also published the first essay in Taiwanese literary history that was written in Taiwanese vernacular. Lai was a prolific writer of essays, poetry, and novels. He wrote a great deal about the life of common people and often expressed anti-colonial and anti-authoritarian sentiments.

醫師、作家與革命份子。自台北總督府醫學校(台大醫學院前身)畢業後開始執業,因不滿日籍與台籍醫師薪資差異,回到故鄉彰化創立「賴和醫院」,並加入台灣文化協會,投入社會運動與《台灣民報》的編輯工作。賴和力倡以台灣話進行創作,發表台灣文學史上第一篇白話散文、新詩與小說,他的作品關懷小人物生活,充滿反殖民、反權威的精神與態度,被譽為「台灣新文學之父」。

Li Ang, one of Taiwan's most celebrated feminist writers, was born into a literary family in Lukang and known as the youngest of the Three Shi Sisters. Li is her mother's maiden name and ang means to hold one's head high. Quite unlike her peers, who wrote about love in subtle and veiled language, Li explores topics of lust, self, and even forbidden affairs in a bold and brutally honest manner. *The Butcher's Wife* and *Beigang Incense Burner of Lust* are some of her most iconic works that not only depict—but also invert—inequality between the sexes. In her latest work, *Sleeping Pan*, Li continues to explore feminism with a focus on the bodies and desires of mature women.

鹿港文壇「施家三姐妹」的老么。筆名「李」是母親的姓,「昂」象徵昂首挺胸。有別於當時女性作家寫作情愛題材,李昂的小說故事多半圍繞在情慾、自我,甚至是禁忌的愛戀糾葛,《殺夫》和《北港香爐人人插》是經典作品,用意是透過寫作反轉不平等的兩性關係,2017 新作《睡美男》依舊以女人為題,寫熟齡女性的身體與慾望,被文壇認為是台灣最重要的女性作家之一。

In 1990, Lim Giong released his debut album, *Marching Ahead*, which heavily influenced the New Taiwanese Song movement. The titular song became a national soundtrack that symbolized financial success and encouraged youths from central and southern Taiwan to make a name for themselves in the big city. In recent years, Lim Giong has composed several award-winning movie scores that garnered international acclaim, including the soundtrack for *The Assassin* which won the Cannes Soundtrack Award. Lim also composed the open credit sequence for *Millennium Mambo*, which was selected by French fashion house Chloé as their Spring-Summer 2018 runway soundtrack.

1990 年首張專輯《向前走》帶起台灣「新聞南語搖滾」風潮,同名歌曲〈向前走〉全台傳誦,象徵經濟起飛,呼應中南部青年往城市尋夢發展的決心。近年來投身幕後,進入電影配樂領域,結合自己最愛的電子音樂,作品屢獲國際肯定,包含以《刺客聶隱娘》榮獲坎城影展最佳電影原聲帶殊榮;電影《千禧曼波》開場配樂被時尚品牌 Chloe 選為 2018 春夏大秀的走秀音樂。

Poet Wu Sheng, a Changhua native born in Hsichou Township, grew up in the fields and amidst nature. His abiding love for his land and mother nature inspired and enriched his poetry which has gone on to touch the hearts of generations of readers. Wu Sheng passed down his love for the land to his son Wu Zhi Ning, a folk rock musician who incorporates current events, social justice, and literature into his lyrics. Wu Sheng's daughter, Wu Yin Ning, an agricultural expert published author in Taiwanese agriculture, was the CEO of Taipei Agricultural Products Marketing Corporation. In spite of certain political controversies, she was a successful business woman who performed her duties diligently till the end. This family's creative attitude is one of the land's most tender yet unwavering forces.

詩人吳晟是溪州鄉人,田野生活深刻影響他的創作觀,他對於農村土地的濃厚感情成就了無數動人作品。兒子吳志寧承襲父親對於土地的關愛,將台灣時事與文學詩詞寫入民謠搖滾;女兒吳音寧奠基親身田野經驗,著作台灣農業觀察專書,更曾任台北農產連銷公司總經理一職,儘管備受政治攻訐,但她仍低調行事直至任期最後一天。這一家人的創作態度是台灣土地上最溫柔且堅毅的力量。

LUKANG

鹿港鎮——老派才是新時尚

Photo credit

For a lot of people, the historical town of Lukang is synonymous with Changhua. Popular tourist spots such as Lukang Mazu Temple, Mo Ru Lane, and Yu Zhen Zhai Pastry are just a few examples of the many historical and cultural treasures Lukang has to offer. In recent years, locals have been making a real effort to keep this ancient town fresh by revamping old buildings and creating a strong online presence for Lukang on social media.

Xi Shi Book and Tea is a charming second-hand bookstore housed in a revamped residence. The owner kept the building's original layout as well as the spotted brick floor, water well, courtyard, and air-raid shelter. They even preserved the old, chipped paint on the walls to reflect the years the building has seen. Come browse old books, drink slow tea, and experience an elegant afternoon as literatis would in the olden days.

The Kids From Lukang (TKFL) is a local organization dedicated to the cultural preservation of Lukang. The founders of TKFL started The Lukang Renaissance in 2012 and have since organized numerous events such as workshops and community film festivals to help locals re-establish a connection with their community.

提到彰化旅遊，大家可能會直覺地想到有著許多古蹟、老街與老店的舊城鹿港，像是天后宮、摸乳巷或是玉珍齋糕餅等，都是觀光客必訪的景點。但對於一個古都而言，近期不少老屋翻新的店家，或是社群平台上的熱門打卡點，都只是錦上添花。如何「修舊如舊」，讓老派風情延續不滅，才是真學問。

「書集囍室」就是一個老派又迷人的二手書店。店主人買下了古宅，保留老厝格局，斑駁的紅磚地、水井、庭院與防空洞。不刻意刷漆翻新，把時光的痕跡留在屋裡，再擺進二手書籍，泡壺茶邀請旅人入座喫茶，好像經歷了舊日時光的文人雅士生活。

「鹿港囝仔」也是個致力維護鹿港文化的團體。秉持著為家鄉做點事的初衷，創辦人發起「保鹿運動」，從 2012 年底至今，發起多場工作坊、社區巡迴影展等活動，建立在地人與鹿港的連結。

Photo credit：書集囍室

XI SHI BOOK AND TEA 書集喜室

A charming second-hand bookstore in a revamped historical residence 老宅邸改建的迷人二手書店

📍 彰化縣鹿港鎮杉行街20號 | 11:00-17:30 (Closed on Mon. & Tue.)
No. 20, Shanxing St., Lukang Township, Changhua County

Photo credit：勝豐吧

HOME BAR LUKANG 勝豐吧

A popular local bar in a revamped space
活化廢棄空間，讓在地人到這裡喝杯酒聚聚

📍 彰化縣鹿港鎮民族路131號 | 20:00-00:00 (Closed on Tue. and Thur.)
No. 131, Minzu Rd., Lukang Township, Changhua | •886-4-778-5232

TIANWEI

田尾鄉—內行人的花園

SPECIAL FEATURE
CHANGHUA
彰化特輯
SPECIAL FEATURE

An architect friend of mine in Taipei once told me: "Changhua's Tianwei Township is incredible!" I was somewhat dubious about this statement as I had always thought of Tianwei as a small town where people my grandparent's age went strolling and nature-watching on weekends. One day, another friend and I decided to go to Tianwei to purchase plants for an interior design project. We discovered an abundance of nurseries and greenhouses selling an incredible variety of succulents, trees, and flowers. That was when I, Changhuanese born-and-bred, finally realized the treasure that is Tianwei Township.

Central Taiwan is Taiwan's largest floral and plant production area; up to 40% of Changhua's land is dedicated to floral production. Changhua also has one of Taiwan's four major flower and plant wholesale markets. Compared with its northern counterpart, Taipei's Neihu Flower Market, Tianwei's flower industry benefits from longer daylight hours and more land for cultivation. Interior designers and floral designers with inside knowledge will make special trips to Tianwei to hunt for plants at a relatively approachable price-point and look for the latest imported varieties.

一個在台北執業的室內設計師朋友，曾經帶著驚嘆的口氣跟我說：「你們彰化田尾非常厲害！」我半信半疑，私以為這只是個長輩們假日散步賞花的小鎮。有天我與友人同行，到田尾採購空間設計用的植栽。搭著車蜿蜒在田間小徑，到處都是園藝行，無論是多肉植物、大型林木或是切花，品種豐富，讓我這個土生土長的彰化人開了眼界。

台灣中部是最大的花卉產區，光是彰化縣的種植面積就占了 40%。這裡同時也是台灣四大花卉批發市場之一。相較於台北的內湖花市，田尾因為日照時數長、地域廣大，所以到處都是植物培育場，可以開車逛一整天。有的規模好比大型植物園，藏有各式林木，必須花點時間「挖寶」。許多懂門路的室內設計師或花藝師，會專程到田尾營業主挑植栽，這裡的價格相對親民，最新引進台灣的品種也能在這裡找到。

MANGROVE FLORAL AND GREENHOUSE 紅樹林園藝
Great variety at a wholesale price, specializing in bonzai
價格多為實惠的批發價，以盆景為大宗

⌐ 彰化縣田尾鄉民生路一段486號 | 11:00-17:30 (Closed on Mon. & Tue.)
No. 486, Sec. 1, Minsheng Rd., Tianwei Township, Changhua County

GARDEN CENTER LANDSCAPE COMPANY 合利園藝
A large-scale greenhouse offers an impressive variety of plants
腹地廣大，植物種類多，容易挖到寶

⌐ 彰化縣田尾鄉公園路一段26號 | +886-4-822-3098
No. 26, Sec. 1, Gongyuan Rd., Tianwei Township, Changhua County

Photo credit：徐芳閣

南投
NANTOU

THE HIDDEN GEM OF INLAND TAIWAN

─────── Chia-Fang Li 李佳芳 (Text 文字)
─────── Pei-Ling Guo 郭佩怡 (Planning 企劃)

The word inland had different meanings in different periods of time in Taiwan. At the time, large numbers of Taiwanese focused their business or career in China, and some started to use the word inland to refer to China. Many Taiwanese found this offensive because of China's ideology of denying the sovereignty of Taiwan, and tried to correct this by reassigning the term to Nantou, the only county in Taiwan landlocked by other counties. Inland Rock, the rock music festival held in Nantou's Jiji Township from 2015 to 2017, derives its name from this idea. This also unexpectedly put Nantou in the headlines of news media and developed a connection with the younger generations of Taiwanese who believe in Taiwan's sovereignty.

Without any coastline, the mountainous Nantou terrain used to be inhabited by the indigenouse people who guarded the abundant natural resources in the forests. The Assam black tea of Yuchi Township, the logging industry in Checheng Village, and the bamboo product industry in Zhushan Township accounted for three important exports that helped build up Taiwan's international trade. Furthermore, at the center of this green land, there is embedded an azure gem: Sun Moon Lake, the biggest natural lake in Taiwan. The trail around the lake is listed as one of the 10 best cycling routes in the world by CNN.

Undergoing the severe trauma of the Jiji Earthquake on September 21st, 1999, Nantou is now welcoming young locals back to their hometown to develop their careers and livelihoods. With the establishment of Taomi Eco-village in Puli Township, the community building activities in Zhushan Township, to the emerging unique shops and bazaars in Zhongxing New Village in Nantou City, not to mention the well-known beauty of the mountains and waters, Nantou is on its way to becoming an even more vibrant and charming county. Why not visit Nantou and let the mountains touch your heart in so many surprising ways!

「內地」在台灣不同時期有著不同意思，在越來越多人到中國發展的同時，也開始有些人使用內地一詞代稱中國，這樣的說法讓部分台灣人感到不舒服，似有矮化主權的意味，遂提出「台灣內地是南投」的說法來抵制，甚至還有單位在 2015 年以「內地搖滾」為名，於南投集集接連 3 年舉辦了搖滾音樂祭，讓南投意外躍上版面，與天然獨一代有了全新的連結。

沒有海岸線的南投只有滿滿的山稜線，這裡曾經是原住民族的居住地，長久以來守護著森林裡的豐富資源。從魚池的阿薩姆紅茶、車埕的伐木業，到竹山的竹加工業，這幾項名聞遐邇的產業，都曾是台灣外銷世界的重要支柱。除此之外，在這片綠色版圖中央，還鑲飾著一顆湛藍寶石：台灣第一大天然湖泊「日月潭」，環著湖畔的遊憩路線更被 CNN 譽為全球十大最美自行車道。

走過 921 大地震的重創，一波又一波的年輕人返回南投，從埔里桃米生態村的建立、竹山的地方創生運動，到近期中興新村出現許多有趣小店與市集，都讓好山好水的南投更為有趣、有活力。來南投吧！讓山，用各種方式感動你。

TRANSPORTATION
交通

When departing from Taipei, it takes about an hour to travel by HSR to Taichung Station in Wuri District. Then take Taiwan Tourist Shuttles, which offers Sun Moon Lake and Xitou routes, to travel around Nantou. However, renting a car to travel between towns and mountains is highly advisable.

台北往南投可搭乘高鐵至台中烏日站（約1小時），台灣好行巴士提供日月潭線與溪頭線兩條轉乘路線；但強烈建議租汽車代步，橫跨山區鄉鎮旅行會更加方便。

RECOMMENDATIONS
推薦

READING LIST 旅遊書籍

VISIT NANTOU · SHORT TRIPS (UPDATED EDITION)
《來去南投·小旅行》
Introducing detailed Nantou travel routes along Provincial Highway 16 and Provincial Highway 21
詳細介紹台16線與台21線為主軸的南投旅行路線
⌐ books.com.tw/products/0010667164

LOCAL PUBLICATIONS 在地刊物

《LOCAL WORD》
Published by a local team in Zhongxing New Village, documenting local people and happenings
由中興新村地方團隊發起製作，記錄地方人事物
⌐ localword.weebly.com

TRAVEL WEBSITES 旅遊網站

WELCOME TO NANTOU 走進南投
Official Nantou travel website. Multiple language versions available
南投旅遊官方網站，有多國外語資訊
⌐ travel.nantou.gov.tw

NANTOU WELCOME 樂旅南投
Official Facebook page of the Department of Tourism of the Nantou County Government
南投縣政府觀光處的官方臉書粉絲團
⌐ facebook.com/nantouwelcome

NT TRAVELER 南投旅行誌
Operated by a local team, providing comprehensive sightseeing information
由在地團隊經營，提供完整景點資訊
⌐ nttraveler.com

GUIDED TOURS 導覽

SHORT TRIPS IN CHUNGHSING NEW VILLAGE
中興新村小旅行
In-depth tours led by cultural and historic workers, leisurely explore the garden city on a bike
文史工作者帶路，騎上單車深度漫遊花園城
⌐ facebook.com/chunghsingnewvillage

545 PULI BIKE 順騎自然探索體驗
An eco-friendly bike tour in Puli Township, enjoy local delicacies while cycling
在埔里來趟低碳單車旅行吧，還能邊騎邊吃在地美食！
⌐ www.545bike.com

ANNUAL EVENTS 年度活動

RURU STROLL MARKET (THE 4TH WEEK OF EACH MONTH)
籠籠散步市集 (每個月第4週)
Local bazaar organized by Good York & Friends' Studio
好約作伙工作室主辦的地方市集
⌐ facebook.com/rurustrollmarket

SUN MOON LAKE INTERNATIONAL SWIMMING CARNIVAL (SEPTEMBER)
日月潭國際萬人泳渡嘉年華 (9月)
Popular annual sporting event attracting swimmers from around the world
年年吸引國內外游泳愛好者的運動盛事
⌐ facebook.com/sunmoonlake.swimming

SUN MOON LAKE FIREWORKS FESTIVAL (OCT.–NOV.)
日月潭花火音樂嘉年華 (10月-11月)
Festive firework marathon lasting from morning to night
從白日馬拉松到夜晚煙火秀的不間斷盛會
⌐ www.sunmoonlake.gov.tw (see activities for details)

NANTOU GLOBAL TEA EXPO (OCT.)
南投世界茶業博覽會 (10月)
Biggest tea arts and culture expo in Taiwan
全台最大的茶藝文化展演
⌐ teaexpo.mmweb.tw

Photo credit：交通部觀光局日月潭國家風景區管理處

Photo credit：92 向陽高山咖啡

A SITOU NATURE EDUCATION AREA 溪頭自然教育園區
Bamboo-themed nature education site, great for strolls
以竹子為主題的自然教育園區，適合散步

南投縣鹿谷鄉森林巷9號
No. 9, Senlin Ln., Lugu Township, Nantou County
facebook.com/sitoucenter
07:00–17:00

B CHECHENG OLD STREET 車埕老街
Most beautiful train station along the Jiji line, witnessing
the rise and fall of Taiwan's logging village
南投集集線最美車站，見證台灣去村的興衰繁華

南投縣水里鄉車埕村民權巷
Minquan Ln., Shuili Township, Nantou County

C IN GOOD HANDS CAFE 映古子咖啡
Offering home roasting coffee and handmade desserts
and holds sporadic exhibitions and events
提供自家烘焙咖啡與自製甜點，不定期舉辦展覽與活動

南投縣草屯鎮育才巷54號 | facebook.com/ingoods
No. 54, Yucai Ln., Caotun Township, Nantou County
11:00–18:00, Fri. 12:00–19:00 (Closed from Tue. to Thur.)

D MOUNTAIN BOUTIQUE 山間良物 國姓咖啡咖手造所
Delicious coffee made with beans grown in their own
fields and roasted in-house
供應自家種植並烘培的美味咖啡

南投縣國姓鄉乾溝村中西巷7-3號 | +886-4-9272-1952
No. 7-3, Zhongxi Ln., Guoxing Township, Nantou County
10:00–17:00, weekend 10:00–18:00 (Closed from Mon. to Wed.)

E 92 CAFÉ 92 向陽高山咖啡
Specialty coffee from Jioufenershan (mountain)
來自九份二山的精品咖啡

南投縣國姓鄉中正路一段206之5號
No. 206-5, Sec. 1, Zhongzheng Rd., Guoxing Township, Nantou County
09:00–18:00 (Closed on Tuesdays)
+886-4-9272-1430

F YOSHAN TEA 遊山茶訪
A brief history, processing and different types of
Taiwanese tea
一覽台灣茶的發展簡史、製成和種類。

南投縣竹山鎮延平路19號 | +886-49-264-3919
No. 19, Yanping Rd., Zhushan Township, Nantou County
09:00–17:30

A JU BA-WAN 菊肉圓

Local ba-wan recipe paired with vegetable broth
肉圓淋上蔬菜高湯的南投在地吃法

南投縣埔里鎮西安路一段33號
No. 33, Sec. 1, Xi'an Rd., Puli Township, Nantou County
11:30–17:00 (Closed on Tuesdays)
+886-4-9299-2111

B AZHANG YI-MIEN 阿章意麵

Authentic yi-mien highly recommended by the master
chef of the Yuan restaurant
元YUAN餐廳主廚蕭淳元力推的道地意麵

南投縣南投市民權街126號 | +886-4-9222 -6558
No. 126, Minquan St., Nantou City, Nantou County
07:00-16:30, weekends 07:00-17:00

C TUNG'S KITCHEN 雋茗廚房

Delicious and friendly private kitchen service. Reservation
one week prior to visiting is required
親切又美味的私廚，至少要一週前電話預約

南投縣埔里鎮樹人路16號 | +886-4-9290-1758
No. 16, Shuren Rd., Puli Township, Nantou County
11:00–14:00, 17:00–21:00 (Closed from Mon. to Thur.)

D 30 TEPPANYAKI 式食鐵板料理

Popular teppanyaki with a refreshing style
風格清新的人氣鐵板燒

南投縣草屯鎮成功路一段130號
No. 130, Sec. 1, Chenggong Rd., Caotun Township, Nantou County
11:00–14:00, 17:00–20:30 (Closed on Wednesdays)
+886-4-9233-0335

E MAL-U KITCHEN 慢午廚房 X 野食

Sophisticated indigenous Bunun-style cuisine made with
wild vegetables
精緻布農野菜風味料理

南投縣信義鄉望美村望和巷31-1號 | +886- 0980-774-911
No. 31-1, Wanghe Ln., Xinyi Township, Nantou County
11:00–14:00, 17:00–21:00, Tue.-Wed. 17:00-21:00 (Closed on Thursdays)

F XIJUEZHI PLUM ORCHARD FEAST STUDIO
喜覺支梅園梅宴工作室

Surprising meals made with plum available exclusively
during plum season (Reservation only)
只有梅花季才會推出的神祕梅餐

南投縣信義鄉自強村陽和巷2號 | +886-4-9279-1115
No. 2, Yanghe Ln., Xinyi Township, Nantou County | 11:30–14:00

Photo credit：HYAKU YAMA

Photo credit：野之光

Photo credit：旅物 SHOP

A HYAKU YAMA

A vintage prop shop opened by an artist couple, the space and selection are both worth savoring

由藝術家夫婦開設的古道具店，空間與選物都值得細細品味

⌐ 南投縣草屯鎮太平路一段462號 | instagram.com/hyakuyama
No. 462, Sec. 1, Taiping Rd., Caotun Township, Nantou County
需事前預約 Advanced reservation is required.

B LUWU SHOP 旅物

A craftsmanship and curio shop nurtured by the land

一間由土地孕育而生的工藝選物店

⌐ 南投縣草屯鎮中正路573號 | +886-4-9233-4141
No. 573, Zhongzheng Road, Caotun Township, Nantou County
09:00–20:00 (Closed on Mondays)
luwushop.ntcri.gov.tw

C YUANTAI BAMBOO 元泰竹藝社

30-year-old factory reborn through youthful design (cute bamboo cups!)

30年老工廠文創轉型 (竹杯很可愛！)

⌐ 南投縣竹山鎮頂橫街1號 | +886-4-9265-8681
No. 1, Dingheng St., Zhushan Township, Nantou County
10:00-12:00, 13:00-17:00 | facebook.com/ybamboo557

D FIELD OF LIGHT ART SPACE 野 之 光

A gallery and pottery studio amidst the fields, sharing beautiful crafts and lifestyle

田野間的藝廊與陶藝工作室，分享美好的工藝與生活

⌐ 南投縣草屯鎮玉屏巷65-19號 | facebook.com/FOL.artspace
No. 65-19, Yuping Ln., Caotun Township, Nantou County
需預約參觀 Visits by appointment only

E GOANG XING PAPER MILL 廣興紙寮

Make a piece of paper for yourself at the paper mill

來紙寮親手製作一張屬於自己的紙

⌐ 南投縣埔里鎮鐵山路310號 | +886-4-9291-3037
No. 310, Tieshan Rd., Puli Township, Nantou County
facebook.com/taiwanpaper
09:00-17:00

F TRIP EXPLORING 省府日常散策

Ideal starting point to explore Zhongxing New Village with hands-on activities and bicycle rental

認識中興新村的最佳起點，可預約手作活動與租借單車

⌐ 南投縣南投市光明二路84號 | +886-4-9231-2476
No. 84, Guangming 2nd Rd., Nantou City, Nantou County
10:00-18:00 (Closed on Mondays) | facebook.com/tripexploring

Photo credit：溪山行館

A FLEUR DE CHINE 雲品溫泉酒店

5-star hotel with breathtaking lake views
擁抱絕美湖景的五星級酒店

⌖ 南投縣魚池鄉中正路23號
No. 23, Zhongzheng Rd., Yuchi Township, Nantou County
www.fleurdechinehotel.com
+886-4-9285-6788

B THE LALU 涵碧樓

Taiwan's top resort beside Sun Moon Lake designed by world-class architect Kerry Hill
由國際建築大師Kerry Hill操刀，日月潭頂級度假酒店

⌖ 南投縣魚池鄉中興路142號
No. 142, Zhongxing Rd., Yuchi Township, Nantou County
+886-4-9285-5313 | thelalu.com.tw

C SUNNY DAY B&B 溪頭有晴天民宿

A tranquil B&B hidden in the Forest in Chitou
隱身在溪頭森林裡的恬靜民宿

⌖ 南投縣鹿谷鄉興產路32-12號
No. 32-12, Xingchan Rd., Lugu Township, Nantou County
+886-910-562-762 (張小姐 Ms. Chang)
shirleychang58@gmail.com

D KOYA XISHAN 溪山行館

A hidden gem in the Xitou forest, this stylish lodging is themed around tea
隱身溪頭山林，以茶為主題的質感旅宿

⌖ 南投縣鹿谷鄉興產路23-1號
No. 23-1, Xingshan Rd., Lugu Township, Nantou County
www.koya-xishan.com | +886-4-9261-2399

E OLDFIVE B&B 老五民宿

Quaint and simple Japanese-style-inspired B&B in the mountains
樸實靜默的和風山居

⌖ 南投縣水里鄉福田路29號
No. 29, Futian Rd., Shuili Township, Nantou County
+886-4-9282-1005

F THE PAVILION OF PHOENIX 蟬說：鳳凰亭序

Dreamlike cabin situated in a conserved forest
座落在保護林裡的夢幻小木屋

⌖ 南投縣鹿谷鄉仁義路1號
No. 1, Renyi Rd., Lugu Township, Nantou County
+886-4-9275-5990

CAOTUN AND ZHUSHAN TOWNSHIPS

草屯與竹山周邊

ZHUSHAN ARTS, CULTURE, AND LOCAL-LIFE DAY TRIP　竹山地味 文創一日遊

水沙連高速公路
Shuishalian Freeway

Zhongtan Highway
中潭公路

草溪路
Caoxi Rd.

Zhongzheng Rd.
中正路

集山路一段
Sec. 1, Jishan

濁水溪
Zhuoshui River

大智路　Dazhi Rd.

用手機掃描 QR code，存取推薦路線的 Google M
Scan the QR code to access this recommended route on Google Ma

1) **09:00**   Visit Taiwan Craft Research and Development Institute to learn about Taiwan's crafts

2) **10:30**   Head to Yu-Hsiu Museum of Art and appreciate the architecture and exhibitions (by reservation only)

3) **12:30**   Enjoy lunch in Caotun and have some handmade mochi for dessert

4) **14:00**   Have a nice cup of coffee for your after-meal ritual

5) **16:00**   Pray for good fortune at Zhushan's Zi Nan Temple

6) **17:00**   Shop at unique shops in Zhushan and try local street food in front of Lianxing Temple for dinner

---

1) **09:00**   一早先到「台灣工藝文化園區」認識各式台灣工藝

2) **10:30**   再轉往「毓繡美術館」欣賞建築與展覽（須事先預約）

3) **12:30**   回到草屯享用午餐，吃完別忘了來一顆手工麻糬

4) **14:00**   悠閒地在咖啡店坐坐，幫助消化

5) **16:00**   前往「竹山紫南宮」求發財金，祝你賺大錢

6) **17:00**   逛逛竹山小店，晚餐到連興宮廟口吃一輪在地小吃

Note 備註：

Due to the considerable distance between itinerary spots, driving or scootering is advisable.
因景點間稍有距離，建議自行開車或騎車較為方便。

09:00
TAIWAN CRAFT RESEARCH AND DEVELOPMENT INSTITUTE
1. 台灣工藝文化園區

Located in Caotun Township, Taiwan Craft Research and Development Institute is an important base for preserving Taiwanese craftsmanship and fostering professional craftspeople. The Craft Hub in the park delivers themed exhibitions, craft-groups-in-residence programs, and experiential educational classes. Weekend are a better time to visit as you get to explore the lively weekend bazaar, Red Bean Campo.

位於草屯的「台灣工藝文化園區」，是台灣保存工藝技術與培育工藝人才的基地，園區裡的地方工藝館除了有主題展覽之外，也有工藝團體進駐，舉辦體驗學習課程。週末園區也固定舉辦「小紅豆創意市集」，若時間允許建議假日造訪，更為熱鬧！

10:30
YU-HSIU MUSEUM
2. 毓繡美術館

Situated in Jioujiou Peaks Nature Reserve, Yu-Hsiu Museum is a private museum of realistic art housed in an architecture designed by Taiwanese architect Wei-Li Liao. Inside the museum, you can appreciate the dance of light and shadows between the artwork and the architecture. In the outdoor area of the museum, you will discover the delightful-duo plays presented by the sculptures and the surrounding nature. Its distinctive ambiance is incomparable to any other art museums in the cities.

位於九九峰自然保留區，由台灣建築師廖偉立設計的「毓繡美術館」，是一座以寫實主義為主題的私人美術館。美術館內外皆有風景，內部可欣賞藝術與建築的光影對話，外部可欣賞自然與雕塑的趣味共演，氣氛有別於城市裡的美術館。

12:30
LUNCH IN CAOTUN
3. 草屯午餐

Head back to the downtown area of Caotun, and enjoy your lunch at Wushi, a white-building restaurant offering delicious pastas, stewed rice, and other food. 30 Teppanyaki with two stylish chefs making quick-fried meat and vegetable dishes is also a potential option. After your meal, Jo-Way Mochi's signature handmade Gold Bullion mixed with fine-ground sesame, fine-ground peanut, and adzuki bean purée should be your choice of dessert.

回草屯享用午餐，白色小屋建築的「武食」供應美味的義大利麵與燉飯等料理。鐵板料理店「弎食」也是好選擇，兩位型男主廚臨場熱炒，熱騰騰的肉食與炒時蔬超下飯。飯後甜點推薦「草屯久味大姐手工麻糬」混合了芝麻粉、花生粉跟紅豆泥的「招牌金條」口味。

14:00
THE POT&PAN BAKERY AND DINING
4. 衛蕾原味攻坊

Travel through the Green Tunnel and come to the Pot&Pan Bakery and Dining to taste its delicious cakes and cookies. The store also regularly holds Front Yard Market to promote local farmers' produce and local artists' works. If you long to see more of this kind of unique café, the Log café that doubles as a Northern Europe antique furniture store, displaying a beautiful collection of tableware from Northern Europe, will make you want to bring them all home.

轉移陣地來到中興新村，穿越綠色隧道來「the Pot&Pan Bakery and Dining」來吃新鮮美味的蛋糕或餅乾吧，店裡也固定舉辦支持小農與在地創作的「前院市集」。但如果你渴望看得更多，另一家結合北歐古董家具店的「深港浮木」咖啡館，現場展示漂亮的北歐食器，各個都令人想帶走。

16:00
ZI NAN TEMPLE
5. 紫南宮

A must-see spot on your way to Zhushan, Zi Nan Temple is in fact a temple worshiping Tudigong, the lord of the local soil and the ground. Despite the rather small scale, it's a very popular temple among Taiwanese folks. Large numbers of people visit to pray for great fortune by offering donations or doing exchanges for mother money, a small amount of money lent from the temple, and therefore blessed by the temple god, that is supposed to duplicate when you use it to do business, or simply place it in your wallet. Since it doesn't matter which currency you use, why not come and give it a try!

前往竹山，再怎麼樣都要路過「紫南宮」。紫南宮其實是座土地公廟，而這座規模不大的廟宇相傳十分靈驗，因此在台灣擁有高人氣，吸引許多人前來添香油錢換發財金，只要把「錢母」放在錢包就能「以財生財」，不論哪國的錢幣都可以，快來試試看吧！

17:00
A STROLL IN ZHUSHAN
6. 竹山走逛

As the center of the Zhushan cultural creative cluster, the old Taisi Bus Station relinquished its main hall and underwent conversion to host Taisi Ice Shop and Taisi Select Shop. On the second floor, you will find the Be Young Garden restaurant. There are also shops like Yuantai Bamboo nearby. When it's dinner time, give the ba-wan and rice pudding from the Jili ice shop a try. If you still have an appetite, all sorts of street foods await you in front of Lianxing Temple.

「竹山文創聚落」以舊台西客運站為核心開展，候車大廳改建成「台西冰菓室」與「台西選貨店」，2 樓司機休息室則運用竹編打造成「竹青庭人文空間」，周邊還有「元泰竹藝社」等小店。晚餐可到「吉利冰菓店」吃肉圓與米糕；若還不滿足，可到「連興宮」廟口大啖各式小吃。

SUN MOON LAKE

日月潭——台灣最美的湖光山色

Photo credit：p

SPECIAL FEATURE
NANTOU
南投特輯
SPECIAL FEATURE

Xiangshang Visitor Center beside the mountains and the lake is a fair-faced concrete building designed by Japanese architect Norihiko Dan specially for the landscapes of Sun Moon Lake. Take a bike ride around the lake from the visitor center, and visit Shuishe Pier, Ita Thao Pier, and Xuanguang Temple Pier along the way to discover the changing mountain scenery around the lake.

Sun Moon Lake is the most popular check-in spot in Taiwan. There are several check-in spots you simply must collect when traveling here, such as a picture of the bright-orange flying roof ridge contrasting the azure-blue lake on top of the Wenwu Temple, documenting the national representative rowing team's intensive training on the Crescent Bay, making photographic records of the indigenous Thao culture at Ita Thao Pier, and snapping a mountain-surrounded-lake birdseye shot of the entire Sun Moon Lake from the Sun Moon Lake Ropeway. Or visit the living basin of Toushe, a rare geological phenomenon where the ground moves when you step due to its overflow underground water and peat soil stratum, located not far from Sun Moon Lake and offering kayaking activities between farmers' fields.

Not only famous for Sun Moon Lake, Yuchi Township is also known as the hometown of Taiwanese black tea. If time permits, the Antique Assam Tea Farm surrounded by betel nut orchards is an elegant tea factory constructed during the Japanese colonial period that still operates its tea-making machines. Have a sip of the graceful Red Jade tea with its flowery aroma, also known as Taiwanese Tea No.18, and let mind and body comfortably stretch out in the space filled with the scent of tea.

For more information, please check out the official website of Sun Moon Lake National Scenic Area: www.sunmoonlake.gov.tw

依山傍水的「向山行政暨遊客中心」，這座清水混凝土的前衛現形，是日本建築師團紀彥依照日月潭風景打造的舞台。從這裡出發單車遊湖，沿途拜訪水社碼頭、伊達邵碼頭、玄光寺碼頭，隨著湖光山色變幻，用不同角度看日月潭。

日月潭是台灣打卡率最高的地方之一，幾處不可思議的祕境必定要蒐集，登上「文武廟」的屋頂，拍下橙豔飛簷與湛藍湖景的強烈對比；到神祕的「月牙灣」，拍下西式划船國家代表隊魔鬼訓練；到「伊達邵碼頭」，可記錄台灣原住民族之一的「邵族」文化；倘若搭上「日月潭纜車」，從高空視角更可一覽山環水繞的日月潭全貌。如果到距離日月潭不遠的「頭社活盆地」，還能親身嘗試在灌溉大排划獨木的神奇體驗。

魚池鄉除了日月潭外，還有「台灣紅茶故鄉」的美名，若時間充裕，建議造訪遺留在檳榔林間的「日月老茶廠」，這座日治時代建造的優雅茶廠，昔日的製茶機器依舊運轉著。浸潤在充滿茶香的空間裡，飲一口花香淡雅的紅玉紅茶，讓身心跟著茶葉在茶湯裡舒展開來。

更多資訊可參考日月潭國家風景區：
www.sunmoonlake.gov.tw

XIANGSHANG VISITOR CENTER 向山行政暨遊客中心
The first stop for anyone traveling in Yuchi Township and to Sun Moon Lake
魚池鄉與日月潭旅遊的第一站

▛ 南投縣魚池鄉中山路599號
No. 599, Zhongshan Rd., Yuchi Township, Nantou County
09:00-17:00 | +886-49-234-1256

ANTIQUE ASSAM TEA FARM 日月老茶廠
Buy some Taiwanese Tea No.18, also known as Sun Moon Lake Red Jade tea, as gifts
來買日月潭紅玉——台茶18號當伴手禮

▛ 南投縣魚池鄉中明村有水巷38號
No. 38, Youshui Ln., Yuchi Township, Nantou County
08:00-17:00 | +886-49-289-5508

SAVORING STATE-DINNER DELICACIES IN A SMALL TOWN

PULI TOWNSHIP

埔里——順遊小鎮，吃國宴級美食

credit：Ming-yen Hsu

Situated at the heart of Taiwan, Puli Township underwent the severe trauma of the Jiji Earthquake over 20 years ago. The resilient Puli residents took the crisis as an opportunity to grow by working with Newhomeland Foundation and transforming Taomi community into an eco-village. In addition, after the Paper Dome that accompanied Japanese people during the Great Hanshin Earthquake was relocated to Puli, more and more tourists have been attracted to this small town while traveling to Sun Moon Lake.

Puli is famous for its beautiful mountains and waters. There are few industrial factories but abundant clean and pure spring water contributing to the plentiful agricultural harvests. Under the hills, simps, the galled stems of Manchurian wild rice harvested as vegetables, are grown in wet farmlands. On the Dapingding hills, acres of passion fruit orchards compose magnificent scenery. Puli Brewery also uses local spring water to make the acclaimed Shaoxing wine. Local produce is often used in local restaurants, like the reputable Jin-Du Restaurant established in 1994 or the Vegan Bowl vegetarian eatery, to make various delicious dishes.

When in town, you might want to make a trip to Rest Book & Bed operated by book lovers, and Shuang Nu's handmade bittern douhua made with organic soy beans.

Outside of the town, you can appreciate lotus flowers and the Paper Dome architecture in summer time (better be prepared for mosquitoes). Nomad Festival (facebook.com/Nomadfestivaltaiwan), held every other autumn at National Chi Nan University, is a music event combined with camping activities. If you enjoy outdoor activities, Puli Tiger is another good site for camping, also offering paragliding service.

埔里位居台灣最中心位置，20多年前在921大地震時遭到重創，然而堅韌的埔里人化危機為轉機，與新故鄉基金會一起將桃米社區打造成生態村，加上曾陪伴日本走過阪神大地震的紙教堂遠渡重洋來到埔里，漸漸吸引了不少遊客前往，結合日月潭成為經典的二日遊行程。

埔里以好山好水聞名，這裡鮮少工廠，純淨甘甜的山泉水，灌溉出豐產的農業。山腳下的水田裡，有俗稱「美人腿」的茭白筍；大坪頂的丘陵上，有壯闊的百香果園；埔里酒廠更是汲取泉水，釀造出聞名的紹興酒。走進創立於1994年的老字號餐廳「金都」，或是「一碗食舖」蔬食小店，都能品嚐到運用在地物產烹煮成的道道佳餚。

小鎮上，有愛書人經營的「籃城書房」和使用有機黃豆的「雙女號手工鹽滷豆花」。

小鎮外，夏季可在「紙教堂」賞建築兼賞荷花（夏日記得防蚊），而每隔兩年在秋季時節於暨南大學大草原舉行的「游牧森林音樂祭」(facebook.com/Nomadfestivaltaiwan)，則結合了露營與音樂活動。若喜愛戶外運動的朋友，也可到「虎嘯山莊」，晚上露營，白天還可以玩飛行傘！

JIN-DU RESTAURANT 金都餐廳
State-dinner-level restaurant in Puli offering old-time Taiwanese dishes
埔里國宴級的餐廳，品嚐古早味台灣菜

⌐ 南投縣埔里鎮信義路236號 | www.jindu.com.tw
No. 236, Xinyi Rd., Puli Township, Nantou County
11:00–14:30, 17:00–21:00

PAPER DOME 紙教堂
A commemorative church, relocated from Japan to Taiwan, awaits your visit along with a beautiful lotus ecological pond
從日本移築台灣的紀念性教堂，還有美麗的荷花生態池

⌐ 南投縣埔里鎮桃米巷52-12號
No. 52-12, Taomi Lane, Puli Township, Nantou County
09:30-17:00 | paperdome.homeland.org.tw

SOUVENIRS

伴手禮——山城裡的好食好酒，不買對不起自己

SPECIAL FEATURE
NANTOU
南投特輯
SPECIAL FEATURE

Chocolate: Feeling 18

Founded in the mountainous town of Puli, this famous chocolate brand Feeling 18 expanded their business from online to offline, developing into a cluster of subordinate dessert brands including Feeling 18, the Baumkuchen 18 cake shop, and the handmade Gelato 18 all made with local ingredients to satisfy your taste for sweets.

⌐ www.feeling18c.com

Pineapple cakes: SunnyHills' courtyard house in Nantou

Operating a shop in the most fashionable shopping district in Tokyo, Omotesando, SunnyHills, the Taiwanese pineapple cake brand, actually originated in Nantou's Bagua Mountain. When entering this old courtyard house in the simplicity of the countryside, you will be greeted by a piece of freshly baked pineapple cake and a cup of warming tea, allowing you to feel warm appreciation for the beautiful pineapple-field scenery outside.

⌐ www.sunnyhills.com.tw

Wine: Nantou Winery & Distillery and Tsai's Actual Brewing

If you enjoy an alcoholic beverage, you shouldn't miss these two products in Nantou: the whiskey at Nantou Winery & Distillery, and the craft beer at Tsai's Actual Brewing. The former, OMAR Single Malt Whisky, is a unique fruit-based whisky finished in liqueur barrels, and a multiple-time international wine and spirit competition winner. Curious about how it tastes? Just come visit the winery.

⌐ Nantou Winery & Distillery | event.ttl.com.tw/nt
⌐ Tsai's Actual Brewing | facebook.com/Tsais.Actual.Brewing

Dry noodles: Forest Noodles

Established 90 years ago in the town of Zhushan, this fourth-generation traditional noodle-making shop transformed itself into a new brand called Forest Noodles under the current management . They have infused the spirit of making sun-dried noodles with local produce and developed various flavors like squash, sweet potato, green tea, among others, not to mention a favorite of local parents: salt-free noodles for babies. (by Chia-Fang Li)

⌐ www.forestnoodles.com

巧克力：Feeling 18（18 度 C 巧克力工房）

埔里山城馳名的職人巧克力品牌 Feeling 18，從網路發跡到開設實體店，如今在鎮上發展成規模不小的美食聚落，裡頭集合了旗下品牌：18 度 C 巧克力工房、木輪 18 蛋糕店、Gelato 18 義式手工冰淇淋等，可品嚐使用台灣在地食材製作的美味甜點。

⌐ www.feeling18c.com

鳳梨酥：微熱山丘 南投三合院

展店到日本最時尚商圈表參道的台灣鳳梨酥品牌「微熱山丘」，最開始的原點就在南投的八卦山上！來到純樸農村裡的老式三合院，在店員熱情奉茶招待下，品嚐一塊現烤鳳梨酥與一杯溫熱的茶，可細細感受台式糕餅的美味與鳳梨園風景的美麗。

⌐ www.sunnyhills.com.tw

酒：南投酒廠、蔡氏釀酒

酒精飲料愛好者的你，絕不能錯過以下兩個重點：南投酒廠的威士忌以及蔡氏釀酒的精釀啤酒；尤其前者的「OMAR 單一麥芽威士忌」以台灣水果酒為基礎發展出的獨特風味桶威士忌，更是連年獲得國際烈酒競賽大賞。好奇滋味如何？來觀光酒廠就能逐一品嚐。

⌐ 南投酒廠 event.ttl.com.tw/nt
⌐ 蔡氏釀酒 facebook.com/Tsais.Actual.Brewing

乾麵：森林麵食

原為南投竹山鎮 90 年歷史的傳統製麵所，在第四代的接承之下開創新品牌「森林麵食」，以日曬麵的製作精神結合地方物產，研發出南瓜、番薯、綠茶、蔬菜……等麵條口味，另外還有深受地方媽媽們歡迎的無鹽寶寶麵。(文／李佳芳)

⌐ www.forestnoodles.com

UMESHU

梅酒食譜——懶人釀梅酒

credit : sayotsu

SPECIAL FEATURE
NANTOU 南投特輯
SPECIAL FEATURE

Xinyi Township of Nantou is famous for its plum produce. Every year around April is Guyu, the 6th of the 24 solar terms of the traditional Chinese calendar. During this period, plum fruits turn from green to yellow, signalling the perfect and only time of year to make homemade umeshu. Below is the recipe I've practiced myself over the years that I'd love to share with everyone. Cheers!

Ingredients:

Wine 1 bottle (600cc)

Any wine over 40% ABV will do. I personally recommend Wu Feng Rice Shochu made by Wu-Feng Farmer's Association Distillery.

80% ripeness fresh plum fruits 1 catty (600 g)

Order green plums from Xinyi Township or other organic plums by the catty online between mid-March and late-April.

Rock Sugar half catty (200–300 g)

You can adjust the amount of rock sugar to your liking. My preferred proportion of wine:plum:rock sugar is 1:1:0.5, which makes it perfect for adding ice cubes when drinking.

The math is done for you:

A regular umeshu bottle is approximately 750 ml, allowing 300 ml of wine, 300 g of plums, and 100 to 150 g of rock sugar, which means 1 catty of plums can make 2 bottles of umeshu.

Tools:

2 Glass bottles (750 ml. Available at the Station Rear Shopping District of Taipei Main Station), label stickers (to mark the date), toothpicks, hairdryer, scale and paper towels

Steps:

Rinse the glass bottles thoroughly and dry them completely with hairdryer (boil the bottles before drying if you want to save time).

Rub dust off plums with paper towels, or when quantity is larger, rinse with water and air dry (a hairdryer may help).

Remove the remains of the stem of plums with a toothpick.

Place plums and rock sugar into the bottles (no need to arrange them in layers).

Pour wine into the bottles and seal the lids. Wait patiently for half a year and it's ready to drink. It will be even more aromatic if you let it sit for a year or more! (by Pei-Ling Guo)

南投信義鄉是著名的梅鄉,每年穀雨青梅轉黃,是酒鬼們自己釀梅酒的好時節,以下是作者多年以來的私房食譜,在此分享給大家,乾杯!

材料:

• 酒 1 瓶 (600cc)

可用任何酒精濃度大於 40 度的酒類,私心推薦霧峰初霧燒酎,可向霧峰農會酒莊訂購(www.twwfsake.com)。

• 新鮮 8 分熟的梅子 1 斤 (600 g)

3 月中旬至 4 月底可網路訂購信義鄉青梅或其他有機青梅 (www.52313.com.tw)。

• 冰糖半斤 (200-300 g)

甜度可以依照自己口味調整冰糖多寡,酒:梅子:糖的比例約 1:1:0.5,這個比例加冰塊剛好,不喜歡太甜的,糖可以放少一些。

幫你算好好:

一般梅酒瓶約 750 ml,可放 300 ml 酒、300 g 梅子、100~150 g 冰糖(意即 1 斤梅子可以釀 2 瓶。)

小道具:

玻璃罐 x2 (750 ml,台北後火車站買得到)、標籤(標上日期)、牙籤或竹籤、吹風機、磅秤、紙巾

步驟:

空玻璃罐洗乾淨,用吹風機將水氣完全吹乾(求快的話,可以用熱水先燙過,再以吹風機吹乾)。

將梅子用紙巾擦乾淨,若數量多可用水清洗後晾乾(可以吹風機吹乾)。

用牙籤將梅子的蒂頭挑掉。

將秤好的青梅與冰糖放入玻璃瓶中(不需要一層糖一層梅子地放)。

將酒注滿,蓋上蓋子密封,耐心等待半年後可飲用,能放一年以上更為香醇!

(文 / 郭佩怜)

北漂不怕
有土就能生根的雲林人

雲林
YUNLIN

THOSE WHO CALL YUNLIN HOME GROW STRONG ROOTS TO GRIP THE EARTH

— Chia-Fang Li 李佳芳

When asked of their impressions of Yunlin, nine people out of ten might reply that they have none. The last person will likely have a standard answer: it's the capital of agriculture. However, in my opinion, the word capital is overstating things, because as a matter of fact, most people might be bored when surrounded by the plain country scenes of Yunlin. Yet, if what you seek is the most authentic side of Taiwan, Yulin is certainly the place to go.

Yulin locals are very friendly and unreasonably generous. They tend to offer the best to others instead of keeping it for themselves. For instance, they bring their biggest and prettiest fresh produce to market to sell to customers, or send their hard-working, outstanding children away to work in other cities. They've always shared whatever they have, and done their best as if willing to risk everything to achieve their goals. Indeed, this spirit has contributed to some of Yunlin's marvelous achievements which include the development of several renowned old towns, such as: Xiluo Township, the kingdom of soy sauce; Huwei Township, the city of sugar; and Beigang Township, the former center of ocean trading activities in Yunlin. The locals remember the prosperity of olden days, but they don't flaunt it. Traces of those golden times are now only visible on the magnificent façades of the buildings in those little old towns.

According to Taiwanese culture, people say that the fate of the Yunlin locals is governed by the earth element, which explains their stubbornness and their resolve. Like strong plants, Yunlin locals extend roots deep into the ground wherever they go. No matter how poor the land is, they've always believed in the deep, root-shaped calluses of their hands as they hold tightly to the rich Taiwanese earth. In case you've ever wondered what down-to-earth means, the people of Yunlin will tell you that they are the definition.

若是問大家對雲林的印象是什麼？10 個有 9 個會回答「沒印象」，而剩下 1 個最可能的形容就是「農業首都」。個人認為，用「首都」來形容雲林太言過其實，你可能會對這兒的樸素感到無聊，但如果想認識最真實的台灣，這裡肯定是不摻一滴水的純。

雲林人有種莫名的熱情與慷慨，那大概是雲林人總習慣把最好的留給別人，最大、最漂亮的蔬菜水果拿出來賣，最認真、最打拚的年輕人送出去東南西北漂。雲林人「拚命」、動輒賭注身家的懸命精神，讓雲林人創造了許多奇蹟。幾座老城如有醬油王國之稱的「西螺」、糖都「虎尾」和曾是雲林海線貿易中心的「北港」，當年是如何繁榮，雲林人知道，但雲林人不說。只有老街上仍看得出當時氣派的建築，隱隱透露了往日的風華。

雲林人命中帶土，頑固強韌，哪兒漂泊就哪兒扎根。無論種地多旱，無論海水多鹹，雲林人相信自己一雙厚繭的手，那深痕掌紋就像植物的根，把台灣的土地牢抓著。你要找什麼叫接地氣，這裡的人會告訴你：「本人就是地氣。」

It takes one hour and 15 minutes to travel from Taipei to Yunlin by High Speed Rail. In Yunlin's downtown area, if you prefer not to be limited to the bus routes, there are scooter rental companies situated right outside TRA Douliu Train Station. Taiwan Tourist Shuttle Service also offers plans for two travel routes in Yunlin; the Douliu–Gukeng route that departs from TRA Douliu Train Station, and the Beigang–Huwei route that departs from HSR Yunlin Station. Please check out their official website for more information.

台北搭高鐵前往雲林約 1 小時又 15 分鐘。市區內移動若不想受限於公車路線，在斗六火車站外有短期機車出租。另外台灣好行推行兩條套票路線，分別是由台鐵斗六火車站出發的「斗六古坑線」，以及由雲林高鐵站出發的「北港虎尾線」，詳細資訊可上官網查詢。

RECOMMENDATIONS
推薦

■ READING LIST 旅遊書籍

SHORT TRIPS IN YUNLIN: YUFU'S HAND-DRAWN MAPS FOR WALKS《雲林輕旅行：魚夫手繪散步地圖》
Reveals the secrets of Yunlin's historic buildings
雲林歷史建築身世大解密

⌐ books.com.tw/products/0010738441

■ LOCAL PUBLICATIONS 在地刊物

YUNLIN TABERU《雲林食通信》
Package of local farming news and fresh produce delivered to your door
產地消息與新鮮食材一起打包送到手中

⌐ facebook.com/yunlintaberu

■ TRAVEL WEBSITES 旅遊網站

TRAVELING IN YUNLIN 雲林文化旅遊網
First-hand information about Yunlin's culture, tourism, and festivals
雲林文化觀光節慶的第一手消息

⌐ tour.yunlin.gov.tw

YUNLIN TIME 漫步雲林
Platform for Yunlin's delicacies and sight-seeing spots operated by multiple contributors
多位部落客共同經營，分享雲林美食景點

⌐ facebook.com/yunlintime

■ GUIDED TOURS 導覽

LOUYOUNG CULTURAL AND EDUCATIONAL FOUNDATION 螺陽文教基金會
Cultural tours along Xiluo's Yanping Old Street
出發西螺延平老街文化巡禮

⌐ louyoung.org.tw | sightseeing_reservations.php (需前一週申請 Reservation one week prior to the tour is required)

HUWEI SALON 虎尾厝・SALON
Walks through the small town of Huwei led by local culture and history workers
在地文史通領路漫步虎尾小鎮

⌐ huwei.salon (需先申請 Please make a reservation in advance)

■ ANNUAL EVENTS 年度活動

CHENGLONG WETLANDS INTERNATIONAL ENVIRONMENTAL ART PROJECT (MAY–JUNE) 成龍濕地國際環境藝術節 (5月-6月)
Outdoor exhibition with landscape installation artwork to raise environmental awareness
喚醒環境關懷的大地藝術

⌐ facebook.com/chenglong.artproject

SUMMER THEATRE FESTIVAL (JUNE–SEPTEMBER) 夏至藝術節 (6月-9月)
Collaborative theater project by four cities and counties
四縣市「雲嘉嘉營」劇場連線計畫

⌐ facebook.com/yacctheater

YUNLIN INTERNATIONAL PUPPET ARTS FESTIVAL (OCT.) 雲林國際偶戲節 (10月)
Performing channel for local and international puppetry art groups
本土與外國偶藝表演大拼台

⌐ www.ylccb.gov.tw

A BEIGANG CHAO-TIAN TEMPLE 北港朝天宮

Bustling, festive pilgrimage parade for goddess Mazu in the third month of the traditional Chinese calendar
農曆3月來可以看到熱鬧出巡盛況

雲林縣北港鎮中山路178號
No. 178, Zhongshan Rd., Beigang Township, Yunlin County
+886-5-783-2055

B CHENGLONG WETLANDS 成龍濕地

Mutual paradise for both the environmental arts and the local waterfowl
環境藝術與水鳥共舞的天堂

雲林縣口湖鄉 | +886-5-797-0856
Kouhu Township, Yunlin County
全天候開放 | Accessible 24/7

C JIAN GUO VILLAGE 虎尾建國眷村

New cultural base reconstructed from a deserted veteran's village
由眷村改造而成，虎尾新興文化基地

雲林縣虎尾鎮建國一村55號
No. 55, Jianguo 1st Vil., Huwei Township, Yunlin County
facebook.com/jian.guo.village

D XILUO EAST MARKET 西螺東市場

Former traditional market located at Xiluo Old Street transformed into a creative cultural center
位於西螺老街，由菜市場轉型而成的文創聚落

雲林縣西螺鎮延平路35-49號
No. 35–49, Yanping Rd., Xiluo Township, Yunlin County
多數店家在五點左右結束營業 | Most stores/shops close around 5 pm

E HUWEI SALON 虎尾厝沙龍

Bookstore focused on environment, gender, and alter-globalization issues
關注生態、性別、另類全球化的議題書店

雲林縣虎尾鎮民權路51巷3號 | +886-5-631-3826
No. 3, Ln. 51, Minquan Rd., Huwei Township, Yunlin County
10:00–17:30 (Closed on Mon. and Tue.)

F TUKU FIRST MARKET 土庫第一市場

The historic market building in Tuku City has a long history and is now home to many emerging shops
土庫市街歷史悠久之市場建築，現有許多新興店家進駐

雲林縣土庫鎮大同路62號
No. 62, Datong Road, Tuku Township, Yunlin County

A WANG'S ANGELICA DUCK NOODLES 王家當歸鴨肉麵線

50-year-old shop with unique and refreshing Chinese-herb-based broth

50年老字號獨家清爽藥膳湯頭

雲林縣虎尾鎮民生路37-8，37-9號 | +886-5-631-4629
No. 37-8 & 37-9, Minsheng Rd., Huwei Township, Yunlin County
11:00–20:30 (Closed on Fridays)

B YC BEEF 芸彰牧場台灣牛肉料理

Enjoyable fresh beef dishes from raw to stir-fried

從沙西米到熱炒的溫體牛美味絕贊

雲林縣虎尾鎮光復路370號
No. 370, Guangfu Rd., Huwei Township, Yunlin County
+886-5-633-3825
11:00-14:00, 17:00-21:00 (Closed on Mondays)

C BEIGANG FU-AN DUCK RICE 北港福安鴨肉飯

Miraculously tasty combination of rice, duck and soy sauce

白飯、鴨肉與醬油結合的奇蹟美味

雲林縣北港鎮中山路37號 | +886-919-800-101
No. 37, Zhongshan Rd., Beigang Township, Yunlin County
11:00-18:30

D BEIGANG HUASHENG JIANPANGUO 北港華勝煎盤粿

Local brunch choices from griddled sticky rice cakes and braised pork intestines, to rice and pork sausages

在地早午餐，煎粿、滷腸、米腸、香腸一次滿足！

雲林縣北港鎮華勝路107號 | +886-912-740-120
No. 107, Huasheng Rd., Beigang Township, Yunlin County
05:30–11:30 (Closed on Tuesdays)

E XILUO TRIANGULAR BA-WAN 西螺三角大水餃

Gelatin-textured potato starch dough filled with savory pork and bamboo shoots. Goes well with or without soup

Q彈外皮包豬肉、筍丁，乾吃、湯吃都美味

雲林縣西螺鎮觀音街12號 | +886-5-586-3955
No. 12, Guanyin St., Xiluo Township, Yunlin County
Fri.-Sun. 10:00–15:00

F DOULIU CHANG-XING TANGYUAN ICE 斗六長興圓仔冰

Hot and iced combo for traditional rice snacks

傳統米食甜點的冰熱雙吃法

雲林縣斗六市中華路136號 | +886-5-533-9445
No. 136, Zhonghua Rd., Douliu City, Yunlin County
11:00-22:30

A ENCHANTED CAFÉ 著迷食間

Stylish and refreshing vegetarian brunch
質感清新的蔬食早午餐

⌂ 雲林縣斗六市鎮東路81巷1號 | +886-5-534-5623
No. 1, Ln. 81, Zhendong Rd., Douliu City, Yunlin County
營業時間洽臉書 For business hours, please refer to FB page
facebook.com/enchantedcafetw

B QIU SHAN JIAO COFFEE HOUSE 丘山角珈琲室

A charming café located near Tuku First Market, where you
can enjoy a cup of coffee and then visit Shuntian Temple
土庫第一市場附近的老宅咖啡店，喝完咖啡可順遊順天宮

⌂ 雲林縣土庫鎮中山路167號 | +886-922-746-661
No. 167, Zhongshan Road, Tuku Township, Yunlin County
10:00-17:00 (Closed on Mondays)

C JML WATCH CAFÉ 金茂利鐘錶咖啡

Creative integration of 70-year-old clock shop and café
70年鐘錶老舖與咖啡的創意結合

⌂ 雲林縣土庫鎮中正路133號 | +886-5-662-2508
No. 133, Zhongzheng Rd., Tuku Township, Yunlin County
10:00-18:00 (Closed on Tuesdays)

D MAIMENLA CAFÉ

Homey, carefree café operated exclusively by the owner
一人咖啡工作室，有家的自在感

⌂ 雲林縣斗六市警民街38-1號
No. 38-1, Jingmin St., Douliu City, Yunlin County
14:00-23:30 (Closed on Tue. and Wed.)
+886-938-300-949

E R.ANGLE DESSERT STUDIO 方島 R 角甜點工作室

Come to the hometown of peanuts and taste local
homemade desserts
來花生的故鄉品嚐在地私宅甜點

⌂ 雲林縣元長鄉22-1號 | +886-9-284-383-087
No. 22-1, Yuanchang Township, Yunlin County
Fri.-Sun. 13:00-18:00 | www.instagram.com/r.angle2020

F BARRE PEANUTS GELATO 巴蕊花生 手作義式冰淇淋

Incorporating Taiwan's peanuts and other ingredients into
foreign sweets with various flavors
以異國甜食手法呈現台灣花生與食材，有多種口味

⌂ 雲林縣斗六市民生南路217號 | +886-5-535-0101
No. 217, Minsheng S. Rd., Douliu City, Yunlin County
13:00-20:00

A **DOUNAN DEEP-FRIED STEAMED BREAD 斗南炸饅頭**

Devilishly good late-night snack tucked away down an urban alley

等級相當邪惡的隱藏版消夜

⌐ 雲林縣斗南鎮中正路117號 | +886-5-596-3299
No. 117, Zhongzheng Rd., Dounan Township, Yunlin County
21:30–05:00 (CLosed on Sun. and Mon.)

B **HOUYUAN 後院**

Stylish café renovated from an old residence that transforms into a bar after dark

老宅改建的氣質咖啡廳，晚上變身調酒吧

⌐ 雲林縣虎尾鎮忠孝路2號 | facebook.com/thehouyuan
No. 2, Zhongxiao Rd., Huwei Township, Yunlin County
+886-5-596-3299 | 19:00-02:00

C **AZEROTH BAR 艾澤拉斯小酒館**

Skillful, fancy cocktails that will satisfy the finicky drinker

手法高明的精緻雞尾酒，可令酒徒滿意

⌐ 雲林縣六市內環路772號 | +886-5-925-006-289
No. 772, Neihuan Rd., Douliu City, Yunlin County
20:30–02:00 (Open year-round)

D **KHOKAK PANORAMAS BUG TWO 華山觀止 虫二行館**

Taiwanese emerging architect's award-winning work located in the coffee town of Gukeng

位於咖啡重鎮古坑的villa，台灣新銳建築師得獎之作

⌐ 雲林縣古坑鄉松林路54-5號
No. 54-5, Songlin, Gukeng Township, Yunlin County
+886-5-590-0000

E **HUWEI HOTEL 虎尾春秋・布袋戲文創設計旅店**

Design hotel with Taiwanese hand puppetry theme

融入布袋戲文化的設計旅店

⌐ 雲林縣虎尾鎮信義路69號
No. 69, Xinyi Rd., Huwei Township, Yunlin County
+886-5-636-0618
facebook.com/huweihotel

F **TRIACADEMY 三學舍**

The pilgrims' building of Beigang Wude Temple offers accommodation space combining arts and culture and religious belief

北港武德宮香客大樓，結合藝文與信仰的旅宿空間

⌐ 雲林縣北港鎮華勝路330號 | facebook.com/triacademy
No. 330, Huasheng Rd., Beigang Township, Yunlin County

BE A YUNLINESE FOR A DAY! 來當一天雲林人！

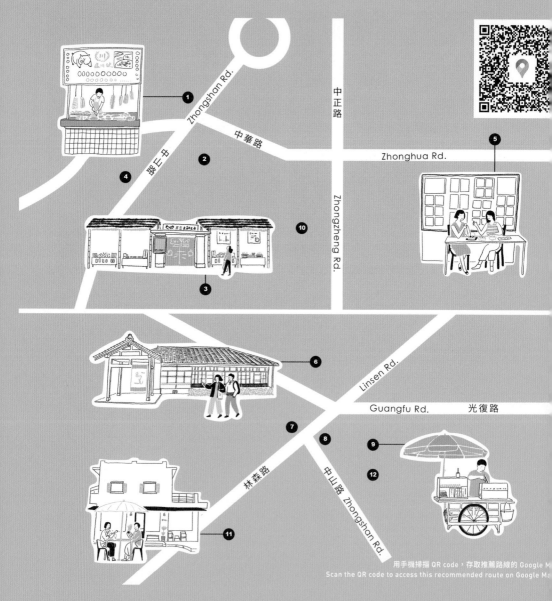

Zhongshan Rd.

中正路

中華路

Zhonghua Rd.

中山路

Zhongzheng Rd.

Linsen Rd.

Guangfu Rd.　光復路

林森路

中山路 Zhongshan Rd.

用手機掃描 QR code，存取推薦路線的 Google M
Scan the QR code to access this recommended route on Google Ma

1) **08:00** Early in the morning, have a nice warming bowl of lamb broth at Douliu West Market to start the day

2) **09:00** Take a walk on Taiping Old Street and appreciate the gorgeous, detailed façades of the Japanese architecture

3) **10:00** Join the farmer's market and discover local delicacies for perfect gifts

4) **11:00** Head to Yunzhong Street Cultural Village and enjoy a cup of single-origin brewed coffee at Otto Café

5) **12:00** Order sashimi plates for lunch at Fukudoden Japanese restaurant

6) **14:00** Head to Huwei Township and visit Yu-Sui-Kaku, a former high-class governmental guesthouse

7) **15:00** Yunlin Hand Puppet Museum is a must-see place when traveling in Yunlin

8) **16:00** Don't miss the bookstore hidden inside a fire department for an artsy afternoon

9) **17:00** Satisfy your craving for snacks at the First Bank plaza

10) **18:30** For dinner, savor tasty meals made with local ingredients at Migu Organic

11) **20:00** Enjoy a few drinks at Houyuan, a café which transforms into a bar after dark

12) **22:00** Discover Yunlin's history at Diamond Inn, a former cabaret, or book a room to stay overnight

---

1) **08:00** 一早就在「斗六西市場」喝碗羊肉湯,開始認識雲林

2) **09:00** 散步「太平老街」,欣賞日式建築外壁的華美細節

3) **10:00** 來逛逛農學市集,帶點好吃的雲林伴手禮

4) **11:00** 前往「雲中街文創聚落」,在「凹凸咖啡」悠閒地喝杯手沖單品

5) **12:00** 午餐就去「福道田日式料理」吃生魚片吧

6) **14:00** 吃飽搭車前往虎尾,到曾是招待所的「湧翠閣」參觀

7) **15:00** 來到雲林一定要到「雲林布袋戲館」認識這門藝術

8) **16:00** 文藝的下午少不了藏在消防局裡的書店「合同廳舍」

9) **17:00** 嘴饞的話先到虎尾人的美食小天地「第一銀行廣場」吃小吃

10) **18:30** 晚餐在「米穀」吃在地食材做的美味料理

11) **20:00** 來白天是咖啡廳,晚上是氣氛酒吧的「後院 houyuan」小酌兩杯

12) **22:00** 到曾是虎尾歌廳的「鑽石背包客」感受歷史,或就住下來吧

08:00
DOULIU WEST MARKET
1. 斗六西市場

The best place to start your trip in the capital of agriculture is no doubt a traditional market. Douliu Second Market, also known as the West Market, is within walking distance from TRA Douliu Train Station. With over 60 years of history, the market has become a bustling convergence of reputable and established shops and local produce stalls. Take a seat at Ayi Lamb and order a nice warming bowl of broth while you listen to vendors peddling their goods. The hospitality and enthusiasm in the air are warmer than the sun.

旅行農業首都自然要從菜市場開始走逛。斗六火車站步行可達的「第二市場（西市場）」，結市歷史超過 60 年，匯聚的名攤老店與嘉南物產不少，而坐在「阿義羊肉」來碗湯暖胃，聽著叫賣聲節奏，感覺炙熱的人情味，完全不輸豔陽。

09:00
TAIPING OLD STREET
2. 太平老街

Cross the street and you arrive at Taiping Old Street which used to be the most popular commercial district in Douliu one hundred years ago. The history of the fair-faced brick street buildings can be traced back to the 1970s. Spend some time to appreciate the diverse and sometimes whimsical flowers, animals and human figures sculpted of clay on the building façades.

過一條馬路，來到老街所在的太平路，這裡是一百年前斗六最繁華的商業區，大街建物以清水磚建造，歷史可追溯至 1972 年代，而華麗的泥作雕飾有花草、人物或動物圖騰，充滿著奇幻的神祕色彩。

10:00
A WALK TO LOCAL STORES
3. 逛在地小店

Constructed in 1927, Duoliu House of Citizen-Memorial Hall of Attendance transformed itself into a contemporary cultural site for the citizens, and holds weekend market with musical performances. Continue your journey at Tri-small Market, renovated from three red-brick houses and a dugout, for some creative local produce, then to the petite yet copious 2 Hand Book Seller to pick out your next read.

1927 年建造的「斗六公民會館」，從昔日慶典集會場所轉型為當代市民藝文遊園地，週末假日常有音樂市集。接著散步到改造三棟紅磚屋與防空洞為店面的「三小市集」採買雲林本地農創品後，再晃到小巧的「哲美系二手書店」，為自己挑本書吧。

11:00
YUNZHONG STREET CULTURE VILLAGE
4. 雲中街文創聚落

Walking on Yunzhong Street is like traveling back in time as you behold the nostalgic wood police dormitories built during the Japanese colonial period. After its reconstruction project, Yunzhong Street has been reborn as a new home for numerous stylish stores and shops. I recommend having a cup of aromatic coffee at Otto Café and tasting Banana Pound Cake under the eaves at Offer Bananie Cake Shop.

來到雲中街就像穿越時空，日治時代建造的警察局宿舍群，有著古老木造房舍的懷舊氛圍。歷史建築經活化之後，有不少風格小店進駐。推薦到「凹凸咖啡館」來杯香醇咖啡，或到「猿樂作」的簷廊下吃份有趣的創意磅蛋糕「猿糕丸」。

12:00
FUKUDODEN JAPANESE RESTAURANT
5. 福道田日式料理

The fervent Yunlin sun might make you crave a refreshing meal for lunch, and sashimi with wasabi at the local favorite Japanese restaurant, Fududoden, may be the perfect idea. The young owner/chef used to be an apprentice in a high-end Japanese restaurant, in which he gained impressive cooking skills and an eye for good ingredients. With satisfying portions and economic prices, Fukudoden is also suitable for solo travelers.

雲林豔陽太火熱，只想來份清爽感午餐，像是生魚片加上微嗆芥末，這時自然不可錯過在地人大推的超人氣丼飯店「福道田」。年輕的老闆曾在高檔料亭修業，技術與食材眼光不差，料滿實在的丼飯在價格上卻是相當經濟，一個人去也能無壓力地點菜。

14:00
HUWEI TOWNSHIP
6. 轉往「虎尾鎮」

To get to the neighboring Huwei Township, take a one-hour trip by bus starting from Taisi Bus Service's Douliu Station, and ending when you hop off at the Shengyuan bus stop. Then, hike up the hill to Dalunjiao Park from where you will see the octagon-shaped Huwei Street Old Water Tower which used to be the main reservoir for this area. Also visit Yu-Sui-Kaku, the former royal family's guesthouse, and appreciate the exquisite details of Japanese governmental architecture as well as the art exhibition in the tatami room.

到台西客運斗六站搭車前往隔壁虎尾鎮（在勝源站下車，車程約1小時），登上小山丘的「大崙腳公園」，遠眺古代水源地的八角狀「虎尾街貯水塔」後，可到皇室招待所改造的「涌翠閣」，欣賞日式官舍建築的美麗細節以及榻榻米房間的創作展。

- ## 15:00
YUNLIN HAND PUPPET MUSEUM
7. 雲林布袋戲館

Take a leisurely walk to the bustling train station area where Taisi Bus Main Station located, and discover the vibrant, creative energy of this small town. Pay a visit to Yunlin Hand Puppet Museum, Yunlin Story House and Yunlin Memory Cool, converted from the old district office and official residences, for traditional hand puppet shows, storytelling activities and classic old-fashioned toys to get an in-depth experience of local culture.

漫步到虎尾最熱鬧的「車頭」（台西客運總站），這裡已然成為小鎮文創能量最高漲的區塊，由日治時代建築虎尾郡役所、郡守官邸與登記所活化成的「雲林布袋戲館」、「雲林故事館」與「雲林記憶 Cool」，可以看布袋戲、聽故事、玩童玩，深刻感受地方文化。

- ## 16:00
JOINT OFFICE BUILDING
8. 合同廳舍

Right across from the Yunlin Hand Puppet Museum sits the legendary bookstore inside a fire department. Also known as the Joint Office Building, the space was converted from an old firehall and is home to a "Hoango," an antique shrine used to preserve and worship sacred pictures of the Japanese Royal family during the Japanese colonial period.

就在雲林布袋戲館的正對面，這棟名為「虎尾合同廳舍」就是傳說中「開在消防局裡的書店」，由老消防局整修完成的空間，祕藏著一座古代保險箱「奉安庫」的遺跡，想知道藏在哪裡，不妨進來找找！

- ## 17:00
FIRST BANK PLAZA
9. 第一銀行廣場

The First Bank plaza is a bustling hub where locals gather day and night to enjoy delicious food. Don't forget to get some duck egg waffles at the street stand to snack on with the coffee you are soon to purchase, and to admire the vendor's masterful, nearly-extinct technique with traditional iron tongs and charcoal.

第一商業銀行的街口，是虎尾人日夜打牙祭的美食廣場，強烈建議去買包「炭烤鴨蛋糕」，除了滋味配香醇的咖啡正好，還可以順道欣賞老闆用鑄鐵夾與木炭烤糕的瀕臨失傳手藝。

18:30
MIGU ORGANIC
10. 米穀

It's dinner time! If you are a vegetable-lover, I recommend the restaurant Migu Organic which focuses on rice and grains in its concept. They offer delicious hot pot dishes, such as their flavorful Tajine pot, made with a variety of fresh local vegetables. Don't forget to try their homemade rice noodles as well! After a satisfying meal, you can head to Barre Peanuts Gelato in Huwei for some delicious Italian gelato.

虎尾哪裡有好吃晚餐？如果你是喜愛品嚐大量蔬菜的健康族，推薦以米食和穀物為概念的餐廳「米穀」。使用大量在地新鮮蔬菜創作的塔吉鍋口味鮮美，自行研發的「米麵條」也值得一試！吃飽還可到附近的「巴蕊花生」虎尾店來口義式冰淇淋！

20:00
HOUYUAN
11. 後院

Wondering where to go to have fun in the evening? No worries. Just pay a visit to Houyuan, a cozy day-time café which dims the lights and transforms itself into a tipsy bar after dark. Their choice of classic cocktails and craft beers might surprise you.

入夜的虎尾會不會沒地方去？別擔心。白天是咖啡館的「後院」，到了夜晚換上調酒師站吧，提供數款經典雞尾酒與精釀啤酒，而轉為昏暗模式的設計感空間，瞬間變身成為舒服到醺然的小酒吧。

22:00
DIAMOND INN
12. 鑽石背包客

After a few drinks, take a walk to the February Drink & Food neighborhood, and check out this special backpackers' hostel, Diamond Inn. This ordinary four-story building was once a cabaret that caused an uproar in Huwei. Years after its prime, Maggie, the granddaughter of the previous owner, came back to Huwei and decided to take over the space which she has revived by converting it into a venue offering entertainment and accommodations to travelers.

稍微散步一下，來到在貳月咖啡館附近、特色強烈的背包客旅店，那今日看來不起眼的 4 層樓建築，其實是 50 年代虎尾最轟動的「鑽石歌廳」，如今由返鄉青年的老闆娘 Maggie 重新活化開放，重新提供南來北往的旅人住宿與娛樂使用。

ATTENTION, MARKET SHOPPERS!
FOUR MUST-KNOW PRODUCTS FROM YUNLIN

PRODUCTS FROM YUNLIN

菜籃族注意！不可不知的 4 種雲林物產

You might not have enough time to tour around the entirety of Yunlin County, but you can bring a taste of this marvelous county back with you. Buy a bag of high-quality rice, a bottle of soy sauce, a piece of meat, or even a pack of mullet roe, all the basics for a tableful of delicacies. Just get your appetite ready, and set out on a journey with your chopsticks.

1. Soy sauce: a century-old, dark-colored, flavorful ferment

An essential condiment on every Taiwanese dinner table, soy sauce is mainly produced in Yunlin. Xiluo Township is even called the kingdom of soy sauce to pay homage to its over one-hundred-year history of soy sauce making. Important local brands like Rueichun, Wuan Chuang, Ta-Tung Can, Chen Yuan-Ho and Yu-Ding-Shing produce various products, such as Japanese soy-wheat sauce, black bean wood-fired soy sauce, etc. with wide flavor spectrum of saltiness, sweetness and richness. In courtyards under the hot sun, the savory aroma of soy sauce sitting in vats permeates in the air. This aged and fermented smell might be interesting to foreigners, but it reminds all Taiwanese of a good rice meal.

Future Dining Table project initiated by Yu-Ding-Shing is a monthly soy-sauce-based vegetarian gathering. Please visit the Future Dining Table Facebook page for more information.

雲林很大，如果你沒時間走遍，建議把味道買回家細嚐。買包好米、帶瓶醬油、切塊肥肉，如果還有銀兩，定要買塊烏魚子犒賞。如此，一桌好菜的基本架構有了，接下來你只需要準備好胃口，就能用筷子開始旅行。

1. 百年陳釀的黑滋味：醬油

台灣人餐桌必有的調味料「醬油」，最主要的生產地就在雲林，尤其是被稱為醬油王國的西螺鎮，產業發展已有百年以上歷史，此地醬油品牌就有瑞春、丸莊、大同、陳源和、御鼎興等，從日式豆麥醬油到柴燒黑豆醬油，薄厚、濃淡、甜鹹各種滋味任選。來到烈日下缸埕，正曝曬的甕釀醬油溢出一股熟悉的鹹香氣，那陳放發酵的味道對外國人而言很特別，但對台灣人來說，可是一聞就想吃飯的味道。

御鼎興發起「飛雀餐桌行動」，每月舉辦「全醬油」的蔬食料理聚餐活動，有興趣可參考 facebook.com/FutureDiningTable

2. Mullet roe: gold-like ingredient condensed from the ocean

Being described as shiny as gold, mullet roe plays an important role in Taiwan's banquet culture. The seaside township of Kouhu is the primary mullet roe supplier in Taiwan. Not only does it contribute 60% of Taiwan's total mullet roe production, but has also won multiple awards for its premium mullet roe products. Winter is the time of year to see mullet harvests in Kouhu. With their white bellies reflecting the winter sun by the ponds, the plump mullet will soon be delivered to factories for a process which includes removing the roe, and then salting, pressing and dehydrating it. This condensed delicacy is one of Taiwan's classic seafood flavors. Furthermore, Chongwen Road, also known as black gold street, is the place to see processed mullet roe sunbathing in courtyards in the ocean breeze under the piercing sun like a colorful pointillist painting.

3. Meat: marbled delicacy melting on the tip of your tongue

As the primary base of Taiwan's animal husbandry and dairy farming industries, Yunlin is a meat-lover's heaven. There is YC Beef's Taiwanese beef, Fun Sun's Taiwan Chicken, Nice Garden's Choice Pig and Just Milk Ranch's milk products, to name a few of your choices. Moreover, Yunlin's excellent meat industry is not only demonstrated by what you see on dining tables, but also in the reinvention of an industry image by creating such educational venues as the Nextland pork processing factory, in which you can learn fun facts about pork production and taste some delicious pork dishes.

4. Rice: pearls harvested from black paddies

Yunlin's farmlands are also nicknamed black-meat fields as a result of Zhuoshui River's alluvial plains which are composed of dark-colored clay and provide the perfect natural conditions for growing high-quality rice. Considered to be Taiwan's rice storehouse, Yunlin is famous for an old rice cultivar in Xiluo called Zhuoshui rice, as well as various emerging breeds like Dounan's koshihikari rice. Besides having a decent bowl of plain rice in Yunlin, you should also try other rice products like Douliu's rice pudding with lamb, Xiluo's steamed rice cake, and Beigang's griddle-fried rice cakes. The variety of tastes from light to sophisticated will definitely blow your mind.

2. 海味凝結的黃金食材：烏魚子

橘澄色澤有如黃金的烏魚子，是台灣宴席料理絕對不可缺少的一味，雲林濱海的口湖鄉是台灣烏魚子的主產地，不只是產量占全國 6 成，品質更贏得多次全國烏魚子評鑑。冬日來到口湖鄉，自養殖池採收的肥美烏魚閃亮著銀白鱗光，趁新鮮送到加工廠裡取卵、抹鹽、壓漬、日曬，濃縮成為一片片的台灣海味。在擁有「烏金一條街」的崇文路，可見大大小小曬埕鋪滿了烏魚子，在海風吹拂與烈日曝曬下，形成一幅豔麗壯觀的點彩畫。

3. 融化舌尖上的霜降美味：肉

肉食主義者來到雲林，簡直就是置身天堂！雲林是畜牧與酪農業的大本營，無論是芸彰牧場的台灣牛、凱馨實業的桂丁雞、祥圃實業的究好豬，以及嘉明牧場的純鮮乳，無論想吃哪種肉，通通都能滿足。此外，雲林的肉食文化不只表現在餐桌，在顛覆傳統養豬場印象的「良作工場農業文創館」，集合各種關於豬肉的冷知識，並可現場品嚐美味的豬肉料理。

4. 黑肉田採收的白珍珠：米

濁水溪滾滾沖積的平原，一鋤頭翻起是又黑又黏的土，使得雲林的田又有「黑肉田」的綽號，而這也成了孕育好米的天然條件。雲林是台灣的米倉，古來有「西螺濁水米」聞名，近來有「斗南越光米」崛起，新品種如後浪推前浪。來雲林必定要吃碗好飯，也不可錯過各種米食，斗六的羊肉米糕、西螺的碗粿、北港的煎盤粿等，從素雅到濃豔的滋味變化，米食在農鄉超精彩。

Photo credit：飛雀餐桌行動

FUTURE DINING TABLE 飛雀餐桌行動

⌐ facebook.com/FutureDiningTable | +886-5-588-19162

ISLAND 77 良作工場農業文創館

⌐ 雲林縣大埤鄉豐田路57號 | +886-5-552-9586
No. 57, Fengtian Rd., Dapi Township, Yunlin County
09:30-17:00 (closed on Mon. & Tue.) | facebook.com/nicenextland

AN AGED YET VIBRANT TOWN

BEIGANG
古老卻充滿生命力的城市

Photo credit｜KerotoTW

SPECIAL FEATURE
YUNLIN
雲林特輯
SPECIAL FEATURE

Almost 365 days a year, you may see religious events at different temples in Beigang. I have a preference for staying close to a temple square to feel the fireworks explode. With red paper fragments blowing around in the air, my sight is fixed on the tongji, a spirit medium between gods and men, enacting his dramatic ritual movements. The powerful essence of religion connecting life and death, good and evil can be perceived even from a distance.

Beigang is aged yet alive. The established hand-drawn lantern shop and farming tool store near Chao-Tian temple and the old Chinese medicine shop and oil pressing workshop on Beigang's eight winding old streets give the town a vibrant energy. Under Beigang Main Bridge, there is the former cattle market, now a lively outdoor market where you can find swimming bighead carp, cages of young chicks for sale and mysterious snake soups. Except for the lack of traditional costumes, this place truly looks like a historical drama being performed right before your eyes.

No doubt Beigang is also an incubator for new things. There are plenty of spots worth visiting as well as B&Bs hidden down urban alleys, such as An Jie Zhai Nei, Houda Hostel, Soo Home, Bao Sheng Hall Café, Guangming Bookstore, and a surprising mosaic garden on the roof of Zhu Yuan Medical Department Hospital.

一年 365 天裡頭，這裡幾乎天天都有迎神進香活動，我喜歡貼緊著廟埕感受鞭炮的爆炸，在紅紙炸裂紛飛的煙霧瀰漫，用目光追逐乩童起駕的激昂動作，牽掛著生死善惡的信仰本質，距離再遠都能感受到那份強烈的震撼。

北港的古老是活著的。圍繞大廟（北港朝天宮）的老號商鋪有手工彩繪的燈籠店、賣鋤頭鐮刀的農具店，而錯綜的北港八街有還營業中的老中藥房、榨花生芝麻的油車間，以及大橋下的牛墟可見地攤集市生猛景象：活跳的大頭鰱、籠賣的小黃雞、望之生畏的蛇湯，真心覺得除了行人沒有穿古裝之外，北港簡直是一部現實上演的穿越劇。

當然，北港也孕育了許多新事物，幾家隱藏店鋪與民宿很值得瞧瞧，暗街宅內、好住民宿、手厚商號、保生堂漢方咖啡館、北港傳薪學院－光明屋等，在諸元內科醫院的屋頂上還有座神祕的馬賽克花園，是個會讓你驚訝的地方。

Photo credit：北港傳薪學院 - 光明屋

GUANGMING BOOKSTORE 北港傳薪學院 - 光明屋
Independent bookstore converted from an old clinic
由老診所改建而成的獨立書店

雲林縣北港鎮光明路122號｜+886-5-783-7556
No. 122, Guangming Rd., Beigang Township, Yunlin County
09:00–17:00 (Closed Mondays and Tuesdays)

Photo credit：保生堂漢方咖啡館

BAO SHENG HALL CAFÉ 保生堂漢方咖啡館
Lovely café converted from an old Chinese medicine shop
原為中藥行，現為有茶、有咖啡的美好空間

雲林縣北港鎮中山路61號｜+886-5-783-3827
No. 61, Zhongshan Rd., Beigang Township, Yunlin County
11:00–19:00, Fri.-Sat. 10:00–20:00, Sun. 10:00-19:00 (Closed on Wed.)

XILUO

台灣味道原鄉

SPECIAL FEATURE
YUNLIN
雲林特輯
SPECIAL FEATURE

Walking through the dim corridor of the East Market, you smell the underlying soy sauce aroma from the braised pork of the triangular ba-wan dumplings and Ah-Min Grandma's steamed rice cakes. If every town has a signature taste, Xiluo's would be called the original Taiwanese flavor. Xiluo is at the border of Yunlin, with red Xiluo Main Bridge guarding the river banks. The bridge bids farewell to countless agricultural trucks traveling to other cities and welcomes the return of stacks of money. Xiluo provides one-third of the fruit and vegetables of Taiwan's total market. It's fair to say that Xiluo is a convergence of merchants who weigh the plates on your table and determine the quality of your meals.

In the Qing Dynasty, Xiluo residents used the harbors to hold markets. During the Japanese colonial period, the government built up the East Market building and other gorgeous street houses throughout this town. Nowadays, you can still see the beautiful Western-style street views on Yanping Old Street. Take a closer look and you will find astonishingly detailed sculptures on the façades; from exotic flowers and fruit to brand names spelled out in English, you may wonder just how international this small town used to be. Beneath the turning wheel of time, the East Market resigned from its original tasks, and was transformed into an innovative site for cultural workers and artists. Several local shops such as Maha Box with artists in residence, Yongfong Rice Shop promoting grain-based diet and Xiluo Culture Museum situated in Jie Fa Qian Ji Tea Shop across the street compose a casual day-to-day scene.

走進東市場的幽暗穿廊，聞著「三角大水餃」傳來的肉燥香以及「阿敏婆」炊碗粿的米香，沉鬱在味道底蘊的醬油釀味，把西螺浸潤出一種熟悉感。這裡是台灣味道的原鄉。西螺是雲林的邊界之城，一座紅色西螺大橋駐守著河岸，揮別一輛又一輛的菜車，換得一張又一張的草紙；這裡運銷著全國三分之一量的瓜果蔬菜，聚集著雲林最精明厲害的商賈，秤斤打兩盤算著你的飯桌子，每天吃好吃壞都由他們說了算。

從清領時代以來，西螺人就開始在渡船頭結市，直到日治時期建起美麗的市街與東市場，在西螺延平老街留下一座座豪邸洋樓。仔細欣賞西螺街屋，藻飾的山牆精緻得令人咋舌，從雕琢的奇花異果到英文拼寫店號，推想著古代的西螺曾是何等國際化的城市？在世代轉替下，東市場解除原有任務，轉型成為文創聚落，有藝術家進駐的「馬哈文創小商店」、推廣五穀飲食的「永豐米糧行」，以及對街進駐捷發乾記茶莊的「西螺延平老街文化館」等等，沒了叫賣人的庸庸碌碌，卻多了份愜意自在的生活感。

MAHA BOX 馬哈文創小商店
Small shop exhibiting illustration artwork and cultural products run by locals 在地人用心經營的插畫、文創小鋪

⌜ 雲林縣西螺鎮延平路45-1號 | +886-5-587-8663
No. 45-1, Yanping Rd., Xiluo Township, Yunlin County
10:00–17:00 (Closed Mondays and Tuesdays)

YONGFONG RICE SHOP 永豐米糧行
Hundred-year-old shop offering local produce and dishes
百年老商行，提供在地小農產品與現煮料理

⌜ 雲林縣西螺鎮延平路57號 | +886-5-587-6229
No. 57, Yanping Rd., Xiluo Township, Yunlin County
Wednesday to Friday: 11:00–17:00, weekend 10:00–18:00

不只是雞肉飯和阿里山

嘉義
CHIAYI

MORE THAN CHICKEN RICE
AND ALI MOUNTAIN

————— Joanna Sun 孫育晴

Located in the southwestern part of Taiwan, Chiayi lies north of the Tropic of Cancer and is home to the Chianan Plain, Taiwan's largest agricultural plain. Despite its proximity to Tainan, people don't often associate Chiayi with anything more than the region's turkey rice and Ali Mountain. Travelers seem to forget that it's well-worth the trip!

The beauty of Chiayi is not the loud or bold kind, but rather a humble beauty that needs to be discovered and savored. Take a stroll alongside the railroads and imagine the olden days when Chiayi's logging and brewing industries boomed and the smell of cypress trees and liquor filled the air. Explore the many alleys of the city and observe the continuation of traditional arts and crafts such as embroidery and carpentry and feel the energy that comes from revitalizing historical buildings with creativity. A quick train or car ride will transport you from city center to must-visit destinations such as Ali Mountain or Budai Beach in Dongshi Fishing Harbor.

If you are interested in experiencing traditional Taiwanese culture in an authentic way, make sure to include Chiayi in your trip to southern Taiwan. Beyond its good food and captivating scenery, Chiayi also offers a glimpse into how locals balance modern development and traditional living.

Let's head over to Chiayi!

位於台灣西南部的嘉義，地處台灣糧倉嘉南平原、北回歸線橫貫，聊到「嘉義」，許多人首先聯想到「火雞肉飯」、「阿里山」等印象，卻對於這個比鄰台南的城市不那麼熟悉，在規劃南台灣旅遊時，也不常想到可以「在嘉義待一晚」。

然而「嘉義」的美，是不鋪張奢華的，是隱藏於街道中、需要停留才能細細品味的。出了嘉義火車站沿著鐵道閒逛，遙想在地長輩們口中，過往充滿檜木香及酒香的產業榮景；穿梭於市區巷弄看見刺繡或木工等傳統工藝，在舊建物創意改裝中感受年輕活力；無論搭乘小火車前往阿里山，或驅車前往東石布袋海岸，皆能快速便利到達目的地，瞬間遠離塵囂，覓得一片平靜。

若想細細品味台灣傳統文化，體驗不過分矯揉造作的創新，不妨將「嘉義」規劃為從中台灣進入南台灣的行程。除了樸質實在的美食和引人入勝的山水風光，你將深刻體驗如何在城市發展與傳統生活間取得平衡。來吧，走進嘉義！

Watch the fifth episode of Netflix's Street Food EP05 Chiayi, Taiwan to get an in depth look at Chiayi's most delicious street food and the people behind them. 「netflix.com/tw/title/80244996

可觀看由 Netflix 出品的美食節目《世界小吃》第 5 集台灣嘉義，認識認真做小吃的嘉義人與在地美食。

TRANSPORTATION
交通

It takes roughly an hour and a half to get to Chiayi from Taipei via the high speed rail. Take the free shuttle bus for around 20 minutes and you will arrive at the city center where YouBikes and scooters are available. You can also take the Alishan Forest Railway or various tour buses to travel outside the city center.

搭乘高鐵從台北至嘉義約 1.5 小時，搭乘免費 BRT 接駁車至嘉義市區約 20 分鐘，租借 YouBike 或機車便於市區移動，可轉搭阿里山林業鐵路或觀光巴士至周邊景點。

RECOMMENDATIONS
推薦

◤ READING LIST 旅遊書籍

CHIAYI, NOT A TRAVEL GUIDE《嘉義，非旅遊書》
An in-depth publication created by locals who work in the art and cultural fields. Available for purchase at shopee
在地文化工作者撰寫的深度地方誌，可在蝦皮商城購買

⌜ shoppee.tw (search "嘉義,非旅遊書")

WALK INTO CHIAYI《裏嘉義：從藝文空間、巷弄小吃到山海風景，走進在地人眼中的生活角落》
Chiayi local Ekang Woman shows you a unique perspective of Chiayi
嘉義在地人「下港女子」帶你看見與眾不同的嘉義

⌜ books.com.tw/products/0010962384 | FB: ekangwoman

ISLANDERS' MIGRATION: SAVORING A NEW LIFE IN CHIAYI《島內移民：移住嘉義美味新人生》
Written by influencer Outsider in Chiayi, the southern-bound art manager. Find more info on her social media!
南漂藝術經理人「嘉義異鄉人」撰寫，社群也有許多資訊

⌜ books.com.tw/products/0010985072 | FB: outsiderinchiayi

◤ LOCAL PUBLICATIONS 在地刊物

《+1+1+1》
+1+1+1, a lifestyle annual magazine, takes its name "+1" from the homophone of Chiayi, guiding readers to delve into this small town with a rich history
生活風格年刊，刊名「+1」取自嘉義諧音，引領讀者深入探索這座悠久歷史的小城。

⌜facebook.com/extraordinarychiayi

◤ TRAVEL WEBSITES 旅遊網站

CHIAYI CITY TRAVEL WEBSITE《嘉義觀光旅遊網》
The official travel website of Chiayi City offers useful information and downloadable maps
嘉義市政府官方旅遊網站，連結有些不錯的地圖可下載

⌜travel.chiayi.gov.tw

◤ GUIDED TOURS 導覽

TOAH TOURS
Reed, a US native who resides in Chiayi, offers a customized guided tour full of insight and packed with activities in English
來自美國現居嘉義的Reed，提供最道地的英文客製化及套裝行程服務

⌜ toahtours.com

PERCEPTION OF CHIAYI 發現嘉義
An in-depth bilingual guided tour focused on local culture and history
提供深度人文歷史中英文導覽

⌜ facebook.com/PerceptionCYI

◤ ANNUAL EVENTS 年度活動

THE GRASSTRAW FESTIVAL (MARCH)
草草戲劇節 (3月)
Founded by local theatre group Our Theatre in 2009, Grasstraw Festival is held each March to celebrate theater, dance, music, film, aesthetics, and folk art
由嘉義青年返鄉成立的「阮劇團」主辦，自2009年開始每年3月舉辦融合戲劇、舞蹈、音樂、電影、美學、學習的民間藝術節

⌜ facebook.com/GrasstrawFestival

CHIAYI INTERNATIONAL BAND FESTIVAL (DECEMBER)
嘉義管樂節 (12月)
Hosted by the Chiayi City Government, the Chiayi International Band Festival is an annual event that takes place at the end of December
由市政府主辦，每年活動包含室內外管樂演出、踩街等精彩內容，是每年12月下旬聞名全世界的盛大古典音樂節

⌜ facebook.com/chiayiband

Photo credit：勇氣書房

Photo credit：洪雅書房

A CHIAYI CULTURAL & CREATIVE PARK
嘉義文化創意產業園區
Japanese-style buildings and interesting shops
來這裡看日式建築也逛逛有趣小店

⌂ 嘉義市東區中山路616號 | +886-5-216-0500
No. 616, Zhongshan Rd., East Dist., Chiayi City
10:00-18:00 (Closed on Mondays)

B CHIAYI ART MUSEUM 嘉義市立美術館
A contemporary art museum, repurposed from the Taiwan
Tobacco & Wine Monopoly Bureau
原菸酒公賣局嘉義分局古蹟改建的當代美術館

⌂ 嘉義市西區廣寧街101號 | +886-5-227-0016
No.101, Guangning Street, West Dist., Chiayi City
09:00-17:00 (Closed on Mondays)

C 25X40 ART AND CULTURAL SPACE 25X40 藝文空間
A café in an old Chinese juniper building that often hosts
exhibitions and events
檜木老屋中的咖啡店，時常舉辦展覽與藝文活動

⌂ 嘉義市西區中正路554號 | +886-905-188-033
No. 554, Zhongzheng Rd., West Dist., Chiayi City
13:00-21:00 (Closed on Wed. and Thur.)

D COURAGE BOOKSHOP 勇氣書房
A bookstore/select shop in the cultural and creative park
位於文創園區內的複合式書店，有好書也有生活選品

⌂ 嘉義市西區中山路616號K棟2樓 (嘉義文創園區內)
No. 616, Zhongshan Rd., West Dist., Chiayi City
13:00-20:00 (Closed on Mon. and Tue.)
facebook.com/couragebookshop

E HONG YA BOOKSTORE 洪雅書房
An impressive curation of local culture and history books,
with a weekly lecture on Wednesday nights
齊全的嘉義歷史文化書籍，每週三晚定期舉辦講座

⌂ 嘉義市東區義教東路110號 | FB: hoanyabookstore
No. 110, Yijiao East Rd., East Dist., Chiayi City | +886-5-277-6540
13:00-20:00, Wed. 13:00-21:30 (CLosed on Mon. and Tue.)

F YO-HOO TSHEH TIAM 島呼冊店
An independent bookstore and studio that also sells
locally sourced soy milk
販售台灣友善耕種豆漿的獨立書店與在地工作室

⌂ 嘉義市西區北興街86號 | +886-5-231-1031
No. 86, Beixing St., West Dist., Chiayi City
14:00-20:00 (Closed on Mon. to Thur.)

LIFESTYLE AND COFFEE
生活風格與咖啡

Photo credit : ChengYu Li

A SHIIIIIBI 拾筆
A stationery shop specializing in fountain pens
小巧可愛的鋼筆、文具選品店

⌐ 嘉義市東區垂楊路156號
No. 156, Chuiyang Rd., East Dist., Chiayi City
13:00-19:00, Sun. 13:00-18:00 (Closed on Mon. and Tue.)
+886-5-225-2522

B HUNTER GOODS & CO.
A charming select goods shop on the second floor; the
first floor is Archers Kitchen
迷人的2樓選品店，1樓是餐廳「弓箭手」

⌐ 嘉義市西區北榮街191號 | facebook.com/huntergoodsco
No. 191, Beixing St., West Dist., Chiayi City
13:00-20:00 (Closed on Tue. and Wed.)

C UNIQUE ANTIQUE 舊美好.生活器物.古道具
A beautiful antique shop hidden in Chiayi city
藏身在嘉義的美麗古道具店，造訪前記得電聯！

⌐ 嘉義市西區西榮街2號 | No. 2, Xirong St., West Dist., Chiayi City
+886-922-900-246 小芳 Fang (Please call before visit.)
每月營業日會公布於臉書書專頁 | facebook.com/VintangeLife
Opening days of the month will be announced on its FB page

D FORWARD ROASTERS 往前咖啡製作所
An industrial-style café serving high quality pour-over
coffee and delicious desserts at a reasonable price
低調工業風咖啡館，平價享受高質感手沖咖啡與甜點

⌐ 嘉義市東區興中街205號 | +886-5-278-6920
205, Xingzhong St., East Dist., Chiayi City
13:30-21:00 (Closed on Tuesdays)

E JIOU CAFÉ 玖咖啡
Rebuilt from an old village, this café has large windows
that surround you and make you feel like you're in a
greenhouse 由眷村老屋改建，大片玻璃採光如同溫室花房

⌐ 嘉義市東區興業東路387號 | +886-5-216-2626
No. 387, Xingye E. Rd., East Dist., Chiayi City
13:00-22:00, Sun 13:00-18:00 (Closed on Thur. and Fri.)

F SHIMO SORA CAFÉ 霜空
A charming dessert and coffee café, transformed from an
old clinic, with a cozy backyard
老診所改造、有著愜意後院的甜點咖啡廳

⌐ 嘉義市西區國華街132號 | +886-5-225-5507
No. 132, Guohua St., East Dist., Chiayi City
12:00-18:00 (Closed on Wed.and Thur.)

Photo credit : 嘉義黃記涼麵涼圓

Photo credit : Eureka Home

A DA REN WEI JAPANESE / INDIAN CURRY 大人味日・印珈哩

Get here early because their delicious curry runs out quickly

提早到才能搶到每日限量的美味咖哩料理

⌂ 嘉義市東區成仁街94號
No. 94, Chengren St., East Dist., Chiayi City
11:00-14:00, 17:00-20:00 (Closed on weekends)
FB：大人味 日・印珈哩

B A-FEIFEI RESTAURANT 阿肥肥二通食堂

This menuless restaurant serves food that is reminiscent
of a mother's cooking

如媽媽料理般美味的無菜單老屋餐廳

⌂ 嘉義市西區中正路556號 | +886-963-843-332 (建議預約)
No. 556, Zhongzheng Rd., West Dist., Chiayi City
11:00-14:30, 17:00-20:30 (Closed on Mon. and Wed.)

C YUAN LE HUT 元樂庵

Brunch in the day and comforting Japanese cuisine at night

「早晨小姐」早午餐，夜間提供療癒日式料理

⌂ 嘉義市東區延平街198號 | +886-5-223-0605
No. 198, Yanping St., East Dist., Chiayi City
11:00-19:00, Sun. 11:00-16:30 (Closed on Tue. and Wed.)

D CHIAYI-HUANG COLD NOODLES 嘉義黃記涼麵涼圓

Try the Chiayi-exclusive white vinegar cold noodles, along
with liangwan (cool dumplings) and tapioca pearl ice!

試試嘉義限定白醋涼麵，還有涼丸和消暑粉圓冰！

⌂ 嘉義市東區興中街6號 | +886-5-224-0620
No. 6, Xingzhong St., East Dist., Chiayi City
09:00-18:00 (Closed on Mon. and Tue.)

E YUAN-SHENG MEDICINAL HERB RESTAURANT 元生補湯

This restaurant features medicinal herbs in their cuisine

提供養生藥膳料理，該好好補一下了～

⌂ 嘉義市東區大雅路二段579號
No. 579, Sec.2, Daya Rd., East Dist., Chiayi City
11:00-20:00
+886-5-277-9597

F EUREKA HOME

To savor the seasonal flavors of Chiayi, make a
reservation through Facebook page before visiting

來此品嚐嘉義時節風味，需在臉書專頁預約

⌂ 嘉義市西區北榮街137號 | FB: Eureka Home
No. 137, Beijung St., West Dist., Chiayi City
18:00-20:30

Photo credit：斗酒

Photo credit：承億文旅桃城茶樣子 Hotelday+．Teascape Chiayi

Photo credit：CASA

Photo credit：阿里山英迪格酒店

A　BAR DOUJIOU 斗酒

Indulge in the flavors of local cocktails at this cozy bar, transformed from an old quilt shop
在棉被老店改造成的舒適酒吧，品嚐在地調酒風味

⌐ 嘉義市東區成仁街82號 | +886-5-227-7299
No. 82, Chengren St., East Dist., Chiayi
19:30-02:00 (Closed on Mon. and Tue.)

B　CASA

Come taste award-winning cocktails inspired by Chiayi
來喝調酒冠軍的特調與嘉義的味道

⌐ 嘉義市東區光彩街132號 | +886-5-278-6588
No. 132, Guangtsai St., East Dist., Chiayi City
19:00-01:00 (Closed on Sun. and Mon.)
Reservation: inline.app/booking/chiayi/CASA

C　COP BAR-COCKTAILS OF PIONEERS

A nice new spot for a drink in Chiayi
在嘉義想小酌一杯的質感新據點

⌐ 嘉義市西區西門街54-1號 | +886-919-267-786
No. 54-1, Ximen St., West Dist., Chiayi City
19:30-02:00 (CLosed on Sundays)

D　HOTELDAY+．TEASCAPE CHIAYI 承億文旅 桃城茶樣子

A stylish tea-themed hotel, have a drink at N23.5 Lounge Bar at night
以「茶」為主題的人文設計旅店，晚上可到樓上的N23.5 Lounge Bar小酌

⌐ 嘉義市東區忠孝路516號 | +886-5-228 0555
No. 516, Zhongxiao Rd., East Dist., Chiayi City

E　ANTIK 私人旅宿

A select goods shop that mixes antique goods with daily objects
隱身於舊市場內，美好交疊古董老件與生活日常

⌐ 嘉義市西區中央第一商場39號
No. 39, Zhongyang 1st Market, West Dist., Chiayi City
facebook.com/antik39

F　HOTEL INDIGO ALISHAN 阿里山英迪格酒店

Experience the breathtaking mountain scenery at the five-star hotel located in Alishan National Scenic Area
位於阿里山國家風景區的五星飯店，在此享受山景風光

⌐ 嘉義縣番路鄉公田村龍頭20號 | +886-5-258-6800
No. 20, Longtou, Gongtian Village, Fanlu Township, Chiayi County
info@inalishan.com

CHIAYI STATION AREA
嘉義火車站周邊

FEEL THE CHARM OF THE LUMBER CITY ALONG THE RAILROAD
沿著鐵道感受木都魅力

Linsen W. Rd.
林森西路
Minquan Rd.
民權路
吳鳳南路
Wufeng S. Rd.
Minzu Rd.
民族路

用手機掃描 QR code，存取推薦路線的 Google
Scan the QR code to access this recommended route on Google

1) **10:00** Explore all the exhibitions, shops, and creativity that Chiayi Cultural & Creative Park has to offer

2) **11:00** Visit the Museum of Ancient Taiwan Tiles and Hinoki Village to get a glimpse into the once flourishing forestry industry

3) **12:00** Head over to the East Market—a.k.a. Chiayi's Central Kitchen—and experience the energy of local Chiayi food culture

4) **13:30** Visit Chiayi Old Prison, a wooden prison from the Japanese colonial period, and learn about its historical significance from professional guides

5) **15:00** Enjoy some afternoon tea, Chiayi-style

6) **16:00** Stroll through Chiayi Park for some history lessons or visit Chiayi Botanical Gardens for fun nature exploration

7) **18:00** Prepare to feast at the Wenhua Road Night Market

8) **21:00** Enjoy a post-feast night cap!

---

1) **10:00** 到舊酒廠「文創園區」看展演、逛店家、玩創意

2) **11:00** 逛「花磚博物館」和「檜意森活村」遙想林業盛況

3) **12:00** 前往嘉義人的大灶咖「嘉義東市場」，補足一整天的嘉義元氣！

4) **13:30** 參觀日治時期木造「嘉義舊監獄」，專人導覽揭開神祕面紗

5) **15:00** 來份「嘉義人的下午茶」

6) **16:00** 逛「嘉義公園」走讀嘉義歷史，或到「嘉義植物園」自然探險趣

7) **18:00** 噴水圓環美食大集合，「文化路夜市」越夜越美味

8) **21:00** 散步後小酌一下！

10:00
CHIAYI CULTURAL & CREATIVE PARK

1. 嘉義文化創意產業園區

Kick off your Chiayi trip by taking a three-minute walk from Chiayi Cultural & Creative Park, a former sorghum liquor distillery turned local cultural and creative hub. There are stores, workshops, and exhibitions that are mostly free. Visitors can spend some time at Roi Café, Courage Bookshop, performance art space Sinkagitso and the former office of the Taiwan Tobacco and Liquor Corporation. With the nearby Chiayi Art Museum, this area is sure to become a major stronghold of arts and culture in Chiayi.

嘉義首站來到火車站步行 3 分鐘、運用高粱酒廠改造的「嘉義文化創意產業園區」，除特殊展演之外免費開放參觀。園區內有人文咖啡館「國王蝴蝶祕密基地」、在地創意品牌獨立書店「勇氣書房」、表演藝術劇場「阮劇團－新嘉義座」與原舊酒廠單位「台灣菸酒公司」等，與周邊的「嘉義市美術館」將形成嘉義最有看頭的文化聚落。

11:00
MUSEUM OF ANCIENT TAIWAN TILES
AND HINOKI VILLAGE

2. 台灣花磚博物館 與 檜意森活村

Follow the railway and you will arrive at the Museum of Ancient Taiwan Tiles, a gorgeous and historic building built from Chinese juniper. Walk farther down Linsen East Road and you will arrive at Hinoki Village which was rebuilt from the dormitories around the former Beimen Station—the starting point of the old railway route used to transport logs during the Japanese colonial period. Adjacent to Hinoki Village is the Alishan Forest Railway Garage Park, where a wide variety of trains are permanently parked, reminding us of Chiayi's past. Multitudes of trains used to converge and dispatch from this location to transport logs. If you're looking for a place to stay or just a good cup of coffee, go to Jade Mountain Hostel, a budget-friendly hostel that has recently become a popular local platform for arts and cultural exchange.

沿著鐵道步行可抵達檜木古厝「台灣花磚博物館」，再往林森東路行走，即是昔日森林鐵路蒸汽小火車起點「北門車站」，連結運用宿舍群改建的「檜意森活村」，以及可近距離接觸各式火車的「阿里山森林鐵路車庫園區」，遙想過往阿里山鐵路貨運集散盛況，體驗當代創意與鐵道文化撞擊出的特殊能量。而車站前的「玉山旅社」近年轉身為藝文平台及背包客宿舍，不住宿也可以進去喝杯咖啡！

12:00
CHIAYI EAST MARKET
3. 嘉義東市場

The century-old Chiayi East Market is a common thread in the memories of countless Chiayi locals because it is where they spent their childhoods shopping with their parents and exploring the stalls. Apart from groceries and produce, the markets also have food stalls; some notable ones include Wang's Family Secret Locally Sourced Beef Soup, serving delicious and rich beef broth. There is also Local Mutton, serving meaty mutton soup perfectly balanced with Chinese medicinal herbs that are good for the body and soul. If rice is your passion, then be sure to sample Yuan's Bamboo Rice Cake with Crispy Pork and order their rice cake paired with pork marinated with medicinal herbs that are fried to a crisp.

Once your savory palette has been satisfied, it's time to take care of your sweet tooth. Try East Market Guo Dong Sweet Rice Balls, Vermicelli, and Rice Cakes. Made with all natural ingredients using traditional methods, their desserts are not only delicious but also reminiscent of the olden days. I also recommend East Market Star Fruit Ice, made with sweet, tangy, and slightly savory star fruit juice known for its thirst-quenching properties. This century-old drink shop has also developed new recipes such as star fruit hibiscus soda that are sure to delight your taste buds.

擁有百年歷史的「東市場」，乘載無數嘉義人共同成長回憶，其中家傳4代的「王家祖傳本產牛肉湯」湯頭鮮而不腥。超過60年「本產羊肉」現宰羊肉湯調和中藥，無羊臊味、暖胃又暖心。喜愛米食的別錯過「袁家筒仔米糕排骨酥」，來份鹹香四溢的現蒸米糕與中藥香料配方的現炸排骨酥。

吃完鹹食，不妨嚐嚐「東市國棟湯圓、粉條冰、甜米糕」，純天然不加色素的古早冰品讓人回味無窮。這裡也推薦「東市場楊桃冰」，鹹甜古早味楊桃汁生津解渴，近百年老飲料店還發展出楊桃 / 洛神加汽水的雞尾酒式喝法，新奇又清涼消暑。

13:30
CHIAYI OLD PRISON
4. 嘉義舊監獄

Follow the railway eastwards to visit Chiayi Old Prison, they offer four scheduled guided tours through the prison cells built in a circular row around and connected to a central platform where wardens and guards were stationed. After-wards, visit independent bookstores Hong Ya Bookstore to discover interesting volumes and creative goods.

沿著鐵道再往東行，可到免費開放的「嘉義舊監獄」，每日4場次定時團進團出導覽參觀，一窺中央扇形台管理手掌狀放射出去的神祕囚房。接著可到嘉義的獨立書店「洪雅書房」逛逛，尋找在地文史書籍與設計小物。

15:00
AFTERNOON TEA, CHIAYI-STYLE
5. 嘉義人的下午茶

Speaking of afternoon tea, you have to try Hei Ren Cooked Meat located on the Nan Men Roundabout. This restaurant has been around for over six decades and still follows the recipes of the original owners. They are known for classic banquet dishes such as crab cakes, marlin intestine, and three-meat rolls. They are also known for serving delicacies—such as pig large intestine and trachea—that are tricky to process but simply scrumptious when done right. Also, don't forget to order their famous bottle gourd rice noodle soup. A testament to their deliciousness, there is always a queue outside as soon as they open at 2 pm and they are often sold out by 5 pm. Next door is Xin Wei Sausage, which serves fresh homemade sausages roasted over charcoal and rice sausages with a lima bean filling. Located on the other side of the roundabout, also try Nan Men Star Fruit Juice for their authentic traditional star fruit juice recipe.

說到「嘉義人的下午茶」，就不得不提南門圓環的「黑人魯熟肉」了！超過 60 年的老店，依循著第一代老闆的傳統純手工製作，經典辦桌手路菜如蟳粿、旗魚腸、三絲捲，還有處理乾淨的腹內如大腸頭、脆管、松阪肉等，再來碗匏瓜米粉湯，每天下午 2 點開賣即大排長龍，不到 5 點就全數完售。一旁的「信味香香腸鋪」，每日現做炭烤香腸及包皇帝豆的米腸，以及圓環對側的古法釀製「南門楊桃汁」，也是饕客必點美味。

16:00
CHIAYI PARK
6. 嘉義公園

If you want a history lesson on Chiayi, go to the eastern suburbs of Chiayi City and stroll through Chiayi Park. Here you will find a great deal of historical in-formation and relics, such as the Chiayi City Historical Relics Museum, which used to be a temple during the Japanese Ruling Era, and Shôwa 18 Café, a café named after the year in which the building was built. If time allows, climb up the 62-meter-tall Sun-Shooting Tower to get a great view of the entire city. You could also stroll through the Chiayi Botanical Garden, built during the Japanese colonial period, to experience the experimental and exploratory ambiance of the garden.

到位於市區東郊的「嘉義公園」深入認識嘉義歷史！公園內仍保存眾多不同時期的史蹟資料，如日治時期的神社附屬館修復成為「嘉義市史蹟資料館」，近期以建造年「昭和十八」為名經營咖啡館。若還有時間，可登上高達 62 公尺的「射日塔」眺望嘉義市全景，或漫步至「嘉義植物園」，感受過往日治時期充滿實驗探險氛圍的南方想像。

18:00
NIGHT MARKET
7. 文化路夜市越夜越美味

Kick off your night-long feast near the central water fountain on Wenhua Road (featured in the movie *KANO*) by getting yourself a cup of grapefruit green tea from Yu Xiang House. Then, head over to Lin Cong Ming Fish Head Casserole Stew for fried silver carp or fish head soup made with bone broth paired with homemade satay sauce. Then, for something lighter, try shrimp and pickled mustard greens soup, healthy assorted vegetable plate, or turkey rice. The delicacy of an over 60-year-old restaurant featured on Netflix series *Street Food*. The family's story can be found in the book: *Lin Tsongming Fish Head Stew: A Story of Traditional Family Flavor*.

Known as the place to satisfy your ultimate late night cravings, Zhen Zhen Seafood Congee serves seafood congee made with seafood broth as well as noodle soups, oyster omelette, milkfish, and fish intestines. A-Eh Tofu Pudding offers delicious soy milk and tofu pudding; Rainbow 500 cc Specialties serves homemade pudding and papaya milk; and Zhuang Yuan Juices serves fresh fruit juices and desserts.

從電影《KANO》中曾出現的「中央噴水池」出發,買杯「御香屋」葡萄柚綠茶,再到三代老店「林聰明沙鍋魚頭」,可選炸過的大頭活鰱魚肉或魚頭,加上特製沙茶醬,香濃醇口的大骨高湯讓人一嚐成主顧,別怕胖再來份清爽的冬菜蝦仁湯及阿菁健康涼菜盤,以及限量供應的火雞肉飯。超過一甲子的好滋味甚至被收錄在 Netflix 紀錄片《世界小吃》中,其奮鬥歷程可見於《林聰明沙鍋魚頭,家的味道》(日日學出版)專書中。

號稱「嘉義最強消夜」的「珍珍海產粥」,除了新鮮海味湯頭熬煮粥品和湯麵,蚵仔煎、虱目魚肚與魚腸也是必點!吃完鹹的還有「阿娥豆花」的豆漿豆花、懷舊老店「七彩 500cc 專賣店」的手工布丁和木瓜牛奶、圓環入口處「狀元果汁」等甜品,絕對讓你意猶未盡。

21:00
TIME FOR A NIGHT CAP
8. 散步後小酌一下

Once your appetite has been fully satisfied, head over to CASA on Guangtsai Street for award-winning and wallet-friendly cocktails made by owner Xiao Mao, a winner of the Edrington Bartender Competition. Go to N23.5 Lounge Bar for delicious cocktails accompanied by the view from the side of an infinity pool atop a skyscraper. Additionally, I recommend O'bar Lounge for customized cocktails and cigars, and Charcoal Old Soul, a great place for late night hangouts.

吃飽可以到光彩街旁的「CASA」以親民價格品飲特調酒品,店主人小毛曾獲台灣愛丁頓調酒大賽冠軍;或在位於高樓層的「N23.5 Lounge Bar」無邊際泳池畔,俯瞰嘉義夜景;另外客製化調酒與雪茄的「O'bar Lounge」、炭烤小酒館「Charcoal Old Soul」,也是夜間放鬆的好去處。

SPECIAL FEATURE

CHIAYI
嘉義特輯

SPECIAL FEATURE

A-An Rice Cake
阿岸米糕

嘉義市東區民族路420號
No.420, Minzu Rd., East Dist., Chiayi City
16:00-00:00
+886-5-225-9359

Huang's Cold Noodles and Ba-Wan
黃記涼麵涼圓

嘉義市東區興中街6號
No.6, Xingzhong St., East Dist., Chiayi City
09:00-18:00 (Closed on Mon. and Tue.)
+886-5-224-0620

Taiwnaese Sweet Potato Ball Soup
台灣人蕃 (番) 薯糖圓仔湯

嘉義市東區蘭井街249號
No.249, Lanjing St., East Dist., Chiayi City
12:30-20:30 (Closed on Wednesdays)
+886-5-222-2773

嘉義人氣小吃與伴手禮
Chiayi's most popular eats and gifts!

Nan Men Roasted Almond Tea
南門包氏炭燒杏仁茶

嘉義市東區民族路191號
No.191, Minzu Rd., East Dist., Chiayi City
06:00-10:00 (Closed on Mondays)
+886-973-808-696

Chiayi eatery food 嘉義小吃

在地人推薦從下午 4 點營業到深夜的「阿岸米糕」、嘉
義特有的美乃滋涼麵及涼肉圓；甜品部分有陳澄波故居
中的古早味番薯糖，加了蛋黃的杏仁茶配油條，以及由
木瓜、芭樂、鳳梨、檸檬共譜的嘉義特別版四味果汁。

As a local, I recommend trying A-An Rice Cake, open
from 4 pm to midnight as well as mayonnaise-coated
cold noodles and chilled ba-wan, a unique Chiayi
specialty. In terms of dessert, I recommend traditional
candied sweet potato, especially the ones sold at
Tan Ting Pho's former residence. You also have to
try almond tea made with egg yolk and served with
youtiao as well as Chiayi's unique blend of juice,
consisting of papaya, guava, pineapple, and lemon.

Four Fruit Juice
涼麵四味果汁

嘉義市西區信義路48號
No.48, Xinyi Rd., West Dist., Chiayi City
09:00-19:00 (Closed on Wednesdays)
+886-5-285-1919

Gifts 伴手禮

若要買伴手禮，首推以手工蛋捲及福椒餅聞名的「福義
軒」；另外將早期眷村燒餅輕巧化的「老楊方塊酥」，
酥脆多層次餅皮，散發樸實風味，兩者都是在地人與遊
客的最愛。

If you're interested in getting some gifts, I highly
recommend Fuyushan, known for their homemade egg
rolls and pepper pastry, and TK Food, for their cubic
pastry. Cubic pastry is a traditional pastry that can be
quite dense, but TK Food has developed a recipe that
is light, flaky, and delicious.

Fuyishan
福義軒

嘉義市西區成功街98號
No.98, Chenggong St., West Dist., Chiayi City
08:00-20:00, Sun. 08:00-17:00
+886-5-285-1919

TK Food Cubic Pastry
老楊方塊酥

嘉義市西區中山路506號
No.506, Zhongshan Rd., West Dist., Chiayi City
09:30-21:30
+886-5-227-5121

Turkey Rice 火雞肉飯

說起雞肉飯，每個嘉義人心中都有自己的排行榜！在眾多店家中，嘉義人總能比較出米飯軟硬 Q 度、醬汁鹹度、油量、使用雞腿或雞胸等些微差異，分出勝負！如果胃容量足夠，歡迎來嘉義進行雞肉飯 PK！以下是參戰名單：

Turkey rice is a true Chiayi staple and every local has his or her favorite. Based on the rice, sauce, leanness, and which part of the turkey is used, different restaurants cater to different preferences. If your stomach can handle it, give these places a try and pick out your own favorite:

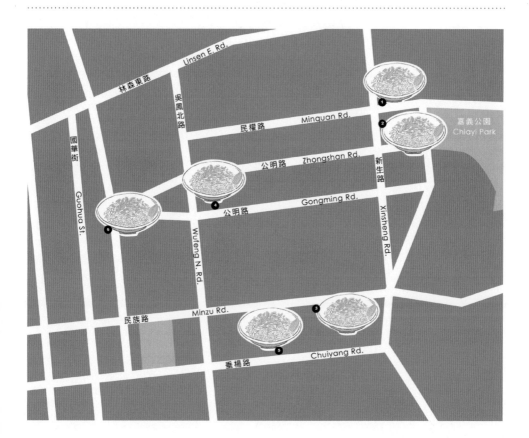

1 Park Turkey Rice
公園火雞肉飯

⌐ 嘉義市東區忠孝路338號
No.338, Chungxiao Rd., East Dist., Chiayi City
06:00-13:30 (Closed on Tuesdays)
+886-5-278-1372

2 Chiayi People's Turkey Rice
嘉義人火雞肉飯

⌐ 嘉義市東區垂楊路157號
No.157, Chuiyang Rd., East Dist., Chiayi City
05:30-14:00
+886-5-223-1737

3 Nam Men Tao Cheng Turkey Rice
南門桃城火雞肉飯

⌐ 嘉義市東區安和街24號
No.24, Anhe Rd., East Dist., Chiayi City
05:00-13:00 (Closed on Wednesdays)
+886-5-278-3080

4 Tao Cheng Three Grain Turkey Rice
桃城三禾火雞肉飯

⌐ 嘉義市東區民權路97號
No.97, Minquan Rd., East Dist., Chiayi City
10:00-19:00 (Closed on Thursdays)
+886-5-278-6846

5 Chief Liu's Turkey Rice
劉里長火雞肉飯

⌐ 嘉義市東區公明路197號
No.197, Gongming Rd., East Dist., Chiayi City
07:00-14:30, 16:30-18:30 (Closed on Mon.)
+886-5-222-7669

6 A-Xia's Turkey Rice
阿霞火雞肉飯

⌐ 嘉義市東區文化路119號
No.119, Wenhua Rd., East Dist., Chiayi City
17:40-22:30

SUNRISES, SEAS OF CLOUDS, RAILROADS, FORESTS, AND ROSE-TINTED SUNSETS

ALISHAN

阿里山——日出、雲海、鐵路、森林、晚霞

Photo credit: J

SPECIAL FEATURE
CHIAYI
嘉義特輯
SPECIAL FEATURE

Crossing the four townships of Chiayi County, you encounter the wonderland-like beauty of the Alishan National Scenic Area starting from low elevation and rising to over 2,000 meters. You watch as the forest cover transforms from deciduous trees to a mixture of deciduous and coniferous vegetation, until finally only conifers remain, the mountain scenery causing all who pass to gaze on in wonderment. There are many ways to get to Alishan: you can drive yourself, take the forest train or the Taiwan Tourist Shuttle. Whether or not you travel to the top of Alishan, places such as Zhuqi, Zhangnaoliao, Dulishan, and Fenqihu, the scenery is gorgeous year-round, with bursts of sakura blossoms, wisteria flowers, maple leaves, and more at different times of year. In any case, you can see the fusion of local business and natural environs which gives rise to scenery unique to such mountain towns.

Besides the famous five natural scenic attractions of sunrises, seas of clouds, railroads, forests, and rose-tinted sunsets, Alishan is also home to a settlement of the Cou indigenous tribe deep in the mountain forests, with exquisite thatched buildings and fully-preserved sacrificial rituals. In February, the Mayasvi war ritual is held, and in October, the Bean of Life Festival. Due to the disparity between daytime and nighttime temperatures and relatively short sunlight hours of this blessed environment, in addition to the self-governed planting and harvesting of crops and excellent roasting skills, the tea produced in Alishan is fragrant and sweet, while the coffee is pure and rich. As such, both are well-known products, giving rise to a diverse experiential culture of streamside tea tastings, bamboo-forest tea ceremonies, and first-hand coffee roasting. Travel here is a sensual experience for travelers both from Taiwan and from abroad. More reccomendations :

AIR LIBRARY

Traversing the thirty-six bends of mountainous Meishan township, discover the Air Library beside the Taiping Bridge

⌈ 2, Xiakengzai, Meishan Township, Chiayi County | 09:00-18:00 (closed on Wed.)

HANA VILLAGE KITCHEN

A South African girl met with a Cou youth and settled in Pnguu (Laiji) Tribe. Their restaurant serves amazing barbecue platter, pizza, and red-wine risotto, while its kiln-baked bread is also a must-eat

⌈ Laiji, Alishan Township, ChiayiCounty | 11:00-17:00 (closed on Mon.&Tue.)

橫跨嘉義縣四鄉鎮、美如仙境的「阿里山森林風景區」，海拔高度一路攀升超過 2000 公尺，沿途可見森林植被從闊葉林、針闊葉混合至針葉林，豐富多樣的山林景緻令人神往不已。前往阿里山可以自行駕車，也可搭乘懷舊森鐵小火車或台灣好行等大眾交通工具，無論是否到達頂端的森林遊樂區，沿途的竹崎、樟腦寮、獨立山、奮起湖等地，一年四季櫻花、紫藤、楓葉等花期輪番上陣，皆能見在地產業與自然景觀融合出的特殊山城景緻。

除了阿里山五奇：日出、雲海、鐵路、森林、晚霞外，不妨也深入山林，探訪鄒族部落，認識以茅草為頂的部落建築景觀，或參與完整保存的傳統祭儀，如 2 月的「瑪雅斯比祭（或稱戰祭）」及 10 月的「生命豆季」。阿里山因晝夜溫差大且平均日照短，得天獨厚的環境條件，加上自我自種品質控管及優良烘培技術，阿里山產製的「茶」清香回甘、「咖啡」香醇濃厚，是遠近馳名的在地產業，如今更有結合溪邊品茶、竹林茶席、現場烘豆等多元化體驗方式，提供國內外旅客豐富的五感體驗之旅。更多推薦：

空氣圖書館

攀過崎嶇的梅山 36 彎，太平雲梯旁結合綠植栽與美食的複合式景觀餐廳。

⌈ 嘉義縣梅山鄉太平下坑仔2號附12
09:00-18:00 (closed on Wednesdays)
facebook.com/airlibrary36

HANA 廚房

南非女孩與阿里山鄒族相遇而定居來吉部落，取自在地食材的烤肉盤、披薩、紅酒燉飯皆令人驚豔，窯烤手工麵包更是必買。

⌈ 嘉義縣阿里山鄉來吉村三叉路
11:00-17:00 (Closed on Mon. and Tue.)
facebook.com/hanavillagekitchen

MANIFESTATION OF OIL PAINTING, PROMINENT MODERN TAIWANESE PAINTER

CHEN CHENG-PO

陳澄波——油彩的化身，台灣近代重量級畫家

Chen Cheng-po, born in Chiayi in 1895, graduated from the Art Teacher Training Program at Tokyo School of Fine Arts in 1924. In his third year (1926) he represented his hometown of Chiayi through oil painting in the series *Outside Chiayi Street (1)* which was the first Taiwanese artist to have work featured in the 7th Empire Art Exhibition in Japan.

Having been a postgraduate at the Tokyo School of Fine Arts and held teaching positions in Shanghai, he returned to Taiwan to live in 1933 and in the following year, established the Tai-Yang Art Association. After the end of World War II in 1945 and the KMT regained possession of Taiwan, Chen Cheng-po proactively promoted the arts while planning to raise funds to build an arts school. In 1947, he was killed as a result of the February 28 Incident at the age of 53, having born witness to some of the greatest fluctuations in Taiwanese history as well as the development of the arts in Taiwan.

Chen Cheng-po incorporated the avant-garde ideological trend of experimental art into his strong art school foundation in painting. Through his warm and sensitive eyes, and his enthusiastic and free-spirited brush, his paintings were composed of the landscapes of Taiwanese houses, streets, natural scenery, including the lively streets in Chiayi lined with traditional townhouses and wooden buildings, Chiayi Park with winding trails and canals, Jade Mountain, the parade and ceremonies of the City God, and sunsets over the Tamsui River. All of these Taiwanese landscapes were documented truthfully and beautifully in a large number of watercolor and oil paintings, allowing us to revisit the simple purity of an earlier era.

Nowadays, you will not only find audio guide services and installations comparing the paintings and the landscape sites where Chen Cheng-po painted decades ago, but also board games, books, and educational activities dedicated to his achievements, all of which are accessible and easy ways for foreign visitors to learn about this important Taiwanese artist and the olden days of Taiwan.

陳澄波，1895 年出生於嘉義，1924 年考入東京美術學校圖畫師範科，並於三年級時（1926 年）以描繪家鄉嘉義為主題的〈嘉義街外（一）〉，成為第一位入選帝國美術展覽會的台灣籍畫家。

歷經東京美術學校研究生及上海任教等過程，於 1933 年返台定居、次年組成「台陽美術協會」。1945 年二次大戰結束國民政府接收台灣，陳澄波積極宣導美術，並計畫籌建美術學校，1947 年受 228 事件牽連而罹難，得年 53 歲，是台灣本島動盪歷史與美術發展的見證。

陳澄波以其扎實學院派繪畫基礎結合實驗性前衛思潮，透過溫暖豐厚的雙眼、熱情揮灑的畫筆，融入水彩、油畫等各式技法，大量為當時台灣房屋街道與山川田園留下身影，包括多幅描繪傳統店屋與木造建築的熱鬧嘉義市街，有蜿蜒小徑與河道交錯的嘉義公園，玉山、城隍遶境祭典、淡水夕照等風景皆被完整封存記錄，絢爛多彩且充滿情感，至今仍能藉由數量龐大的藝術作品遙想過往台灣質樸年代。

現今於嘉義市多處有畫作與現今場景對照裝置及語音導覽系統，全台更有多樣化創意模式介紹陳澄波的故事，如：實境解謎、桌遊、青少年叢書等，不妨透過各種淺顯易懂的方式來趟陳澄波藝術之旅，共感時代記憶。

CHEN CHENG-PO CULTURAL FOUNDATION
陳澄波文化基金會

f facebook.com/chengpofoundation

台南
TAINAN
PROUD TO BE A TAINANESE

———— Huang Jung 黃蓉

Established in the 17th century, Tainan was the capital of Taiwan during the Qing Dynasty. Till this day, the city boasts rich ancient architecture, craftsmen who continue to practice arts and crafts that have been passed down for generations, and the largest number of temples of any city in Taiwan. Locals are still leading their lives in pace with the traditional customs and religious festivals. Some refer to Tainan as Taiwan's little Kyoto, however, as a local Taiwanese, I would say that Tainan is a city that is thoroughly and uniquely itself.

If you were to ask me to describe the quintessential Tainan experience, I would say it's having a bowl of beef noodle soup—a real Tainan staple—at four o'clock in the morning. Food is one of the main reasons Taiwanese and international tourists choose to visit Tainan. In recent years, long queues can be seen outside famous local restaurants and eateries on any given weekend and holiday, and everyone has their own private list of the best places to go for food.

With its almost anachronistic charm of nostalgia, Tainan has attracted tourists from Hong Kong, Macau, Japan, and Korea. There has also been an increasing number of local youths and outsiders who have decided to stay in Tainan. As a result, new cafés and boutiques are popping up all over this ancient city, starting from the Central and Western District and radiating outwards to the East District, Annan District, and Anping District. Come to Tainan, even if it means running the risk of canceling the remainder of your trip and staying for good.

17世紀初建城的古都台南，有著各式建築與古蹟、傳承幾十載的職人工藝，還有全台數量最多的宮廟，台南人也依循著神明的節日與習俗，緩慢、優雅地過日子。有人說台南是台灣的「小京都」，但在我心中台南有著獨樹一格的風情，許多台南人也以出身台南（相當）自豪。

如果問什麼最能感受到台南的個性與味道，那就在凌晨4點來一碗都不知道是消夜還是早餐的台南代表小吃「牛肉湯」吧。「食物」可說是國內外旅人造訪台南的最大原因，近年來每逢假日知名店家無不大排長龍，人人心中都有一張吃不完的美食清單，就像每位台南人也都有一份不外流的私房名單。

有著老派生活感魅力的台南，近幾年讓港澳日韓的觀光客趨之若鶩，吸引越來越多的在地青年與外地人於此定居，新型態的咖啡店、選物店也在巷弄間百花齊放，以「中西區」為起點，向外輻射至「東區」、「安南區」，甚至「安平區」，讓台南越來越有趣迷人。來台南吧，就算可能會舒服到取消後面的行程，或不小心就（永遠）留下來了。

TRANSPORTATION
交通

It takes about an hour and a half to arrive at Tainan's Jente Station from Taipei via the High Speed Rail. Another 20-25 minutes will get you from the station to downtown, where buses and YouBikes (which run on EasyCard) are available.

台北搭乘高鐵至台南仁德站約一個半小時，轉乘到市區約需 20 ～ 25 分鐘。市區移動可搭乘公車，或騎乘 YouBike（可使用悠遊卡）。

RECOMMENDATIONS
推薦

◤ READING LIST 旅遊書籍

LOVE TAINAN《LOVE 台南：在台灣的京都吃喝玩樂》
A lively illustrated guide to Tainan by a Japanese illustrator
日本插畫家以活潑的手繪插圖詳實呈現台南
⌐ books.com.tw/products/0010812073

WHEN TO VISIT TAINAN?《什麼時候去台南？一青妙的小城物語》
A fascinating look at Tainan through the perspective of an author of mixed Taiwanese and Japanese heritage
台日混血作者眼中的台南，驚奇有趣
⌐ books.com.tw/products/0010788230

DISCOVER THE FLOWERS IN TAINAN《花現台南：貓編的追花筆記》
Get to know Tainan through seasonal flora
從台南四季花期認識台南
⌐ books.com.tw/products/0010800057

《TAINAN BY DAY》
An English guide to Tainan based on daytime and nighttime activities
以日、夜為主題策畫的台南英文旅遊指南
⌐ e-book: goo.gl/4PhxaF

◤ LOCAL PUBLICATIONS 在地刊物

MADE IN TAINAN《美印台南》
A bimonthly magazine that offers information on Tainan's arts and cultural events and local affairs
深度介紹台南藝文與地方資訊的雙月刊
⌐ culture.tainan.gov.tw/form/index.php?m2=39&sid=91

TOU SOUTH WIND《透南風》
A magazine that offers in-depth stories on all things local, published intermittently
深入台南地方的人文誌，不定期發刊
⌐ FB：透南風工作室

◤ TRAVEL WEBSITES 旅遊網站

TRAVEL TAINAN 台南旅遊網
Tainan's official travel website with printable information sheets
台南旅遊官方網站，文宣摺頁區有許多資料可下載
⌐ twtainan.net | facebook.com/traveltainan

TAINAN YOYOYO 妳好南搞
A Tainan tourism information platform run by locals
由地方團隊經營的台南旅遊情報平台
⌐ sstainan.com | facebook.com/TainanYoYoYo

TRIP HOSPITAL 台南接古所
A guide to Tainan, curated by local youths (they also offer lodging)
在地青年經營的台南生活指南（也有民宿）
⌐ triphospital.com | facebook.com/triphospital

◤ GUIDED TOURS 導覽

OLD HOUSES, OLD SHOPS, AND OLD LIFESTYLES
「老屋，老店，老生活」散步路線
A bilingual guided walking tour organized by the Tainan Tourism Bureau
由台南市觀光旅遊局主辦的中英雙語導覽
⌐ Sign up for a tour 預約：twtainan.net/en/application

◤ ANNUAL EVENTS 年度活動

YUE JIN LANTERN FESTIVAL (SECOND MONTH OF THE LUNAR CALENDAR) 月津港燈節（農曆2月）
This annual lantern festival is held in Yanshui Township and invites artists to collaborate in the festivities
在鹽水舉辦的燈節，每年邀請國內外藝術家參與創作
⌐ facebook.com/yuejinlanternfestival

PUJI DIAN LANTERN FESTIVAL (SECOND MONTH OF THE LUNAR CALENDAR) 普濟殿燈會（農曆2月）
Held at Tainan's oldest Wangye Temple, it is famous for the beautiful tunnel, lit with hand-painted lanterns
台南最早王爺廟舉辦的元宵活動，手繪花燈隧道相當美麗
⌐ www.facebook.com/phochetian

Photo credit：國立臺灣文學館

Photo credit：Wang Yu Ching

A NATIONAL MUSEUM OF TAIWAN LITERATURE
國立臺灣文學館

Originally the Tainan Prefecture Hall during the Japanese colonial period

日治時期的臺南州廳，現今作為臺灣文學博物館

⌂ 台南市中西區中正路1號 | 09:00-18:00 (Closed on Mondays)
1, Zhongzheng Rd., West Central Dist., Tainan | +886-6-221-7201

B THE SPRING 河樂廣場

Designed by the architectural team MVRDV, the old shopping mall was transformed into a waterfront park inspired by the concept of an urban lagoon

由 MVRDV 操刀，以城市潟湖概念將舊商場改建成親水公園

⌂ 台南市中西區中正路343-20號
No. 343-20, Zhongzheng Road, Central-West District, Tainan City

C TAINAN ART MUSEUM 臺南市美術館

It hosts shows about Taiwanese and overseas artists, with an emphasis on southern Taiwanese masters

展出國內外藝術家作品，並以南台灣大師為核心焦點

⌂ 台南市中西區忠義路二段1號
No. 1, Sec. 2, Zhongyi Rd., West Central Dist., Tainan City
+886-6-221-8881 | 09:00-17:00, Sat. 09:00-21:00 (Closed on Mondays)

D QIAN QI ZHONG ZI GUAN 千畦種籽館

A fantastic museum that collects a wide variety of seeds; by appointment only

收藏各式種子的奇幻博物館，需電話預約

⌂ 台南市北區東豐路451巷29-1號
No. 29-1, Ln. 451, Dongfeng Rd., North Dist., Tainan City
+886-6-236-0035 | 10:00-17:00

E B.B. ART

A gallery and performance space housed in a revitalized building

老屋轉型重生的藝廊展演空間

⌂ 台南市中西區民權路二段48號
No. 48, Sec. 2, Minquan Rd., West Central Dist., Tainan City
+886-6-223-3538 | 10：30~18:00 (Closed on Mondays)

F CHUANMEI CINEMA 全美戲院

Where film director Ang Li's love for film originated, the cinema is also famous for their hand-illustrated movie posters

導演李安電影夢的起點，以手繪電影海報聞名海外

⌂ 台南市中西區永福路二段187號
No. 187, Sec. 2, Yongfu Rd., West Central Dist., Tainan City
+886-6-222-4726 | 12:30-23:00, weekends 10:30-23:00

A HAYASHI DEPARTMENT STORE 林百貨

Taiwan's first department store to be equipped with elevators, now sells creative and design merchandise

全台灣第一座有電梯的百貨公司，如今改賣創意與設計

⌐ 台南市中西區忠義路二段63號

No. 63, Sec. 2, Zhongyi Rd., West Central Dist., Tainan City

+886-6-221-3000 | 11:00-21:00

B DAY BREAK 18 TEAHOUSE 奉茶・十八卯

A Japanese tea house that is always hosting cultural events

文化活動舉辦熱絡的日式茶屋

⌐ 台南市中西區民權路二段30號

No. 30, Sec. 2, Minquan Rd., West Central Dist., Tainan City

+886-6-221-1218 | facebook.com/18Teahouse

10:00-18:00 (Closed on Mondays)

C BEAUCOUP

A minimalist select goods store with a small bookstore on the second floor

簡約風格選物店外加2樓小書店

⌐ 台南市中西區民生路一段205巷13號

No. 13, Ln. 205, Sec. 1, Minsheng Rd., West Central Dist., Tainan City

facebook.com/Beaucoup | 13:30-18:00 (Closed on Mondays)

D ERROR22 （鼴鼠）

A gallery café that is quite otherworldly

以為來到外太空的藝廊咖啡館

⌐ 台南市中西區開山路11號2樓

2F., No. 11, Kaishan Rd., West Central Dist., Tainan City

14:00-23:00, Fri.-Sat. 14:00-00:00

facebook.com/error22mole

E ASUKA ANTIQUES 鳥飛古物店

An antique store that will transport you directly into the past

令人不小心邊尋寶邊掉進舊時光的古物店

⌐ 台南市中西區忠義路二段158巷62號1樓-1

1F.-1, 62, Ln. 158, Sec. 2, Zhongyi Rd., West Central Dist., Tainan City

+886-6-221-1814 | IG : asukaantique

13:00-19:00 (Closed from Tue.-Thur.)

F ROOM A

A reading library that charges by the hour—prepare to be inspired

靈感迸發空間，計時收費的閱讀圖書館

⌐ 台南市中西區康樂街21號3樓 | +886-6-220-9797

3F., No. 21, Kangle St., West Central Dist., Tainan City

11:00-18:00 (Closed on Tuesdays)

A TEA MAGIC HAND 茶的魔手

Tainan boba tea shops with a higher density than convenience stores

在台南比便利商店還要密集的台茶手搖杯

⌂ 台南市中西區府前路二段42號 | 各店營業時間略有不同
No. 42, Sec. 2, Fuqian Rd., West Central Dist., Tainan City
09:00-22:00 (Opening hours vary from store to store.)

B BOG 波哥 (台南勝利店)

For Tainan's old-timers, the bubble milk tea was a must-drink when they go on a date as students

台南人吃的是學生時期約會回憶的珍奶

⌂ 台南市東區勝利路58號 | +886-6-274-4300
No. 58, Shengli Rd., East Dist., Tainan City
07:30-22:20

C SHUÀNSÊN BEVERAGES 双生綠豆沙牛奶

Creamy green bean smoothie mixed with local Hu-San milk is great to have on a hot day

濃郁的綠豆沙配上在地虎山鮮乳超級消暑

⌂ 台南市中西區民族路二段281號 | facebook.com/ShuansenBeverages
No. 281, Sec. 2, Minzu Rd., West Central Dist., Tainan City
11:00-18:00 (Closed on Mon. and Tue.)

D XUANFUJU MILK TEA 宣福居

A traditional tea shop selling black tea and black milk tea only

只賣紅茶和紅茶牛奶的濃厚系傳統茶鋪

⌂ 台南市中西區民生路二段125號
No. 125, Sec. 2, Minsheng Rd., West Central Dist., Tainan City
+886-6-225-6411 | 12:00-22:30 (Closed on Tuesdays)

E XIADA DAO HERB TEA 下大道青草茶

In hot summer days in Tainan, have some lotus root tea or Chinese herbal tea to cool yourself down

炎夏台南解熱來杯蓮藕茶或青草茶退火吧

⌂ 台南市中西區西門路一段775號
No. 775, Sec. 1, Ximen Rd., West Central Dist., Tainan City
+886-6-223-4260 | 08:00-23:00

F CHINGJI FRUIT ICE DESSERTS 清吉冰果室

Peach Yakult and milk mixed with various fruits are all tasty

來杯水蜜桃養樂多或者各種水果牛奶都好喝

⌂ 台南市中西區府前路一段294號
No. 294, Sec. 1, Fuqian Rd., West Central Dist., Tainan City
+886-6-227-1608 | 11:00-00:00 (Closed on Sundays)

Photo credit: 太陽牌冰品

A MEMORY 206 ALMOND JELLY ICE 懷舊小棧杏仁豆腐冰

Almond, matcha, and milk flavored tofu ice are all worth trying

杏仁、抹茶、鮮奶口味豆腐冰缺一不可

台南市中西區五妃街206號 | +886-6-215-8157
No. 206, Wufei St., West Central Dist., Tainan City
10:30-22:00

B SUN ICE 太陽牌冰品

Cube-shaped Caohu taro ice, so good that you can't eat just one

方塊狀的草湖芋仔冰一口接著一口吃

台南市中西區民權路一段41號
No. 41, Sec. 1, Minquan Rd., West Central Dist., Tainan City
10:00-21:20 | +886-6-225-9375

C NINAO 蜷尾家 甘味処。。。散步甜食

Diverse flavored ice sweets originated in Tainan. They even opened up branch stores abroad

口味多樣台南發跡遠征海外的冰品界驕傲

台南市中西區正興街92號 | www.ninaogroup.com
No. 92, Zhengxing St., West Central Dist., Tainan City
Mon.-Thur.11:00-18:00, Fri.-Sun.11:00-20:00

D LIAN DE TANG BAKERY 連得堂煎餅

Handmade miso cookies baked in the century-old style

百年手工古法製作的味噌煎餅

台南市北區崇安街54號
No. 54, Chong'an St., North Dist., Tainan City | +886-6-225-8429
Mon.-Fri. 08:00-20:00, Sat. 08:00-18:00, Sun. 08:00-15:00
每人限購兩包煎餅 (There is a limit of two packs per customer.)

E MERCI KITCHEN 木溪

Assorted flavored scones are their signature products

以各種風味英式司康作為本店主打

台南市北區自強街30號
No. 30, Ziqiang St., North Dist., Tainan City
13:00-18:00 (Closed on Thur.)
+886-6-221-9319

F MARSH 沼澤

One would be on cloud nine when having its delicious pudding in the green-toned space

綠色調的空間加上美味布丁意圖使人融化

台南市中西區西寧街28號2F
2F, No. 28, Xining St., West Central Dist., Tainan City
12:00-18:00 (Closed on Thur.) | facebook.com/marshhenri

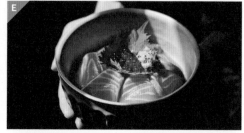

A YEH FAMILY GRILL 台南葉家燒烤

Eat and cheers with the Gods in front of the temple

在廟埕前和神明一起吃飯乾杯

台南市中西區開山路130-1號

No. 130-1, Kaishan Road, Central-West Dist., Tainan City

18:00-22:00 (Closed on Mon. and Tue.)

+886-6-227-3060

B MIN SHENG YI-MEIN 民生路無名意麵

Traditional yi-mein (noodle) flavored with lard and served with braised foods

台式豬油意麵加上滷味非常登對

台南市中西區民生路二段112號

No. 112, Sec. 2, Minsheng Rd., West Central Dist., Tainan City

15:30-01:30 (Closed on Wednesdays)

C YEH CHIA NERITIC SQUID NOODLES 葉家小卷米粉

Squid noodles in a broth that is so fresh and rich you'll want seconds

湯頭鮮甜指數破表的小卷米粉

台南市中西區國華街二段142號 | +886-6-222-6142

No. 142, Sec. 2, Guohua St., West Central Dist., Tainan City

08:30-16:00, weekends 08:30-14:00 (Closed on Mondays)

D AI TZU CHENG SHRIMP RICE 矮仔城蝦仁飯

Experts say to order a half-cooked duck egg to go with your shrimp rice

炭火香的蝦仁飯要加點半熟鴨蛋才是內行

台南市中西區海安路一段66號

No. 66, Sec. 1, Hai'an Rd., West Central Dist., Tainan City

+886-6-220-1897 | 08:30-19:30 (Closed on Tuesdays)

E ZYUU TSUBO 十平

A Japanese rice bowl restaurant in a small space with big flavors

店鋪雖小日式蓋飯俱全的美味料理

台南市中西區忠義路二段158巷22號

No. 22, Ln. 158, Sec. 2, Zhongyi Rd., West Central Dist., Tainan City

facebook.com/zyuutsubo | 11:30-14:00,17:30-20:00

F YI LING WU 串工房 一鈴屋

A secluded but excellent Yakitori restaurant

隱藏在神祕大門裡的日本職人串燒

台南市中西區赤崁東街43號

No. 43, Chikan E. St., West Central Dist., Tainan City

+886-6-221-6226 | 18:00-01:00 (Closed on Wed. and Sun.)

Photo credit : MOONROCK

Caoji Book Inn

A BAR HOME

Be transported back to the olden days in this traditional courtyard bar

在傳統宅院裡品嚐黃金年代的醉意

⌐ 台南市中西區中山路23巷1號 | +886-6-223-2869
No. 1, Ln. 23, Zhongshan Rd., West Central Dist., Tainan City
19:00-01:00

B HĒRÁ

A sophisticated bar with a grayscale aesthetic, serving coffee during the day and cocktails in the evening

灰白色氣質酒吧，日間主打咖啡，夜間享用調酒

⌐ 台南市中西區民族路二段260號2F | +886-06-223-2421
2F, No. 260, Sec. 2, Minzu Rd., Central-West Dist., Tainan City
11:00-01:00, Fri. and Sat. 11:00-02:00 (Closed on Wednesdays)

C MOONROCK

Sip exceptional cocktails at this top-ranked bar in Asia (2022), and be transported to a moonlit paradise

2022年亞洲50大酒吧，跟著口味鮮明的調酒，上月球吧

⌐ 台南市北區成功路22巷42弄13號 | +886-6-222-9528
No. 13, Aly. 42, Ln. 22, Chenggong Rd., North Dist., Tainan City.
20:00-02:00 (Closed on Sundays)

D TAINAN OLD HOUSE INN 台南謝宅

Experience the incomparable elegance of an old home

沒有人能夠抵擋住在台南老房子的優雅

⌐ +886-922-852-280
facebook.com/TainanOldHouseInn
oldhouseinn2008@gmail.com

E U.I.J HOTEL & HOSTEL 友愛街旅館

A hotel with a 24-hour reading room as well as a spacious garden

設有24小時書房與寬敞花園平台的質感住所

⌐ 台南市中西區友愛街115巷5號
No. 5, Ln. 115, You'ai St., West Central Dist., Tainan City
+886-6-221-8188 | uijservice@uij.com.tw

F BOOK INN 艸祭

A bookshelf next to your bed will help you sleep soundly

床鋪旁就是書櫃令人睡得特別香

⌐ 台南市中西區南門路71號
No. 71, Nanmen Rd., West Central Dist., Tainan City
facebook.com/caojiBookinn
+886-6-222-2909

XIMEN ROUNDABOUT
AND MINZU ROAD AREA

西門圓環與民族路周邊

OLD-SCHOOL LIVING INFUSED WITH NEW VITALITY 老派生活與台南新意

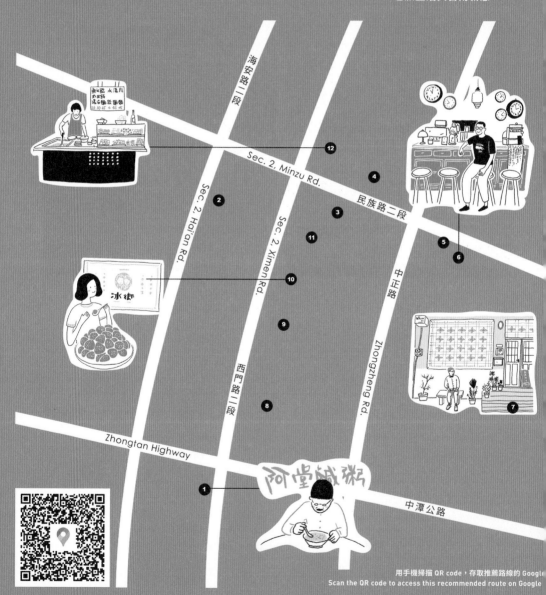

海安路二段

Sec. 2, Minzu Rd.

民族路二段

Sec. 2, Hai'an Rd.

Sec. 2, Ximen Rd.

中正路

Zhongzheng Rd.

西門路二段

Zhongtan Highway

中潭公路

12
4
2
3
11
5
6
10
9
7
8
1

用手機掃描 QR code，存取推薦路線的 Google
Scan the QR code to access this recommended route on Google

1)	09:00	Have milkfish congee for breakfast (observe as locals demonstrate how to get rid of all the tiny fish bones)
2)	10:00	Check out Shuixian Temple Market
3)	11:00	Visit the God of War Temple and the Grand Mazu Temple
4)	12:00	Emjoy Japanese or Italian cuisine on Xinmei Street
5)	13:30	Gift shopping for tea, herbal remedies, and pastries
6)	14:30	Time for some coffee to help with digestion
7)	16:00	Explore Japanese antiques and tableware
8)	17:00	Shop at a Tainan-style boutique
9)	18:30	Head over to the temple square for BBQ and satay hot pot
10)	20:00	Try fruit and shaved ice for dessert at Ice Country
11)	21:00	Go to Bar TCRC and Pista Alcohol
12)	23:00	Still up for midnight snack? Explore Minsheng Road and Hai'an Road

1)	09:00	早餐來碗虱目魚粥，領略台南人的挑刺（挑剔）功夫
2)	10:00	再戰早市「水仙宮市場」
3)	11:00	到「祀典武廟」和「大天后宮」拜拜
4)	12:00	在「新美街」享用日式或義式美食
5)	13:30	吃不完帶著走：買茶、買藥、買糕點！
6)	14:30	是時候需要喝杯咖啡消化消化了
7)	16:00	尋找日式老件和可愛餐具
8)	17:00	逛逛台南風格的選品店
9)	18:30	轉往廟埕廣場附近吃炭烤或沙茶火鍋
10)	20:00	到「冰鄉」品嚐台南式的水果冰
11)	21:00	去「Bar TCRC」或「畢氏酒精」喝杯酒吧
12)	23:00	還想吃消夜？請前往「民生路」或「海安路」

09:00
A-TANG, A-XING AND A-HAN
1. 阿堂、阿星 或 阿憨鹹粥

Tainan is known as the home of the milkfish. The locals utilise various parts of the fish—including its head, stomach, and intestines—and turn them into must-try delicacies. If you are not particularly adept at picking out little fish bones, you're in luck because most restaurants pick out the majority for you. A-Tang, A-Xing, and A-Han are three locally famous milkfish congee restaurants that each have their loyal supporters; you can't go wrong with any of these choices.

台南以虱目魚的故鄉為名,魚頭、魚肚、魚腸皆可單飛各成一道料理。在台南吃虱目魚的懶人特別有福,因為多半魚刺已被店家挑除。知名店家如「阿堂鹹粥」、「阿星鹹粥」或「阿憨鹹粥」各有其擁護者,無論哪家都新鮮美味!

10:00
SHUIXIAN AND YONGLE MARKET
2. 水仙宮市場 與 永樂市場

There's no better place to authentically experience the life of Tainanese locals than at the Shuixian Market, a morning market that has served the local population for over three centuries. Kick off your morning feast at Noodle King's Seafood Noodles and Rice Cakes, then head over to Yongle Market for Jin De Spring Rolls, Fu Sheng Rice Cake, and A-Song Gua Bao—just don't forget to bring your appetite!

要體驗台南常民生活與無敵小吃,就先來一趟有著三百多年歷史的早市「水仙宮市場」吧!先吃「麵條王海產麵」和「粽葉米糕」墊墊胃,再轉往一旁的「永樂市場」吃「金得春捲」、「富盛號碗粿」和「阿松割包」等小吃,在這裡只會恨自己胃不夠大啊!

11:00
GRAND MAZU TEMPLE
AND
GOD OF WAR TEMPLE
3. 大天后宮 與 祀典武廟

Both the Grand Mazu Temple, which was the very first Mazu temple to be built in Taiwan, and its neighboring temple, the God of War Temple, have attracted constant streams of pious believers for decades. It is rumored that the Yue Lao (Matchmaker God) enshrined in the Grand Mazu Temple can help bring to fruition ambiguous relationships. The Yue Lao in the God of War Temple specializes in fixing unrequited love, so write to him if you need his help.

台灣第一座官建媽祖廟「大天后宮」和一旁被稱為「大關帝廟」的「祀典武廟」香客絡繹不絕,但更多遊客來此是向月老祈求感情順利。據傳天后宮的月老能加速曖昧中的雙方修成正果;武廟內的月老則專治單相思,還可以寫信給月老請祂多幫忙!

12:00
XINMEI STREET
4. 百年米街「新美街」

The century-old Xinmei Street was once known as the bustling rice street. After the rice vendors became dispersed throughout the city, Xinmei Street was left desolate until a recent revitalization project. For lunch, try tsukemen restaurant Nani Noodles, or Qing Ting Japanese Family-style Restaurant, or Takoyaki Shao for delicious takoyaki, and then head to Yusaku Chaya for a refreshing matcha drink.

這條一度落寞的老街近幾年因為年輕人進駐重新活絡了起來，午餐就到主打日式沾麵的「Nani 麵」、日式家庭料理館「蜻亭お食事どころ」或章魚燒專門店「蛸屋本舖」，吃飽還可以去「宇作茶屋」喝杯抹茶納涼，這些店家讓新美街充滿了活潑濃烈的日式風情！

13:30
CHIHKAN TOWER AND THE OLD SHOPS
5. 赤崁樓 與 老店們

Visit the historical Chihkan Tower (built in the 17th century during the Dutch Formosa Era)and its neighboring shops that have been around for over a century. Check out Long Xing Ya Lead Shop for plant watering cans, Yi Fong Winter Melon Tea for tea bricks, Wu Wan Chun Incense for exquisitely reformulated traditional incense, Bo Ren Chinese Medicine for herbal medicinal packs, and Jiu Lai Fa Pastry for Taiwanese pastries.

吃飽到荷治時期興建的「赤崁樓」走走，記得到附近的老店採買伴手禮，像是「隆興亞鉛行」的澆花器、「義豐冬瓜茶」的茶磚、「吳萬春香舖」改良研發的精緻線香、「博仁堂中藥舖」的藥膳包和「舊來發餅舖」的各種傳統糕點。。

14:30
REST YOUR FEET
AND
GET SOME COFFEE
6. 來杯咖啡歇腳吧

In recent years, Tainan has really upped its café game; you have numerous options to choose from for a coffee break. I highly recommend the heavily Japanese-influenced Paripari apt., café/b&b Maison the Core, SWALLOW TAINAN and Gan Dan Coffee, which is right next to Kai Long Temple.

台南的咖啡店也是一間比一間厲害，這一帶推薦瀰漫濃濃厚昭和感的「Paripari apt.」、有著美麗天井的「鬼咖啡」、兼營旅宿的「果核抵家」、下午賣咖啡晚上變身酒吧的「嗍·台南」，以及開隆宮旁的「甘單咖啡」。

16:00
TREASURE HUNTING
7. 到選物店尋寶

After your coffee break, head over to Asuka Antiques. The owner visits Japan on a regularly basis to curate and collect furniture and antiques from the Taisho and Showa eras. Stroll over to Deer House and check out their fairly priced and exquisitely designed pieces of tableware.

休息完前往「鳥飛古物店」尋寶，老闆定期前往日本，收藏大量大正、昭和等年代的物件，舉凡擺飾、沙發、櫥櫃等家居用品應有盡有。接著走點路到「餐桌上的鹿早」採購價格公道又可愛的各式餐具，餐具控要小心在此失心瘋。

17:00
LOCAL BOUTIQUES
8. 台南風格選品店

Tainan's preserved traditional culture and rustic charm have fostered the vibrant growth of vintage clothing stores. In the Central-West District, there are numerous vintage shops, such as Xinzhuangli Buyhopehon where you are welcome to embark on a treasure-hunting journey. Also check out Beaucoup, a select good shop so committed to Minimalism that they only carry one book a season—a place like this truly could only exist in Tainan.

台南保存傳統文化的質樸性格，也助長了懷舊古著店的蓬勃發展。中西區一代有許多的古著店，例如「新裝裏百貨行」，歡迎大家前往挖寶。而崇尚減法生活，連選書都只有一季一冊的選品店「Beaucoup」，也很像是台南才能孕育出來的店家。

18:30
A SUBSTANTIAL DINNER
9. 豪氣晚餐

Have dinner at the temple plaza and experience how locals do dinner. In the scorching summer, I would recommend trying Yeh Family Grill. Sit at the large red table and indulge in fresh Taiwanese-style stir-fried dishes, perfectly paired with a refreshing beer. In the winter, I would recommend going to How Chou Satay Hot Pot for their unique broth and fresh, never-frozen beef.

來廟埕前面晚餐，體會台南式的澎湃萬千。炎炎夏日推薦「台南葉家燒烤」，坐在馬公廟前的大紅桌，吃著新鮮的台式熱炒配啤酒才對味。冬天則推薦隱身廟宇旁的「小豪洲沙茶爐」，新鮮的溫體牛豪氣下鍋，是台南才有的霸氣。

20:00
OLD-SCHOOL ICE AND FRUIT JUICE SHOP
10. 老派冰果室

Ice and fruit juice shops are old-school hangout spots that are still popular. Lily Fruit, Tai Cheng Fruit Store, and Yu Cheng Fruit Store are all long-standing local favorites, each with their team of loyal customers. My personal favorite is Ice Country, a shaved ice and fruit dessert place that offers generous portions of seasonal fruits (get strawberry in the winter and mango in the summer).

在過往曾是年輕人約會好去處的冰果室,今日仍深受歡迎,其中老牌的「莉莉冰果室」、「泰成冰果室」、「裕成冰果室」各有擁護者,我最愛的則是季節感鮮明的「冰鄉」,老闆用料大方,總將水果鋪成一座小山,冬天來首選草莓冰,夏天當然要點芒果冰!

21:00
POSH BARS
11. 時髦酒吧

Tainan has no shortage of posh bars. I recommend the highly popular Bar TCRC. Listed as one of the top 50 bars in Asia in 2016, Bar TCRC is always packed, so get there early if you want a seat. I also recommend Pista Alcohol, a bar where you can eat ice cream and enjoy craft beer at the same time.

台南近來出現了許多時髦酒吧,總是一位難求的「Bar TCRC」以及結合酒精冰淇淋與精釀啤酒的「畢氏酒精」,都是值得前往的有趣店家。其中 Bar TCRC 曾在 2016 年獲選為亞洲 50 大酒吧,不想錯過的話記得提早去排隊等候嚕!

23:00
MINSHENG ROAD OR HAI'AN ROAD
12. 民生路 或 海安路

Noticed that Tainan has fewer 24/7 convenience stores than other Taiwanese cities? That's because countless eateries stay open until the wee hours. Can't sleep? Head over to Min Sheng Yi-Mein for a delicious plate of assorted braised foods. For a true Tainan experience, take a midnight stroll along Hai'an Road and enjoy some roadside BBQ, skewers, or braised delicacies. It's the perfect way to savor the charm of Tainan's vibrant nightlife!

有發現台南市區的便利商店相比其他地方少了一些嗎,因為開到凌晨的小吃處處皆是!晚上睡不著可以到「民生路無名意麵」點盤滷味。夜裡還可沿著海安路一帶漫步,隨意在路邊吃點炭烤、串燒或滷味,感受台南夜晚的風情!

TAINAN CONFUCIAN TEMPLE AND SUBURBS

孔廟周邊與台南近郊

HISTORY, FOOD, AND NATURE　歷史、美食和自然通通有

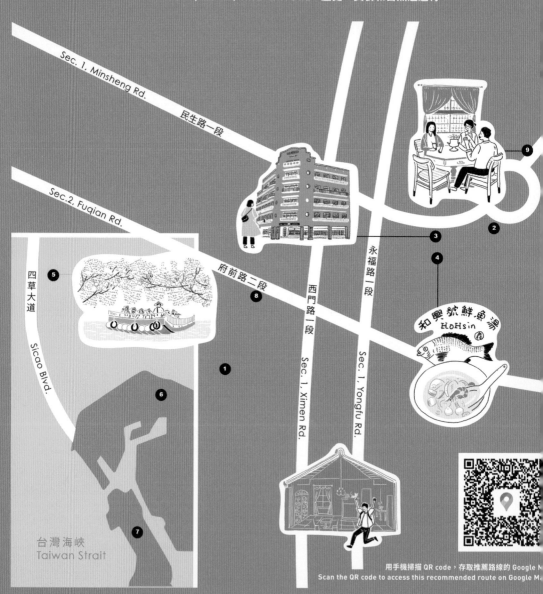

Sec. 1, Minsheng Rd.
民生路一段

Sec.2, Fuqian Rd.

四草大道

Sicao Blvd.

府前路二段

西門路一段

永福路一段

Sec. 1, Ximen Rd.

Sec. 1, Yongfu Rd.

和興號鮮魚湯
HoHsin

台灣海峽
Taiwan Strait

用手機掃描 QR code，存取推薦路線的 Google M
Scan the QR code to access this recommended route on Google M

1)	06:00	Early birds get beef soup for breakfast
2)	09:00	Experience old and new Tainan at the same time
3)	11:00	Shop at the legendary Hayashi Department Store and traditional canvas stores
4)	12:00	Have lunch, standing-style, around the Confucian Temple
5)	14:00	Explore the gorgeous Sicao Wetland
6)	16:00	Get to know the historical Anping County
7)	17:30	Capture a stunning sunset at the beach on Yuguang Island
8)	19:30	Arrive at Bao'an Street, a mecca for food
9)	21:30	Time for a night cap

1)	06:00	早起的人兒吃牛肉湯
2)	09:00	在台南新舊文化地標感受府城氣質
3)	11:00	逛傳奇的「林百貨」與傳統帆布行
4)	12:00	孔廟商圈尋覓中餐，一站式吃到底
5)	14:00	出發嘍，四草生態之旅
6)	16:00	認識荷蘭時期的安平
7)	17:30	漁光島落日攝影就定位，沙灘走走吹海風
8)	19:30	終於來到，傳說中的美食聖地「保安街」
9)	21:30	府城買醉生活起跑

06:00
SIX THOUSAND BEEF SOUP
1. 六千牛肉湯

Legend has it that if you want Six Thousand Beef Soup, you'll have to get up at four a.m. to get it...but it's totally worth it! However, if that's a bit too extreme for you, A-Cun Beef Soup on Bao'an Road also comes highly recommended. If you fancy yourself a beef soup connoisseur, check out this Facebook page: beefsouptn.

「六千牛肉湯」是傳說凌晨４點即必須開始排隊的名店，是否有幸吃到得看個人造化。但也非得單戀一枝花（一隻牛），鄰近的保安路「阿村牛肉湯」也頗受好評。對於牛肉湯有興趣深究的朋友，可到臉書專頁「我要征服台南牛肉湯！！！」看看。(facebook.com/beefsouptn)

09:00
TAINAN ART MUSEUM
2. 臺南市立美術館

The newly inaugurated Tainan Art Museum (facebook.com/TainanArtMuseum) was designed by the Pritzker Architecture Prize-winning Japanese architect Shigeru Ban and Taiwanese architect Joe Shih. Building 1 of the museum was formerly the Tainan Police Department while building 2 is a unique pentagon inspired by the royal poinciana (also known as the phoenix flower). The neighboring National Museum of Taiwan Literature (facebook.com/NmtlTainan) was formerly the Tainan prefecture hall during the Japanese colonial period. Both museums will offer a glimpse into the rich history of Tainan and give you a view of exciting modern developments.

2019 年甫開放的「臺南市立美術館」(facebook.com/TainanArtMuseum) 由普立茲克獎得主日本建築師坂茂與台灣建築師石昭永設計，一館原為臺南警察署，二館以市花「鳳凰花」為概念設計成五角形的特殊建築；鄰近的「國立臺灣文學館」原為日治時期的臺南州廳，兩者無論是建築本體與館藏都相當精彩。(facebook.com/NmtlTainan)

11:00
HAYASHI DEPARTMENT STORE
3. 林百貨

Shop at the historical Hayashi Department Store—the first department store to be built in the south of Taiwan—as well as awesome local select goods shops. In the old city of Tainan, you can find craftsmen practicing traditional crafts that are part of their heritage, such as the art of creating canvas bags. Head over to the famous He Cheng Canvas Store and Yung Sheng Canvas Store to shop around for a sturdy and gorgeous canvas bag.

到南台灣第一間百貨公司「林百貨」感受日式建築與風情，逛逛精選的在地好物。古城台南也傳承了許多職人工藝，手工帆布包便是其中之一，接著就到遠近馳名的「合成帆布行」與「永盛帆布行」，為自己添購一個耐看耐用的布包。

12:00
LUNCH AROUND THE CONFUCIAN TEMPLE

4. 孔廟周邊美食

Traditional Taiwanese lunch options abound in the area around the Tainan Confucian Temple—Klin Tai Bao, Fu's Ba-wan, Huang's Rice Cake, Yong's Milkfish Ball, and Shan Ji Fresh Fish Soup are all long-standing local favorites that you should try. After you've eaten your fill, take a post-lunch walk in the Confucian Temple and enjoy the awe-inspiring architectural detail.

午餐來到全台首學「臺南孔廟」覓食,周邊的「克林台包」、「福記肉圓」、「黃家碗粿」、「永記虱目魚丸」和「山記魚仔店」都是台式古早味,全部吃完一輪後再轉進孔廟散步消化,欣賞明清時期的建築。

14:00
SICAO GREEN TUNNEL

5. 四草綠色隧道

Make your way to Sicao Dazhong Temple by bike or car and catch a 2:30 p.m. tour boat that takes you down the Sicao Green Tunnel, also known as Taiwan's own modest version of the Amazon River. The green tunnel is a river that boasts the largest variety of mangrove tree species. Along the river you will also see historical remnants of the Dutch Ocean Castle and internal tariff bureau. Get your camera ready because the staff of the boat are known to make stops at all the best places for pictures. Another more modern sight to behold is the Taijian National Park tourist center, a scaffolded white building built above the river. The boat fare is NTD 200 per person (4grass.com).

吃飽喝足騎車或搭車前往「四草大眾廟」,買票等待下午兩點半的固定船班,準備搭著竹筏穿越號稱是台灣版的亞馬遜河(稍嫌誇大)的「四草綠色隧道」。這裡的紅樹林種類數量為全台之冠,沿岸也可見荷蘭海堡和鯤金局等歷史遺跡,貼心的工作人員還會在拍照最漂亮的河段停下來讓大家拍個夠。另外周邊的「台江國家公園遊客中心」,以蓋在水面上的白色水上高腳屋建築聞名,若有時間也可停留造訪。綠色隧道船票:新台幣 200 元 (4grass.com)

16:00
A QUICK TOUR OF ANPING

6. 快閃安平

If you have time to spare, I would highly recommend scheduling a good half day to explore the Anping area. Start from the Anping Old Fort (formerly known as Fort Zeelandia), built during the Dutch colonial era in the 17th century. Make your way to the beautifully preserved Former Tait & Co. Merchant House, which was founded during the Qing Dynasty when Anping harbor became one of the first Taiwanese harbors to be opened to international trade. Over the years, the warehouse of the former merchant house has been overtaken by banyan trees and is now known as the Anping Tree House.

其實時間若充足, 更為悠閒緩慢的安平值得安排半日遊。探訪台南最早開發的安平地帶, 不妨先從 17 世紀遊荷蘭人建置的堡壘「安平古堡」(舊名熱蘭遮城)開始逛起。接著前往保存完善的「英商德記洋行」, 安平在清領時期開港, 吸引各國洋商來此建立商行。德記洋行的倉庫如今也成為觀光熱門景點「安平樹屋」, 建築與榕樹交融共生的特殊景觀為其特色。

17:30
RELAX
ON
YUGUANG ISLAND

7. 漁光島放風放空

Yuguang Island, about 15 minutes away from Anping by bike, offers a smooth beach from where you can admire a stunning Tainan sunset. Sunset-chasers will start appearing at dusk, so get here early and secure a good spot. If you're lucky, you will be here for one of the rare fiery red sunsets.

從安平騎車約 15 分鐘即可抵達舊稱三鯤鯓的「漁光島」海邊, 有著能光腳踩踏的細沙和美麗的日落, 坐擁漁光島的台南市民真是令人羨慕啊! 每到傍晚時分, 追逐夕陽人潮漸漸湧現, 運氣好的話可在此觀賞火燒雲的特殊景象。經過今日白天充實的行程, 就讓我們在此和台南的太陽好好說聲再見。

19:30
BAO'AN STREET
8. 保安街

Bao'an Street is the perfect place to sample a wide variety of local dinner staples. A-Ming's Pig Heart Vermicelli is one of the most popular options—you have to order their pork knuckle dish. Go to A-Feng Milkfish Soup for soup with generous chunks of fresh milkfish and A-Long Sausage and Cured Meat for their assorted plate—which includes sausage, pork intestine, sticky rice sausage, shrimp rolls, and crab balls—paired with sweet soy paste and wasabi. Afterwards, sit on a bench and sip on one of my personal favorite drinks from is A-Qing Almond Tea and watch the foodies eat their way through Bao'an Street. If you're a little too stuffed, walk it off in Blueprint Culture and Creative Park.

晚餐在保安街一路吃到底，「阿明豬心冬粉」為排隊首選，豬腳必點。接著到「阿鳳浮水虱目魚羹」，品嚐有整塊虱目魚的甘甜魚湯，再到「阿龍香腸熟肉」吃俗稱「黑白切」的各式小菜，香腸、粉腸、糯米腸、蝦捲和蟳丸應有盡有，配上甜甜的醬油膏和哇沙米，非常合嗜甜的台南人口味。我個人最愛「阿卿杏仁茶」（冰），坐在門外的小板凳上，看著追逐美食的吃貨，穿越其中，怪有情調。如果不小心吃得太撐，可以到鄰近的「藍晒圖文創園區」散散步。

21:30
COCKTAILS OR SNACKS
9. 調酒 或 消夜

There's been a recent influx of bars in Tainan and many are located in difficult-to-find spots— you may need to rely on Google Maps and a bit of luck to locate them. Bar Home is located in a spacious courtyard, they offer refreshingly unique cocktails that incorporate seasonal and local fruits such as hibiscus and pineapple. I also highly recommend Bistro in the Back, a secluded bar that offers a wide variety of delicious cocktails. If you're still up for a snack, I suggest trying out Yi Ling Wu, a Yakitori restaurant owned by a Japanese Yakitori chef; their chicken sashimi is to die for.

近年來台南酒吧一家家開，多數藏在很難找到的位置，必須靠 Google Maps 和一點運氣才能入內，「Bar Home」為「TCRC」調酒師新開的大宅院，同樣熱門，許多調酒皆選用在地當季的新鮮水果，像是洛神花、鳳梨等，讓人驚喜。酒吧也推薦「後面還有小酒館」，美味的調酒讓人期待後面還有沒有。消夜則有日本師傅開立的串燒店「串工房 - 一鈴屋」，其「生雞片」堪稱一絕。

沒有變胖的決心不要來台南！
If you're determined not to gain weight, don't visit Tainan!

如果要把小吃記錄成冊，台南一定是部百科全書。台南的小吃種類多元，口味多數偏甜，常讓人分不清究竟在吃正餐還是甜點，但也令許多旅客回家後念念不忘，成為下次要再回訪台南的最大誘因。以下介紹10樣道地的台南小吃：

If you want to write a book about street foods, Tainan could fill an encyclopedia. There are an abundance of street foods available in Tainan, most of which are on the sweet side, and many blurring the line between snack and meal. What we can be sure of is that the street foods of Tainan are remembered fondly by a great number of travelers to the area, and provide strong enticement to return again in the future. What follows is an introduction to ten authentic Tainan street foods:

Sheng's Pork Cartilage Over Rice
聖記軟骨飯

⌐ 台南市中西區民生路二段110號
No.110, Sec. 2, Minsheng Rd.,
W.Central Dist., Tainan City
11:00–21:00 (Closed on Sun.)
+886-6-226-7379

Melt-in-your-mouth braised pork cartilage with delicious bamboo shoot goes very well with a bowl of rice. Don't miss their signature cold-dressed pork liver.

軟骨富含膠質，滷得相當軟嫩可入口即化。再配上附的筍絲，非常下飯可口。店內的涼拌豬肝也是主打，也推薦一定要點。

Shijingjiu Rice in Mushroom Soup
石精臼香菇飯湯

⌐ 台南市中西區國華街三段182號
No. 182, Sec. 3, Guohua St.,
West Central Dist., Tainan City
07:00-19:00
+886-6-223-5679

A generous and extraordinar bowl of rice with rich umam flavor containing local velve shrimp, shiitake mushroom fror Puli Township, braised pork, an bamboo shoot.

台南本地的火燒蝦，搭配埔里
香菇與滷肉條、竹筍，香菇飯湯
的湯頭鮮美甘甜，是一碗用料大
方、不平凡的湯泡飯。

Zhipinji Angelica Duck
至品記肉燥麵當歸鴨

⌐ 台南市中西區民生路一段152號
No. 152, Sec. 1, Minsheng Rd.,
West Central Dist., Tainan City
11:00-15:00, 17:00-20:30
(Closed on Saturdays)

Angelica duck is a popular winte dish in Taiwan. Although it's har to experience low temperature during wintertime in Tainan Songzhuhao's generous portion of angelica duck in rich medicina broth are worth trying. Their por knuckle, duck intestine, and pi blood tofu are also tasty.

雖然台南很難感覺到真正的冬
天，但松竹號的當歸鴨值得令人
流汗。濃郁的藥膳湯頭，配上用
料大方的鴨肉，豬腳、鴨腸、米
血也相當美味。

A-He Stewed Pork Over Rice
阿和肉燥飯

⌐ 台南市中西區府前路一段12號
No. 12, Sec. 1, Fuqian Rd., West
Central Dist., Tainan City
06:00-15:00 (Closed on Wen.)
+886-6-220-2619

A-He's stewed pork over rice i prepared using fatty minced pork but never tastes overly greasy The fish skin soup can be orderec with cooked or raw skin, and mus be paired with doubanjiang, the broad bean chili sauce beloved b Tainan locals.

肉燥飯使用新鮮肥美的豬碎肉
但卻不感油膩順口。魚皮湯可任
選生魚皮和熟魚皮，必要搭配台
南人最愛的豆瓣醬。

Guo's Zongzi
郭家粽

Offering over 70 years of great taste, Guo's zongzi contain peanut and are wrapped in bamboo or shell ginger leaves, generously topped with cilantro and thick soy sauce, and a bowl of miso soup.

糯米加土豆,淋上滿滿的香菜與油膏,郭家粽的好味道已延續超過 70 年。菜粽還可分桃葉或竹葉包裝,再搭配味噌湯,非常講究。

台南市中西區友愛街117號
7, You'ai St., West
al Dist., Tainan City
-15:00 (Closed on Mon.
ue.)
6-221-3516

A-po's Noodles in Thick Soup
阿婆魯麵

Offering relatives and friends noodles in thick soup on wedding day is a tradition unique to Tainan. Ingredients in A-po's thick soup include carrots, daikon, wood ear, napa cabbage, and chunks of pork leg battered in milkfish paste, offering great incentive for everyone to get married.

在結婚當天招待親友吃魯麵,是台南才有的禮俗。羹湯有紅白蘿蔔、木耳、白菜,搭配虱目魚漿裹上的豬後腿肉羹,讓人想趕快求婚(或被求婚)。

台南市中西區國華街三段51-2號
51-2, Sec. 3, Guohua St.,
st Central Dist., Tainan City
00-16:00 (Closed on Tue.)
6-6-220-4090

A-Jiang Stir-Fried Asian Swamp Eel
阿江炒鱔魚

Asian swamp eel and yi-mein in thick sweet-and-sour soup offers a smooth texture. Or try the aromatic quick-fried version, a dish both savory and sweet which makes a good choice to experience the crunchy texture of Asian swamp eel.

鱔魚搭配意麵,融入在酸甜的湯頭中,雖然勾芡但相當順口。生炒鱔魚則鹹香甜三味皆有,歡迎體會鱔魚的爽脆口感。

南市中西區民族路三段89號
9, Sec. 3, Minzu Rd., West
al Dist., Tainan City
-00:00 (Closed on Mon.)
-937-671-052

Xia's Shantou Fish Noodles
夏家汕頭魚麵

Al dente noodles made of bombay duck. Topped with celery and seaweed, and paired with soup containing fish balls and dumplings, this meal exhibits the pinnacle of mouth-watering flavors from the ocean.

魚麵的原料是狗母魚,由魚漿製成的麵口感 Q 彈滑順,沒有魚的腥味。拌上芹菜和紫菜,以及搭配魚丸、魚餃、魚冊的綜合湯,是最正點的海味。

台南市中西區民生路一段158號
No. 158, Sec. 1, Minsheng Rd.,
West Central Dist., Tainan City
11:30-17:00, 11:30 15:00 on Sat.
(Closed on Sun.)
+886-6-221-5997

Lu's Narrow-Barred Spanish Mackerel Thick Soup
呂記土魠魚羹

This meaty narrow-barred Spanish mackerel, harvested in fall and winter, is battered and deep-fried and then added to a thick, sweet soup paired with a choice of rice noodles or alkaline noodles. Are you drooling yet?

土魠魚秋冬季盛產,魚肉扎實,裹粉後炸得酥香,再放進勾芡甜甜的湯頭,可自選米粉或是油麵,看到這裡還沒流口水嗎?

台南市中西區郡西路47號
No. 47, Junxi Rd., West Central
Dist., Tainan City
06:00-13:00
+886-6-224-5582

Young-Le BBQ Pork Rice
永樂燒肉飯

Aromatic barbecue pork fillet grilled over old-fashioned charcoal paired with Taiwanese-style salad and miso soup make for a satisfying meal.

以傳統木炭炭烤,使里肌肉肉具有炭燒香氣。搭配台式十足的生菜沙拉與味噌湯,足以飽餐一頓,口齒留香。

台南市中西區民族路三段16號
16, Sec. 3, Minzu Rd., West
Central Dist., Tainan City
10:00-21:00 (Closed on Wed.)
+886-6-228-1516

PROUD TAINANESE

台南人跩什麼？

SPECIAL FEATURE
TAINAN
台南特輯
SPECIAL FEATURE

When people from around the world visit Tainan, they all have the same question in mind: "What on Earth are the Tainan people so cocky about?" Beef soup shops that open before daybreak and close for the day rather than cover their shortfall, and stores that are more often closed than open are some unique challenges that travelers encounter when visiting Tainan, making travelers wonder: "What kind of cocky blood flows through the veins of the people of Tainan?" We were honored to be able to interview the owner of Asuka Antique (p.181, E), Pipi Yeh, and the principal manager of Nuo Fu Rice Pudding, Liu Yu-Qiao. After all, they were born and raised in Tainan, and give their all every day in their given professions, so who better to represent the new generation of Tainan business owners and to sit down and explain everything to us.

Can you describe the people of Tainan in a single sentence?

Pipi Ye (hereafter referred to as Pipi): Eat well, rest well, live well.

Liu Yu-Qiao (hereafter referred to as Yu-Qiao): Cocky. We are of the opinion that Tainan is the only place on Earth. We see Tainan as a country and have pride in our blood. However, we are friendly and generous at the same time. We like to talk about ourselves, our city, and our lives, all of which are contradictory yet lovable.

Why do the people of Tainan have such pride?

Pipi: In my opinion, our history and culture are the two main factors. Our culture, gradually-developed over time, has nurtured the distinctive character of Tainan. The hundred-year history of Tainan has given rise to its unique qualities. The people of Tainan live their life in the city where they grew up. Sometimes they have to fight to earn a living or to create the future they dream of, but they never forget to live their lives. Tainan might be smaller, slower, and messier than other cities, and it might be full of strong opinions, but it is still lovable.

Yu-Qiao: The people of Tainan view the whole city as their home. The unique pace of this city is immutable. The people of Tainan are not only in love with their city but also obsessed with the life here. Tainan is a place where you can live well, dream well, and work hard. Why wouldn't anyone who lives here be proud?

全世界來到台南都有同樣的心聲：「台南人到底在跩什麼？」凌晨開賣、賣完就不再補貨的牛肉湯、公休日比營業日還要長的商店，種種在台南獨有的觀光「挑戰」，讓旅客不禁在心中好奇：「台南人流的到底是什麼樣的傲骨血液？」本篇特輯邀請到兩位土生土長並在台南創業的新生代：「鳥飛古物店」（p.181, E）老闆葉家宏與「糯夫米糕」主理人劉雨樵，請他們來跟我們說明白。

Q1：一句話形容台南人？

葉家宏（以下簡稱葉）：好好吃飯，好好休息，好好生活。

劉雨樵（以下簡稱劉）：自以為是，以為全世界只有台南這個城市，把台南當成了一個國家。雖然台南人流著傲慢的血液，但卻相當富有人情味，可以熱情地向每個人介紹台南這座城市與生活，可說是既矛盾又可愛。

Q2：台南人為何能如此「理直氣壯」地跩（有性格）？

葉：我想歷史脈絡與文化占了很重要的因素。慢火溫煮的城市文化底蘊，醞釀出台南特有的個性；百年歷史衝擊及堆積下，產出了自己的氣質。在台南，大家為了理想與生計努力工作，但也沒有忘記要過好自己的生活，這是跟其他地方不一樣的想法。台南步調慢一點，城市規模小一點，樣子亂一點，卻一切都可愛可愛的。

劉：其實台南人真的都把台南這座城市當成自己的家，不允許任何外力進入破壞改變。台南人不僅愛著自己的城市，也迷戀著台南人獨有的生活氣息。台南是個可以好好作夢、好好過日子以及工作的城市，擁有如此生活的台南人，你說，能不理直氣壯嗎？

Can you give an example of an aspect of Tainan with which you have a love-hate relationship?

Pipi: There are all kinds of foods in Tainan, with everyone interpreting Taiwanese cuisine in their own way, and this has developed into the typical flavors associated with Tainan. As people say: "The city, the food, and the people of Tainan will all stick with you." What I hate about it is that all of the eateries know how to live their lives better than we do. They take turns to have days off and close business for the day as soon as supplies run out, which means I have to wait and deal with my cravings.

Yu-Qiao: Tainan is an enchanting city, possibly because it's a place where you can live your life properly. Life here is about heading out on a scorching day, riding a scooter down alleyways lined with tall trees, appreciating the sun shining on the ground and the historical sites you see along the way. When described in this way, who wouldn't love it? As for what I hate about Tainan, I hate the highly palatable food which I can't help but to devour. I hate that Tainan is making me fat!

What are your observations on the people of Tainan while developing your career there?

Pipi: As an antique collector, I get excited whenever I find local objects. You can tell how the people of Tainan lived their lives in olden times by carefully examining those objects. However, life in Tainan in olden times was always elegant, you can also see how much they cared about the little things, the details of the daily items they used.

Yu-Qiao: As a member of the younger generation, it's a challenge to enter the restaurant and catering industry, and it's a path of no return. The people of Tainan have a tendency to reject new things, which means extra time is required if you want to enter their territory. Of course, your efforts will be paid back in due time. I've been challenging the people of Tainan with my local blood, telling the story of Nuo Fu Rice Pudding through my industrious efforts and diligent food preparation. My vision is for my shop to become one of the establishments that exhibits the priceless hospitality of this city.

How do you suggest visitors might best experience the true significance of Tainan when they travel here?

Pipi: Besides tasting all the well-known street foods, staying here for a week or more and blending into the day-to-day life of the locals might be even better. You might find that, when it comes time to leave, a part of your heart has become attached to Tainan. To enjoy the flavors cultivated over decades and to learn about the new ideas and visions emerging in Tainan will provide you with a feeling of contentment. The charm of Tainan is actually found in the daily life of the city.

Yu-Qiao: Put down your electronic devices, rent a bike, and thoroughly explore Tainan. Hop off the bike whenever you feel like it and experience the city's ambiance.

Q3：請各舉一例對台南的又「恨」又「愛」？

葉：台南用自己的角度詮釋全台灣的食物，並衍生出屬於台南的味道。「台南會黏人，食物會黏人，人與人之間的感覺會黏人。」恨的是那些老口味、小店總是一個比一個更會過生活，大家輪流公休，每天準備的分量售完就休息，有時候突然很想吃某家店，就被迫要忍耐。

劉：台南是個迷人的城市，迷人之處或許是這裡是個可以好好生活的地方。我們很習慣台南炎熱的天氣，或是騎著機車在大街小巷穿梭，經過擁著大樹並被陽光穿透的街道，被一座座歷史古蹟包圍，你能不愛嗎？說恨，我恨台南的食物都那麼好吃，又想不克制地大快朵頤，恨台南讓我體重一直上升！

Q4：經營自己志業對台南人的觀察？

葉：經營古物若是收到台南在地的物件，總是讓人興奮。從古物可以細細觀察以前的台南人如何生活。老台南人的生活方式總是很優雅，從物件細節就可以看得出來那個時代多麼講究。

劉：身為新生代的年輕人，踏入台南餐飲界根本是條不歸路，挑戰也高。台南人不太接收新事物，新店要進入台南人的生活，確實是需要時間醞釀的。當然，我相信時間久了大家能感受你的用心，我會繼續努力訴說「糯夫米糕」的故事，希望有朝一日成為台南富有人情味的老店。

Q5：期許國內外旅客來台南能夠感受到的真正內涵？

葉：除了品嚐台南美食外，希望旅客能來台南住上一週甚至更長的時間，並試著融入台南的生活。離開的時候就會發現，身心靈有個地方似乎已經被台南黏住了。請去細細品味那些老味道、看看在台南萌芽的想法與理念。台南的魅力，其實就是台南的日常。

劉：請放下手邊充斥著各種科技的電子產品，租台單車，好好深入台南。用走走停停的速度，感受這城市帶給你的味道。

NUO FU RICE PUDDING 糯夫米糕
台南市中西區府前路一段359巷22號 | nuofu.co
No. 22, Ln. 359, Sec. 1, Fuqian Rd., West Central Dist.,
Tainan City
10:00-till sold out (Closed on Wen. and Thur.)

不按牌理出牌、一身爽快的氣魄

高雄
KAO
HSIUNG

JUST YOLO IT IN
THE CHARISMATIC BREEZE

———————— Trista and Nato

People from outside Kaohsiung always say that coming here is a breeze. The streets are broad, the sea is at your doorstep and the weather is sunny all the time. Embracing the largest seaport in Taiwan, Kaohsiung lives and breathes the ocean. The starting point of industrialization for Kaohsiung was the opening of the harbor during the Japanese colonial period. Then after WW2, the American troops stationed here brought in free trade and open culture. The city has also changed a lot during recent years. Pier2 Art Center, Kaohsiung Exhibition Center, Kaohsiung Music Center and other significant infrastructure project in the harbor area promise great things for the future development of Kaohsiung.

The area which extends from the harbor further into the vastness of the heartlands is a treasure trove of tropical ingredients. Towards the mountains, there exists abundant natural wildlife habitat, as well as Hakka villages and indigenous settlements. The all-encompassing arrangement of mountains, creeks, harbor and sea has gathered the Minnan and Hakka, the indigenous and recent migrants, to take part in the creation of a flourishing harbor scene, which has since become the largest city in Southern Taiwan: Kaohsiung.

In the easy-going, culturally cultivated city of Kaohsiung, people appear to possess a certain pioneering YOLO—you only live once—spirit. The Kaohsiung Incident, that called for the lifting of martial law, took place here, turning the tide for Taiwanese democracy. The spirit of "this is the way I like it" that arose in the aftermath can still be seen from the many interesting and ambitious independent stores.

Come feel the comfortable and liberating aura of Kaohsiung, but be advised: quite a few days await you.

外地朋友總說，來到高雄，就覺得爽快。這裡有大條馬路、近在咫尺的海，還有總是晴朗的天氣。坐擁全台最大的海港，高雄的發展與海洋息息相關。日治時期築港後開啟了高雄工業，二戰後美軍駐守則帶來了自由的文化與貿易。近年都市轉型，港邊的「駁二藝術特區」、「展覽館」及「高流中心」等重大建設，都讓人十分期待高雄港灣的未來發展。

除此之外，從海港往內陸一路延伸，是腹地寬廣的熱帶食材寶庫；再深入山邊，還有豐富的自然生態、客家農村與原住民聚落。身為台灣南部第一大城的高雄，備齊了山、河、海、港的大格局，聚集於此的閩、客、原與新移民也共同打拚，創造出今日港都的繁華風貌。

在熱情爽朗、文化多元的高雄，我們似乎也有種不按牌理出牌、勇於開創的性格，大至呼籲終結戒嚴、促成台灣民主化的「美麗島事件」就在高雄發生，小至「我就是喜歡這樣，來試試吧！」的精神，都可以從許多有趣又有想法的獨立小店中看見。

來高雄感受這樣自在輕鬆的氣息吧，一不小心，就會多待上好幾天！

TRANSPORTATION
交通

Train ride from Taipei to Zuoying Station takes two hours via Taiwan High Speed Rail. Direct line takes 95 minutes. After arriving to Zuoying, passengers can access Kaohsiung City by transferring to the MRT. EasyCard, iPASS, mobile payment and credit card can be used to access the MRT stations. For convenient transportation, a motorbike can be rented, or one can utilize the public bicycle system, YouBike.

台北搭高鐵至左營站約 2 個小時，若搭直達車 95 分鐘就能抵達，到左營後可轉乘捷運到高雄市區，捷運可使用悠遊卡、一卡通、電子支付與信用卡刷卡進站。若想更方便移動也能租借機車，或是使用公共自行車系統 YouBike。

RECOMMENDATIONS
推薦

◤ READING LIST 旅遊書籍

THE ALLEY LIFE IN KAOHSIUNG《高雄巷弄日和：文創聚落、朝氣小舖、輕食咖啡，暢遊陽光海港城新亮點》
Introduction to little-known spots and shops in Kaohsiung's four major districts in order of MRT lines
以捷運線為經緯，分4大區介紹高雄私房好點店

⌐ books.com.tw/products/0010673084

MUST-EAT IN KAOHSIUNG《雄合味：橫跨百年，包山藏海，高雄 120 家以人情和手藝慢燉的食飲私味》
Another thorough guide to snacking in Kaohsiung.
另一本完整了解高雄在地小吃的飲食指南

⌐ books.com.tw/products/0010960694

HISTORY OF KAOHSIUNG IN COMICS《漫畫高雄歷史》
Humorous and easy to read introduction to Kaohsiung's past and present
淺顯易讀，用詼諧的方式認識高雄的前世今生

⌐ books.com.tw/products/0010361985

◤ LOCAL PUBLICATIONS 在地刊物

MEGAO《大雄誌》
New publisher with interesting editorial plans that focus on Kaohsiung. Has also set up an online media hiông hiông
一本高雄主義、企劃有趣的刊物，也成立網媒「雄雄」

⌐ facebook.com/megatakao

FLAVOR KAOHSIUNG《旬味，高雄》
Kaohsiung City Government issued monthly illustration introducing local small farms and produce
高雄市農業局發行的質感月刊，介紹高雄在地小農與食材

⌐ e-book: agri.kcg.gov.tw/?pn=ebook_more

BENSHI《本事》
National Kaohsiung Center for the Arts - Weiwuying issued quarterly publication with different topics. Great layout and content
衛武營發行的季刊，每期都有不同主題，設計內容俱佳

⌐ Purchase online 線上購買：https://pse.is/JXSMA

◤ TRAVEL WEBSITES 旅遊網站

KAOHSIUNG TRAVEL 高雄旅遊網
Kaohsiung City Government's official website
高雄官方旅遊網站，有多國語言資訊

⌐ khh.travel

HERENOW KAOHSIUNG | HERENOW 高雄
Japanese creative community hosted quality website about Kaohsiung. Also available as a downloadable app
日本藝文網站製作的高質感高雄城市網站，有app可下載

⌐ herenow.city/zh-tw/kaohsiung

◤ GUIDED TOURS 導覽

WALK THE KITCHEN 塩埕。行灶腳
Guided tour to Yancheng District hosted by 3080s
由參捌地方生活主辦的鹽埕區在地導覽

⌐ thirtyeighty38.wix.com/walkingtour

CHILL CHILL KAOHSIUNG PROJECT 去去高雄
A seasonal tour introducing Kaohsiung flavors, from markets to kitchens
不定期推出節氣食旅，從菜市場到廚房，認識高雄味

⌐ chillchillkh.com

◤ ANNUAL EVENTS 年度活動

MEGAPORT FESTIVAL (MAR.-APR.)
大港開唱 (3月-4月)
One of Taiwan's best music festivals – make sure to get your tickets early!
台灣最棒的大型音樂祭之一，務必要搶票！

⌐ https://megaportfest.com

KAOHSIUNG FILM FESTIVAL (OCT.) 高雄電影節 (10月)
The largest film festival in southern Taiwan. In addition to the Short Film Competition, it also has held VR Competition in recent years
南台灣最大影展，除知名的短片競賽外近年也推出VR競賽

⌐ www.kff.tw

Photo credit：othree

Photo credit：陳彥君

Photo credit：莉莉周（高雄市立美術館提供）

Photo credit：James Lin

A KAOHSIUNG MUSEUM OF HISTORY 高雄市立歷史博物館
Architecture fans won't be disappointed with this oriental, palace-like building from the Japanese colonial period
台灣日治建築少有的東方宮殿風格，建築迷不能錯過

⌐ 高雄市鹽埕區中正四路272號
No. 272, Zhongzheng 4th Rd, Yancheng District, Kaohsiung City
facebook.com/khmorgtw | 09:00-17:00 (Closed on Mon.)

B KAOHSIUNG MUSEUM OF FINE ARTS 高雄市立美術館
Professional and international venue for carefully curated contemporary fine art in Kaohsiung
高雄當代藝術的國際級專業場館，策展用心

⌐ 高雄市鼓山區美術館路80號
No. 80, Meishuguan Rd, Gushan District, Kaohsiung City
facebook.com/KaohsiungMuseum | 09:30-17:30 (Closed on Mon.)

C HOLY ROSARY CATHEDRAL 玫瑰聖母堂
Located on the bank of Love River, it is the oldest Catholic church-building in Taiwan
位於愛河畔，天主教會在台灣所建的第一座教堂

⌐ 高雄市苓雅區五福三路151號
No. 151, Wufu 3rd Road, Lingya District, Kaohsiung City
facebook.com/cathedralminorbasiliica

D TAKAOBOOKS 三餘書店
The most representative independent bookstore in Kaohsiung with an abundance of independent magazines
高雄最具代表性的獨立書店，有豐富的獨立小誌

⌐ 高雄市新興區中正二路214號 | facebook.com/takaobooks214
No. 214, Zhongzheng 2nd Rd, Xinxing District, Kaohsiung City
13:30-21:00, Fri.-Sun. 13:30-21:00 (Closed on Tuesdays)

E YENCHENG FIRST PUBLIC RETAIL MARKET 鹽埕第一公有市場
Explore Traditional Stalls and Trendy Boutiques!
菜市場活化再生，來逛老攤位與風格小店！

⌐ 高雄市鹽埕區瀨南街141之7號 | Instagram: yymkt_1949
No. 141-7, Sainan St., Yancheng Dist., Kaohsiung City
07:00-12:00, 16:00-22:00, Mon.-Tue. 07:00-12:00

F TAKAO RENAISSANCE ASSOCIATION 打狗文史再興會社
A base for local history and monument research that provides guided tours to the old Hamasen area
在地文史、研究的基地，提供哈瑪星街區導覽

⌐ 高雄市鼓山區捷興二街18號 | facebook.com/TakaoKaisha
No. 18, Jiexing 2nd Street, Gushan District, Kaohsiung City
Sat.-Sun. 11:00-16:00 (Closed on weekdays)

Photo credit：李佳芳

A　SKB 文明鋼筆

An old-fashioned stationery brand which begun with hand-crafted fountain pens

以製作手工鋼筆起家的老字號文具品牌

⌐ 高雄市鹽埕區五福四路155號
No. 155, Wufu 4th Road, Yancheng District, Kaohsiung City
+886-7-521-8271 | 10:30–19:00, weekends 11:00-19:00

B　ABBEY ROAD RECORD STORE 艾比路唱片行

A vast collection of foreign and domestic second-hand vinyl albums. Very fascinating owner

有豐富的海內外二手黑膠收藏，老闆非常有趣

⌐ 高雄市新興區錦田路11之1號 | facebook.com/abbeyroadrecordstore
No. 11-1, Jintian Road, Xinxing District, Kaohsiung City
12:00–21:00 (Closed on Sun. and Mon.)

C　GOÖOD TIME 龜時間

A diner/Café inspired by the farm-to-table concept selling sake and goodies from the 60s to 80s

以產地到餐桌為概念的食堂咖啡館。販售清酒和 60s-80s 的古物選品 (每月營業時間請洽臉書 FB: gooodtime.kh)

⌐ 高雄市新興區中正四路41號1F | Thur.-Mon. 11:00-19:00
1F, No. 41, Zhongzheng 4th Rd, Xinxing District, Kaohsiung City

D　MOONMIST 泊・月白

Tea ceremonies, crafts, and all things beautiful – regular exhibitions held

茶道、工藝與所有美好的事物，定期舉辦展覽

⌐ 高雄市鹽埕區2-2號 駁二藝術特區大義倉庫C8-12
Pire-2 Art Center C8-12, Kaohsiung | FB : moonmist.atelier
13:00 - 19:00 (CLosed on Mon. and Tue.)

E　MLD 台鋁生活商場

Reinvented from the old plant formerly owned by Taiwan Aluminum Corporation, now a shopping mall integrates with restaurants, cultural and creative stores, and cinema

由台灣鋁業公司舊廠房改造的美食、文創與娛樂商場

⌐ 高雄市前鎮區忠勤路8號 | 11:30-21:30
No. 8, Zhongqin Rd., Qianzhen Dist., Kaohsiung City | mld.com.tw

F　BOOKING

Bookstore with a focus on manga rentals. Even their instant noodles are designed by a Kaohsiungese chef of French cuisine, Thomas Chien

超講究漫畫書店，連泡麵都是高雄法餐主廚簡天才設計

⌐ 高雄市鹽埕區瀨南街177號 | 11:30-19:00 (Closed on Wednesdays)
No. 177, Lainan St., Yancheng Dist., KHC. | facebook.com/bookingbookstore

A **BREEZE MARKET** 微風市集
Southern Taiwan's largest and longest running organic farmers' market
南台灣最大、歷史也最悠久的有機農夫市集

⌐ 高雄市鳳山區光復路二段120號 (鳳山婦幼青少年活動中心)
120, Section 2, Guangfu Road, Fengshan District, Kaohsiung City
facebook.com/breezemarket | Sat. 07:30-11:00

B **GIEN JIA BISTRO** 挑食餐酒館
Meticulous Italian dishes made with selected ingredients sourced from southern Taiwan in a relaxed atmosphere
精選南台灣在地食材，店內氣氛輕鬆，義式菜色細緻美味

⌐ 高雄市前金區中正四路80號 | +886-7-288-5252
No. 80, Zhongzheng 4th Rd, Qianjin District, Kaohsiung City
facebook.com/GienJia | 11:30-14:30, 17:00-21:30 (Closed on Mon.)

C **THOMAS CHIEN RESTAURANT / THOMAS. 簡 法式餐廳**
Focuses on presenting the beauty of Taiwanese ingredients by means of the French cuisine
以講究的法菜手法呈現台灣食材之美

⌐ 高雄市前鎮區成功二路11號 | +886-7-536-9436
No. 11, Chenggong 2nd Road, Qianzhen District, Kaohsiung City
facebook.com/thomaschien2012 | 11:30-14:30, 18:00-22:30

D **TAKE SWEET TIME BAKERY TST麵包店**
European-style bakery which cultivates its own natural yeast
自家培養天然酵母的歐式麵包專賣店

⌐ 高雄市苓雅區廣東一街115號
No. 115, Guangdong 1st Street, Lingya District, Kaohsiung City
facebook.com/TakeSweetTime | 10:00-17:00 (Closed on Thur.)

E **R.RUYO CAFÉ** 有。咖啡
Founded by local young people, this café does drip-brewing in Kōno style
在地青年開設，河野 Kōno 式手沖咖啡館

⌐ 高雄市苓雅區中正二路56巷11號 | facebook.com/rruyocafé
No.11, Lane 56, Zhongzheng 2nd Rd, Lingya District, Kaohsiung City
12:00-18:00 (Closed on Mondays) | +886-7-223-6808

F **TAIWAN NATIVE MOUNTAIN TEA**
哈娜谷台灣原生野山茶工坊
Liouguei District's rare, hundred-year old wild Camellia, a tea with a distinctive honey aroma
六龜山區稀有的百年野生山茶，茶湯有獨特的蜜香

⌐ 高雄市桃源區寶山里41號 | facebook.com/BununTea
No. 41 Baoshanli, Taoyuan District, Kaohsiung City.

Photo credit：MARSALIS BAR

Photo credit: 屋物清酒

A ISLAND BAR/B&B/CHAMBRE D'HÔTES 小島公寓/小島茶酒

An atmospheric inn which caters afternoon tea and evening drinks

下午賣茶、晚上賣酒的氣氛民宿

⌐ 高雄市新興區六合一路148號 | +886-7-238-8166
No. 148, Liuhe 1st Road, Xinxing District, Kaohsiung City
facebook.com/island148 | 20:00-02:00, Fri,-Sat 20:00-03:00

B WUWU SAKE 屋物清酒

A stylish sake bar, with the nearby must-visit 55mobler Studio for furniture, art and lifestyle goods

時髦的清酒店，一旁家具行「屋物工作室」也別錯過

⌐ 高雄市苓雅區青年一路261巷1號 | +886-7-531-0300
No.1, 261 alley, 1st Qingnian Street, Lingya District, Kaohsiung City
facebook.com/wuwuSake | 11:00-23:00

C ATMAN SPACE 三千

A hipsterisque pub with lots of books and whiskies

有很多書和威士忌的文青風格小酒館

⌐ 高雄市前金區文武三街194號 | +886-7-221-6456
No. 194, Wenwu 3rd Street, Qianjin District, Kaohsiung City
facebook.com/AtmanSpace | 19:00-02:00

D MARSALIS BAR 馬沙里斯爵士酒館

A jazz bar tucked away on the second floor and a den for the Kaohsiung nightlife

藏身在2樓的爵士酒吧，高雄夜晚最想窩的角落

⌐ 高雄市新興區中正四路71號2樓 | +886-7-281-4078
2F, No. 71, Zhongzheng 4th Rd, Xinxing District, Kaohsiung City
facebook.com/marsalisbar | 19:00-02:00

E HOK HOUSE 鶴宮寓

An old hotel renovated into a cozy space to which one wants to return

老飯店改造，去過就會想一直再去的舒適空間

⌐ 高雄市新興區中正四路41號2樓 | +886-7-201-1988
2F, No. 41, Zhongzheng 4th Rd, Xinxing District, Kaohsiung City
facebook.com/hokhouse

F BRIO HOTEL

Kaohsiung's highly acclaimed business hotel with a good location

高雄深受好評的質感商旅，地理位置佳

⌐ 高雄市新興區中山一路14-26號 | +886-7-281-7900
No. 14-26, Zhongshan 1st Road, Xinxing District, Kaohsiung City
facebook.com/briohotel1

QIANJIN, DAGANGBU, YANCHENG AND HAMASEN

前金、大港埔、鹽埕埔和哈瑪星周邊

STROLL IN KAOHSIUNG'S OLD TOWN AREA 漫步高雄老城區

市議會站
City Council
Station

美麗島站
Formosa
Boulevard
Station

Zhongzheng 4th Rd.

中正四路

中華三路

Zhonghua 3rd Rd.

愛河 Love river

路山鼓

五福四路

Gushan 1st Rd.

鹽埕埔站
Yanchengpu
Station

Wufu 4th Rd.

高雄港
Kaohsiung Harbor

用手機掃描 QR code，存取推薦路線的 Google
Scan the QR code to access this recommended route on Google

1)	08:30	Local light bites for breakfast at the Gongyou Qian Jin Market
2)	09:30	Have a cup of coffee or tea, and tour the revitalized old market
3)	11:00	Proceed to Kaohsiung's creative hotspot, Pier2 Art Center
4)	12:30	A street food adventure awaits you for lunch in Yancheng District
5)	13:30	Wander the alleyways of Jiu Kujiang Shopping District in search of interesting shops run by young people
6)	14:30	Experience the feel of a Japanese-colonial-period kissaten that also doubles as a coffee shop, at Xiaodi Café
7)	15:30	See the fine paintings exhibited at ALIEN Art Centre
8)	17:00	Stroll the Hamasen, a name which means "the shoreline" in Japanese
9)	18:00	Behold Kaohsiung's sunset scenery at Sizihwan bay
10)	19:30	Return to Dagangbu to feast on home-style cooking
11)	21:00	Eat street food from the well-established vendors at the Liuhe Night Market next to the Formosa Boulevard metro station
12)	22:30	Raise a toast to Kaohsiung in Dagangbu

1)	08:30	早上在「前金市場」吃在地小吃當早餐
2)	09:30	吃飽喝咖啡或喝杯清茶，再逛逛改造回春的老市場
3)	11:00	前往高雄的創意熱點「駁二藝術特區」散步
4)	12:30	午餐在鹽埕埔來場小吃大冒險
5)	13:30	散步舊堀江，在巷弄裡尋找在地青年開設的有趣店家們
6)	14:30	在「小堤咖啡冷飲」感受日治時代喫茶店的風情
7)	15:30	到「金馬賓館當代美術館」看用心策畫的展覽
8)	17:00	來到名稱由日語濱線 (Há-má-seng) 而來的哈瑪星走逛
9)	18:00	在西子灣欣賞高雄的夕陽美景
10)	19:30	返回大港埔吃口味一點都不簡單的家庭料理
11)	21:00	在美麗島站旁的六合夜市吃老字號攤販的美食
12)	22:30	在大港埔跟高雄乾一杯

08:30
QIAN JIN MARKET
1. 前金市場

After WW2, the local judicial court relocated to near Love River, where many legislative buildings soon sprang up nearby, thus attracting various low-key, yet outstanding signature Kaohsiung restaurants to settle here. Serious eaters favor Qianjin Rouzaofan, Cai Zong He Tang Rou Yuan, or Xiao Zhang Hai Chan Zhou where the customer can select their favorite seafood ingredients to go with a pot of noodles. Around here, one can also thrift for old tableware treasures.

二戰後地方法院遷址愛河，周邊律師樓林立，開始聚集許多低調、出色的高雄經典美食。像是老饕客們喜愛的「前金肉燥飯」、「前金肉圓肉粽專賣店」、還有可以客製海鮮選料的「小張海產粥」鍋燒意麵。周邊的老餐具行也有一些寶可以挖。

09:30
YANCHENG 1ST PUBLIC RETAIL MARKET
2. 喝咖啡兼逛菜市場

Near the entrance to the Gongyou Qian Jin Market, you'll find Ruh Café, a rock-and-roll-spirited coffee roaster which sells takeaway cold-brew. For refreshing tea, old Bishan Cha Zhuang tea house across the street is recommended. Afterward, take a leisurely walk to the rejuvenated Yancheng 1st Public Retail Market, where you can explore a variety of emerging shops. (I also recommend the unique guesthouses and coffee shop House of Takao Ginza nearby.)

前金菜市場的入口有間自家烘豆、搖滾風格的冰滴咖啡外帶吧「路人咖啡 2 號店 Ruh Cafe」，也推薦對街老鋪「碧山茶莊」的清茶。之後散步到重新改造回春的「鹽埕第一公有零售市場」，探訪各式進駐的新興店家。（也順道推薦在附近的特色民宿與咖啡店「銀座劇場」。）

11:00
PIER2 ART CENTERS
3. 駁二藝術特區

Yancheng District's Pier2 used to be a commercial warehouse building for storing sugar products bound for shipment overseas during the Japanese colonial period. After gathering dust for sixty-odd years, it was born anew with an influx of shops, bookstores, diners, live music venues, cinema, art galleries, co-working spaces, and a space for culture and arts for foreign and domestic artists-in-residence. Be sure not to miss this site.

接著進入鹽埕埔的「駁二」，曾是日治時期商會儲存砂糖物資、裝船出海的專用倉庫，在塵封了一甲子後再生，成為承載設計商店、書店、餐廳、音樂展演空間、電影院、藝廊、共同工作空間及海內外駐村藝術家的藝文場域，千萬不可錯過。

12:30
LOCAL DELICACIES IN YANCHENG
4. 鹽埕埔小吃大冒險

Old towns always have the densest and the most talent-rich assortment of eateries. Qingzhou Xiaocai, Gang Yuan Beef Noodle Restaurant, and Ben's Duck are recommended. Entering the Dagouding area within the Jiu Kujiang Shopping District, options include Dagouding rice noodles with milkfish, Lekami (Shantou soy sauce noodles), Lotus Root Teas & Juices, and Sister's Breakfast (be sure to order the bun with egg).

老城總有密度最高、最講究的小吃，推薦五福大路上的「高雄清粥小菜」、「港園牛肉麵」和「鴨肉珍」與「鴨肉本」。鑽進大溝頂舊堀江，還有「大溝頂虱目魚米粉湯」、「樂咖咪」（汕頭乾拌麵）、「老牌蓮藕茶，真饗菓菜汁」和「姊妹老五冷飲早餐店」（烘蛋堡必點）。

13:30
JIU KUJIANG SHOPPING DISTRICT
5. 散步舊堀江

Jiu Kujiang Shopping District and Ginza Shopping Mall were built during the Japanese colonial period, and it is easy for visitors to imagine the colorful jubilation that once took place. Nowadays, young people are attracted to start a business here, examples include the second-hand vintage store Nan Gua, the design studio for the Dagouding shopping street, Push Pin Diner, and Amain Mochi. We also love digging for treasures on Wufu Road, also known as the Bamboo Street, near the Hamasen area.

「舊堀江商店街」與「銀座商場」發展於日治時期，走進鹽埕埔的巷弄，不難察覺這裡曾有的華美歡騰。如今這裡吸引了年輕人在此創業，像是專營舊貨選物的「南瓜百貨與南瓜鐘錶」、大溝頂商店街的設計工作室與「阿綿麻糬」。我們也愛到五福路靠近哈瑪星一帶的「竹器街」挖寶。

14:30
HAVE A CUP IN YANCHENG DISTRICT
6. 鹽埕埔喝一杯

Established in the 70s, Xiaodi Café is probably Kaohsiung's first bookstore/kissaten specializing in Japanese literature. They serve syphon coffee with few options available: hot or cold, acidic or not. To this day, Xiaodi retains the classic kissaten breakfast combination of ham and eggs over easy. That is romantically old-school, right there.

創立於1970年代的「小堤咖啡冷飲」，可能是高雄最早專營日本圖書的書店喫茶。當家吧檯手二姐經典的吸虹式咖啡，只有酸、不酸、冰、熱等簡單的選擇。小堤至今還保有喫茶店「火腿荷包蛋」的經典組合，可來此重溫老派的浪漫。

15:30
ALIEN ART CENTRE

7. 金馬賓館當代美術館

This art center used to be a boarding site for mobilized Taiwanese troops. In 2018, the local Yuimom Group transformed it into a contemporary art center exhibiting domestic and foreign works, such as American contemporary artist James Turrell's light installation *Corinth Canal, 2016 / Diamonds (Squares on point)*. The accompanying eccentric Alien café deserves a try.

「金馬賓館」曾是台灣軍人收到「金馬召集令」後，搭船前往部隊的「候船營區」。2018 年在地的御盟集團將它改造成一座當代藝術中心，展示國內外當代藝術，像是美國當代藝術家 James Turrell 的光與空間裝置《科林斯運河——鑽石》。附設的 Alien café 餐點別出心裁，值得一試。

17:00
WALK AROUND HAMASEN

8. 哈瑪星散步

Hamasen used to be the financial and political center of Kaohsiung during the Japanese colonial period. Walking from the kendo building (Kaohsiung Wude Hall) towards the seaside, checkered streets, Yamagataya Bookstore Relic, trade buildings, and Japanese machia-style buildings appear. The nearby Gushan Daitian Temple used to host Kaohsiung's first city government, and to this day it remains a religious center for its people. In the square in front of the temple can be found many delicious things to eat. The Japanese oden-stews topped with peanut powder by vendor D is recommended, alongside Shantou Fish Ball Soup.

哈瑪星曾是日治高雄的政經中心，從劍道館「武德殿」往海邊走，可見棋盤式街道、山形屋、貿易商樓與日式町屋。附近的「代天宮」曾是高雄第一個市府所在地，至今仍是居民的信仰中心。廟前廣場有幾攤美味的廟口小吃，推薦灑了花生粉的炭烤黑輪「D」還有「汕頭麵魚丸湯」。

18:00
HAVE A DRINK IN HAMASEN

9. 哈瑪星喝一杯

See the fantastic sunset at Kaohsiung's famous Sizihwan. Sizihwan Lookout and The British Consulate at Takow are both absolutely stellar vantage points for the occasion. Inside National Sun Yat-sen University, near the Shanhai Temple at Chaishan Fishing Pier, there is the scenic Terroir café (by reservation only), where one can enjoy the romantic sunset over a cup of coffee.

來看高雄名景——西子灣魔幻夕陽。「西子灣觀景台」和「英國領事館」都是很不錯的賞陽景點。往中山大學裡面走，近山海宮的柴山小漁村有一家海景咖啡店「Terroir 流浪吧」（預約制），在此邊看夕陽邊喝咖啡也相當浪漫。

19:30
ZHAO MING HOME-STYLE RESTAURANT
10. 昭明海產家庭料理

Arrive in Dagangbu to have dinner at Zhao Ming home-style seafood restaurant which was originally located near Sapphire Grand Ballroom, the scene of the most popular song and dance show of the 1970s led by Chu Ko-Liang, where the biggest stars of the era were all guests. Perhaps the secret to Zhao Ming's over 40 years of flavor is their ability to turn stir-fried pork with garlic, tomato eggs, braised fish, and other mundane dishes into something elegant.

回到大港埔,在「昭明海產家庭料理」吃晚餐,因原址近「藍寶石大歌廳」(豬哥亮發跡地,70 年代台灣最重要的歌舞秀場),當時的明星都是座上賓。能把「蒜苗炒五花肉」、「番茄炒蛋」、「紅燒魚」等家常菜做得講究風雅,也許是昭明能飄香逾 40 年的祕訣。

21:00
LIUHE NIGHT MARKET
11. 六合夜市

Dagangbu has become the center of city development since WW2. Having its own newspapers, a hospital, restaurants which are open at all hours, and ahead-of-the-curve entertainment, Liuhe Night Market has certainly risen to the occasion. Here, one can experience the charm and character of many established vendors, including Dong Dong Mini Hotpot with tableside service, Fuji Duntang, Kaorouzhi Jia, and Nong-hou-pu Herbal Tea, who even at two o'clock in the morning on a stormy night are reluctant to call it a day.

大港埔是戰後高雄的發展核心,有報社、醫院、日夜輪番的飲食店與前衛的娛樂場所,「六合夜市」也應運而生。來此可體驗老攤販的魅力與風骨,像是保有桌邊服務的「東東迷你石頭火鍋燒烤」、「富記燉湯」、「烤肉之家」和「濃厚舖青草茶」,即使颱風下雨,不到半夜 2 點不會輕易打烊!

22:30
CHEERS TO DAGANGBU
12. 大港埔乾一杯

Lastly, have a tasty drink at Hway Coffee with delicious drinks, carefree atmosphere, and good taste in music. This late-night café is frequented by many artistic and well-cultured young folk. Similarly hidden in an alleyway is FEWdrink which provides craft beers from around the world and spirits with accompanying snacks for you to enjoy on a tranquil Kaohsiung night.

最後在瀰漫自由氛圍、好聽音樂與好喝飲品的深夜咖啡廳「灰咖啡 Hway Coffee」喝杯小酒,這裡你會遇到許多充滿想法的文藝青年。同樣也隱身巷弄的「小酌 FEWdrink」,提供來自世界各地的精釀啤酒與可單杯品嚐的烈酒,配著下酒菜,享受高雄靜謐的夜晚。

TWIN TOWN ROUTE
雙城路線

ZUOYING AND FENGSHAN AREA
左營和鳳山周邊

EXPLORE HISTORIC SITES AND RENOWNED ATTRACTIONS IN KAOHSIUNG
探索高雄古蹟與經典景點

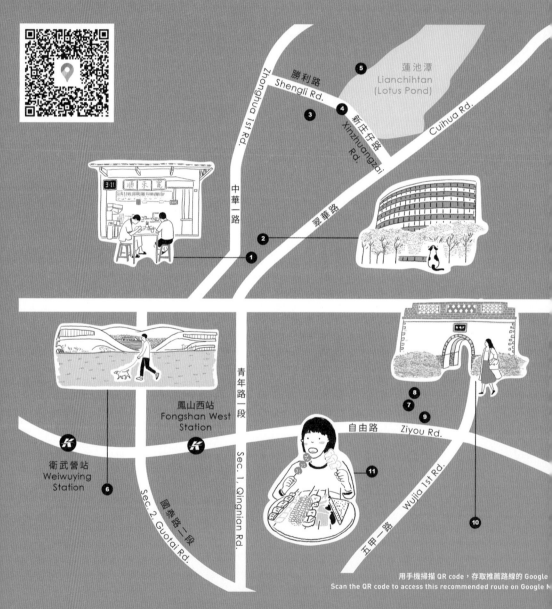

用手機掃描 QR code，存取推薦路線的 Google
Scan the QR code to access this recommended route on Google M

1)	08:30	Breakfast at Kuan Lai Shun Breakfast Restaurant in the Old City of Fongshan County
2)	09:30	Take pictures at the Guomao Community, a former navy dependents' village
3)	10:00	Learn the history of the Old City of Fongshan County
4)	10:30	Head to the Lotus Pond and the Dragon and Tiger Pagodas which are much liked by foreign visitors
5)	11:30	Traditional char-grilled shortcakes or local noodles for lunch
6)	13:30	En-route to the New City of Fongshan County, be sure to stop by at Weiwuying National Kaohsiung Center for the Arts to experience the energy of the Southern Taiwanese art scene
7)	14:30	Prior to entering the New City, pay your respects to the City God at the Fengyi City God Temple
8)	15:30	Imagine the life of an olden-day scholar in the Fengyi Academy and learn about the history of Fengshan
9)	16:30	Come the time for afternoon tea, grab yourself a cold douhua or a grilled sausage
10)	17:30	Take a walk to the East Gate and stroll through the 100-year-old neighborhood
11)	18:30	Dine at the Zhongshan Street Night Market and finish the day with a tasty meal in the midst of Fengshan

1)	08:30	早上先到鳳山縣舊城邊的「寬來順」吃早餐
2)	09:30	到老眷村改造的「果貿社區」拍張網美照
3)	10:00	到「鳳山縣舊城」認識舊城歷史
4)	10:30	轉往深受外國遊客喜愛的「龍虎塔」與「蓮池潭」
5)	11:30	午餐時間吃老字號炭烤酥餅或在地麵店
6)	13:30	前往新城途中，務必停留「衛武營」感受南台灣藝文能量
7)	14:30	進入新城，先來「鳳邑城隍廟」跟城隍爺打聲招呼
8)	15:30	在「鳳儀書院」想像早期讀書人的生活並認識鳳山歷史
9)	16:30	下午茶時間到，來點冰豆花或是烤香腸吧
10)	17:30	散步「東便門」，穿梭百年老街區
11)	18:30	在鳳山中山路夜市吃晚餐，在今日鳳山與美食中結束雙城之旅

INTRODUCTION
簡介

Kaohsiung consists of two ancient Qing dynasty cities within the former Fongshan County. Due to differing periods of construction, the one in Zuoying District is called the Old City, and the other in Fengshan District is called the New City. Having experienced the eras of the Qing dynasty, the Japanese colonization, and the nationalist government that followed the war, each of the twin towns houses different ethnic groups and emcompasses a diverse culture and history. This route lets you tread the twin cities and encounter their unique history and life.

高雄市內有兩座清代古城，一座在左營，一座在鳳山，都叫做鳳山縣城，惟因建造時間不同，而有新與舊之分。歷經了清領、日治和戰後國民政府各個時期，雙城各自聚集了不同族群，也揉和許多歷史文化。 這條路線能讓你一日踏查雙城，遇見城邊獨特的歷史與生活。

08:30
KUAN LAI SHUN BREAKFAST
1. 寬來順

First, get to the Old City of Fongshan County for breakfast. Have pancake fritters, carrot cake or soy milk at the Kuan Lai Shun breakfast shop, and be prepared for a lengthy queue. A wide variety of pastries are also available here. Carry your bowl to find a seat in the shade and enjoy the authentic, wheaty northern-Chinese-style breakfast. Many visitors are fascinated by the spontaneous atmosphere of this place. Other busy nearby breakfast vendors include Meihong Doujian and Lailai Breakfast.

一早先到左營舊城邊吃早餐！ 來總是大排長龍的「寬來順」吃燒餅油條、蘿蔔糕和豆漿，這裡還有琳瑯滿目的點心。端了餐盤在樹蔭下就坐，享用道地的北方麵食早點，這種隨興的氣氛讓人著迷。附近的早餐人氣店還有「美紅豆漿」與「來來早點」。

09:00
GUOMAO COMMUNITY
2. 果貿社區

Guomao Community was renovated from a navy dependents' village back in the 1960s. Various food cultures and lifestyles originating in different provinces of China converged and took shape in a spectacular way in the navy dependents' village buildings. The ring-shaped, hive-like arrangement of the tall buildings is a popular check-in destination among today's internet celebrities. Guomao market inside the community has an agrarian feel to it and deserves a look, especially given the weekend flea market.

海軍眷村改建的「果貿社區」，始於 60 年代。各省的吃食與生活樣貌都匯聚在這彷若立體版的眷村樓宇之中，十分壯觀。環狀的蜂巢式大廈，是現今網紅必到的打卡熱點。社區內的果貿市場，有濃濃的眷村味，很值得一逛，如果能遇到週末限定的跳蚤市集就更棒了。

10:00
THE OLD CITY OF FONGSHAN COUNTY

3. 鳳山縣舊城

A first-class heritage site, the Old City of Fongshan County is the earliest and the largest well-preserved ancient city in Taiwan. It can be called the ancestor of all Taiwanese cities. The East Gate entrance to the Old City is a mere ten-minute walk from the Guomao Community. One can further explore the history of the Old City and Zuoying areas by visiting The Center of Old Fongshan City History inside the city wall.

一級古蹟「鳳山縣舊城」是全台年代最早及保存面積最廣之古城,堪稱台灣的城池之祖。從果貿社區只需步行 10 分鐘,就能來到舊城的東門口。如果對左營地區的發展想更深入了解,還能到城牆內的「見城館」,體驗更多關於舊城與左營的歷史過往。

10:30
DRAGON AND TIGER PAGODAS

4. 龍虎塔 與 蓮池潭

Located at the North Gate of the Old City, Dragon and Tiger Pagodas are a must-see in many foreign travel guides. Though the cute dragon and tiger seem plastic on the outside, the safeguarding symbolism of the dragon entrance and tiger exit, coupled with the many folk stories which were turned into ceramics displays inside the twin pagodas, makes the trip an interesting artistic voyage. Lotus Pond includes many other temples and monuments for those who are interested in such culture.

被許多國外旅遊書列為必訪的景點「龍虎塔」,位於舊城北門邊上。外型可愛的龍虎雖然塑膠感略重,但龍口進、虎口出的消災解厄意涵,搭配塔內許多交趾陶製成的民間故事,走一趟等於逛了一回廟宇的藝術之旅,其實挺有意思的。若對廟宇文化有興趣,「蓮池潭」除了龍虎塔,還有許多特別的廟宇與古蹟。

11:30
JINHUA SU-BING

5. 金華酥餅

Now that you have walked to the Lotus Pond side, ordering a char-grilled shortcake at Jinhua Su-bing is recommended. These handmade shortcakes have tasted the same for over sixty years, and with each limited batch coming in hot, it would be inexcusable not to have one. In addition, one can try Fenyang Huntun, an old wonton vendor, or opt for noodles at San Niu Beef Noodle Restaurant or Xi'an Mianshi Guan, both recommended by locals.

既然已步行到蓮潭邊,建議先來「金華酥餅」預約炭烤酥餅! 60 多年口味不變的手工酥餅,每次出爐數量有限,沒吃到會令人扼腕吶。除此之外,中餐可以嚐嚐市場老店「汾陽餛飩」,或者想吃麵食的話,在地人推薦「三牛牛肉麵」跟「西安麵食館」。

13:30
WEIWUYING
6. 衛武營

Once aboard the MRT from the Old City en-route to the New City, one ought to stop in at the former military base, Weiwuying. After ten years of renovations, it has become South Taiwan's first international-level venue for performing arts. World-class performances and local arts and culture assemblies are enjoyed here since opening in late-2018. With its distinctly fantastic architecture design, it has become a must-visit place for fans of architecture and photography.

從舊城搭乘捷運往新城移動，途中必經曾為軍事基地的「衛武營」，是南台灣第一座國家級表演藝術場館。2018 年底開幕之後，從世界級的表演乃至在地的藝文小聚，都能在這裡欣賞。其奇特的屋頂造型與奇幻感的建築載體，也成為許多建築迷與攝影迷必訪之處。

14:30
FENGYI CITY GOD TEMPLE
7. 鳳邑城隍廟

Upon entering the area of the New City, report for duty to the One who watches over everything. To commemorate the fifth year of the Qing dynasty's Jiaqing Emperor, the Fengshan temple was built and the county administration was relocated to the New City, Fengshan. The incense offerings have continued until today. The carvings in the temple are exquisite and elegant. Among them, the "you are here" wooden sign and the big abacus are special cultural relics which remind us to abstain from evil and pursue virtue.

進到新城的範圍內，先來跟城池的守護神城隍爺報到。「鳳山城隍廟」建於清嘉慶 5 年，隨當年縣治移至新城（鳳山）後建立。時至今日依然香火鼎盛。廟裡頭各項雕琢細膩雅緻，其中抬頭可見的「你來了」木匾與「大算盤」都是廟裡的特殊文物，在在提醒諸惡莫作、眾善奉行。

15:30
FENGYI ACADEMY
8. 鳳儀書院

For those interested in learning more about Fengshan, the Fengyi Academy next to the Fengyi Temple is a worthwhile visit. Built in 1814, it is the oldest and most intact academy in Taiwan. In the renovated academy, visitors walk past cute puppets which recount the history of Fengshan. The site has preserved its original layout from the Qing dynasty, which is very rare.

想多認識鳳山，位在城隍廟旁的「鳳儀書院」也相當值得一看。建於 1814 年，是台灣現存書院中，年代最早且規模完整之書院。歷經修復後，鳳儀書院內透過可愛風格的人偶，讓參觀者能夠想像過往書院運作方式，同時述說著鳳山歷史。此外，書院的建築與空間安排依然維持著清代原有的格局，非常難得。

16:30
FUQUAN BINGPIN DOUHUA
9. 福泉冰品豆花

If you tire of strolling around and need a place to rest, head next door to the Fuquan Bingpin Douhua. This vendor is loved by the locals for its fresh fruits and genuine ingredients. If mango is in season, be sure to try ice flakes topped with fresh mango . Alternatively, take a few extra steps to Dadong Arts Center and eat at the nearby Qiaobian Xiangchang, a popular sausage stall which has been in operation for over fifty years and often sells out early in the evening.

走逛累了想暫歇，就來書院旁的「福泉冰品豆花」。水果新鮮、用料實在，是當地人的愛店。假如碰到芒果產季，新鮮芒果加上雪花冰推薦必嚐。除此之外，多走幾步路可以到大東文化藝術中心附近吃「橋邊香腸」，在地 50 年的人氣香腸攤，晚到就賣完囉。

17:30
THE EAST GATE
10. 東便門

The East Gate, a category-three historic monument, is the lone surviving gate from the old city wall, and still serves as an important passage for the local residents. The oldest streets in the city include Datie, Fanshu, Fuju, Jiaju, greeting all visitors entering the gate with a sense of the olden times of this centennial city.

三級古蹟「東便門」是新城內僅存的古城門，時至今日依然是當地居民往來的主要通道。從城門走入，會遇見幾條鳳山城內最古老的街道，像是打鐵街、番薯街、佛具街和家具街。來這一帶走走，還能感受百年古城的舊時生活風貌。

18:30
YUCHUAN VEGETARIAN RESTAURANT
11. 昱川素食

Returning to Zhongshan Road, you immediately feel the full vitality of the modern Fengshan. At sunset, the street turns into a night market from which the locals seek out delicacies, making it less of a touristy, sightseeing affair and more of a relaxing, leisure activity. Here, Yuchuan vegetarian restaurant is especially recommended for its confluence of vegetarian night market foods. Dining amidst the locals creates a beautiful scene by which the day's tour of the twin cities comes to its end.

回程往中山路去，馬上就能感受現今鳳山的滿滿活力。入夜後的中山路自然聚集成為在地人覓食的夜市，少了市區夜市的觀光氣息，多了幾分悠閒輕鬆。這裡特別推薦西園宮前的「昱川素食」，簡直是夜市版的素食總匯。今日的雙城之旅，就在庶民美食中畫下美好句點。

MEINONG DISTRICT, QISHAN DISTRICT AND FO GUANG SHAN IN ONE DAY

KAOHSIUNG EXCURSION

郊遊高雄：美濃、旗山與佛光山一日散策

Photo credit：Ma

SPECIAL FEATURE
KAOHSIUNG
高雄特輯

For those visitors with more time in Kaohsiung, we recommend visiting locations in Meinong and Qishan districts. Foreign travelers with an interest in Buddhism can stop by the Fo Guang Shan Buddha Museum to attend classes or experiential programs tailored to foreign nationals. The day trip offers Hakka culture and spiritual scenery different from downtown Kaohsiung.

Here are our picks:

Morning: take the Meinong express line from Kaohsiung Main Station to Meinong, get a taste of the local specialty breakfast of papaya pancakes, visit the Guangjinsheng paper umbrella factory and the Meinong Hakka Cultural Museum and behold the famous paper umbrellas and Hakka culture.

Noon: eat handmade Meinong rice noodles at Xuanweiwu and proceed to walk around the area.

Afternoon: traverse to Dashu District and gain a deeper understanding of Buddhist culture by strolling around Fo Guang Shan Buddha Museum.

Evening: one can have tasty vegetarian food in the temple area for an early dinner, then visit the old streets of Qishan District and enjoy a cup of pour over coffee.

每次客人來訪高雄，若有多一點時間，我們都會推薦大家往美濃、旗山一帶走，尤其外國朋友若對佛教有興趣，也能順道去「佛光山佛陀紀念館」參觀，參加為外籍人士量身打造的課程或體驗營，看見有別於高雄市區的客家農村與心靈風景。

以下是我們的推薦走法：

早上：從高雄車站搭「美濃快線」到美濃，先品嘗美濃特色早餐「木瓜粄」，再到「廣進勝」油紙傘、「美濃客家文物館」看遠近馳名的紙傘與客家文化。

中午：在「軒味屋」享用手工自製美濃粄條，吃飽繼續散步美濃。

午後：轉往大樹區，參觀「佛光山佛陀紀念館」，深度認識佛教文化。

晚上：晚餐可早點在紀念館內享用美味素食餐點，或到旗山逛老街、喝手沖咖啡。

Meinong is an authentic Hakka town where one can feel the rich Hakka culture and tastes, such as the iconic indigo garments and preserved foods. This agricultural area is known for its highly environmental and community-oriented spirit. Locals cultivate the prestigious water lotus (one of the most famous Taiwanese stir-fry ingredients) and orange cherry tomatoes. In protest to the construction of a water reservoir in 1992, artists in favor of ecological preservation held a festival, the Yellow Butterfly (organized between March and August annually), a brave gesture in the period immediately following the lifting of martial law. Following suit, Hokkien indie-rock band The Labor Exchange Band (whose lead vocalist later founded Sheng-xiang & Band) was established, which sings in traditional Hakka tones about matters close to the hearts of the Meinongese and of all farmers alike.

Recently, many shops run by younger folk have emerged in Meinong, such as Yellow And Black Guest House with its collection of four thousand vinyl records, Yaolan Café x Huiru Hut which was once a Japanese era police station, and Encore Café with its delicious cakes. For those travelers interested in Meinong's produce, all you have to do is to visit the Meinung Farmers' Association to get a hold of the fresh stuff.

Qishan was once an internationally renowned banana town, bringing considerable income to the farmers. The ways of the past can still be seen along the old street which resembles the baroque style. These days, Qishan's banana industry is not as prevalent as it used to be, but it is still an important source of income. In addition to strolling down the old street, it is also recommended to visit Youthbanana Creativity Store which was started by a group of caring young locals who also set up the Youthbanana orchestra in order to highlight the banana industry and Qishan's way of living. The beauty of Qishan is also reflected in the 70-year-old shop, Chang Mei Ice Shop, which has been passed down through three generations. Their traditional-style banana ice dessert carries a sweet and unforgettable taste.

Lastly, Dashu District's Fo Guang Shan Buddha Museum is recommended. This impressive temple has a 50-hectare park which hosts the tallest sitting Buddha statue in the world and a majestic group of pagodas. Facilities with modern technology and an abundance of cultural relics on display inspire visitors with awe. The temple arranges different kinds of activities such as meditation retreats which—given enough time—are definitely worth attending.

美濃是道地的客家小鎮，在這裡能感受到濃厚的客家文化與飲食特色，如客家藍衫與各式醃製品等。這裡也是極有環保、社區意識的高知識農業區，當地居民種植經濟價值高的野蓮（台灣熱炒名菜）與澄蜜香番茄，更在1992年因為反對水庫興建，舉辦了以藝術守護生態的「黃蝶祭」運動（每年3至8月），在剛解嚴不久後的台灣社會，可說是相當前衛且勇敢。此活動還衍生了以客家八音為音樂基礎的獨立搖滾樂團「交工樂隊」（主唱後來成立生祥樂隊），唱出美濃與農民的心聲。

美濃近期也有許多在地青年經營的店家，像是有著四千多張黑膠的「香蕉與黑膠三合院」、由日治時期派出所改造的「搖籃咖啡x惠如小屋」以及有著好吃米蛋糕的「慢熟咖啡」。另外若對美濃食材有興趣的旅人，只要走一趟「美濃農會」便能一次買齊新鮮農產。

隔壁的旗山曾是享譽國際的香蕉重鎮，為農民帶來了可觀的收入，在有著仿巴洛克式建築的旗山老街上，可看得出昔日風華。如今旗山香蕉產業不若以往風光，但仍是重要經濟來源。來這裡除了逛老街，也推薦到「旗山台青蕉香蕉創意工坊」，一樣由一群關心在地的年輕人發起，還成立「台青蕉」樂團，透過音樂讓大家更專注香蕉產業與旗山文化生態。旗山的美好也體現在70年老店「常美冰店」，傳承三代的古早味香蕉冰，甜蜜滋味令人難忘。

最後推薦位於大樹的「佛光山佛陀紀念館」，這裡不只有大家印象中的佛寺，佔地50公頃的園區有著世界最高坐佛與壯觀佛塔群，現代化的設備與豐富的文物展示都讓人驚嘆，館方也舉辦各種相關活動如禪修營等，若有時間千萬別錯過了！

YELLOW AND BLACK GUEST HOUSE 香蕉與黑膠三合院

⌐ 高雄市美濃區興隆一街112巷34號
No. 34, Ln. 112, Xinglong 1st St., Meinong Dist., Kaohsiung City
+886-912-823-556

Photo credit：慢熟咖啡

ENCORE CAFÉ 慢熟咖啡

⌐ 高雄市美濃區自強街一段442號｜facebook.com/ENCORECAFE1921
No. 442, Sec. 1, Ziqiang Street, Meinong Dist., Kaohsiung City
Open on Fri. and Sat. 12:00-18:00

HIDDEN GEMS OF
KAOHSIUNG FLAVORS

這些日常小吃，都飄著台式美國味

SPECIAL FEATURE
KAOHSIUNG
高雄特輯

Once in Kaohsiung, many recommend Lao Chiang's signature breakfast of black tea coupled with toast topped with an egg sunny side up. Many do not know that the shop's toaster, which turns white bread into crispy, golden yellow toast, was actually removed from a US warship. Looking back at 1953, Lao Chiang's founding year, it was the beginning of the US garrisons in Taiwan, for the Korean war had just broken out. As many US soldiers found themselves in Kaohsiung, bringing with them their preferred tastes for food and entertainment, different kinds of bars, restaurants, and clubs started to appear.

American soldiers were not used to Taiwanese food. With them, they brought in wheat flour, milk, condensed milk, toast and even their own chefs. The warships also carried over beef steaks, salads, sandwiches, and other such foods. The openness and creativity of the Taiwanese allowed them to incorporate local flavors into these new elements. Thus, when excess papaya crops were added to milk, the now-ubiquitous night market favorite—papaya milk—was born; those wanting to make sandwiches but lacking a toaster simply used a charcoal grill instead (they couldn't have imagined that it would become a modern Taiwanese favorite, the grilled sandwich); not used to eating medium rare beef, the Taiwanese introduced well-done teppanyaki steak alongside noodles and an egg sunny side up; ice cream alone was a bore, so it was orchestrated into an ice cream cake.

Since then, these food items have made their way into the daily diet of many Taiwanese. However, in Kaohsiung there are a number of make-shift cuisines and vendors from that era still going strong. For an old-school get-together, the old Kaohsiungers' meeting places Mimi's Steakhouse is recommended. And as for your sweet tooth, head on over to Kaohsiung Milk King or Bresler's Ice Cream and get a mouthful of that Taiwanese fusion sweetness.

來高雄玩，許多人都會推薦到老牌早餐店「老江紅茶」喝杯招牌紅茶牛奶搭配半熟蛋吐司，但大家可能不知道，將白吐司烤得金黃酥脆的土司機，竟是從美軍軍艦上拆下來的！回顧老江成立的1953年，正是美軍因韓戰開始駐守台灣的初期，大量美國軍官從高雄港上岸，應運而生的飲食、娛樂需求，促成了各式酒吧、餐廳與俱樂部的出現。

吃不慣台灣食物的美國大兵帶來了小麥粉、牛奶、煉乳、吐司甚至是美國大廚，軍艦也帶來了牛排、沙拉、三明治等西方飲食。而充滿創意的台灣人當然不免俗地加入了台味元素，靈巧的台灣人在牛奶裡嘗試加入了生產過剩的木瓜，竟搖身一變成為夜市飲料之王木瓜牛乳；想做三明治但沒有吐司機的商家就用炭火直烤（沒想到現在台灣正當紅的可是炭烤吐司）；吃不慣有血水牛肉的台灣人於是推出鐵板全熟牛排，旁邊還要放麵和荷包蛋；冰淇淋單吃太無聊，我們就做成冰淇淋蛋糕！

如今這些食物已成為台灣日常風景，但在高雄還有不少在那個年代應運而生的西餐廳與店仍然屹立不搖。想要老派約會的推薦老一輩高雄人的約會勝地「新統一牛排館」；如果想來點甜的就到「高雄木瓜牛乳大王」或是「百樂冰淇淋」，吃一口台美混血的香甜滋味。

LAO CHIANG MILK TEA 老江紅茶牛奶
高雄市新興區南台路51號 | +886-7-287-7317
No. 51, Nantai Rd., Xinxing Dist., Kaohsiung City
24 hours

MIMI'S STEAKHOUSE 新統一牛排館
高雄市鹽埕區五福四路31號 | +886-7-551-9479
No. 31, Wufu 4th Rd., Yancheng Dist., Kaohsiung City
11:30-14:30, 17:30-21:30 (Closed on Tue. to Thur.)

SEEFOOD

KAOHSIUNGERS LEAD YOU IN ON THE FOUR SCHOOLS OF SEAFOOD

跟著高雄人吃海產，4 大派別報你知

SPECIAL FEATURE
KAOHSIUNG
高雄特輯

When coming to the harbor area, people, especially non-locals, usually haphazardly search for a recommended seafood restaurant online. This sort of ordeal simply will not do in the eyes of the Kaohsiungers: here, eating seafood is a battle of different schools.Have you ever noticed how the restaurants add the word "Penghu" to their name signs? This is in reference to the Penghu Islands and comes from the many Penghu migrants who have started restaurants, and translates as: fresh seafood flown over from Penghu daily. In the wake of city development, the restaurants have also become finer in class, such as the Sea World Seafood Restaurant and Crab's House Restaurant, both of which can be said to belong to the gentry of seafood cuisine. Common dishes in the Penghu faction of seafood include narrow-barred Spanish mackerel, Iniistius trivittatus, cold-dressing crowned turban shells, boiled calamari, braised pork with octopus, oysters with seaweed, fried eggs with sea urchin, and rice noodles with squash, all of which are rarely found on the menus of other seafood restaurants.

In addition, Kaohsiung is also home to the Qijin, Donggang, and Tainan schools of seafood. Qijin fish comes mainly from the Qijin and Ch'ien-chen fishing harbors, and the most bountiful catch has the tendency to end up in the tummies of the Qijin residents. Donggang has tuna, sakura shrimp, marlin oden and an assortment of sashimi. The Tainan school is about knife skills and exquisite technique in preparing peculiar delicacies such as eel noodles. In contrast, Penghu and Donggang cuisines prepare seafood in a relatively straightforward manner, not using starch to thicken soup stocks and adding only minimal seasoning. The following list of recommended restaurants from Kaohsiung's different seafood schools should help you cherry-pick your seafood just like the Kaohsiungers do.

來到港都，不免俗地一定要吃個海產，身為外地人，大家可能找家網路推薦的海產店就草草了事，這種行為在高雄在地人眼裡簡直搞不清楚狀況，在這裡，連吃個海產可都是有派系之爭的！你曾經注意過某些海產店的招牌上，除了大大的名字外，還寫著「澎湖」兩個字嗎？是的，高雄其實有許多來自澎湖的移民，這些由澎湖人開設的海產店，因為熟悉當地門路，使用的都是當日從澎湖空運而來的新鮮海產。而隨著都市發展，澎湖海產店也發展成更高級精緻的餐廳，如「海天下」與「蟳之屋」，簡直可說是海產店的仕紳化。澎湖派系的常見菜色有土魠魚、紅新娘、涼拌珠螺、汆燙小卷、魠鮔滷肉、紫菜鮮蚵、海膽炒蛋和金瓜米粉也都是其他海產店沒有的料理。

除此之外，高雄也有旗津派、東港派與台南派的海產店，旗津的漁獲多來自旗津與前鎮漁港，而且最好的漁獲通常都留在旗津被當地人吞下肚；東港則有黑鮪魚、櫻花蝦和旗魚黑輪（裡面包蛋！）等，也提供生魚片料理；台南派則是在切工、料理手法上較為細膩，也有特色料理如鱔魚意麵。相比之下，澎湖、東港系統的海產店，通常都以較簡單的方式烹調海鮮，也不見勾芡或放太多調味。以下我們推薦幾間高雄不同派系的海產店，讓你像個高雄人一樣，挑嘴吃海鮮。

QIJIN SCHOOL-HAIBIN SEAFOOD 旗津派-海濱海產
⌖ 高雄市旗津區中洲巷68-16號 | +886-7-571-3485 | 10:00-20:30
No. 68-16, Zhonggang St., Qijin Dist., Kaohsiung City

TAINAN SCHOOL-TAINAN WANG 台南派-台南旺
⌖ 高雄市前金區六合二路187號 | +886-7-272-0999
No. 187, Liuhe 2nd Rd., Qianjin Dist., Kaohsiung City
17:00-21:30 (Closed from Mon. to Wed.)

PENGHU SCHOOL-WEISIEN SEAFOOD 澎湖派-味鮮澎湖海產
⌖ 高雄市新興區民生一路214號 | 17:00-01:00 (Clsoed on Mon.)
No. 214, Minsheng 1st Rd., Xinxing Dist., Kaohsiung | +886-7-282-3131

DONGGANG SCHOOL-FOODIE SMALL CAFÉ 東港派-福得小館
⌖ 高雄市苓雅區和平一路179號 | +886-7-222-0089
No. 179, Heping 1st Rd., Lingya Dist., Kaohsiung City
11:30-14:30, 17:30-21:30

背山面海的熱帶之都

屏東
PING
TUNG

TROPICAL LAND WITH HILLS BEHIND AND THE OCEAN IN FRONT

——————— Ming Chang Huang 黃銘彰

Located at the very south of Taiwan, the oblong county of Pingtung has the privilege of enjoying nice weather year round. The residents here consist of indigenous, Minnan, Hakka and other ethnic groups, giving this land a diverse culture. Instead of hastily pursuing industrialization like other cities in Taiwan, Pingtung retains its original character and shows endless possibilities.

In the Pingbei area under the hill of Dawu Mountain that is also called Kavulungan in the indigenous Paiwan language, you will find the oldest church in Taiwan and some of the best-quality chocolate in the world. By the sea in Donggang Township, a new landmark has formed—The Goddess of the Sea, a lantern art installation built with 350,000 oyster shells. In the sunny Hengchun Township, the well-preserved, century-old town walls, nowhere else to be found in Taiwan, accompany you on your journey. Kenting (Kending) National Park, the first national park to open in Taiwan, is the place to meet surfers from around the world, all come to challenge the azure ocean.

Besides the worth-mentioning natural scenery and fresh produce, an abundance of cultural activities have been emerging in this area over the past few years, such as stylish shops and stores, and the Isenasena indigenous music festival which started in 2015. It was even decided that the 2019 Taiwan Design Expo would open in Pingtung for the first time. These active cultural scenes bring a fresh new look to Pingtung. If you are tired of bustling city life, just come to the south of the island and let the southern sun rejuvenate your exhausted body and mind.

位處台灣最南端的屏東縣，南北狹長、四季如春，這裡散居著原住民、閩南、客家等多元族群，擁有豐富的文化面貌。這裡並不像台灣其他城市迅速走上工業化之路，反而處處充滿性格，蘊藏意想不到的可能。

像是大武山腳下的屏北地區，不但有現存最古老的教堂建築，更種植出世界上品質最優良的可可；沿海的東港地區，由 35 萬顆蚵殼打造的燈會主燈「海之女神」成為地方新地標。向南來到陽光燦爛的恆春鎮，不時會望見全台保存最完整的百年城牆；再往南抵達台灣首座國家公園所在地——墾丁，隨處都能碰上被湛藍海洋吸引而來、曬得一身黝黑的國內外衝浪愛好者。

屏東除了引以為傲的生態景觀與蔬菜農產外，近期也有許多風格小店出現，15 年開始舉辦原民藝術音樂祭典「斜坡上的藝術節」，台灣設計展也在 2019 年首度於此開展，讓屏東展現有別於以往的風貌。總之要是膩了大城市的生活，就來國境之南吧，讓南方的陽光，療癒疲憊的身心。

TRANSPORTATION
交通

To get to Pingtung from Taipei by public transportation, first catch the HSR to Zuoying Station, which takes about 2 hours. Then transfer to the TRA and travel to Pingtung Station, which takes about 40 minutes. When traveling in Pingtung City, although YouBike (public bike-sharing service) is available around town, renting a scooter or a car is highly advisable in the event you decide to travel further south to Hengchun or Kenting.

台北往屏東可搭乘高鐵至高雄左營站（約 2 小時），再轉搭台鐵至屏東站，約需 40 分鐘左右。市區內有公共自行車 YouBike 可租借，但強烈建議租汽、機車代步，若打算繼續前往恆春或墾丁，會方便許多。

RECOMMEMDATIONS
推薦

◤ READING LIST 旅遊書籍

THE PLACE: PINGTUNG《本地 THE PLACE：屏東》
Currently one of the best Pingtung travel guides, covering the culture, the customs and the people
從人文、習俗等多角度切入，目前最棒的屏東深度旅遊書

⌐ books.com.tw/products/0010820636

◤ LOCAL PUBLICATIONS 在地刊物

VERY PINGTUNG《屏東本事》
Diligent quarterly magazine covering local affairs published by the Pingtung government
由屏東縣政府發行的季刊，編輯用心，可線上閱讀

⌐ e-book：reurl.cc/6vXXDO

AMAZING PINGTUNG
Diligent bimonthly magazine covering local affairs published by the Pingtung government
由屏東縣政府發行的在地資訊雙月刊，可線上閱讀

⌐ e-book：reurl.cc/4rYY32

TOURISM BROCHURE OF PINGTUNG
《關於屏東的 6 件事》
Six highly in-demand Pingtung travel brochures titled Coffee, Dessert, Rice, Cuisine, Read, Mountain and Sea
一發刊就被搶光的旅遊手冊，共有咖啡、甜點、米食、閱讀、山、海 6 本

⌐ e-book：issuu.com/pthgwebsite

NEW WAYS TO EXPLORE SOUTHERN TAIWAN
《南島新玩樣》
Kenting's community ecotourism guide for 2019. On-line versions are available in Chinese and English
2019墾丁社區生態旅遊手冊，中英文版皆可線上閱讀

⌐ 中文：issuu.com/lishaneco/docs/kenting_ecotourism-ch-2016
⌐ English：issuu.com/ lishaneco/docs/kenting_ecotourism

◤ TRAVEL WEBSITES 旅遊網站

I-PINGTUNG TRAVEL GUIDE 屏東縣觀光旅遊網
Pingtung government's official online travel guide (one of the better looking ones)
屏東市旅遊官方網站，少數比較好看的政府網頁

⌐ i-pingtung.com

UUKT 悠遊墾丁
One of the most comprehensive Kenting and Hengchun travel websites. An essential planning tool
最完整的墾丁、恆春旅遊資訊網站，規劃墾丁行程必備

⌐ uukt.com.tw

TAIWAN NEW FOOD 平食樂趣
Facebook page sharing information about good food and restaurants in Pingtung
分享屏東美食店家的臉書粉絲專頁

⌐ facebook.com/taiwannewfood

◤ GUIDED TOURS 導覽

PEARL PINGTUNG 南國小藝思・沐光私旅行
Providing short, irregularly scheduled local/community trips and recommended itineraries
不定期舉辦社區、在地小旅行，網站也有推薦行程

⌐ facebook.com/pearlpingtung

LISHAN ECO COM 森社場所
Local team promoting the Satoyama Initiative and ecotourism
以里山為中心思想，推廣生態旅遊的在地團隊

⌐ facebook.com/LiShanEcotourism

◤ ANNUAL EVENTS 年度活動

HEAR HERE FEST (OCT.) 半島歌謠祭 (10月)
International world music festival in Hengchun that welcomes everyone
在恆春舉辦的國際民謠音樂節，邀請大家一起來同歡

⌐ facebook.com/hearherefest

A **WANCHIN BASILICA OF THE IMMACULATE CONCEPTION**
萬金聖母聖殿
Oldest church preserved in Taiwan, conferred the title of
basilica by Pope John Paul II
台灣現存最古老的教堂，受教宗若望保祿二世列為聖殿

📍 屏東縣萬巒鄉萬興路24號 | +886-8-783-2005
No. 24, Wanxing Rd., Wanluan Township, Pingtung County

B **BREEZY BLUE** 藍皮解憂號
Take the oldest train in Taiwan from Fangliao Railway
Station and enjoy the scenic beauty of the South Link Line
with a refreshing breeze
從枋寮車站搭乘台灣最老火車，迎著微風感受南迴風光

📍 請預先上網購票 | +886-2-8793-2565 (Phone reservation is
required for booking tickets)

C **PINGTUNG COUNTY LIBRARY** 屏東縣立圖書館總館
Taiwan's only forest-themed library, a unique venue that
regularly hosts vibrant markets and events
全台唯一森林系圖書館，不定時舉辦各式市集活動

📍 屏東縣屏東市大連路69號 | www.cultural.pthg.gov.tw
No. 69, Dalian Rd., Pingtung City, Pingtung County
09:00-21:00 (Closed on Mondays)

D **SSUN VILLE** 小陽。日栽書屋
Vibrant bookstore converted from an old house and
holding frequent cultural events
完整保留老屋結構，經常發起藝文活動，能量充沛

📍 屏東縣屏東市清營巷1號 | facebook.com/ssunville
No. 1, Qingying Ln., Pingtung City, Pingtung County
14:00-20:00 (Closed from Mon.to Wed.)

E **AKAUW BOOKS** 繫。本屋
Offering a rich selection of books on folk culture, with the
must-visit Fāng Gēn Fā Coffee Bar in the backyard
擁有豐富民俗文化選書，後院「方根發咖啡」不可錯過

📍 屏東縣屏東市青島街112號 | +886-908-839-267
No. 112, Qingdao St., Pingtung City, Pingtung County
10:30-18:30 (Closed on Mon. and Tue.) | facebook.com/akauwbooks

F **LE BALLONROUGE** 紅氣球書屋
Discover local history and culture, engage in community
events at this vibrant bookstore
在這裡認識在地歷史文化，店裡不定時舉辦各式交流活動

📍 屏東縣恆春鎮北門路110巷86號 | +886-934-149-657
No. 86, Ln. 110, Beimen Rd., Hengchun Township, Pingtung County
Fri. to Sun. 11:00-18:00

Photo credit：Johnson Wang

Photo credit：御木軒冰室

A **MEI-JU'S NOODLE SHOP 美菊麵店**
Praised as the most beautiful noodle shop in Taiwan, they put their whole heart into each serving
號稱「全台灣最美麵店」，用心煮好一碗麵

屏東縣屏東市協和東路99號｜facebook.com/meiju88
No. 99, Xiehe East Road, Pingtung City, Pingtung County
11:00-18:30 (Closed on Tue. and Wed.)

B **A BOWL OF TOFU 一碗豆腐**
The reinvention of stinky tofu at a Japanese-street-style stand
改良傳統臭豆腐，攤販設置擁有日本街町的特殊氛圍

屏東縣屏東市濟南街2-6號｜+886-916-199-318
No. 2-6, Jinan St., Pingtung City, Pingtung County
14:30-21:00 (Closed on Wednesdays)

C **YE'S STEAMED RICE CAKE 葉家肉粿**
The favorite steamed rice cake of the Donggang locals, established 50 years ago
擁有 50 年歷史，是東港在地人指名的人氣店家

屏東縣東港鎮光復路三段156號｜+886-8-832-9218
No. 156, Sec. 3, Guangfu Rd., Donggang Township, Pingtung County
09:00-14:30

D **BAI-YANG-DAO MOCHI 白羊道柴燒麻糬**
Made with natural, local ingredients and lots of patience. Waiting time required
運用天然在地食材製作，需耐心等待

屏東縣恆春鎮中山路188號｜+886-8-889-9992
No. 188, Zhongshan Rd., Hengchun Township, Pingtung County
12:00-18:00 (Closed on Tue. to Thur.)

E **AUTHENTIC CHAO ZHOU COLD & HOT ICE 正老牌潮州冷熱冰**
Don't miss this amazing cold-and-hot-mixed-flavored ice that you will never forget
不可錯過這冷熱交融的絕妙滋味，包準讓你畢生難忘

屏東縣潮州鎮新生路120號｜+886-8-788-6117
No. 120, Xinsheng Rd., Chaozhou Township, Pingtung County
09:00-22:00, weekends 09:00-22:30

F **YU MU XUAN ICE SHOP 御木軒冰室**
Indulge in sweet shaved ice at the old house built in the early Showa period
在昭和初期建造的老房子大口吃甜蜜剉冰

屏東縣屏東市勝利路133號｜+886-933-123-182
No. 133, Shengli Rd., Pingtung City, Pingtung County
12:00-18:30, weekends 12:00-20:30 (Closed on Mon. and Tue.)

Photo credit : Le Son

Photo credit : 驛前大和咖啡館

Photo credit : 三平咖啡

A ESKE PLACE COFFEE HOUSE
Australian and local fusion Café with higher-quality coffees and sweets
融入在地風情的澳式咖啡館，咖啡甜點皆在水準之上

⌂ 屏東縣屏東市民享路142號 | +886-8-722-6266
No. 142, Minxiang Rd., Pingtung City, Pingtung County
09:00–17:00 (Closed on Mon. and Tue.)

B CHUN JO COFFEE 春若咖啡
Diligent, sophisticated café with a lovely yard and various brewed coffee choices
手沖咖啡選擇多，用心講究的精品庭園咖啡館

⌂ 屏東縣屏東市天津街6號 | +886-968-758-310
No. 6, Tianjin St., Pingtung City, Pingtung County
11:00-19:00

C YAMATO COFFEE 驛前大和咖啡館
A boutique coffee shop transformed from an 80-year-old historic hotel
由80年歷史旅社改建而成的精品咖啡館

⌂ 屏東縣屏東市民族路163號 | +886-8-766-9777
No. 163, Minzu Rd., Pingtung City, Pingtung County
09:00-18:00

D AKAME
Contemporary indigenous cuisine, well worth the trip. By reservation only
值得專程前往的原住民當代料理，只接受預約用餐

⌂ 屏東縣霧台鄉古茶柏安街17巷8號 | facebook.com/akame.in
No. 8, Ln. 17, Guchabo'an St., Wutai Township, Pingtung County
18:00–00:00 (Closed on Mon. and Tue.)

E LE SON
Modern European cuisine featuring Taiwanese ingredients. By reservation only
台灣食材入菜的歐洲現代料理，只接受預約用餐

⌂ 屏東縣屏東市豐榮街12號 | www.instagram.com/le_son_tw
No. 12, Fengrong St., Pingtung City, Pingtung County
預約請洽Line For reservations, please contact via LINE, ID : @lesontw

F SANPEI CAFÉ 三平咖啡
Nostalgic, elengat Japanese-style café makes you feel like you're in a museum. Lunch and dinner by reservation only
如個人美術館般的日式咖啡廳，用餐需預約

⌂ 屏東縣潮州鎮育才路86號 | facebook.com/sanpeitaiwan
No. 86, Yucai Road, Chaozhou Township, Pingtung County
11:30–17:30, Sat.&Sun.till 20:00 (Closed on Tue.) | +886-8-789-8363

ACCOMMODATIONS

住宿

Photo credit：鈕扣倉庫

Photo credit：James Lin

Photo credit：窩墾丁

Photo credit：德旅店

A NEW CUT WAREHOUSE 鈕扣倉庫
Tropical-island-style bistro converted from an abandoned warehouse
廢墟空間重生，充滿濃濃半島風情的餐酒吧

⌂ 屏東縣恆春鎮恆西路12號｜+886-8-888-3578
No. 12, Hengxi Rd., Hengchun Township, Pingtung County
18:30–01:30 (Closed on Wed.)

B WOOKT BARISTRO 窩墾丁
Proud branch of Woo Taipei, a chic bar in Taipei City
台北質感酒吧「窩台北」的墾丁得意之作

⌂ 屏東縣恆春鎮恆北路8-16號
No. 8-16, Hengbei Rd., Hengchun Township, Pingtung County
11:30–20:00
+886-8-888-1980

C GLORIA MANOR 華泰瑞苑
Design hotel in the mountains offers a pleasurable holiday experience
想享受一些的話，請來這家在山腰上的設計旅館

⌂ 屏東縣恆春鎮公園路101號｜+886-8-888-3666
No. 101, Gongyuan Rd., Hengchun Township, Pingtung County
gloriamanor.com

D WANDERING WALLS 灣臥
A serene and secluded retreat, nestled between mountains and the sea
背山面海，遺世獨立的祕境旅宿

⌂ 屏東縣恆春鎮崁頭路270號｜+886-8-889-9270
No. 270, Kantou Rd., Hengchun Township, Pingtung County
thewanderingwalls.com

E DE HOTEL 德旅店
Experience the charm of rural culture and Hakka cuisine at a boutique guesthouse converted from an old rice mill
老碾米廠改建的質感民宿，體驗鄉野人文與客家美食

⌂ 屏東縣竹田鄉豐明路22 號｜+886-975-502-083
No. 22, Fengming Road, Zhutian Township, Pingtung County
www.dehostel.com.tw

F SUMMER POINT
Located in the popular surfing spot of Jialeshuei, the hearty owner shows you the charm of the ocean
位於衝浪聖地佳樂水，老闆親切熱情，帶你感受海洋魅力

⌂ 屏東縣滿洲鄉港口村茶山路252號｜+886-936-416-006
No. 252, Chashan Rd., Manzhou Township, Pingtung County
facebook.com/summerpoint

PINGTUNG ROUTE
屏東路線

PINGTUNG CITY
AND HENGCHUN AREA
市區與恆春周邊

A NATURE AND CULTURE DAY TRIP IN PINGTUNG 屏東山海人文一日遊

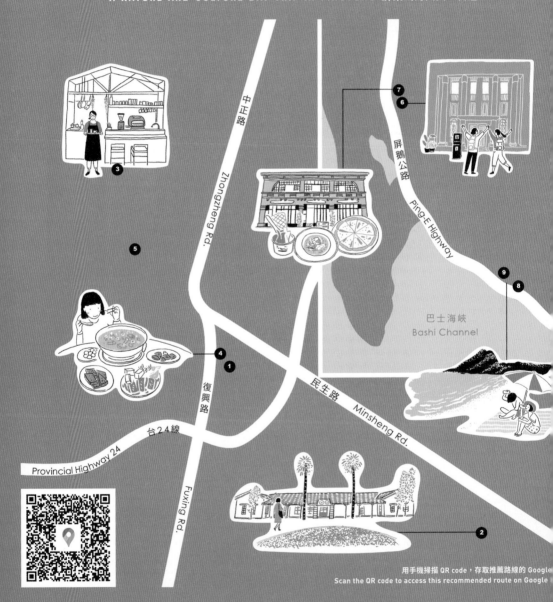

用手機掃描 QR code，存取推薦路線的 Google
Scan the QR code to access this recommended route on Google

1)	08:30	Start your day in the night market for Authentic Pingtung Ba-wan, while supplies last
2)	09:30	Visit the old-looking, creatively-renewed Pingtung Tobacco Factory
3)	10:30	Wander the reconstructed veteran's village and check out some bookstores
4)	11:30	Taste the delicious authentic beef hotpot and some rich papaya milk afterward
5)	13:00	Get some scrumptious bread from Mei-Ju Bakery on your way to Hengchun
6)	15:30	Take a leisurely walk through Hengchun Old Town and enjoy a cup of coffee
7)	17:00	Have dinner at Kitchen Swell for some sunny Mediterranean cuisine
8)	19:30	Linger on the beach or at the light-pollution-free meadow under starry skies
9)	22:00	Embraced by the southern evening breeze, end your day with some drinks

---

1)	08:30	來夜市吃早餐，可別錯過早早就賣光的「正老牌屏東肉圓」
2)	09:30	妥善保留舊風貌又具有新氣象的「屏東菸葉廠」
3)	10:30	漫步老眷村活化後的園區，靜心感受書香氣息
4)	11:30	品嚐湯頭迷人的道地牛肉火鍋，再來杯香醇木瓜牛乳
5)	13:00	買個麵包等等去恆春的路上吃
6)	15:30	恆春古城散心，享受愜意的咖啡、閱讀走逛時光
7)	17:00	在「波波廚房」享用充滿陽光味道的地中海料理
8)	19:30	到墾丁海邊散步，在無光害的大草原抬頭仰望星空
9)	22:00	南方晚風輕拂下，怎能不小酌一杯

PINGTUNG CITY
屏東

After taking the HSR to Zuoying Station, transfer to the TRA or a bus to Pingtung City. Pingtung City was never a popular travel destination, but a cultural tourism trend has emerged here over the past few years. Meticulous shops hidden down old alleys and reputable local food vendors offer the most charming scenes.

搭乘高鐵至左營站後,可轉乘台鐵或客運抵達屏東市區。近年來,過往在旅程安排時常被忽略的屏東市,吹起來一股濃濃的文化旅行氣息,藏身古老巷弄間用心經營的小店,以及飄香多年的美食,是這裡最迷人的風景。

08:30
AUTHENTIC PINGTUNG BA-WAN
1. 正老牌屏東肉圓

Early in the morning, head to the lively Pingtung Night Market and have some Authentic Pingtung Ba-wan for breakfast. The typical southern Taiwanese steamed ba-wan is smaller in size, so a regular serving consists of five ba-wans. If that is not enough for your stomach, try A-Gou Sliced Food for an assorted plate of sliced delicacies, stir-fried rice noodles, hot garlic sauce and a bowl of aromatic broth.

透早來逛從早熱鬧到晚的「屏東夜市」,早餐就先來吃「正老牌屏東肉圓」,南部的「蒸肉圓」尺寸迷你,一次來 5 顆是基本分量。肚子還餓可以到附近的「阿狗切仔擔」切盤黑白切,搭配炒米粉、辣蒜醬和免費的濃醇清湯就是完美組合。

09:30
PINGTUNG TOBACCO FACTORY
2. 屏東菸葉廠

Bearing witness to the history of Taiwan's tobacco monopoly, the old Pingtung Tobacco Factory keeps a well-preserved assembly hall, boiler room, stem-removing room, and curing room. After completion of the reconstruction plan several years ago, the factory is now open to the public as a new culture and design venue that holds arts and culture events and exhibitions on an unfixed schedule.

見證台灣菸葉專賣歷史的「屏東菸葉廠」,中山堂、鍋爐室、菸草葉除骨及復薰加工區等舊有廠區結構保存完整。近年在活化整理後對外開放,不定期舉辦藝文活動及各式特展,是屏東文化與設計的新基地。

10:30
VICTORYSTAR IN PINGTUNG ZONE
3. 勝利星村創意生活園區

Formerly an old veteran's village, Victorystar in Pingtung Zone, also called V.I.P. Zone, has many stores and shops that are worth exploring, such as Akauw Books, an independent bookstore with a wide selection of folk culture and local history books, and Gadu Studio that promotes indigenous tribe ecotourism and provides farm products from indigenous tribes, and other creative products.

原先是老眷村的「勝利星村創意生活園區」，在活化後有許多有趣店家進駐。像是選書遍及民俗文化及在地歷史的獨立書店「繁。本屋」，還有致力於推動原鄉部落生態旅遊並在空間提供部落簡單農產品及文創商品的「奧山」等，都值得逛逛。

11:30
BEEF HOTPOT AND QIU-LIN MILK BAR
4. 牛肉鍋 與 秋林牛乳大王

Pingtung locals have a thing for hotpot. Xin-Yuan Beef Hotpot and Long-Xing Shantou Hotpot consisting of generous chunks of beef and delicious broth are local favorites. After a hotpot feast, visit Qiu-Lin Milk Bar, the locals' go-to dating place, for a glass of the signature papaya milk or a big bowl of mango shaved ice. I personally adore the frozen taro, a recipe much improved by the owner!

屏東人特愛吃鍋，有著豪邁現切牛肉與鮮美湯頭的「新園牛肉爐」及「隆興汕頭火鍋」是不容錯過的必訪名單。吃完再到老屏東人的約會地點「秋林牛乳大王」，來杯招牌木瓜牛乳或大碗芒果冰，其實我也愛老闆精心研發的冷凍芋，好吃！

13:00
MEI-JU BAKERY
5. 美菊麵包店

Head to the most beautiful bakery in Taiwan, Mei-Ju Bakery, which is named after the owner's grandmother, for some of their signature bagels or soft bread before you head to Hengchun. (During a summer visit to Pingtung, if the weather gets too hot and you're looking for a simple yet delicious meal for lunch, you can head to the nearby Mei-Ju Noodle Shop, opened by the same owner of Mei-Ju Bakery. Enjoy a satisfying bowl of noodles and braised dishes!)

接著到有屏東最美麵包店之稱、以阿嬤名字命名的「美菊麵包店」買招牌的貝果或吐司，等等搭車到恆春時可以墊墊胃。（夏天造訪屏東若天氣太熱，中午想吃點簡單但美味的餐點，可到附近同樣由美菊麵包店老闆開設的「美菊麵店」，享用好吃的乾麵和滷味！）

HENGCHUN AND KENTING

恆春 與 墾丁

Heading south till you reach Hengchun, the sun is even brighter here. Behind the ancient walls of Hengchun Old Town, some delightful stores and shops are waiting for you to explore. After dark, it finally quiets down in the popular travel destination of Kenting, allowing you to ease your pace and feel the peaceful sea breeze. Gently embraced by the ocean and mountains, you realize why so many people have decided to settle down here to pursue their dreams.

從市區搭乘客運一路向南往恆春走，陽光愈發燦爛，古城牆內也有愈來愈多有趣店家。晚上再到觀光勝地墾丁，海洋的氣息沁人肺腑，我們終於可以放慢腳步，被山海溫柔擁抱。不難明白為何有那麼多人選擇移居此地，開始真正地「過生活」。

15:30
TRANQUIL TIME IN A SMALL TOWN

6. 小鎮時光

Several stylish cafés and culture spaces are hidden within the quaint Old Town area of Hengchun. Hop off at Hengchun Bus Station and pay a visit to Lishan Eco Com, a space that promotes local ecotourism and provides farm products from local communities, and other creative products. Then, following the ancient wall clockwise, find a seat and enjoy a cup of coffee at But Who Roasting and Bakery or Glass House, a beautiful café constructed largely of glass under a royal poinciana tree. If you enjoy spending time in renovated old spaces like this, Credit Union Base is also a good option.

The chance to enjoy the limited-production Bai-Yang-Dao Charcoal-roasted Mochi near the west town gate requires some luck. Keep going to the east town gate and you will arrive at Le Ballon Rouge, Taiwan's southernmost independent bookstore. HC Playground and the Hun-Hau Restaurant & Gallery next door are worth checking out as well.

在小小的恆春古城，有幾間極具質感的咖啡廳及空間藏身其中。從轉運站下車後，先到推廣社區生態遊程、販售社區農產品及文創商品的「森社場所」。接著順時針散步小城，首先在老鳳凰樹下的絕美玻璃咖啡屋「樹夏飲事」或「伯虎在二樓，恆春 But Who」喝杯咖啡吧，喜歡老屋空間也可以到「恆春信用組合」坐坐。

在西門附近的「白羊道柴燒麻糬」，每日限量的美味要有緣分才吃得到。繼續往東門走，會來到本島最南的獨立書店「紅氣球書屋」，旁邊的「城東大院子」與「恆。好 餐廳 & 畫廊」也都值得逛逛。

17:00
KITCHEN SWELL
7. 波波廚房

■

Originally operated out of a pizza truck, Kitchen Swell now resides in an old building in the center of Hengchen, bringing new life to the old edifice. They value the original taste of ingredients and put their whole heart into making mediterranean bistro cuisine. If Kitchen Swell is too crowded during weekends, you might venture further south and try either the Japanese restaurant Honnkiya or the homestyle restaurant Migu Village. Making reservations in advance for all above restaurants is advisable.

從墾丁大家披薩攤車起家的「波波廚房」，以恆春中心的一棟古宅為空間，讓老建築有了新生命。這裡的烹調忠於食材原味，賣著有靈魂的地中海餐酒料理。若假日人潮眾多，也推薦南邊一點的日式料理「本氣食堂」或家常菜館「麋谷」（假日建議都先訂位）。

19:30
BEACHES AND CHINIULING MEADOW
8. 沙灘 與 草原

■

After a satisfying meal, why not take a walk along the beach in Kenting! If you'd like to avoid the crowds that fill popular beaches like Nanwan Bay (South Bay) and Baishawan Bay, make a trip to the recently well-managed Xiaowan Beach (Little Bay) or the less-famous Xingshawan Bay. Or head to the vast, light-pollution-free ChiNiuLing meadow and bathe in the tranquil aura under starry skies.

吃飽我們就前往墾丁海邊散步吧！若想避開如南灣、白沙灣等著名沙灘的人潮，可到近年來環境維護管理良好的「小灣沙灘」，或者較少人知道的「星砂灣」。若想看星星，「赤牛嶺」遼闊的草原讓視野一望無際，可盡情徜徉在無光害的漫天星斗之中。

22:00
TIPSY TIME
9. 小酌一杯

■

With the southern breeze blowing by, there's no harm in ending your day over a few drinks with friends. There are plenty of bars and bistros in Kenting, which usually offer a relaxing ambiance and a welcoming owner. I recommend Hold inn Lounge and 30M Bar. If you prefer an even more authentic and carefree tropical style, the mobile Ma Der Barz on Kenting Main Street is a typical Taiwanese choice.

南方晚風輕拂下，適合與三五好友一同小酌來作結。墾丁有不少小酒館，老闆大多親切健談，氣氛放鬆，這邊推薦「猴飲酒館」及「30M Bar」兩家。若想體驗更道地、隨興的熱帶南島風情，墾丁大街上的行動酒吧「馬的吧子」也是相當台式的選擇。

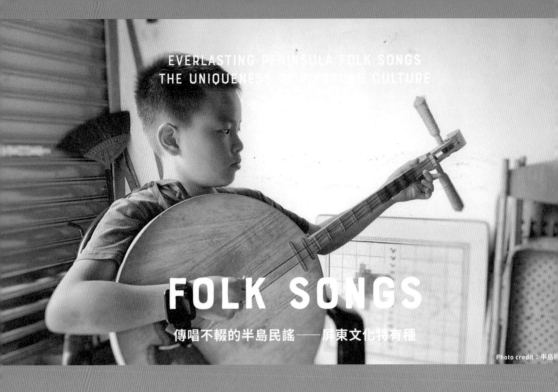

FOLK SONGS

傳唱不輟的半島民謠──屏東文化特有種

Photo credit：半島

Previously known as Longkiau, Hengchun is a peninsula surrounded by the ocean and mountains. Due to historical difficulties in accessing and governing the area, different tribes and ethnic groups reside in harmony here, despite not having clear territorial borders. The peninsula area includes the townships of Hengchun, Checheng, Manzhou, Fangshan, and Mudan, where the mixture of indigenous, Minnan and Hakka people retains peaceful relations. Over time, this land, blown by strong katabatic winds in autumn and winter, has developed a unique, culturally-inclusive style of folk song that stands out among other types of Taiwanese Minnan folk music.

The seven major folk song melodies that have circulated in Hengchun Peninsula are Old Memories, Forever Spring, Swinging Cow Tail, Plains Indigenous Minor (also called Taitung Minor), Five Kong, Fonggang Minor, and Cattle Watching, the last one exclusive to Manzhou Township. Among these seven melodies, countless songs with alternative lyrics have been created through the various performing styles of the free-spirited locals. Some songs aim to express day-to-day emotions, some are for relaxation between toilsome labor jobs, while still others are for ceremonies performed to eliminate bad luck and pray for blessings. Although countless in their variations, all folk songs have a universal purpose—reflecting the genuine presence of society at the time and place to which those people's hearts belong.

古稱「瑯嶠」的恆春，受山海包圍，在歷史上因為地理位置偏遠，治理不易，不同族群間大多共融而居，沒有明顯的區界。在受落山風吹拂的半島地區，包含恆春鎮、車城鄉、滿洲鄉、枋山鄉及牡丹鄉，混居的原住民、閩南人及客家人互動和諧，隨著時間一久，醞釀出多元融合的歌謠風格，在台灣閩南的地區性民謠之中具有高度的特殊性。

在恆春半島流傳的主要民謠曲調有〈思想起〉、〈四季春〉、〈牛尾絆〉、〈平埔調〉（亦常被稱作〈台東調〉）、〈五孔小調〉（亦稱〈五空小調〉）、〈楓港小調〉，以及滿州鄉特有的〈守牛調〉等7種曲調，透過當地人的自由創作與演繹，能夠幻化出無限種可能。有些人透過民謠寄託生活之中的情感，或者調劑勞動時的疲勞，也有一些民謠創作，是為了祭典的消災祈福用。民謠類型千變萬化，唯一的共通點是，每首歌謠都反映當下社會的真實樣貌及身處其中百姓的生命情懷。

Despite the fact that Hengchun's folk songs almost went extinct at one point, thanks to the tireless endeavors of locals working to preserve them, the peninsula folk songs are now preserved in a systematic archive. From pioneering artists such as Chen Da and Chu Ting-shun to modern masters such as Wu Deng-Rong and Chen Ming Chang, the journey of the Hengchun folk song never ends. As local cultural heritage has been receiving more attention over the past few years, local government and schools have realized the importance of preserving and promoting folk songs. As a result, the traditional culture keeps evolving and showing more possibilities nowadays. Take, for instance, Hear Here Fest, the former Hengchun Peninsula World Music Festival that was transformed in 2018. After the transformation, besides the promotion and preservation of Hengchun Peninsula folk songs, Hear Here Fest also connects the local community and the world through inviting foreign art groups from such diverse artistic genres as music, dance, drama and multimedia to provide the audience with a celebration of international culture.

The reason that peninsula folk songs are still circulating today is because, not only are they precious creations intertwined with history and the environment, they also transcend and resonate between different ethnic groups and generations. To conclude, the peninsula folk songs are no doubt worth exploring, appreciating and handing down to future generations.

Hengchun Folk Songs Museum

Important base devoted to promoting and handing down traditional Hengchun folk song culture through comprehensive images, quality exhibitions and soundtrack curation portraying the ongoing folk song history.

Manjhou Folk Songs Museum

After years of searching, Manjhou Folk Songs Museum finally found a home on the ground floor of Manzhou Township Library where venerable seniors and young students alike gather together to hand down the spirit of the local folk songs.

儘管曾經面臨失傳的危機，在地方民謠工作者的積極奔走下，半島民謠終究免於失傳的命運，有系統地流傳下來。從陳達、朱丁順，一路到現在吳登榮老師與陳明章老師，民謠的傳承沒有停下。隨著地方文化資產逐漸受到重視，近年來，學校和政府單位也開始重視民謠文化的傳承。這項傳統文化在各種刺激下不斷碰撞出愈發繽紛的色彩。在地方深耕多年的「恆春國際民謠音樂節」，就在2018年邁入第10年之際，擴張並轉型為「半島歌謠祭」，除了致力傳承及推廣恆春半島民謠文化，也開展出結合音樂、舞蹈、戲劇、多媒體等多種藝術類型的嶄新面貌，持續連結地方與世界，儼然一場國際文化盛宴。

半島民謠傳唱不輟，是自然與歷史交織下的珍貴產物，更是超越世代與族群的深遠共鳴，值得細細品味，讓它持續傳承下去。

恆春民謠館

推廣傳承恆春傳統民謠文化的重要據點，透過豐富的影像、空間規劃與聲音策展勾勒出長久流傳的民謠歷史輪廓。

滿州民謠音樂館

位於滿州鄉立圖書館一樓，這裡可說是滿州民謠經過多年奔走後覓得的「家」，國寶級阿嬤與學生囝仔齊聚一堂，在這裡將地方歌謠傳唱下去。

HENGCHUN FOLK SONGS MUSEUM 恆春民謠館

屏東縣恆春鎮恆南路168號
No. 168, Hengnan Rd., Hengchun Township, Pingtung County
09:00-17:00 | FB：恆春民謠館

MANJHOU FOLK SONGS MUSEUM 滿州民謠館

屏東縣滿州鄉中山路152號
No. 152, Zhongshan Rd., Manzhou Township, Pingtung County
08:00-17:00 (Closed on Mondays) +886-8-880-1362

ECOTOURISM DEVELOPMENT HAND-IN-HAND WITH COMMUNITY BUILDING:
LEARN ABOUT HENGCHUN FROM A DIFFERENT PERSPECTIVE

ECOTOURISM

陪伴社區成長的生態旅遊———用不一樣的方式認識恆春墾丁

Photo credit：

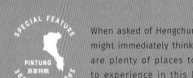

SPECIAL FEATURE
PINTUNG
屏東特輯
SPECIAL FEATURE

When asked of Hengchun Peninsula, many people might immediately think of Kenting. In fact, there are plenty of places to explore and activities to experience in this lively area, such as the fascinating tribes, communities, and natural ecosystems. In-depth ecotours through different communities are one of the best ways for travelers to discover Hengchun Peninsula.

The first community that started to develop ecotourism is Shirding, also spelled Sheding. With the skilled guidance of instructors from Kenting National Park, travelers get to explore the diverse ecosystems, spotting Mycena fungi, golden birdwings and sika deer in this primitive tropical jungle. In September and October, when the seasonal winds start blowing over from the northeast, people gather here to witness the spectacular migrating scene of thousands of Chinese sparrowhawks and grey-faced buzzards from the north, flying over the peninsula and landing on Ling-Xiao pavilion, the highest point of Sheding Natural Park.

The initiator of the ecotourism model is Chen Mei-Hui, a professor in the department of forestry at Pingtung University of Science and Technology. She has worked as a coordinator between the government and the local communities for over 10 years, and established a community forestry model that promotes ecotourism through community empowerment programs that build partnerships between the government and the public.

說到恆春半島，很多人第一個想到的就是墾丁。不過在這個生命力旺盛的半島上，還有許多擁有豐富自然生態和生活風格的社區。而深入在地社區的「生態旅遊」，是旅人認識恆春半島的最佳方式之一。

第一個發展生態旅遊的社區是「社頂部落」，這裡擁有完整的原始熱帶森林，螢光蕈、黃裳鳳蝶、梅花鹿等動植物都在裡頭生活。在墾丁國家公園解說員的帶領下，旅客可以透過遊程認識這裡的生態樣貌。每到 9、10 月，東北季風開始吹拂，北方的赤腹鷹及灰面鵟鷹會飛過半島上空，來到社頂自然公園的制高點凌霄亭，形成數以萬計的「鷹海」，非常壯觀。

事實上，這套生態旅遊模式的幕後推手，是現任屏東科技大學森林系的教授陳美惠。十多年前，她開始擔任公部門與社區之間的橋梁，建立起「社區林業」模式，透過社區培力，讓政府與民間成為夥伴關係，共同推動生態旅遊。

Her student Lin Zhi-Yuan later continued her work on the peninsula, developing various itineraries to recruit more travelers according to each community's needs. With the team's long-term endeavors, there are now more than 11 communities participating in these programs that have developed more than 50 different itineraries. In order to promote their ideas, the team also operates a space called Lishan Eco Com. This successful ecotourism model has not only earned government awards, but has also received ample praise from the ecotourism and environmental protection fields.

Nowadays, several communities have developed their own distinctive ecotours for travelers. These include the Shuiwaku tribe situated next to Longpan Park, the Daguang community with its fascinating intertidal zone ecosystem, the South of the Island community (Eluan) with its unique coastal erosion scenery, Long-Shui Village with its famous organic rice farming, the Houwan community with its beautiful coastal scenery, Lide Community with its stunning forest scenery, the Jiupeng community with its vast meadows, the Gangkou community that grows low-elevation tea, the Manzhou community with its well-preserved historic heritage, and last but not least, the Yongjing community that faces Dajian Mountain.

It should never be said that Kenting Main Street and the beaches are the only places to go in Hengchun. There are numerous ways to explore the ocean and the mountains, offering you a journey both enriching and fulfilling.

Gangkou Community

The tropical jungles along the coastline where land crabs live is a perfect spot for ecological observation. Moreover, you can experience the harvest and taste of Gangkou tea, grown in Taiwan's lowest-elevation tea plantations.

Shuiwaku Tribe

Located between the Pacific Ocean and the Longpan meadow, Shuiwaku Tribe has some breathtaking natural scenery. In the daytime, you may see sika deer gracefully lingering on the meadow; at night, with the comfortable breeze blowing, you may hear frogs under starry skies as mother nature completely lifts all burdens from your heart.

她的指導學生們繼續深耕半島，依照各社區需求開發遊程，同時積極導入遊客；在團隊的長期投入下，目前參與的社區已多達11個，發展出超過50種特色遊程，還在恆春老街開了實體空間「森場場所」，與在地遊客接軌。這套生態旅遊的模式，不但獲得官方獎項肯定，在保育界或生態旅遊界也受到不少好評。

如今，鄰近龍磐公園的「水蛙窟部落」、潮間帶生態繽紛的「大光社區」、海蝕地形獨特的「國境之南社區」、以有機稻作著稱的「龍水社區」、沿岸景致舒適宜人的「後灣社區」、森林景觀傲人的「里德社區」、擁有遼闊草原的「九棚社區」、種植最低海拔茶葉的「港口社區」、歷史痕跡留存完好的「滿州社區」，以及與大尖山遙遙相望的「永靖社區」，都已發展出各有特色的生態遊程。

下次來到恆春半島，別再說只有墾丁大街跟沙灘可以去，山海之間還有好多好多種旅行方式，都可以讓你玩得充實又過癮。

港口社區生態旅遊

港口社區有著大批陸蟹生活在熱帶海岸林之中，適合進行生態觀察；此外，這裡還種有全台灣海拔最低的茶葉「港口茶」，可在此體驗採茶並沖泡品嚐。

水蛙窟生態社區

水蛙窟位在太平洋與龍磐草原之中，擁有絕美的自然景觀。來到這裡，可以瞧見梅花鹿的優雅身影，夜晚時，伴隨著徐徐微風與蛙鳴聲觀看滿天星光，心靈便好像獲得了大自然的完美滋潤。

GANGKOU COMMUNITY 港口社區生態旅遊
facebook.com/gangkou.Ecotourism | +886-963-522-868
https://kko.uukt.com.tw

Photo credit：洪嘉隆

SHUIWAKU TRIBE 水蛙窟生態社區
facebook.com/shuiwaku | +886-909-013-928
shuiwaku@gmail.com

北部慢活，向東移居的第一站

宜蘭
YILAN

WITH ITS RELAXED PACE AND NORTHEAST LOCATION,
YILAN IS THE FIRST STOP ON YOUR JOURNEY TO THE EAST

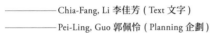

———————— Chia-Fang, Li 李佳芳 (Text 文字)
———————— Pei-Ling, Guo 郭佩怜 (Planning 企劃)

When exiting the Hsuehshan Tunnel, the Yilan Plain stretches in front of your eyes, as the green from the paddies reach up to the horizon in a race to meet the azure Pacific Ocean. In comparison to Taipei, just a short train ride away, the rich and deep colors of this city make visitors believe they have just entered the world of high definition!

From the historical point of view, many influential politicians have come from Yilan, such as Chiang Wei-shui, the co-founder of the Taiwanese Cultural Association and the Taiwan People's Party. Guo Yuxin is a senior statesman outside of party politics as well as Chen Chu, the current Director of the Control Yuan. Geographically speaking, Yilan is the largest agricultural county in the north, and it used to be the first choice for the urbanites who were looking to migrate east.

Yilan has a rich natural and cultural landscape with examples including the Jiaoxi Hot Spring, known far and wide, Su'ao Cold Spring and BulauBulau Aboriginal Village's Tayal culture, which all have contributed to the rapid development of the leisure and tourism industry in the area. In addition, Yilan also has the World Whiskies Awards winner in single malts from the Kavalan whisky owned by the King Car Group. Alsoit's the home of the Taiwanese craft beer brand Jim & Dad's Brew Company. Apart from Yilan's great mountains and waters, its magnificent beverages soothingly charm even the most level-headed, turning the place into a fail-safe destination for those who love to sommelier themselves a glass or two whilst traveling in Taiwan.

穿過雪山隧道，蘭陽平原在眼前舒展，柔軟的稻田綠延伸到天際，承接著蔚藍色的太平洋；對比著方才經過的台北城，宜蘭的色彩又豐富又飽滿，好像來到 Full HD 的世界！

從歷史角度看宜蘭，這裡孕育出許多對台灣政治影響深遠的人物，例如台灣文化協會與台灣民眾黨的共同創立者蔣渭水，以及黨外運動元老之一的郭雨新（現任監察院長的陳菊曾擔任其祕書）；而以地理位置來說，這裡是北部最大的農業縣市，過去是都市人向東移居的第一站。

宜蘭擁有豐富傲人的自然人文風景，像是聞名遐邇的礁溪溫泉、蘇澳冷泉與不老部落的泰雅族文化等，造就了當地休閒觀光產業的蓬勃發展。此外宜蘭還有曾獲得 WWA 世界威士忌競賽 (World Whiskies Awards)「世界最佳單一麥芽威士忌」殊榮的金車噶瑪蘭威士忌酒廠，台灣精釀啤酒品牌「吉姆老爹」的啤酒工廠也設立於此。美酒也讓宜蘭除了好山好水外，還多了令人心醉的香醇風味，成為喜愛小酌一杯的旅客不可錯過的台灣旅遊目的地。

The journey from Taipei Bus Station to Yilan Bus Station takes about 40 minutes. Ticket costs NTD 120. Ask guidance for the daily motorbike rentals inside the Yilan Bus Station; one should cost about NTD 300-400.

從台北車站客運轉運站搭乘至宜蘭轉運站約 40 分鐘，車票費用約 120 元。日租機車：在宜蘭轉運站內詢問「日租機車處」，一天費用約 300~400 元。

RECOMMENDATIONS
推薦

◤ READING LIST 旅遊書籍

TAKE A STROLL IN YILAN OLD TOWN 《舊城散步：食藝・工藝・文藝，走進一座城市的美好旅行》
A comprehensive set of private scenic spots put together by Yilan's art and culture experts
宜蘭在地藝文工作者共同完成，是私房景點的大集合

⌐ 可在Stay旅人書店購買 | Could be purchased at Stay bookstore

GREATER TAIPEI AND YILAN SMALL VILLAGES × 100 TRAILS 《大台北宜蘭小村 × 步道100 》
Explore 100 trails in Northern Taiwan featuring old streets, tea villages, mountain hamlets, fishing ports, and tribes
探索北台灣老街、茶鄉、山村、漁港、部落的100條步道

⌐ books.com.tw/products/0010929165

YILAN NATURE TRAILS 100 《宜蘭自然步道100》
Explore Lanyang! Featuring 100 nature trails across 12 towns and cities in Yilan
悠遊蘭陽！收錄宜蘭12鄉鎮市100條自然步道

⌐ books.com.tw/products/0010598181

◤ GUIDED TOURS 導覽

蘭城歷史廊道導覽
A two-hour stroll through Yilan Old Town, group tours available for ten or more people
2小時漫遊宜蘭老城，10人以上成團

⌐ https://landscapeofyilan.e-land.gov.tw/reserve.php

EXPLORE THE TRADITIONAL MARKET WITH A LOCAL
跟在地人逛傳統市場
The first step to understanding local culture is to explore the traditional markets!
認識一個在地文化的第一步，就是走進傳統菜市場！

⌐ www.kkday.com/zh-tw/product/31343

◤ TRAVEL WEBSITES 旅遊網站

YILAN TOURISM 宜蘭勁好玩：宜蘭旅遊網
The most up-to-date information on news and events in Yilan
最即時的宜蘭新聞與活動資訊

⌐ www.facebook.com/travel.yilan.tw

PLAY YILAN 玩轉宜蘭
A platform for news about Yilanese quality shops
串聯宜蘭質感店家的資訊平台

⌐ www.facebook.com/playilan

CRUSH ON YILAN 宜蘭痴
A Facebook group for sharing news about eating, drinking and having fun in Yilan
臉書分享宜蘭吃喝玩樂消息

⌐ facebook.com/CrushonYilan

◤ LOCAL PUBLICATIONS 在地刊物

《ABOUT：關於地方誌》
Using different points of views, it discusses about the trivialities of Nanfang'ao
用不同的觀點只談南方澳的一件小事

⌐ thenewdays.tw/exhibition

◤ ANNUAL EVENTS 年度活動

INTERNATIONAL CHILDREN'S FOLKLORE & FOLKGAME FESTIVAL (AUGUST) 宜蘭國際童玩藝術節 (8月)
A popular, crazy-fun summer day water party for children
風靡全台兒童的夏季瘋狂玩水日

⌐ facebook.com/YICFFF

TOUCHENG QIANGGU (AUGUST) 頭城搶孤 (8月)
The most exciting folk activities of the Yilan Zhongyuan Festival
宜蘭中元祭典最刺激的民俗活動

⌐ FB：頭城搶孤

A CHUNG HSING CULTURAL AND CREATIVE PARK
中興文化創意園區
An old Chung Hsing paper factory that has become a
cultural and creative park in Wujie Township
中興紙廠舊建築活化的文創園區

宜蘭縣五結鄉中正路二段6-8號 | chccp.e-land.gov.tw
No.6-8, Section 2, Zhongzheng Road, Wujie Township, Yilan County

B SANSHING FOUR SEASONS BLUE & WHITE POTTERY
三星四季青花瓷
A pottery art workshop next to Sanxing Bald Cypress
三星落羽松祕境旁的陶藝工作室

宜蘭縣三星鄉行健二路二段275號 | facebook.com/3s4shome
No.275, Sec. 2, Xingjian Second Road, Sanxing Township, Yilan County
Mon., Tue., Fri.: 13:00-17:30, Sat. & Sun.: 11:00-17:30 | +886-3-989-2789

C ZHUANGWEI TOURIST CENTER 壯圍沙丘旅遊服務園區
An eye-capturing exhibition venue designed by architect
Huang Sheng-Yuan that is worth a visit
黃聲遠建築師設計的展覽場域，適合來此散步發呆

宜蘭縣壯圍鄉壯濱路二段196巷18號 | +886-3-930-8420
No.18, Aly. 196, Sec. 2, Zhuangbin Rd., Zhuangwei TWP., Yilan County
09:00-17:00

D TRAVELER BOOKSTORE 旅人書店
A local cultural brand in Yilan, organizing various lectures
and workshops occasionally
宜蘭在地文化品牌，不定期舉辦各式講座與工作坊

宜蘭縣羅東鎮文化街55號 | +886-3-932-5957
No. 55, Wenhua Street, Luodong Township, Yilan County
11:00-18:00 (Closed on Tue. and Wed.)

E YILAN STYLE 蘭陽原創館
Yilan's first Indigenous Cultural and Creative Park, hosting
regular exhibitions and market events
宜蘭首座原住民文創園區，不定期舉辦展覽與市集活動

宜蘭縣宜蘭市中山路二段430巷1號 | +886-3-936-0098
No. 1, Ln. 430, Sec. 2, Zhongshan Road, Yilan City, Yilan County
10:00-18:00 (Closed on Tuesdays) | facebook.com/yilanstyle

F COME HOME STUDIO 回家生活-書食小舖
Enjoy the farmers' cuisine and share the warm vigor of
returning home
從食農料理的分享感受回家溫暖的力量

宜蘭縣羅東鎮公正路557-8號 | facebook.com/comehomestudio
No. 557-8, Gongzheng Road, Luodong Township, Yilan County
10:00-1:00 (Closed on Weekends) | +886-3-961-0260

Photo credit : 旅人書店

Photo credit : Barn Stay

A NORIMORI SHOP & HOUSE

A charming shop by the harbor, sharing delightful and unique lifestyle items

港灣邊分享美好生活道具的奇妙店鋪

⌐ 宜蘭縣蘇澳鎮江夏路2號 | facebook.com/norimorishopandhouse
No. 2, Jiangxia Rd., Su'ao Township, Yilan County
11:00-17:00 (Closed on Sun. and Mon.) | +886-920-517-573

B 1970'S

A lifestyle store specialized in 1970s vintage and lighting

專售1970年代古物與燈飾的生活道具店

⌐ 宜蘭縣羅東鎮公正路61號2F
2F, No. 61, Gongzheng Rd., Luodong Township, Yilan County
13:00-18:00 (See opening hours on Facebook | 需到臉書確認營業日)
facebook.com/1970years

C BARN STAY

A uniquely designed boutique lodge and café, beautifully transformed from an old granary

設計風格獨到、由穀倉改建的民宿與咖啡廳

⌐ 宜蘭縣員山鄉惠民路429號 | www.instagram.com/barn_stay
No. 429, Huimin Rd., Yuanshan Township, Yilan County
CAFE 12:00-18:00

D MASLOW CAFÉ

A cozy café and select shop, come have a cup of coffee!

舒服的老屋選物咖啡館，來悠閒地喝杯咖啡吧

⌐ 宜蘭縣三星鄉上將路二段433巷17弄12號 | +886-906-931-210
No. 12, Lane 17, Alley 433, Section 2, Shangjiang Road, Sanxing Township, Yilan County
11:00-17:50 (Closed on Tuesdays)

E COFFEE STREET CO. 小揭商行

A dessert and coffee house in the confines of the old city street

藏身在舊市街的甜點咖啡屋

⌐ 宜蘭縣羅東鎮公正街17號
No. 17, Gongzheng Street, Luodong Township, Yilan County
17:30-17:30 | +886-3-955-6938

F CA:SAN 烘培坊

A small and easy-going European-style bakery that uses homemade yeast

使用自製酵母，能吃得安心的歐式麵包小鋪

⌐ 宜蘭縣羅東鎮愛國路186號 | +886-955-164-511
No. 186, Aiguo Road, Luodong Township, Yilan County
Tue.-Fri. 12:00-17:00

Photo credit：阿芳鹹粥

Photo credit：愛法餐廳

A JUST FRESH MEAT DUMPLINGS 正好鮮肉小籠包
Bursting with broth, these xiaolongbao are popular to a
point of never-ending queue
歷久不衰的排隊人氣爆漿小籠湯包

🚩 宜蘭縣宜蘭市泰山路25-1號 | +886-3-932-5641
No. 25-1, Taishan Road, Yilan City, Yilan County
10:00-15:00 (Closed on Mondays)

B FEIYU SHIRAN 飛魚食染-鹽浦豆花專賣店
The store uses natural coloring and bean products to
raise awareness of water consumption
用天然染與豆食品喚醒對水資源的關注

🚩 宜蘭縣冬山鄉中正路42號 | +886-3 959-5020
No. 42, Zhongzheng Road, Dongshan Township, Yilan County
11:30-18:00, Sat. 11:30-21:00 (Closed on Mondays)

C AFANG XIANZHOU 阿芳鹹粥
Traditional country-style congee cooked to perfection
with local Yilanese ingredients (Reservations required)
傳統農家古早味，用在地食材熬煮成綿密鹹粥（需預約）

🚩 宜蘭縣五結鄉西河五路70號 | +886-919-003-829
No. 70, Xihe 5th Rd., Wujie Township, Yilan County
1人350元，4人成行，NT$350 per person, minimum group of four

D MOTHER'S LOVE GARLIC MEAT SOUP
阿娘給的蒜味肉羹（原 北門口蒜味肉羹）
Since its opening for business in 1966, the aroma of garlic
has reigned supreme
民國55年開業蒜香濃郁至今

🚩 宜蘭縣宜蘭市泰山路239-1號 | 09:00-18:00 (Closed on Mon. & Sun.)
No.239-1, Taishan Rd., Yilan City, Yilan County | +886-3-932-4293

E LUODONG ROUGENGFAN 羅東肉羹番
Their signature dish—the meat roll—paired with geng
soup is praiseworthy
招牌肉捲配肉羹絕讚

🚩 宜蘭縣羅東鎮民權路185-1號 | +886-3-954-0262
No. 185-1, Minquan Road, Luodong Township, Yilan County
09:30-14:30

F I-FRANCE 愛法餐廳
A bistronomy featuring French cuisine with local Yilan
ingredients. Reservations required.
融入宜蘭食材的法式料理餐酒館，需事先預約

🚩 宜蘭市中山路二段426之1號 | inline.app/booking/Ifrance/922
No. 426-1, Sec. 2, Zhongshan Rd., Yilan City, Yilan County
11:30-14:30, 18:00-21:00 (Closed on Mon. and Tue.)

A KNIGHT BISTRO 騎士酒吧

All mixed drinks are meticulously prepared with astonishing looks and tastes

用心製作每杯調酒，呈現與口味都令人驚喜

宜蘭縣宜蘭市復興路二段190號 | +886-3-936-5001
No. 190, Sec. 2, Fuxing Rd., Yilan City, Yilan County
21:00-03:00

B HÀNG KHÁU HOTEL 行口文旅

A hotel that is fused with coffee, arts and the scent of books

融合咖啡、書香與文創的旅店

宜蘭縣宜蘭市康樂路14號 | +886-3-936-3610
No. 14, Kangle Road, Yilan City, Yilan County.
facebook.com/hangkhau.hotel

C HOSTEL TOMATO 番茄溫泉旅店

A youth hostel with a design inspired by Jiaoxi hot spring tomatoes

以礁溪溫泉番茄為設計靈感的青年旅店

宜蘭縣礁溪鄉溫泉路10號 | +886-3-988-2171
No. 10, Wenquan Road, Jiaoxi Township, Yilan County.
facebook.com/hosteltomato.tw

D HOUSE&KITCHEN 好春好然

An Yilanese home-stay accommodation with a tasty cuisine

感受宜蘭家常況味的宿所，料理相當美味

宜蘭縣員山鄉深洲二路22號 | +886-3-922-7723
No. 22, Shenzhou 2nd Road, Yuanshan Township, Yilan County
11:30-14:30, 17:00-20:00 (Closed on Tue. and Wed.)

E JUST STAY 呆宅

A house on the riverbank in Dongshan Township suited for napping, daydreaming and meditation

適合打盹、發呆、冥想的冬山河畔居

宜蘭縣冬山鄉幸福六路150號 | +886-966-508-150
No. 150, Xingfu 6th Road, Dongshan Township, Yilan County.
facebook.com/juststay150

F ZHUANGWEI ZHANGZHAI 宜蘭壯圍張宅經典民宿

A beautiful guest house designed by the architect Huang Sheng-Yuan

黃聲遠建築師設計的宜蘭厝民宿

宜蘭縣壯圍鄉過嶺路1巷36號 | +886-3-930-7565
No. 36, Lane 1, Guoling Road, Zhuangwei Township, Yilan County
facebook.com/changhouse999

OLD TOWN ROUTE

舊城路線

YILAN CITY
AND SURROUNDING AREA

宜蘭市區

EXPERIENCE THE BEST OF YILAN IN ONE DAY 讓你一日就懂宜蘭市

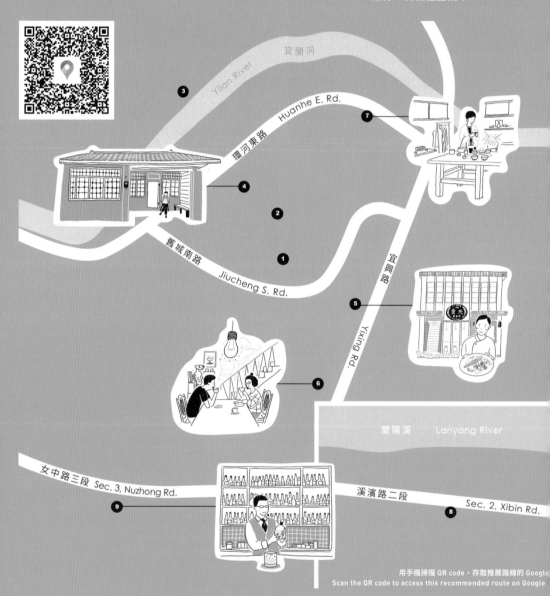

用手機掃描 QR code，存取推薦路線的 Google
Scan the QR code to access this recommended route on Google

1)	**08:00**	Get familiar with Yilan, and eat to your heart's content at the Beiguang Market in the morning
2)	**09:00**	After paying your respects in the City God Temple, have a cup of hanfang medicinal tea at Guangsheng Pharmacy
3)	**10:00**	Walk to the Jin-Mei Pedestrian Bridge and take in the architecture and the view of the river
4)	**11:00**	Take a leisurely stroll to the Yilan Style to learn about Taiwan's Indigenous culture
5)	**12:00**	For lunch, opt for well-known world dishes made of local ingredients, or stick to Yilanese light bites
6)	**14:00**	Once full, in one of the old cafes settle with a cup of coffee
7)	**15:30**	Visit the National Center for Traditional Art for a walk, or head to Heat and Breeze to make pottery
8)	**18:30**	Though a beast of a feast, the Shen Yen Teppanyaki is still a must
9)	**20:00**	Consider having a drink or seeing the romantic Yilan nightfall

1)	**08:00**	一早先到「北館市場」認識宜蘭，順便打打牙祭
2)	**09:00**	接著前往「城隍廟」拜拜，再到「廣生藥房」喝杯漢方茶
3)	**10:00**	散步至「慶和橋津梅棧道」看建築與河景
4)	**11:00**	慢行到「蘭陽原創館」認識台灣原住民文化
5)	**12:00**	午餐有使用在地食材的西式選擇，或來點宜蘭小吃
6)	**14:00**	吃飽在老屋咖啡裡來杯咖啡幫助消化
7)	**15:30**	去「國立傳統藝術中心」走走，或去「慢火雅風」做陶器
8)	**18:30**	晚餐到吃完會很撐，但一定要體驗一次的「饗宴鐵板燒」
9)	**20:00**	小酌一杯，或去看宜蘭浪漫夜景

08:00
BEIGUANG MARKET
1. 北館市場

Built in the showa era, Beiguang Market sells quality vegetables, fruits and ingredients, and it hosts many of the landmark eateries, such as the two major ones: Yishang with its sesame paste noodles and Xinlihao with its mao'er rice noodles with fish-balls. In the outskirts of the market, one can devour Cheng Huang breakfast shop's braised pork rice paired with a coddled egg.

昭和年代落成的「北館市場」在老宜蘭人心中是「貴婦菜市場」，販售高品質蔬果食材，也有許多打牙祭的名攤，「一香飲食店」的麻醬麵與「信利號」的貓耳魚丸米粉為兩大必吃，在市場外圍的「宜蘭城隍早餐店」可大啖控肉飯搭配半熟蛋！

09:00
CITY GOD TEMPLE
2. 城隍廟

After a full meal, take your newly rounded belly for a walk. With 200 years of history, from the establishment of Yilan City to the present day, the City God Temple retains numerous Qing dynasty artifacts and works of artisans. Close by is the historic Guangsheng Pharmacy, though originally striving for transformation through traditional medicine, they also stock a more contemporary gift-set item that conveys health and prestige.

飽餐之後，帶著圓滾肚皮散步去。建廟 200 年歷史的「城隍廟」，隨著宜蘭古城建立至今，內存許多清朝文物與藝匠之作；不遠的「廣生藥房」也有百年歷史，傳統中藥房力拚轉型，把中藥包變時髦禮盒，買來送健康，拿著有面子。

10:00
JIN-MEI PEDESTRIAN BRIDGE
3. 慶和橋津梅棧道

Follow the Chenghuang Street towards Yilan River and turn right at Ximen Road to arrive at what spans between the two banks of Yilan River, the Jin-Mei Pedestrian Bridge designed by architect Huang Sheng-Yuan. The alluring trails and the exciting swings loved by children, merged with the "ruined industry" style of design, make the gallery-ways a popular walking and bucket list destination in Yilan.

沿著城隍街往宜蘭河方向漫遊，右轉西門路，就能抵達由黃聲遠建築師設計、橫跨宜蘭河畔兩端的「慶和橋津梅棧道」，小刺激的鏤空步道與深受小朋友喜愛的鞦韆，加上工業廢墟風格設計，讓棧道成為宜蘭熱門的散步與打卡景點。

11:00
YILAN STYLE

4. 蘭陽原創館

The Yilan Style, formerly government dorms and a Japanese-era school, now showcases Indigenous culture. Enjoy Indigenous-style burgers and millet ice desserts, explore unique craft shops, and catch street performances and holiday markets on weekends. Don't miss the hands-on DIY workshops!

「蘭陽原創館」前身是政府舊宿舍群與日治時期的宜蘭小學校，現在是以原住民文化為主題的園區，集結了多個原民工坊、餐廳與品牌。來這裡可以試試原民風味漢堡和小米冰等美食，喜歡工藝品的話，園區內的選品店也不容錯過。週末時還有街頭藝人演出和假日市集，若有時間，也推薦參加工坊舉辦的手工 DIY 體驗！

12:00
TIME FOR LUNCH

5. 午餐時間

If you're looking for foreign cuisine with excellent quality-to-price ratio, head to the French bistro Le Temps 1998. They serve creative fusion dishes such as fermented tofu and peeled chilies. For a lighter option, you can try the recommended local Yilanese food vendors, including Mother's Love Garlic Meat Soup, A-Mao Rice Noodles Pottage, and Sihaiju Local Dishes.

想吃異國料理可以到高貴不貴的法式餐酒館「Le Temps 食光 1998」，享用有著豆腐乳與剝皮辣椒融合西餐的創意滋味。堅持走小吃路線的你，則推薦宜蘭在地美食「阿娘給的蒜味肉羹」、「阿茂米粉羹」與位於宜蘭北館市場內的「四海居小吃部」。

14:00
HAVE YOURSELF A CUP OF COFFEE

6. 喝咖啡

It is easy to eat too much while in Yilan. Not to worry though, for we got you covered come the time for rejuvenation (or having a nap). In the confines of the Guorong Road's alleyways, an independent coffee roaster Who Café or Café Sanpo—an old building near the train station—can indulge (or comatose) you in the aromas of drip-coffee.

在宜蘭很容易不小心吃太飽！沒關係，下午的提神時間（或打瞌睡時間）也幫你找好了！隱藏在國榮路巷弄的自家烘培「虎咖啡」，以及火車站附近的老屋咖啡館「散步咖啡」，都可以盡興沉醉（或昏迷）在職人手沖的美味中！

15:30
TRADITIONAL ART OR POTTERY
7. 傳統藝術或陶藝

The most frequented cultural spot in Yilan is the National Center for Traditional Art, known for its rich traditional folk art and engaging DIY experiences. For a quieter alternative, visit Heat and Breeze, a pottery-themed venue where you can enjoy coffee in a peaceful setting and try your hand at pottery making without the crowds.

宜蘭藝文旅行最常去就是集結各式傳統民俗技藝與 DIY 體驗的「國立傳統藝術中心」，但如果不想要人擠人，推薦到以陶藝為主題的「慢火雅風陶藝工作室」，在這裡可以邊喝咖啡邊玩陶作，享受不受打擾的靜謐時光。

18:30
SHEN YEN TEPPANYAKI
8. 饗宴鐵板燒

Once in Yilan, a pilgrimage to chef Ayong's cuisine is a must. With a cavalcade of ingredients and their home-made soy sauce, the signature dish of Shen Yen Teppanyaki, cherry duck, is a delicacies one has to try. And on the seafood side of things, there is not much to add, except to dive head first into the cuisine of no menus and keep wondering how come the hand is yet again reaching for another mouthful when the tummy is already full to its brim!

來宜蘭必定朝聖阿勇師的廚藝，標榜上選食材、連醬油都是自己釀造的「饗宴鐵板燒」，招牌櫻桃鴨料理絕對是必嚐佳餚，海鮮食材的料理更是好得沒話說；澎湃到極點的無菜單料理，讓人飽到極點卻還是手停不下來把菜往嘴裡送！

20:00
HAVE A DRINK OR SEE THE NIGHTVIEWS
9. 小酌一杯或看夜景

Not willing to wrap it up just yet? Consider having a drink, listening to music, throwing darts or conversing with the locals in one of the many bars, like Knight Bistro or Get lost in the Whisky. If drinking is not in the cards, you can always drive to Dongshan Township's place for taoist worship, Sanching Temple, which overlooks the Yilan Plain in the night.

還不想那麼快結束行程嗎？幾家在地酒吧如「Knight Bistro」與以威士忌為主題的「威佬 - 威士忌會所」，可以聽音樂、喝調酒、玩飛鏢，在輕鬆飲酒時刻與老闆或當地人交上朋友。若不想喝酒，也能開車到冬山鄉的道教總廟「三清宮」，俯瞰宜蘭平原美麗的夜景。

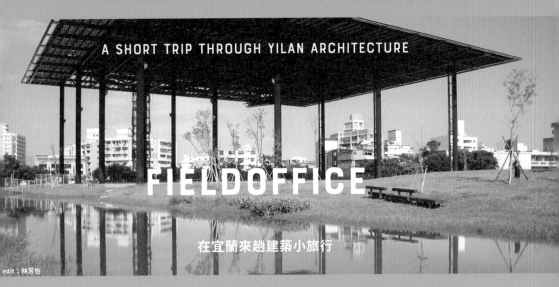

A SHORT TRIP THROUGH YILAN ARCHITECTURE

FIELDOFFICE

在宜蘭來趟建築小旅行

There is no other architect connected with Yilan in such a way as Huang Sheng-Yuan. With Luodong Cultural Working House, Kamikaze Aircraft Shelter as War Museum in Yuanshan, Cherry Orchard Cemetery in Jiaoxi, together with Jimmy Plaza and New Moat in Yilan City, Huang's works span across the Yilan Plain, and it is safe to say that his structures have shaped the way Yilan looks.

Jiaoxi Civic and Public Health Center, a building seemingly crushing down on itself with crooked layers, is a real eye-catcher, while the nearby Jiaosi Township Office is even more indescribable with its mountain-shaped building composed of the imagery of tectonic plates, footbridges and ramps. Both break down the impression of traditional public buildings. After moving to Yilan in 1993, Huang Sheng-Yuan established the Fieldoffice Architects, and the aforementioned two buildings were his starting point in the new city.

Rather than expressing whimsy avant-garde aesthetics, his architecture creates a different lifestyle to serve the need of Yilaners, turning public buildings into places where the locals can gather, rest, come and go at ease. With Cherry Orchard Cemetery on the hill of Jiaoxi, Huang Sheng-Yuan hopes that the children of Yilan can come here to gaze at their hometown. He has also designed a hidden tunnel under the connecting bridge and the cantilever platform of Wei-Shui Chiang Memorial Cemetery, in hopes that people can see and feel Yilan from various angles while passing through these structures.

沒有任何一位建築師能像黃聲遠一樣，可以與宜蘭如此緊密相連的了！從羅東鎮的「羅東文化工場」、員山鄉的「員山機堡戰爭地景博物館」、礁溪鄉的「櫻花陵園」，以及宜蘭市的「幾米廣場」與「新護城河」等，黃聲遠建築師的作品遍及蘭陽平原，也可以說，他的建築改變了宜蘭的地景。

來到「礁溪戶政事務所」，這棟貌似被壓壞的千層派建築，長相歪歪扭扭太惹人注目，而不遠的「礁溪鄉公所」更是難以言語形容，由板塊、空橋以及坡道堆積的山形，打破傳統對於公家機關的印象。1993年黃聲遠移居宜蘭，並在此成立「田中央聯合建築師事務所」，這兩棟建築正是黃聲遠在宜蘭的起點。

他的建築並非為了前衛搞怪，而是想替宜蘭人創造不一樣的生活，讓公家建築成為附近居民休憩的亭仔腳，或是成為歡迎走過、路過、不錯過的通勤動線。甚而，在礁溪丘陵山上的作品「櫻花陵園」，黃聲遠希望這座墓地可以成為宜蘭孩子眺望自己家鄉的高台，他在往來的橋下藏入一條隧道，並加入「渭水之丘」等懸空平台設計，希冀讓人們透過建築，用不同的角度觀看、感受宜蘭。

Recommended Reading 推薦閱讀：

FIELDOFFICE ARCHITECTS
《在田中央：宜蘭的青春‧建築的場所‧島嶼的線條》
Documenting 18 architectural works of Huang Sheng-Yuan and his Fieldoffice Architects
黃聲遠與他的田中央在宜蘭的18件建築作品紀錄

📖 books.com.tw/products/0010739408

A FAMOUS HOT SPRING TOWN

JIAOXI

礁溪——歷史悠久的溫泉名鄉

As far back as the Japanese colonial period, Jiaoxi had hot spring hotels and public baths such as Leyuan and Shengyuelou. With rooms built lavish, there was a time when these establishments tickled the fancy of the gentry and thus became fashionable vacation resorts. Even today, people are very fond of Jiaoxi hot springs. Tangweigou Hot Spring Park has retained the former Shaoshuigou's spring remains, and the neighboring area has countless hot spring establishments of all sizes. Among them, Taiori is an exquisite accommodation also serves Japanese cuisine, while Hot Spring Onion, a creative work of a group of designers and artists, provides a distinctive bathing experience.

Not far from the hot spring area, the Sanjiaolun Mountain at an elevation of about 1,000 meters is another recent popular attraction. From a distance, the mountain just looks like sprinkled with a coat of matcha powder and thus is nicknamed as "Matcha Mountain" among hikers and tourists. Now it has become one of the hottest hiking routes in Yilan. Besides nature's beauty, one can't possibly miss the delicacies in Jiaoxi. Wu's Peanut Ice Cream Wrap and Ke's Scallion Pancake are both famous, so be prepared to wait in long queues. IYouAma in an old village house preserves the traditional life of villagers. Here you may taste the delicious dishes cooked by grandmas and join a short tour of the village, learning more about Jiaoxi.

遠在日治時期,礁溪就有樂園、昇月樓等溫泉旅館與公共浴場,旅館賓室修築富麗堂皇,一時間受到官衙士紳喜愛,而成為時髦風尚的度假勝地。如今,礁溪溫泉依舊深受喜愛,湯圍溝溫泉公園保留從前「燒水溝」湧泉遺跡,而鄰近大大小小溫泉旅館林立,結合日式料理與住宿的「大漁日和」,以及由設計師與藝術家共同注入創意的「蔥澡」,提供有別於溫泉旅館的泡湯體驗。

另外距離溫泉區不遠,海拔高1,000公尺的三角崙山也是近期的熱門景點,遠看貌似被灑上一層輕柔的抹茶粉,而被山友取了個叫「抹茶山」的綽號,成為宜蘭最具話題的登山路線。來礁溪感受山水之美,自然不可錯過口腹之慾,「吳記花生捲冰淇淋」與「柯氏蔥油餅」都是赫赫有名的排隊美食,「番刈田游阿媽藝站」位在小村落裡,老屋子裡保存了村民生活的點點滴滴,還能品嚐婆婆媽媽燒的好菜,有時間也可以參加農村小旅行,更深入認識礁溪。

HOT SPRING ONION 蔥澡

⌐ 宜蘭縣礁溪鄉礁溪路五段77號
No. 77, Section 5, Jiaoxi Road, Jiaoxi Township, Yilan County
Mon.-Fri.: 11:00-23:00, Sat. & Sun.: 10:00-23:30 | +886-3-987-6929

IYOUAMA 番刈田游阿媽藝站

⌐ 宜蘭縣礁溪鄉三民村番割田44號
No. 44, Fangtian, Sanmin Village, Jiaoxi Township, Yilan County
10:00-21:00 | +886-980-446-663

TOUCHENG

頭城——來烏石港衝浪，走逛頭城老街

edit : ladyous

The word "tou" means "first" in Chinese, and as the name implies, Toucheng is the earliest development area in Yilan. Here, many traditional festivals are well preserved, such as Toucheng Qianggu in the seventh lunar month and Toucheng Grand Worship Ceremony in the first lunar month, both are hailed as thrilling events in Taiwan.

Apart from surfing at the Wushi Harbor, another tourist attraction in Toucheng is the Lanyang Museum designed by Taiwanese architect Yao Jui-Chung. Sits at the former site of Wushi Harbor, the museum features a cuesta-shaped building taking after Toucheng's coastal landscape. Not only its appearance is intriguing, but being in the space is also fascinating!

Toucheng also has several cafés with distinctive personalities. The old-house-turned "Treasure of Joy;" "Happy Together" built by a group of sea-lovers; and the lodging/café "Noir Home," are all worth staying and idling away an entire afternoon.

To gain a deeper understanding of Toucheng's culture, come visit Goldfish Space on Zhongyong Street provides guided tours of Toucheng Old Street (Heping Road) for you to experience its long history while strolling around.

「頭」字的意思在中文有第一個之意，所以頭城顧名思義就是宜蘭最早開發的地方，這裡保存了許多傳統節慶活動，每年農曆 7 月有頭城搶孤、農曆正月則有頭城大拜拜等，都是轟動全台的盛事。

頭城最吸引旅人的，除了到烏石港衝浪外，還有由台灣建築師姚瑞中設計的「蘭陽博物館」，座落在烏石港礁遺址的建築，造型取自頭城海岸奇特的單面山，不只外觀十分吸引人，置身空間中的感受更是令人傾倒！

另外頭城還有幾家風格獨具的咖啡館，像是老屋咖啡廳「兌藏」、由一群喜愛大海的浪人共同創設的「白磚屋」，與同時經營民宿的「noir 黑舍」等，都值得在裡面發呆一整個下午。

若想深入理解頭城文化，中庸街有「金魚。厝邊」可帶路導覽「頭城第一街」和平路，透過親身走遊老街區，感受頭城的悠久歷史。

GOLDFISH SPACE 金魚。厝邊

www.facebook.com/goldfishspace

NOIR HOME 黑舍

宜蘭縣頭城鎮朝陽路100號
No. 100, Chaoyang Rd, Toucheng Township, Yilan County
+886-958-093-003 | noirinspiration@gmail.com

Photo credit: 白磚屋

HAPPY TOGETHER 白磚屋

宜蘭縣頭城鎮開蘭東路34號 | FB: HappyTogetherWhiteHouse
No. 34, Kailandong Rd., Toucheng Township, Yilan County
12:30-17:30 (Closed on Thursdays)

A SHORT TRIP IN THE LAID-BACK FISHING VILLAGE

NANFANG'AO
南方澳—— 在悠閒的漁村來趙小旅行

Photo credit : J

SPECIAL FEATURE
YILAN
宜蘭特輯
SPECIAL FEATURE

As part of the infrastructure programs undertaken by the Japanese colonial government, Nanfang'ao was transformed from a small fishing village into a Japanese immigrant town. The fishing port built at that time was Taiwan's third-largest port and then grew into the largest fishing port on the East Coast. In its heyday, Nanfang'ao was the most bustling city in Yilan, with hundreds of fishing boats berthed at the harbor and main streets lined with department stores, hotels, theaters, and ice shops.

When in Nanfang'ao, it is recommended to visit the old-theater-turned accommodation, The New Days. Not only preserving the old building and the old-time memories, but it also offers new services like bike rental, film screening, exhibition, and books. Starting from here, travelers can cycle around the harbor and explore the fishing village. Stop by Time Coffee & Bakery and the writer Wu Xiaomei's CHUN YANG Bookstore, named after an old fishing boat, inviting you to learn the stories of fishermen that may fade in time.

Nafang'ao enjoys bountiful mackerels brought by the Kuroshio Current in the Pacific Ocean and thus wins itself the title of "Homeland of Mackerel." For tasting delicious mackerels, SanSan serves mackerel delicacies, while many seafood vendors around the Nantien Matsu Temple are also worth a visit. Among them, Guanhui Seafood has a rather unobtrusive storefront but offers masterful cuisine that will certainly amaze the epicures. (Be sure to make a reservation in advance!)

受到日治時期的計畫性開發影響,南方澳從原本的小漁村成為日人的移民村,斥資開鑿完成台灣第三大港,使得南方澳逐漸興盛、成長為東岸的最大漁港。全盛時期的南方澳,港邊停泊百來艘漁船,百來公尺的主街林立著百貨、旅店、戲院、冰菓室等,為宜蘭最熱鬧的城市。

來到南方澳可入住由老戲院改造的「日新大飯店」,老建築記憶著往昔時代,卻新加入了電影、藝廊、閱讀、單車租借等服務,成為旅人悠閒漫遊漁村文化的基地。由此為起點,騎著單車繞著漁港,可抵達「與潮珈琲」以及作家吳小枚開的「春陽號漁港小書房」,用老漁船的名字為書店命名,靜靜依在港邊說著即將消逝的漁民故事。

而在太平洋的黑潮暖流下,南方澳可捕撈到豐沛肥美的鯖魚,素來有「鯖魚故鄉」的美稱。若想品嚐鯖魚美味,在「叁三鯖蔥燒」能享用鯖魚製作的小點。金媽祖廟旁小巷則聚集許多海產攤,不起眼的「光輝海鮮料理」,老闆卻是隱藏民間的美食高手,饕客務必前往鑑賞(務必先訂位!)。

SANSAN 叁三文化廚房
Turn grandma's specialty mackerel fillet into a creative snack
把阿嬤拿手的鯖魚肉排變成創意點心

宜蘭縣蘇澳鎮南寧路32號
32, Nanning Rd., Su'ao Township, Yilan County | +886-989-544-319
Weekends 13:00-18:00

THE NEW DAYS 日新大飯店
A refreshing lodging turned from an old theater
老戲院改造成風格清新的青年旅店

宜蘭縣蘇澳鎮江夏路53號
No. 53, Jiangxia Road, Su'ao Township, Yilan County
+886-3-996-2531 | facebook.com/thenewdays.tw

254　　Volume 4: Eastern Taiwan and the Outlying Islands | 第四輯 東台灣與離島

THE NEW YILAN FARMING

宜蘭新農——在宜蘭找到自己的一方田地，安身立命

SPECIAL FEATURE
YILAN 宜蘭特輯

With the boom of the tourism industry in Taiwan, guesthouses and b&bs have risen in popularity in the fields of Yilan and the actual function of farmhouses has become a controversial issue. However, as traditional farmers' perception of the value of agriculture may shift nowadays, Yilan's new migrants from Taipei and elsewhere in search of different lifestyles, have become new farmers and driving forces for the revival of farming.

From Lai Chingsoong's "Ko-Tong Rice Club" to "Land Dyke Feminist Farm," which experiments eco-friendly farming, the new farmers encourage people to pay more attention to the land by inviting people to either join the club. Not only work diligently in the fields, but the new farmers are also good at writing and photography. "Tian Bun Sia" in Shengou Village aims to document farmers' anecdotes and humorously introduce agriculture to draw people to learn more about the value of farming, as their handwritten *Shengou Annual Report* is one of its signature works.

From traditional farming to innovative agriculture, "The Wild Buff" is a group of arts and cultural workers, photographers, and young farmers who lead people into the fields to create art. To promote this spirit, besides visiting them in person, you can support them by purchasing their hand-grown products or handcrafted merchandise from their store, small farmer specialty shops, or their official website, giving them direct encouragement!

在觀光產業的蓬勃發展下，宜蘭民宿如雨後春筍冒出田間，長久累積成為農舍爭議問題。面對傳統農民看待農業價值的鬆動，反倒是來自台北或其他地方的宜蘭新移民，他們到宜蘭尋求不同的生活，並轉換跑道成為新農夫，因而成為復甦土地農用的推手。

從最初賴青松所成立的「穀東俱樂部」到實驗友善種植的「土拉客」，各自以揪夥入會的方式，鼓動人們對於土地的關注。宜蘭新農不僅耐操耐勞，還能拍擅寫，例如駐點深溝村的「田文社」則以捕捉收錄農夫八卦為志，用幽默口吻介紹農業，吸引人們更理解種作的價值，其手寫的《深溝年報》即是經典代表作。

從農業到農創，由藝文工作者、影像工作者、年輕小農所組成「土土野青」，則是帶領人們走進田野創作。如果你也有興趣宣揚這樣的精神，除了親自拜訪他們之外，還有個最簡單的方式——那就是到他們經營的店家、小農選品店甚至是官方網站，購買他們親手種植的農產品或是製作的周邊商品，給他們最直接的鼓勵！

EATDANSU 一簞食-蔬食X生活
Simple and tasty vegetarian cuisine made of fresh local produce
宜蘭米與蔬豆果籽烹煮的樸實味

▗ 宜蘭縣宜蘭市員山鄉尚深路122號
No. 122, Shangshen Road, Yuanshan Township, Yilan County
Weekends 13:00-18:00 | facebook.com/eatdansu

Photo credit：勝美市集

YILAN MART 勝美市集
Take the best of Lanyang local produce with you!
在地小農選品店，蘭陽好物，打包帶走！

▗ 宜蘭縣羅東鎮純精路三段32號 | yilanmart.com
No. 32, Sec. 3, Chunjing Rd., Luodong Township, Yilan County
09:00-19:00, Sun.09:00-17:30 (Closed on Mondays)

不是後山，是迎接太陽，
名副其實的「前山」

花蓮

HUALIEN

THE PREMIER MOUNTAIN RANGE FROM WHICH TO WELCOME THE SUN

—————— Yun-Han, Kao 高韻涵

People often say, "How beautiful are the mountains and waters of Hualien, but how boring it all is!" Yet most travelers limit their exploration to the famous Taroko National Park or a few other well-known scenic spots, where they hurriedly take a few photographs and call it a day. If this is the extent of their travel plans, it's no wonder they feel bored. Besides the beautiful mountains and waters of Hualien, there are many other interesting people, places, and things that are well worth the effort to seek out!

The largest county in all of Taiwan, Hualien encompasses the spectacular mountain ridges of both the Central and Coastal Ranges. Choose a route to follow one or the other of these two mountain ranges and discover two very different, yet equally breathtaking, kinds of scenery. Hualien is also home to multiple indigenous tribes encompassing six different major tribal cultures, namely, the Amis, Truku, Bunun, Sediq, Sakizaya, and Kebalan. With such rich heritage, it is extremely rewarding to undertake small-scale, in-depth tribal tours in order to experience the diversity of local ecology and culture.

In recent years, it is not uncommon for people to move to Hualien for study or work and, as if by accident, eventually end up settling permanently. This piece of land has attracted a large number of people seeking to live rich and fulfilling lives, where they endeavor to match their talents with the unique characteristics of the land in expressing their individual potential. This unique landscape has also given rise to a number of interesting spaces and projects. Three days and two nights of Hualien travel may not be enough. For some, to truly plumb the depths of Hualien may take a lifetime.

常有人說：「花蓮好山、好水、好無聊！」許多旅客常常只來太魯閣國家公園走踏，或是去知名景點拍個照就匆匆離開，如果是這樣難怪會覺得好無聊。花蓮其實除了好山好水，還有更多有趣的人事物，值得好好挖掘！

身為台灣占地最大的縣市，不管是中央山脈與海岸山脈之間的山線，還是鄰近太平洋的海線，兩條路線有著截然不同的壯闊風景。花蓮還有豐富多元的族群文化，這裡光是原住民族就有 6 大族群，分別是阿美族、太魯閣族、布農族、賽德克族、撒奇拉雅族與噶瑪蘭族，如此豐富的人文內涵，非常值得深入當地參與部落小旅行，體驗不同的風土人情。

近年來還有許多人因為念書、工作等因素來到花蓮，結果不小心就被花蓮的土地黏住而定居下來。這片土地聚集了一群想好好過生活的人，並嘗試用自己擅長的事與這片土地交織新的可能，許多有趣的空間與計畫也應運而生。來花蓮 3 天 2 夜可能不夠，對某些人來說，可能要花上一輩子的時間。

Taking the TRA's Tze-Chiang Limited Express, Taroko Express, or Puyuma Express to Hualien Station from Taipei requires about 2 hours. If weekend train tickets are sold out, you can get railway and bus associated tickets at the Taipei Bus Station, and take Kamalan Bus service to Luodong Transfer Station in Yilan, then transfer to the TRA to Hualien. When traveling in Hualien City, renting a scooter or a bicycle is recommended. When traveling in other towns by train or automobile, renting a scooter at the train station after arriving at your destination is advisable.

台北搭乘搭台鐵自強號、太魯閣號、普悠瑪號到花蓮站約需 2 小時。週末若買不到火車票，也可在台北客運站購買鐵路公路聯運票，搭葛瑪蘭客運到宜蘭羅東轉運站後轉乘火車抵達。若有預算搭乘飛機可更快抵達。市區內建議租機車或自行車方便移動，市區外建議以汽車或搭火車後到各站租機車的方式旅行。

RECOMMENDATIONS
推薦

◤ READING LIST 旅遊書籍

Hualien 365：Wonderful Daily Discoveries in Hualien
—Spring and Summer / Fall and Winter
《花蓮 365：每天在花蓮發現一件美好！》
春夏篇、秋冬篇
Season-oriented travel guide focuses on the culture of Hualien
以花蓮人文型態為主、搭配季節的旅遊指南

⌐ books.com.tw/products/0010702114

HAPPY WRITER 寫寫字
A passionate editorial team bringing you in-depth stories of Hualien, with a range of captivating publications
深入介紹花蓮人事物的編採團隊，出版多本相關刊物

⌐ Happy Writer's publications: happywriter.tw

◤ LOCAL PUBLICATIONS 在地刊物

KILAY 奇萊有誌
A quality publication featuring in-depth stories on Hualien's local culture, history, and industries
側寫花蓮在地人文、歷史與產業的質感刊物

⌐ https://reurl.cc/GjZnEp

HUALIEN SAFARI《花蓮趣》
Travel quarterly published by the county government. Available at all Hualien visitor centers
政府發行的觀光季刊，可在花蓮各服務中心索取

⌐ www.hlsafari.com

ENJOY HUALIEN VISITORS GUIDE (ENG)
This PDF guide comes packed with local Hualien travel information for tourists
由在地人製作的全英文花蓮旅遊書，可在網站下載PDF檔

⌐ www.enjoyhualienguide.com/download-now

◤ TRAVEL WEBSITES 旅遊網站

HUALIEN WEBZINE 花蓮旅人誌
Sharing information about local events and daily life, as well as comprehensive food maps of Hualien
花蓮在地活動資訊分享，網站有詳盡的花蓮美食地圖

⌐ facebook.com/hualienfb | www.hl-net.com.tw

HUALIEN TOURIST SERVICE NETWORK 花蓮觀光資訊網
Official Hualien travel website. Multiple language versions available
花蓮旅遊官方網站，頁面設計清晰，有多國外語資訊

⌐ tour-hualien.hl.gov.tw

◤ ANNUAL EVENTS 年度活動

ORGANIK FESTIVAL (APRIL 4月)
Psychedelic music festival held in Hualien's Huting Valas every spring
每年春天在花蓮牛山呼庭舉辦的奇幻音樂生活派對

⌐ facebook.com/OrganikOfficial | smkmachine.com

OCEAN HOME WILD MARKET 海或‧瘋市集 (JULY 7月)
Music and handcrafted market held in summer with enchanting casual ambiance
花蓮夏日的音樂與手作市集，隨興的氛圍讓人著迷

⌐ facebook.com/Ocean.home456

FULI 983 (OCOBER-NOVEMBER)
穀稻秋聲：富里山谷草地音樂節 (10月-11月)
Music party in the countryside for a date in autumn.
花蓮人秋天的約會，去農村的音樂派對！

⌐ facebook.com/fuli983

Photo credit：Jenny Lin in Hualian

Photo credit：花蓮縣石雕博物館

Photo credit：島人藝術空間

A TAROKO NATIONAL PARK 太魯閣國家公園

Otherworldly natural marble cliffs like a magnificent work of God（因地震休園中，出發前請至官網查詢最新訊息）
大自然的鬼斧神工，一定要到這看大理岩峽谷的壯麗景觀

⌂ 花蓮縣秀林鄉富世村291號 | 08:30-17:00 | www.taroko.gov.tw
No. 291, Fushi, Xiulin Township, Hualien County (Closed due to earthquake. Check the official website for updates before visiting.

B PINE GARDEN 松園別館

The only fully-preserved Japanese colonial military building in Hualien County, providing sporadic arts and culture events
花蓮縣僅存的完整日治軍事建築，不定期有藝文相關活動

⌂ 花蓮縣花蓮市松園街65號 | No. 65, Songyuan St., Hualien City
09:00-18:00 (Closed the second Tuesday of each month)

C YOSHINO TEMPLE 慶修院

The most well-maintained Japanese temple in Taiwan, transporting you back to the Edo period
台灣保存完整的日式寺院，彷彿穿越時光到日本江戶時代

⌂ 花蓮縣吉安鄉中興路345-1號
No. 345-1, Zhongxing Rd., Ji'an Township, Hualien County
08:30-17:00 (Closed on Mondays)

D COZY BOOKS 雨樵懶人書店

Independent bookstore in Hualien City great for spending a lazy afternoon surrounded by books
選書推廣台灣文學、詩集及女性書寫

⌂ 花蓮縣花蓮市光復街130號2F | +886-3-833-0721
2F., No. 130, Guangfu St., Hualien City, Hualien County
10:30-17:00, weekends 10:00-18:00 (Closed on Tuesdays)

E STONE SCULPTURE MUSEUM HUALIEN 花蓮縣石雕博物館

The nation's only museum dedicated to stone sculpture, showcasing the endless possibilities of stones
全國唯一以「石雕」為專題進行典藏與展示的博物館，探索石頭的各種可能

⌂ 花蓮縣花蓮市文復路6號 | 09:00-17:00 (Closed on Mondays)
No. 6, Wenfu Rd., Hualien City, Hualien County | stone.hccc.gov.tw

F ISLANDER ART FORCE 島人藝術空間

A local art space promoting Indigenous and Pacific contemporary art exchanges
在地藝文展演空間，推廣原住民族與太平洋當代藝術交流

⌂ 花蓮縣花蓮市光復街80-1號 | +886-928-569-952
2F, No. 80-1, Guangfu St., Hualien City, Hualien County
11:00-18:00 (Closed on Mon. and Tue.) | islander038.com

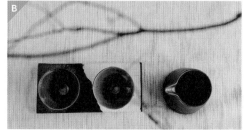

Photo Credit：花蓮日日

Photo credit：山海百貨

A HAKUSUI & CO. 白水商號 X 橋本書屋

The best starting point for delving into Hualien, offering
select books and local products
深度認識花蓮的最佳起點，有精選好書與花蓮選物

⌂ 花蓮縣花蓮市節約街27號｜+886-933-327-221
No. 27, Jieyue St., Hualien City, Hualien County
11:00-19:00, Fri.-Sat. 12:00-20:00 (Closed on Tuesdays)

B HUNSHEN 魂生製器

Unique pottery works made with their own glaze with a
lively organic style
自行研製釉藥、充滿自然生命感的獨特手工捏造陶器

⌂ 花蓮縣吉安鄉建昌路88號｜+886-908-180-882
No. 88, Jianchang Rd., Ji'an Township, Hualien County
Reservation via FB/IG (@hunshen.tw) only.

C SHANHAI.DEPT.STORE 山海百貨

A former Taipower office transformed into a complex
space featuring local products, culture, and dining
舊台電辦事處改造，在地選品、文化和餐飲的複合式空間

⌂ 花蓮縣新城鄉博愛路39號｜+886-3-861-0800
No. 39, Bo'ai Rd., Xincheng Township, Hualien County
10:00-18:00

D HUALIENDAILY 花蓮日日

Discover quality goods, savor simple food, and enjoy
comfortable accommodations here
來這裡找生活好物、簡單食物和舒適住宿

⌂ 花蓮縣花蓮市節約街37號｜hualiendaily@gmail.com
No. 37, Jieyue Street, Hualien City, Hualien County
11:30-20:30

E LONG GONE CAFÉ 龍宮

Laid-back café by Qixingtan to relax your body and mind
in the afternoon
在七星潭旁的慵懶咖啡店，可窩一下午放鬆身心

⌂ 花蓮縣新城鄉七星街79巷3號｜facebook.com/longgonecafe
No. 3, Ln. 79, Qixing St., Xincheng Township, Hualien County
10:00-18:00 (Closed on Tuesdays)

F GIOCARE 義式.手沖咖啡

Café situated in an old house with a lovely yard, offering
delicious desserts
有著可愛院子的老宅咖啡廳，甜點也好吃

⌂ 花蓮縣花蓮市樹人街7號｜facebook.com/giocare.cafe
No. 7, Shuren St., Hualien City, Hualien County
14:00-18:00 (Closed Wed. and Thur.)

Photo credit：定置漁場三代目

A HAIPU OYSTER OMELET 海埔蚵仔煎
Fresh, crunchy local street food with flavorful dressing beloved by the locals
花蓮人氣在地小吃，新鮮、皮脆，搭配醬料非常夠味

⌂ 花蓮縣花蓮市自由街88號
No. 88, Ziyou St., Hualien City, Hualien County
16:30-22:30 (Closed on Tuesdays)

B QIAOTOU STINKY TOFU 玉里橋頭臭豆腐
Stinky tofu that's crunchy on the outside and soft on the inside paired with kimchi and Chinese basil, worth the trip and the wait in line
值得等待甚至專程前往，外酥內軟，更愛九層塔泡菜

⌂ 花蓮縣玉里鎮民權街15號 | +886-3-888-2545 | 10:30-19:00
No. 15, Minquan St., Yuli Township, Hualien County

C 5+ TRADING COMPANY 5+ 商行
Diligently prepared savory and sweet dishes made with local produce from small-scale farms
使用當季小農食材，甜點、鹹點都吃得到用心

⌂ 花蓮縣花蓮市建國路75巷16弄6號 | facebook.com/love5home
No. 6, Aly. 16, Ln. 75, Jianguo Rd., Hualien City, Hualien County
11:40-17:30 (Closed on an unfixed schedule. For more info visit FB page)

D PEACEFUL VALLEY 小和山谷
Enjoy handmade ice cream with caramel in a quaint old Japanese house
在寧靜的日式老屋享用手工冰淇淋與焦糖醬

⌂ 花蓮縣壽豐鄉壽文路43號 | 11:00-18:00
No. 43, Shouwen Rd., Shoufeng Township, Hualien County
+886-3-865-5172

E LIU LIU RESTAURANT 流流社原住民風味餐廳
Surprising and delicious indigenous dishes by reservation only
能吃到意想不到的原民美味菜色，需事先預約

⌂ 花蓮縣花蓮市府前路95-5號 | +886-918-248-563
No. 95-5, Fuqian Rd., Hualien City, Hualien County
11:00-14:00, 17:00-21:00 (Closed on Mon. and Tue.)

F THE FISHERY 定置漁場三代目
Rare restaurant offering fish-broth ramen, using high-quality fish from Dong Chang Fishery Farm in Qixingtan
難得的魚湯拉麵專賣店，使用七星潭東昌定置漁場的鮮魚

⌂ 花蓮縣花蓮市建國路23號 | +886-3-833-5090
No. 23, Jianguo Rd., Hualien City, Hualien County
11:45-14:00, 17:45-20:00

Photo credit：丘丘森旅

Photo credit：緩慢石梯坪

A PEACE ISLE 和嶼

Find tranquility for your soul through cocktails, leaving behind the chaos of urban life

拋下都市生活的紛擾，用調酒找回心靈的平靜

花蓮縣花蓮市光復街80號｜+886-3-832-0183
No. 80, Guangfu St., Hualien City, Hualien County
19:00–01:00 (Closed on Tue. and Wed.)

B BAR SHEPHERD 牧羊人

Savoring kiln-roasted delicacies embraced by the sea breeze by Qixingtan

在七星潭的海邊享受徐徐微風及調酒與窯烤美食

花蓮縣新城鄉七星街9號｜+886-925-810-413
No. 9, Qixing St., Xincheng Township, Hualien County
19:00–02:00 (Closed on Tue. and Wed.)

C CHU RESORT 丘丘森旅

Taiwan's first lodging brand that combines vacation and mindfulness

台灣首家結合「渡假與靜心」的旅宿品牌

花蓮縣鳳林鎮永豐路6號｜+886-3-877-2929
No. 6, Yongfeng Road, Fenglin Township, Hualien County
churesort.com

D MIAOKO HOSTEL

Stylish guesthouse beside Qixingtan operated by a rock musician and an interior designer

七星潭旁，由搖滾樂手與室內設計師開設的風格民宿

花蓮縣新城鄉七星街79巷3號
No. 3, Ln. 79, Qixing St., Xincheng Township, Hualien County
facebook.com/miaokohostel

E THE LEAFF INN 葉宿文旅

Converted from an old dormitory and a barn house with artwork created by different artists in each room

由老宿舍、舊穀倉改造，客房有不同藝術家的創作

花蓮縣花蓮市民生路55號
No. 55, Minsheng Rd., Hualien City, Hualien County
facebook.com/theleafinn

F ADAGIO SHITIPING 緩慢石梯坪

Unwind at the Makotaay tribe, savoring food from the mountains and sea while taking in the boundless ocean views

在港口部落放慢腳步，享用山海慢食與無邊海景

花蓮縣豐濱鄉港口村石梯灣123號｜+886-971-566-188
No. 123, Shitiwan, Gangkou Village, Fengbin Township, Hualien County
www.theadagio.com.tw

HUALIEN TRAIN STATION
AND DOWNTOWN AREA
花蓮火車站與市區周圍

WHO SAYS HUALIEN IS TOO FAR AWAY? JUST BOOK YOUR TICKET AND SET OUT EARLY!
誰說花蓮很遠？趕快訂票一早出發吧！

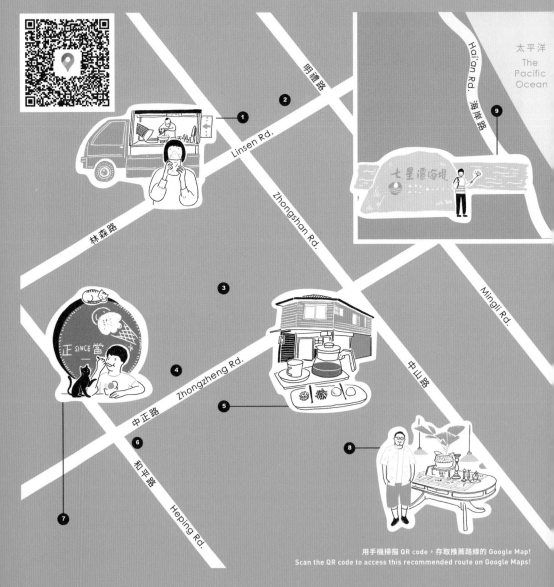

用手機掃描 QR code，存取推薦路線的 Google Map!
Scan the QR code to access this recommended route on Google Maps!

1)	12:00	Rent a scooter when you arrive at Hualien, then head downtown for some local street food
2)	14:00	Visit Shi-Guang Second-Hand Bookstore (you may occasionally find mi na zu ki Market next to the alley)
3)	15:00	Head to Old Railroad Shopping District and discover the unique shops
4)	16:30	Take a stroll at A-Zone Hualien Cultural Creative Industries Park
5)	17:30	Cruise around Gou Zai Wei and sit down in a café along the hipsters' street
6)	19:00	Have dinner at Aaron Kitchen in the A-Zone neighborhood
7)	20:30	Try Italian Sherbet or Taiwanese douhua for dessert
8)	21:30	Enjoy some drinks at the Decryption Room café
9)	05:00	Welcome the sunrise at Qixingtan

1)	12:00	抵達花蓮後先租機車,立刻到市區吃一波花蓮小吃
2)	14:00	逛逛「時光二手書店」（巷弄旁偶爾有「希伯市集」）
3)	15:00	前往「舊鐵道商圈」,沿路尋找特色小店
4)	16:30	漫步花蓮舊酒廠「花蓮文化創意園區」
5)	17:30	「溝仔尾」巡禮,在花蓮「文青街」找間咖啡廳喝下午茶
6)	19:00	到園區周圍的特色餐廳「龍私廚義法餐廳」吃晚餐
7)	20:30	吃飽來點義式雪貝或是台灣豆花
8)	21:30	去「島東譯電所」小酌一杯
9)	05:00	前往「七星潭」看東海岸的日出

12:00
DEEP-FRIED GREEN ONION PANCAKE SHOP
1. 在地午餐

When you arrive in Hualien, your first stop ought to be the deep-fried green onion pancake shop, but be sure to grab a number because the waiting time for this renowned snack is often half an hour or more. While you wait, you can check out the nearby Mei-Hong Vietnamese Foods, or head over to Mr. Goose for a plate of goose meat or a full spread of side dishes. Remember to head back and pick up that evil deep-fried green onion pancake, crispy on the outside and filled with delicious, gooey egg yolk!

到花蓮先來遠近馳名的「炸彈蔥油餅」拿號碼牌吧，因為太熱門通常需要等半小時以上，中間可以先到附近的「美紅越南美食」吃道地越南料理，或是去「鵝肉先生」叫盤鵝肉和滿桌小菜，吃完記得回去拿炸得酥脆、中間留著金黃蛋液的邪惡蔥油餅！

14:00
SHI-GUANG SECOND-HAND BOOKSTORE
2. 時光二手書店

After eating your fill, head to Shi-Guang Second-Hand Bookstore, situated in a renovated old building, to find some books or other publications related to Hualien. Home to occasional thematic book exhibits, Shi-Guang also hosts arts and culture activities. Before heading over, check out their Facebook page to see what's up. Next, you can visit close-by "mi na zu ki," a marketplace selling Japanese zakka as well as plants. Alternatively, consider visiting Little Life Shop where you can purchase cute household merchandise and local farmers' products.

吃飽到老宅改造而成的「時光二手書店」尋找與花蓮相關的書籍、刊物，這裡不時有主題書展，也經常舉辦藝文活動，出發前可先上臉書查詢。附近以日雜與植物為主題的小店「mi na zu ki」與販售可愛雜貨和在地農產的「小一點洋行」也值得造訪。

15:00
OLD RAILROAD
SHOPPING DISTRICT
3. 舊鐵道商圈

In the past, this area was the site of the old eastern railway route. Now, it is the most comfortable part of the market area for pedestrians. While in this area, my first recommendation is to visit Hakusui & Co. located on Bo'ai Street. This store showcases the artwork of local artists and offers a wide range of books and miscellaneous items to explore.The first floor is also home to a household merchandise store, while Hualien Daily B&B can be found on the second floor along with Twine, a fair trade market, and Good Underground, one of the rare performance spaces to be found in Hualien.

曾是舊東線的鐵道現在是市區內最舒服的徒步區，來此首推博愛街上的「白水商號 x 橋本書屋」，這裡展售許多花蓮藝術家作品與好書好物。這一帶還有 1 樓是生活雜貨店、2 樓是民宿的「花蓮日日」、公平貿易店「蠒裏子」與花蓮少有的展演平台「好地下藝術空間」。

16:30
A-ZONE HUALIEN
CULTURAL CREATIVE INDUSTRIES PARK
4. 花蓮文化創意園區

Previously the Hualien Winery during the Japanese colonial period, Hualien Cultural Creative Industries Park was transformed into a public performance space in 2012 which would become the county's local arts and culture center. On top of the multitude of interesting shops that have been set up here, A-Zone also hosts regular marketplace activities. Every autumn, the Original Living Art Festival is held here. If perusing the marketplace has given you an appetite, you can pay a visit to the nearby Daiwa restaurant for some of their famous wanton soup.

前身是日治時期花蓮酒廠的花蓮文創園區，2012 年改造為展演空間對外開放後，成為在的地藝文中心。除了有許多有趣店家進駐還固定舉辦市集活動，每年秋天的「花東原創生活節」也在此舉辦。逛完後若肚子餓了可以去旁邊的「戴記扁食」喝碗招牌餛飩湯。

☐

17:30
GOU ZAI WEI

5. 溝仔尾

Due to its location at the extremity of an irrigation channel, this section of Chenggong Street has been given the name Gou Zai Wei. With proximity to the old Hualien Train Station, it was formerly a relatively bustling area which fell into decline after the railway station was moved away. Yet many young entrepreneurs and newly landed immigrants have come to settle in this area in recent years, converting many of the old buildings into interesting coffee shops such as Choco Choco Handmade Chocolates, Caffe Fiore, Soava Plan, KŌHI, and more. All of this rejuvenation has contributed to Gou Zai Wei's fresh, new look.

早期在圳溝尾端而被稱為溝仔尾的成功街一帶，因鄰近花蓮舊站而相當熱鬧，車站遷移後也跟著沒落。不過近年來不少返鄉青年或新移民將這裡的老房子改造成咖啡廳，像是「choco choco 手工巧克力」、「Caffe Fiore 珈琲花」、「浮室」和「KŌHI 宅」等，賦予溝仔尾全新風貌。

☐

19:00
AARON KITCHEN

6. 龍私廚義法餐廳

For dinner, why not head to Aaron Kitchen, where the indigenous owner combines local ingredients to create his delicate brand of fusion cuisine. For instance, he may create Italian pasta using the local spice Litsea cubeba, also known as mountain pepper or maqaw. I personally recommend the chocolate shrimp. If you're in the mood for something more traditional, you can consider Zhinan for a bowl of braised pork rice or flour dumpling soup!

晚餐就到「龍私廚義法餐廳」吧，有著原住民血統的老闆結合當地食材，做出帶有巧思混搭料理，像是在義大利麵中使用部落常用的香料馬告（山胡椒），我個人也推薦這裡的巧克力蝦。若想吃點傳統的可以在溝仔尾的「痣男」吃碗滷肉飯或麵疙瘩！

☐

20:30
JUSTICECREAM

7. 正當冰

Once you're full, why not have a little dessert? Justicecream, formerly a taro ice factory, has in recent years begun to produce Italian sherbet completely free from chemical additives. This place is also the ideal rest stop for feline friends, allowing you to play with cute cats while you enjoy your icy treat and making for a remarkably relaxing environment. I also recommend Tsai's Tofu Pudding Shop located nearby. Job's tears with milk, and mesona grass milk jelly are their signature flavors.

吃飽來吃點甜品吧，前身為傳統芋冰廠的「正當冰」，近年利用在地食材做出無添加化學物的義大利雪貝，這裡也是貓咪中途之家，來吃冰還可以跟可愛的貓咪玩耍，相當療癒。另外也推薦附近的「蔡記豆花」，薏仁牛奶和仙草奶凍都是招牌。

21:30
DECRYPTION ROOM
8. 島東譯電所

In the evening, head to Decryption Room, a charismatic yet unusually welcoming arts and culture space, for a few cups of the proprietor's own special blend. The owner's mother makes delicious Hakka-style light food that you simply should not pass up. In 2019, Decryption Room also hosted the first annual Gou Zai Wei Street Art Festival in the hopes of allowing visitors to get to know Hualien more deeply as they browse the streets for artwork.

晚上就到充滿個性但又異常溫馨的藝文空間「島東譯電所」，喝幾杯老闆的特調，老闆媽媽做的客家小點也非常好吃，有來千萬別錯過。島東還在 2019 年舉辦了第一屆的「溝仔尾街區藝術節」，希望讓大家在尋找街區角落的作品同時，更深入認識花蓮。

05:00
QIXINGTAN
AND
QINGSHUI CLIFF
9. 七星潭 與 清水斷崖

It's worth the effort to get up early and head out to enjoy the east coast sunrise! For the lazy travelers among us, however, you may choose a guesthouse along the coast where you can enjoy the sunrise from the comfort of your bed. You might also head to Qinxingtan to enjoy beautiful daybreak vistas. For those who are feeling even more vigorous, whale watching tours and canoe trips are available if you head to Qingshui Cliff which ought to make your sunrise experience even more unforgettable! To register for these events, please make your way to Turumoan (facebook.com/turumoan), or Hualien Kayaking (facebook.com/kayakinET).

努力早起看東海岸的日出吧，比較懶惰的旅人可以選擇海岸邊的民宿，躺在房間欣賞日出，或到「七星潭」欣賞晨曦。體力更好的人可前往「清水斷崖」參加賞鯨船或獨木舟行程，讓日出體驗更難忘！活動報名請至「多羅滿賞鯨」(facebook.com/turumoan)，「航海王：花蓮清水斷崖獨木舟」(facebook.com/kayakinET)。

THE MOST BEAUTIFUL HAKKA VILLAGE
AND THE INTERNATIONALLY RECOGNIZED SLOW TOWN

FENGLIN

山線特輯　　東部最美客家村 國際慢城鳳林

SPECIAL FEATURE
HUALIEN
花蓮特輯

Recognized as the first "slow town" in Taiwan by Cittaslow International in 2014, Fenglin Township once had three Japanese immigrant villages and 41 tobacco barns. As lifestyles transformed, younger generations gradually moved out for work, the population has reduced to only about 10,000 people. Local residents even call it "the town that breaks away from the world." That being the case, why not play to its strengths? Therefore, community members unleash their creativity and organize Lost in Tobacco Barns — Ghost Night Parade (facebook.com/BeiLinHyakki) in the seventh lunar month, inviting townspeople and visitors to dress up as ghosts and parade through the streets of tobacco barns. There are also games like watermelon rugby, mud relay race, and tug of war in muddy field, all offering an organic rural atmosphere that can't be found in cities. If you come here on regular days, it is recommended to visit Good Eats, a shop promotes the traditional produce with branding concept, hoping to show the world the rich flavor of Fenglin's peanuts. And the omakase restaurant Si Dai Wu Nong (Farmers of Four Generations) uses locally-grown and seasonal ingredients in its dishes, also echoing with the slow food movement promoted in eastern Taiwan.

Fenglin is the region with the largest Hakka population in eastern Taiwan, while one can easily find the authentic Hakka gourmet foods here. Mama Chuo's Hakka Delicacies provides Hakka rice dumplings, as well as classic Hakka snacks like caozaiguo (herbal glutinous rice cakes), mitaimu (thick rice noodles), Hakka vegetable buns, and glutinous rice cakes. After stuffing the belly, one may take a sightseeing ride on a light-sport aircraft at Fenglin Flight Training Base, taking in the spectacular view of East Rift Valley like an eagle. Lintienshan, formerly one of Taiwan's four major lumbering areas, now has become a forestry culture park, documenting the history of Taiwan's lumber industry. If your feet are sore, make Mingxin Ice and Fruit Shop your final destination of this slow travel and enjoy some refreshing lemon juice and old-fashioned ice desserts. (by Jolin Lin)

2014 年，花蓮小鎮「鳳林」成為台灣第一個成功獲得「國際慢城」認證的鄉鎮，曾擁有 3 大日本移民村與 41 座菸樓的鳳林，由於生活型態轉變，年輕人多外出工作，人口流失到僅剩 1 萬多人。讓鳳林人笑稱這裡是「不小心與世界脫隊的鄉鎮」，不過既然脫隊了，那就自己玩吧！於是鳳林人發揮創意，在農曆 7 月辦起「百鬼夜行菸樓迷路」活動 (facebook.com/BeiLinHyakki)，邀請在地人與遊客扮裝，在菸樓街道遶街遊行，此外還有西瓜橄欖球賽、泥巴大隊接力、泥地拔河等趣味競賽項目，玩出有別於都市的純樸韻味。若是平日前往，推薦將品牌思維帶進傳統產業的「美好花生」，希望讓世界認識鳳林花生的飽滿滋味；另外無菜單料理店「四代務農」，食在地、吃當季的環境共好理念，也呼應東部推行的慢食運動。

鳳林也是全東部客家人口最多的地區，也被稱作「東部最美客家村」，小鎮內可以輕易找到道地的客家美食，「卓媽媽客家美食」提供美味的客家粽與其他經典客家小點如草仔粿、米苔目、客家菜包、年糕與紅豆糕。吃飽後，還可到「鳳林飛行場」體驗輕航機，以鷹的視野，飽覽花東縱谷的震撼美景；曾為台灣第四大林場的「林田山林場」，現則以文化園區的面貌記錄了台灣重要的伐木工業軌跡。逛累了，知名老店「明新冰菓店」提供沁涼檸檬汁與古早冰品，為慢步旅程劃下美好句點。（文／林苡秀）

GOOD EATS 美好花生

花蓮縣鳳林鎮中和路46-1號 | +886-933-528-448
No. 46-1, Zhonghe Rd., Fenglin Township, Hualien County
10:00-17:30 (Closed on Wednesdays)

SI DAI WU NONG 四代務農

花蓮縣鳳林鎮大榮里大忠路1號 | +886-921-750-866
No. 1, Darong Village, Dazhong Rd., Fenglin Township, Hualien County
11:00-14:00, 17:00-20:00

FEEL THE WIND BLOWING FROM THE PACIFIC OCEAN AT SHITIPING'S RICE TERRACE

SHITIPING

海線特輯　來海稻米的故鄉「石梯坪」吹太平洋的風

Situated at the 65-kilometer point of Coastal Highway 11, Shitiping in Fengbin Township, Hualien County is well-known and named after its stunning scene composed of wave-cut platforms and coral reefs, resembling stone steps (what "Shiti" means in Mandarin) protruding into the sea. The Amis of Makotaay tribe are its main residents. It's also the background of the 2015 film *Wawa No Cidal*, which depicts the clashes between economic development and indigenous traditions through the story of reviving the abandoned seaside rice paddies. At the heartfelt ending, the villagers choose to preserve the tribal culture and protect their environment. Its theme song "Aka pisawad" also won the Best Original Film Song of the 52nd Golden Horse Awards, bringing Makotaay instant fame.

Shitiping Park has naturally-formed swimming pools which are rare on the coastline of Hualien. Its famous cuesta is a huge rock of volcanic tuff and has weathered to form the unique landscape with a gentle slope facing the land, and a steep slope on the seaside. Ascend to the highest point on a clear day, one can take in the gifts from the Pacific Ocean—the infinite sky and azure sea.

The works of Makotaay artists often bear oceanic elements, and Necklace Studio is where they often present their works and exchange ideas. Necklace Studio not only offers innovative indigenous dishes and hosts sporadic exhibitions, but it also provides accommodation and Makotaay tours. It is also recommended to visit Ina Fly Fish to taste its smoked fly fish, one of the Amis classic dishes only served in summer. If coming here on the full-moon day, don't forget to check the moonrise time, pick a favorite coast spot, and enjoy the free yet splendid natural theater—the sea of moonlight. (by Jolin Lin)

「石梯坪」位於花蓮縣豐濱鄉台 11 線 65 公里的海邊，是一個由隆起的海蝕平台與珊瑚礁所構成的著名地景，因突然深入海中的岩石排列如梯而得名，港口部落阿美族是居住於此的主要族群。2015 年，電影《太陽的孩子》藉由海稻米復育的故事，述說在經濟發展與傳統文化的衝突中，部落選擇保存文化與守護環境的感人故事，電影主題曲〈不要放棄〉更在當屆金馬獎中獲得最佳電影原創歌曲，讓港口部落一炮而紅。

「石梯坪公園」擁有花蓮海岸線難得一見的安全天然港泳池，園區中著名的單面山，為火山凝灰岩組成的巨大岩石，在風化作用後，造成了近陸地面坡度較平緩，臨海面坡度陡峭的特殊景觀，在晴朗的日子登上最高點，可以一覽太平洋給予的禮物——無際的天空與寶藍色大海。

港口部落的藝術創作者，作品中多帶有海的印記，而「項鍊海岸工作室」是他們經常出沒的地點。這裡提供主打賦予部落傳統料理創新靈魂的風味餐，不定時舉辦展覽，也提供住宿與港口部落導覽。另外也推薦旅人到「升火伊娜現烤飛魚」，品嚐夏季限定的阿美族經典料理燻烤飛魚。若在滿月之時來到石梯坪，別忘了查好月升時間，選一處心儀的海岸，享受免費而精彩的大自然劇場——月光海。（文 / 林苡秀）

INA FLY FISH 升火伊娜現烤飛魚
Local Amis eatery with dishes of fly fish and seafood
阿美族地方小吃，有各式飛魚與海鮮料理

⌐ 花蓮縣豐濱鄉港口村石梯灣118-2號
No. 118-2, Shitiwan, Gangkou Village, Fengbin Township, Hualien County
+886-927-850-136 | 11:00-15:30, 17:00-19:00 (Closed on Wednesdays)

NECKLACE STUDIO 項鍊海岸工作室
A space integrates accommodation, Amis cuisine, and tribal tours
結合住宿、阿美族餐飲與部落導覽的特色空間

⌐ 花蓮縣豐濱鄉石梯坪53-1號
No. 53-1, Shitiping, Fengbin Township, Hualien County
facebook.com/cacagauwen | 10:00-17:30

TRIBAL LIFE

部落特輯——來一趟部落，深入認識原住民文化！

Photo credit：Ljavaus Dare

SPECIAL FEATURE

HUALIEN
花蓮特輯

SPECIAL FEATURE

As Taiwan's economic development shifted its focus, the tribal communities on the east coast are facing serious problems of population aging and outflow. However, in recent years, more and more tribal youths have returned to their homelands, trying to retrieve and pass down their unique cultural heritage. Among them, the Amis tribes of Kaluluwan and Makotaay have been developing local tours to introduce the indigenous culture to more people.

The Amis make up the largest indigenous group of Taiwan with roughly 14,000 members. Although their lifestyles, languages, and cultures vary from tribe to tribe, they all share one thing in common—their respect for living things in nature. The Amis are recognized as skilled gatherers while forests, rivers, and the ocean are like their refrigerators with abundant food. Founded by one of the Kaluluwan tribal youths, Hatila_Life of Kaluluwan, More than You Thought (facebook.com/hatilainkaluluan) offers tours like Mieteng (blocking the stream to catch fish) and Midateng (collecting edible greens in the wild). And Idang (facebook.com/idangexplore), promoting ecotourism and oceanic culture in the Makotaay tribe, brings travelers closer to the Pacific Ocean through kayaking and snorkeling and learn about the stories, legends and wisdom of the Amis people living by the sea.

If you would like to learn more about the indigenous life through food, Atomo Arifowang Canglah, an omakase restaurant in the Cawi tribe founded by chef Chen Yao-Zhong is recommended. Inspired by the traditional Amis food culture while imbued with personal creativity and aestheic, every dish is surprisingly delightful. And nearby The New Pacific 1 is a platform dedicated to presenting tribal cultural products, they also have working holiday programs in tribes from time to time. The optimistic Amis people often say, "What nature bestows has always been sufficient." Come visit the tribes, maybe this saying would become your motto as well. (by Jolin Lin)

台灣東海岸部落隨著經濟發展重心轉移，部落人口老化與流失問題嚴重，但近年也有越來越多部落青年決心返鄉，試圖找回並傳承屬於自己的獨特文化軌跡。其中，屬於「阿美族」的「磯崎部落」與「港口部落」，正如火如荼地發展在地遊程，希望讓更多人認識部落文化。

約14萬人口的阿美族，是台灣原住民第一大族群，儘管部落與部落之間在生活習慣、語言、文化上存在些微差距，但對於自然萬物的敬重，是重要的共通點。阿美族是公認的採集高手，山林、大海、溪流都是他們的冰箱。由磯崎部落青年創立的「Hatila_磯崎生活不只這樣」(facebook.com/hatilainkaluluan)，提供了 Mieteng 堵溪抓魚與 Midateng 野菜採集體驗；在港口部落的生態旅遊與海洋文化推廣組織「Idang 依浪」(facebook.com/idangexplore)，則透過獨木舟、浮潛等活動，讓旅人更親近太平洋，並認識靠海民族的故事、傳說與智慧。

若想要透過食物認識部落，則推薦位於「靜浦部落」內、由廚師陳耀忠創設的無菜單餐廳「陶甕百合春天」，以傳統阿美族飲食文化為底蘊，並加入個人創意與美感，每道菜都讓人驚喜。另外附近的「新太平洋1號店」，致力於挖掘部落文創商品，並且不定時推出部落工作假期。樂觀的阿美族人常說：「大自然給的永遠都夠用。」走一趟部落，這句話或許也會成為你的座右銘。(文／林苡秀)

ATOMO ARIFOWANG CANGLAH 陶甕百合春天

⌐ 花蓮縣豐濱鄉靜浦村3鄰138號 | +886-921-633-406
138, Neighborhood 3, Jingpu Village, Fengbin TWP., Hualien County
Weekends 11:30-15:00

THE NEW PACIFIC 1 新太平洋1號店

⌐ 花蓮縣豐濱鄉靜浦村靜浦8-1號 | +886-3-878-1218
Jingpu No. 8-1, Jingpu Village, Fengbin Township, Hualien County
08:30-17:00

OUTDOOR ACTIVITIES

體驗特輯　　邊學邊玩，一堂沒有教室的自然生活課

SPECIAL FEATURE
HUALIEN
花蓮特輯
SPECIAL FEATURE

Surrounded by the gorgeous scenery composed of mountains and the ocean, Hualien has been a tourist attraction for Taiwanese who want to escape from the bustling cities. In recent years, many young people have returned to their hometowns and devoted themselves to the local ecotourism. Proposing concepts like learning about nature and environmental sustainability, they create in-depth hands-on activities for people to walk into the outdoor and gain an understanding of the land, as well as hunter schools for preserving tribal culture and daily wisdom. Here are two organizations that provide hands-on activities in Hualien's natural environment.

Gao Shan Forest Center

Brought his family back to his hometown, a Bunun retired veteran Ma Tiang has built forest living classes based on the wisdom passed down by the elderly family members. He reformed the unattended forest into the classroom for tree climbing, camping, and adventure using all of the five senses, sharing the indigenous culture and wisdom of Culiu (Gao Shan) tribe with visitors. There is also a secret spot with a grand view of the Pacific Ocean in the Center, so don't miss your chance to make a reservation for the incredible experience.

Fish Bar

Centered around the culture of "set-net fishing," Fish Bar offers freshly-caught seafood, hands-on tours, and knowledge sharing through experiencing the fishing work venue and cooking ocean-friendly fish. The series of activities allow attendees to learn how to maintain a sustainable food resource in an eco-friendly way while avoiding overfishing certain species, as well as how to cook seasonal seafood and discover the tasty secrets of a variety of fish. Bringing together the fishing industry, local culture, and cooking class, the activities provide memorable experiences for tourists of every age group. (by Jolin Lin)

依山傍海的花蓮，一直都是台灣人想逃離繁雜都市時的首選之一，近年來更有許多返鄉青年回到故鄉，提倡認識大自然、永續共存等概念，發展出親山親海的深度體驗，也有為了保存部落文化與生活智慧而創立的獵人學校。以下介紹兩個可親近花蓮山海的體驗單位：

高山森林基地

布農族退伍軍人馬中原，攜家帶眷回到故鄉後，開始思考過去家中父執輩傳授的山林智慧，決定將荒廢多年的山林重新整理成提供體驗課程的場域，透過攀樹、夜宿森林、五感探險等與旅客分享高山部落的傳統文化與生存智慧，園區內有一處觀賞太平洋視野極佳的祕密景點，若有機會預約體驗，千萬別錯過。

洄游吧

推廣「定置漁網」文化，主打鮮撈魚貨、知識分享與課程，實際體驗漁業作業現場，並且親自料理友善海洋的魚種，了解人類怎麼友善地與海洋互動，並在永續的前提下取得資源，練習料理當季的魚種，挖掘每種魚的美味祕訣，避免單一魚種的過度捕抓，結合產業、地方文化與料理的豐富體驗，各種年齡層的遊客都能找到合適的遊程。（文／林苡秀）

GAO SHAN FOREST CENTER 高山森林基地

花蓮縣豐濱鄉磯崎村高山一鄰2號 | facebook.com/g7tribe
2, Gao Shan Neighborhood 1, Jiqi Village, Fengbin TWP., Hualien County
中文 (Chinese) www.gs-forest.com
英文 (English) gsforest.mystrikingly.com

FISH BAR 洄游吧

花蓮市新城鄉海岸路32號
No. 32, Haian Rd., Xincheng Township, Hualien County
service@fishbar.com.tw
facebook.com/fishbar8

台東
TAITUNG

FEELING THE TAITUNG JETLAG!

———— Wen Liu 劉玟苓

Many people think of Taichung as a faraway place that's difficult to get to, especially before Lunar New Year when people working in larger cities are going home since a train ride from Taipei to Taitung can take over three hours. Taitung's distance from other major cities is part of the reason why this gorgeous terrain was one of the last to be developed into a major city and why it has been preserved so beautifully. In the day, the boundless horizon blends ocean into sky; at night, the star-studded sky dazzles the soul. Come stay in Taitung and let its beauty wash away all your urban troubles.

In recent years, a growing number of new and interesting shops and stores have been popping up in Taitung. Lovers of art and music simply cannot miss the Taiwan East Coast Land Art Festival, especially the Moonlight Sea Music event which involves barbecue, beer, and music on the coast of the Pacific Ocean under the moonlight. I would also recommend attending Slow Food Taitung in Tiehua Music Village, a food fest that offers a local experience via food and customs.

Traveling to Taitung is more than just a trip, it's a way of life. This is why whenever I get a work call in Taitung I always apologize for responding late by saying I've got the "Taitung jet-lag." (Just kidding.)

許多人對台東的印象大多停留在「好遠」以及「逢年過節都要搶車票」吧！沒錯，光從台北搭火車到台東就要 3 個多小時跑不掉。但也因為這個距離，讓被山海包圍的台東成為全台最晚被開發的地方，保留了大量的自然景觀。白天的海天一線藍是台東最美的顏色，夜晚的月光星空則是最夢幻的景象。只要待在台東，就算是再汙濁的都市人，也都能被淨化的吧！

近幾年台東還出現了許多有趣的店家與活動，喜愛藝術、音樂的旅人千萬不能錯過夏日的「東海岸大地藝術季」，其中「月光海音樂會」可以邊吃原住民石板烤肉、邊喝啤酒，在灑落月光的太平洋邊聆聽台東最動人的音樂；另外集海線、縱谷超厲害店家於鐵花村的「台東慢食節」，除了品嚐美食更能感受到台東的風土與態度。

懂門路的人都知道，來台東不只是旅行，更是實踐一種心之所向的生活方式，因此只要在台東的時候接到工作電話，我都會跟對方說：「不好意思回比較慢啦，因為我有（台東）時差～」（開玩笑的）

From Taipei, take the Puyuma Express or the Taroko Express for three to four hours to arrive at Taitung Station. A 25-minute cab ride or 50-minute bus ride will get you downtown. Here, buses and bicycles are available although I would strongly recommend renting a car or a scooter.

台北搭乘搭台鐵「普悠瑪號」、「太魯閣號」到台東站約 3 至 4 個小時。到市區車程約 25 分鐘，公車約 50 分鐘。市區移動雖有公車、腳踏車等選擇，但強烈建議租汽、機車代步，會方便許多。

READING LIST 旅遊書籍

THE PLACE 04：TAITUNG《本地 04：台東》
Get a modern and comprehensive look at Taitung through its culture, customs, and characters
從文化習俗、人物等角度切入，介紹最野、最現代的台東
⌐ books.com.tw/products/0010820640

100 LITTLE THINGS ABOUT TAITUNG《台東的100件小事：逛市集、學衝浪、當農夫，一起緩慢過日子》
Experience Taitung through one hundred of its unique events and stories. Written by local media team ZZ Taitung
由在地媒體「台東製造」推薦的100件小事，深度認識台東
⌐ books.com.tw/products/0010798269 | zztaitung.com

LOCAL PUBLICATIONS 在地刊物

SEEINGTAITUNG《臺東藝文》
A quality local publication curating Taitung's arts and cultural events. Visit our website for more information!
彙整台東藝文活動的質感在地刊物，網站有更多資訊！
⌐ culture.taitung.gov.tw/magazine | culture.taitung.gov.tw

TAITUNGTALK《東透可》
Collecting local stories and bringing readers a deeper understanding of Taitung
傾聽台東在地聲音，採集故事，讓讀者更深入認識台東
⌐ e-book : lihi1.cc/nTppp | facebook.com/Taitungtalk

GUIDED TOURS 導覽

TAITUNG WORKING HOLIDAY 台東部落工作假期
An event spanning four days and three nights that allows you a glimpse into indigenous and local culture
4天3夜，透過參與部落活動更了解台東的人事物與生活
⌐ www.jacreative.com.tw/taitungWH

DULAN STROLL 都蘭慢漫走
Dulan tours provided by East Coast National Scenic Area, reservation must be made at least three days in advance
由東管處推出的部落導覽遊程，需3天前預約
⌐ facebook.com/Eastcoast.Taitung4

TRAVEL WEBSITES 旅遊網站

TAITUNG TOURISM 台東觀光旅遊網
Taitung's official travel website, offering great information in many travel categories
台東市旅遊官方網站，有多國外語資訊
⌐ tour.taitung.gov.tw | facebook.com/taitung.tourism

CHIHSHANG PROMENADE 走走池上
An outsider who writes through the perspective of a traveler, letting people learn more about Taitung
一位外地青年，透過旅人角度的書寫，讓大家更認識台東
⌐ zhouzhou.com.tw | facebook.com/zhouzhouTW

ANNUAL EVENTS 年度活動

BOMB HANDAN (ON THE FIFTEENTH OF THE FIRST MONTH OF THE LUNAR NEW YEAR) 炸寒單 (元宵節)
Taitung's most riotous religious event which involves throwing firecrackers at oneself as a means of prayer for prosperity to Lord Handan. Remember: wear a hat, earplugs, and mask for safety!
台東最熱鬧的宗教盛事，用鞭炮炸肉身寒單爺祈求財運亨通，若要去現場記得準備帽子、耳塞和口罩！
⌐ facebook.com/masterhandan

TAIWAN EAST COAST LAND ART FESTIVAL (JUNE) 東海岸大地藝術節 (6月)
An art and music festival that features local, national, and international artists. Enjoy the gorgeous landscape and don't forget to attend the Moonlight Sea Music event
結合國內外藝術家創作、東海岸地景與「月光‧海音樂會」的年度藝術節
⌐ www.teclandart.tw

AMIS MUSIC FESTIVAL (NOV.) 阿米斯音樂節 (11月)
Held by award-winning singer and star of Dulan, Suming, Amis Music Festival is one of Taitung's most popular music festivals
由都蘭明星、金曲歌手舒米恩在家鄉舉辦，是台東最大型熱鬧的在地音樂節
⌐ facebook.com/Amismusicfestival

Photo credit：蔡詩凡（台灣好基金會提供）

Photo credit：台11開放工作室

Photo credit：江賢二藝術園區

Photo credit：白色恐怖綠島紀念園區

A ART CHISHANG 池上穀倉藝術館

Located in a converted barn, this gallery holds superb exhibitions and fascinating lectures

老穀倉改建，時常會有大師藝術作品的展出或講座

台東縣池上鄉中西三路6號 | +886-8-986-2089
No. 6, Zhongxi 3rd Rd., Chishang Township, Taitung County
10:30-17:30 (Closed on Mon. and Tue.)

B DINING BOOKS CAFÉ 食冊CAFÉ書店

A bookstore, café, and roastery all in one serving menuless dinners

身兼書店、咖啡廳、烘焙教室、還有無菜單晚餐的一間店

台東縣台東市洛陽街265號 | +886-8-934-7616
No. 265, Luoyang St., Taitung City, Taitung County
10:00-21:00 (Closed from Mon. to Wed.)

C GREEN ISLAND WHITE TERROR MEMORIAL PARK 白色恐怖綠島紀念園區

A former prison for political dissidents, now preserved as a Human Rights Museum

曾經關押政治犯的監獄，保留為人權博物館

台東縣綠島鄉20號 | +886-8-967 1095 | www.nhrm.gov.tw
No. 20, Ludao Township, Taitung County | 09:00-17:00

D HIGHWAY 11 OPEN STUDIO 台11開放工作室

A curated shop and art space that explores the craftsmanship of the East Coast

發掘東海岸工藝的選品店與藝文空間

台東縣東河鄉61號 | facebook.com/dulanmarkting
No. 61, Donghe Township, Taitung County
Fri. and Sun. 12:00-18:00, Sat. 12:00-21:00

E PAUL CHIANG ART CENTER 江賢二藝術園區

Abstract artist Paul Chiang's studio expansion: a new art landmark in eastern Taiwan

抽象藝術家江賢二工作室擴建，台灣東部藝術新地標

台東縣東河鄉台11線73號 | www.paulchiang.org/art-center
No. 73, Provincial Highway 11, Donghe Township, Taitung County
預計2024年秋天開放 Set to open in fall 2024

F YONGFU WILD STORE 永福野店

Reviving the Amis traditional sea salt making. Sign up for a sea salt experience and cultural tour

阿美族族人復興炒海鹽工法，可預約海鹽體驗與文化導覽

台東縣長濱鄉竹湖村永福5號 | facebook.com/mornoscuisine
No. 5, Zhuhu, Changbin TWP., Taitung County | +886-930-710-512
09:00-18:00

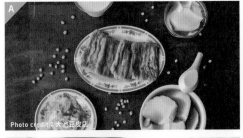

Photo credit：大池豆皮店

Photo credit：陳三月

A DACHI TOFU SKIN SHOP 大池豆皮店
Traditional Wood-Fired Tofu Skin Loved by Local and Travelers
在地人和旅人都愛的古早柴燒豆皮

⌂ 台東縣池上鄉大埔路39之2號 | reurl.cc/GjgRvx
No. 39-2, Dapu Rd., Chishang Township, Taitung County
07:00-14:00 (Closed on Wednesdays)

B KAIANA 蓋亞那工作坊
Get a guided tour and learn how to make millet rice
有導覽，親自體驗如何製作小米飯

⌂ 台東縣海端鄉2鄰中福39號 | +886-989-527-192
No. 39, Zhongfu, Haiduan Township, Taitung County
08:00-20:00 (Closed on Sun.)
facebook.com/GuyanaWorkroom

C WEI YU JI 尾餘記
I'm not joking when I say I can use up an entire jar of their pepper sesame paste in one sitting
吃一碗麵可以配一整罐自製椒麻醬絕對不誇張

⌂ 台東縣鹿野鄉永安村永安路342巷8號 | +886-913-677-757
No. 8, Ln. 342, Yong'an Rd., Luye Township, Taitung County
Weekdays 10:00-16:00 造訪前請先電聯 Please call before visit.

D HAPPINESS KITCHEN 幸福食堂
Delicious and healthy dishes with seasonal ingredients. Reservation is required
使用當季食材、美味又健康的家常料理，需預約

⌂ 台東縣東河鄉興昌村74號 | +886-8-953-0440
No. 74, Xingchang, Donghe Township, Taitung County
12:00-14:30, 17:30-20:00 (Closed on Wed. and Thur.)

E DING LUN BEEF NOODLE SOUP 鼎倫牛肉麵
A little restaurant in Jinlun Village that serves beef noodle soup and appetizers
位於南迴金崙的小餐館，麵食與小菜都非常美味

⌂ 台東縣太麻里鄉金崙村4鄰金崙130-132號 | +886-8-977-1918
No. 130-132, Jinlun, Taimali Township, Taitung County
11:00-14:15、17:00-19:30 (Closed on Tuesdays)

F MEET MARLIN 旗遇海味
Creative seafood cuisine at its freshest
超新鮮的海味創意料理

⌂ 台東縣成功鎮港邊路19-8號 | +886-8-985-2889
No. 19-8, Gangbian Rd., Chenggong Township, Taitung County
11:00-15:00, 17:00-20:00

Photo credit：M' LOMA

Photo credit：草民

Photo credit：海邊咖啡屋

A SINASERA 24
Gourmet French cuisine using locally sourced ingredients
運用在地食材創作出高級法式料理

台東縣長濱鄉南竹湖26-3號 | +886-8-983-2558
No. 26-3, Nanzhuhu, Changbin Township, Taitung County
sinaseraresort.com/sinasera24 | 需預約 Reservation required
18:00-21:30 (Closed on Tuesdays)

B M' LOMA
Savor indigenous flavors through a chef's special
selection of dishes, prepared by a passionate Amis chef
阿美族主廚用心製作的原民風味無菜單料理

台東縣台東市正氣北路109巷60號 | m-loma.com
No. 60, Lane 109, Zhengqi North Road, Taitung City
13:30-21:00 (Closed on Tuesdays)

C FAMILY IN VALLEY 山谷裡的一家人
Experience life with this family, from organic farming to
foraging and cooking food in nature
從採摘自然農法野菜到柴燒晚餐，像一家人一樣一起生活

台東縣鹿野鄉永安村永德路100巷5號 | +886-919-048-656
No. 5, Ln. 100, Yongde Rd., Luye Township, Taitung County
09:00-20:00 (Closed on Mondays) 需預約 Reservation required

D TSAO MIN 草民
Healthy and nutritious brunch made without processed
foods, dinner available on weekends
不使用加工食品的健康營養早午餐，週末提供晚餐

台東縣台東市強國街256巷23號 | +886-8-933-3110
No. 23, Ln. 256, Qiangguo St., Taitung City, Taitung County
08:00-15:00, Fri.-Sun. 08:00-15:00, 18:00-21:00

E CMONDAY COFFEE & FOOD 海邊咖啡屋
A leisurely café in Chenggong Township, perfect for
soaking in the mountain and sea air
成功鎮上的悠閒咖啡廳，來這裡呼吸山海氣息吧

台東縣成功鎮芝田路185之6號 | IG: mondaycoffeeandfood
No. 185-6, Zhitian Rd., Chenggong Township, Taitung County
12:00-18:00 (Closed on Thursdays)

F LI.KA CAFE 力卡珈琲
A café that uses locally sourced and high-quality
ingredients to create Paiwan cuisine
從土地到產桌，堅持用好食材做出不一樣的排灣輕食料理

台東縣太麻里鄉金崙210號 | facebook.com/inLi.kaCafe
No. 210, Jinlun, Taimali Township, Taitung County
08:30-20:00

Photo credit：有海

Photo credit：莊稼熟了

Photo credit：Christine Huang

A YOUR SEA 有海

Moonlight, cocktails, and the sea.

有月光，有調酒，有海

⌂ 台東縣台東市吉林路二段607號｜IG: @your_seaaaaa
No. 607, Sec. 2, Jilin Rd., Taitung City, Taitung
21:00-02:00｜+886-930-702-710
建議先訂位 Reservations recommended.

B BAR CYNIC 吧蟲

A bar opened by a world cocktail champion in his hometown. It's a hidden gem, so be brave and step inside!

世界調酒冠軍回家鄉開的酒吧，店面隱密，勇敢走進去吧

⌂ 台東縣台東市中華路一段376巷23號｜IG: @bar_cynic
No. 23, Ln. 376, Sec. 1, Zhonghua Rd., Taitung City, Taitung County
20:00 - 01:00 (Closed on Sundays)

C TING FENG 聽風．說故事

This hotel in Changbin is so stunning and comfortable you'll never want to leave

位於長濱，是一間美到哭、舒適到哭的旅宿

⌂ 台東縣長濱鄉忠勇村25-1號｜+886-936-147-189
No. 25-1, Zhongyong, Changbin Township, Taitung County
facebook.com/judesign.tw

D FARMING HOSTEL 莊稼熟了

A hostel dedicated to nature and design that offers their guests gardening and farming experiences

非常具有設計感，除了住宿還可以預約農事體驗活動

⌂ 台東縣池上鄉萬安村1鄰1-2號｜+886-936-865-883
No. 1-2, Wan'an, Chishang Township, Taitung County
facebook.com/wei6651

E NORDEN RUDER HOSTEL 路得行旅 國際青年旅館 台東館

Offering a great bang for your buck, this hostel is suitable for solo travelers who don't want to stay in backpackers' hostels

CP值超高，適合獨自旅行又不想住背包客棧的旅人

⌂ 台東縣台東市廣東路162號｜+886-8-933-5162
No. 162, Guangdong Rd., Taitung City, Taitung County
nordenruderhostel.livetaitung.tw

F DAGEDAN HOUSE 打個蛋海旅

A bed-and-breakfast that takes good care of their guests and offers authentic indigenous cuisine

從入住就會被照顧得好好的一間民宿，可體驗原住民料理

⌂ 台東縣太麻里鄉金崙村4鄰金崙128號｜+886-8-977-1551
No. 128, Jinlun, Taimali Township, Taitung County
facebook.com/Dagedanhouse

TAITUNG SUGAR FACTORY
AND TIEHUA MUSIC VILLAGE
台東糖廠文創園區與鐵花村周圍

ENJOY A DAY OF CULTURE AND ART IN TAITUNG! 來個台東一日藝文之旅！

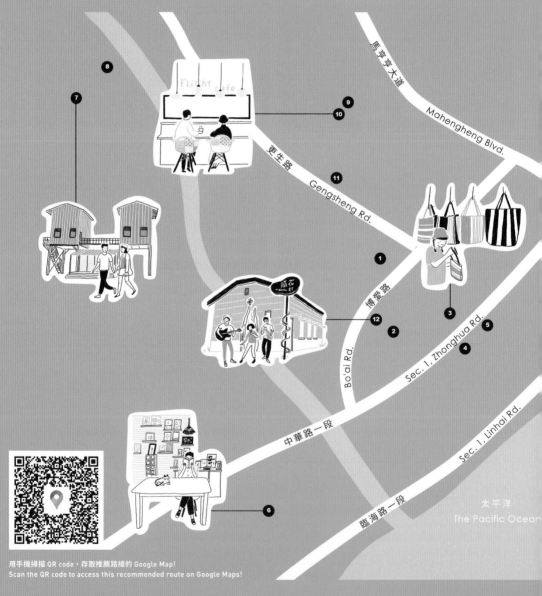

用手機掃描 QR code，存取推薦路線的 Google Map!
Scan the QR code to access this recommended route on Google Maps!

1) **09:00** Have breakfast at Ming Kui Breakfast and Walkabout Café

2) **10:00** Visit Taitung Design Center for their latest exhibition

3) **11:00** Get a custom-made souvenir at Dong Chang Canvas

4) **12:00** Have lunch at Xiang Qi Duck

5) **13:00** Head to Zheng Dong Shan Smoothie and Juice Bar or Lao Dong Tai Sweet House for dessert

6) **14:00** Pick out a good book curated by the owner of Guesthouse Susu, a unique second hand bookstore

7) **15:00** Hail a cab for the Taitung Sugar Factory Cultural and Creative Park and check out The Garage and Ata Beads Studio

8) **17:00** Visit Kung Tung Church, a world-class work of architecture hidden in Taitung

9) **18:00** For groups, I recommend dining at Mi Ba Nai Local Indigenous Food; if you're dining solo, I recommend Flight Café

10) **19:30** After dinner, head over to MùMù Café or Alanger Coffee for a coffee to help with your digestion

11) **20:30** To end the night on a perfect note, go to Tiehua Music Village for performances and markets

---

1) **09:00** 去「明奎早餐店」或「有時散步早午食」吃早餐

2) **10:00** 造訪「臺東設計中心」看當期展覽

3) **11:00** 在「東昌帆布行」訂製專屬台東伴手禮

4) **12:00** 到「香琪鴨肉」享用午餐

5) **13:00** 飯後甜點到「正東山冰屋」或「老東台品甜屋」

6) **14:00** 前往「晃晃二手書店」，買一本主人素選的好書

7) **15:00** 前往「台東糖廠文創園區」，逛「庫空間」與「卡塔文化工作室」

8) **17:00** 前往「公東教堂」，欣賞隱藏在台東的世界級當代建築

9) **18:00** 一群人同遊晚餐推薦去「米巴奈山地美食坊」，自己一個人可前往「福來東咖啡」

10) **19:30** 到「目目咖啡」、「食冊 Café 書店」或「艾蘭哥爾藝文咖啡館」喝杯咖啡幫助消化

11) **20:30** 去「鐵花村音樂聚落」看表演、逛市集，結束完美的一天

09:00
MING KUI BREAKFAST
AND
WALKABOUT CAFÉ
1. 明奎早餐店 與 有時散步早午食

For breakfast, I recommend Ming Kui Breakfast Restaurant for their French toast (which is crispy on the outside and drizzled with condensed milk) and their signature longan fruit tea to balance out the sweetness. If you're interested in brunch, Walkabout Café offers four types of delicious brunch combos with healthy ingredients and delicious bread. Make your stomach and heart happy at the same time!

早餐推薦到「明奎早餐店」吃酥軟口感淋上煉乳的「法式吐司」搭配招牌的「龍眼干茶」，開啟甜而不膩的一天。若想吃西式早午餐，「有時散步」提供4種百元套餐，只能說麵包真的超好吃，健康的食材搭配，讓胃袋與心情都很舒服。

10:00
TAITUNG DESIGN CENTER
2. 臺東設計中心

Taitung's newest contemporary space for humanities-oriented performance and design, Taitung Design Center was rebuilt from the former railway police station and visitor center. The bright and open space holds many interesting exhibitions and studios that are perfect for those interested in gaining insight into local stories and design history.

台東最新的當代展演場所與設計基地，由過去的鐵路警察局與舊台東旅客服務中心改造而成，專注台東的人事物與環境生活。台東設計中心的空間明亮舒適，時常舉辦許多有趣的展覽與工作坊，若想多了解台東的故事與設計力，這裡不容錯過。

11:00
DONG CHANG CANVAS
3. 東昌帆布行

The owner of Dong Chang Canvas has reinvigorated the declining local canvas industry by offering customizable canvas bags that are both stylish and functional. Their bags are even sold in Japan and were recently featured in a Japanese magazine. I recommend getting yourself a custom-made bag as a souvenir.

接著前往有著可愛老闆的「東昌帆布行」，老闆將已逐漸沒落的帆布行轉型成客製環保帆布袋的再生基地，鮮豔有型的實用袋款還紅到日本去，登上日雜成為台東伴手禮推薦，趁早來預訂專屬於自己的帆布袋，裝進滿滿的台東回憶。

12:00
XIANG QI DUCK
4. 香琪鴨肉

Founded by grandfather Zhou Qing Yuan, Xiang Qi Duck is now operated by three granddaughters who take great pride in their family business. This restaurant is a real treasure and a staple for all locals. Some must-order items include zongzi, duck over rice, homemade pig's blood cake, and medicinal angelica soup.

從第一代的周慶源阿公開始，到現在第三代年輕漂亮的 3 個孫女們接手，「香琪鴨肉」可說是老台東的記憶、鄉愁，點上一顆肉粽、一碗鴨肉飯，再加上小菜手工米血糕，以及一碗當歸湯，是肚皮撐破都會吃完的好吃。

13:00
ZHENG DONG SHAN
AND
LAO DONG TAI SWEET HOUSE
5. 正東山冰屋 與 老東台品甜屋

To satisfy you post-lunch sugar cravings, try Zheng Dong Shan Smoothie and Juice Bar for traditional desserts such as shaved ice desserts and tapioca pudding. I would also recommend trying the oldtimers' favorite, American youtiao, a deep-fried sandwich paired with pickled vegetables. I also recommend trying the rice noodle jelly at Lao Dong Tai Sweet House – delicious both hot and cold!

午餐完想來點甜點，可以前往老店「正東山冰屋」，除了剉冰、雪綿冰、西米露等傳統冰品外，還有賣古早味「美國油條」，炸得油香的麵包搭配三明治餡料與台式酸菜，一定要試試！另外也推薦「老東台品甜屋」的米苔目（冷熱都好吃！）

14:00
SUSU SECOND-HAND BOOKSTORE
6. 晃晃二手書店

Susu, owner of Guesthouse Susu, has worked in the local cultural field for over a decade. Her carefully curated inventory reflect not only her taste but also her advocacy for social awareness. The comfortable layout is welcoming and so are the various cats that roam the bookstore. What better way to dodge the heat than spending an afternoon amongst books as cats! In order to keep the cats healthy, please don't touch them!

深耕台東十多年的書店老闆素素，不僅是在選書上有很棒的品味，更努力在這裡推動許多社會議題。晃晃二手書店店內擺設非常的舒適溫馨，店貓一隻比一隻極品，下午太陽正熱，不如進來晃晃買本好書吧！

為了店貓的健康著想，不可以隨意摸店貓喔！

☐

15:00

TAITUNG SUGAR FACTORY CULTURAL AND CREATIVE PARK

7. 臺東糖廠文創園區

Built during the Japanese colonoal period, this sugar factory was once a pineapple processing plant and bore witness to Taitung's rich history until it was shut down in 1996. In 2004, the factory became a cultural and creative park that features a wide variety of arts and crafts workshops and studios such as The Garage and Ata Beads Studio. I highly recommend coming here to check out local brands and try out their workshops.

從日治時代的製糖株式會社，一度成為鳳梨工廠，見證台東開拓發展歷史的臺東糖廠於 1996 年關廠，並在 2004 年轉型為文創園區，邀請許多工藝坊進駐，如庫空間、卡塔文化工作室等，相當推薦來此挖掘在地品牌或體驗手作課程。

☐

17:00

KUNG TUNG CHURCH

8. 公東教堂

Known as Taiwan's Notre Dame du Haut, Kung Tung Church was designed by Swiss architect Justus Dahinden. Within the understated cement exterior is an interior that focuses on natural light and simple lines that evoke a sense of serenity. Before you plan a visit, make sure you go online (chapel.rf.gd) or call Kung Tung High School's campus ministry center (+886-89-222-877) to reserve a spot.

被譽為「台灣的廊香教堂」的公東教堂，由瑞士籍建築師達興登設計，清水模的外觀，重視自然光影與線條的內部設計，走進教堂便能感到平靜。小提醒，如果要入內參觀，記得要先上網 (chapel.rf.gd) 或電洽公東高工宗輔室 (+886-89-222-877) 進行預約喔。

☐

18:00

MI BA NAI INDIGENOUS FOOD

9a. 米巴奈山地美食坊

A third of Taitung's population are indigenous. Among the native people, there are numerous tribes, each with their own unique traditions and cultures. In the Amis language, mi ba nai means a bountiful harvest and this restaurant uses locally sourced ingredients to create traditional Amis dishes with a twist. I recommend trying mountain land rice with pickled fish, betel palm flower, bamboo shoots with muntjac, and roasted springtime bamboo shoots. (reservations needed)

台東有三分之一的人口是原住民，不同族群、部落有著各自的傳統文化與美食。米巴奈是阿美族語「豐收」的意思，美食坊以當地食材為主，自行研發原住民風味桌菜料理，一行人來推薦點「山地飯＋醃魚」、「檳榔花」、「脆筍山羌肉」與很下酒的「烤春筍」，建議先預約。

18:00
2. FLIGHT CAFÉ
9b. 福來東咖啡

For solo travelers, I recommend visiting Flight Café run by a lady from Tokyo, where you can enjoy delicious Japanese-style meals, cake and beverages. I especially recommend trying their specialty hamburger set meal and minced meat curry rice. The owner, Miss Fukunaga, came to Taitung for a short trip and decided to settle down as a new resident. Be careful, as this trip might make you never want to leave Taitung!

若是自己出遊，推薦到由東京女子開設的「福來東咖啡」享用美味的日式簡餐和蛋糕飲品，尤其推薦特製漢堡排定食和肉燥咖哩飯。老闆福長小姐是來台東小旅行之後決定留下來生活的新住民。小心，說不定這一趟也會讓你就此離不開台東！

19:30
MÙMÙ CAFÉ AND ALANGER COFFEE
10. 目目咖啡 與 艾蘭哥爾藝文咖啡館

If you crave a cup of post-dinner coffee, I would recommend trying MùMù Café. They roast their coffee beans in-house and are known for sugarcane coffee, a mixture of local sugarcane juice and coffee. I also love Alanger Coffee, conveniently located in the beautiful Taitung Art Museum. Owner Chang Hong Dian is an advocate for using locally grown coffee beans and is an expert at making pour-over coffee using Taitung golden coffee beans.

吃飽推薦到以販售自家烘焙咖啡豆為主「目目咖啡」，這裡推薦運用台東在地甘蔗混搭的「甘蔗咖啡」，另外我的愛店「艾蘭哥爾藝文咖啡館」進駐在臺東美術館內，老闆張弘典致力推廣台東原生咖啡豆，親手泡製的台東黃金咖啡，讓人驚豔。

20:30
TIEHUA MUSIC VILLAGE
11. 鐵花村音樂聚落

Tiehua Music Village is possibly the liveliest hub for music and bazaars; there are almost always events going on. Check out their website to see what's happening and end your day with a chill evening spent exploring Tiehua Music Village.

「鐵花村音樂聚落」可以說是台東音樂與市集的最大基地，三不五時就有表演可聽、在地市集可逛。晚上還想找點樂子的朋友可以查查網站，看看當天表演節目單有沒有喜歡的團，夜晚散步來鐵花村 Chill 一下，結束有吃有玩有海有表演的一天。

EAST RIFT VALLEY

縱谷特輯　　體驗山谷間的各式理想生活方案

SPECIAL FEATURE
TAITUNG
台東特輯

Between the Central Mountain Range and Coastal Mountain Range, the long and narrow rift valley plain has been a fertile land attracting Taiwan's major ethnic groups to settle for hundreds of years. The alluvial plain, nurtured by the overflow of Hsinwulu River, is the homeland of delicious Chishang rice. Autumn would be the best season to visit Chishang, as the annual Autumn Rice Harvest Arts Festival presents world-class performances in the middle of golden rice paddies with the majestic mountains in the background. The pace of cycling would be just right for exploring Chishang. First, stop at Zhouzhou Chishang café to get travel and events info. At night, stay at Good Farming Day B&B, and the next morning, maybe join the activity organized by the B&B host to experience farm work of the season.

Not far away from Chishang, Haiduan and Yanping Township have long been inhabited by the Bunun people. Millet used to be the staple of their traditional diet, but as it was not easy to grow, it had once been replaced by rice. In recent years, tribal members have begun re-cultivate millet, in hopes of passing on the old wisdom of "setting the rhythms of life by following the growth of millet." If you are interested in millet and Bunun culture, come visit Kaiana Workshop for the tasty millet rice, or Uninag Cultural Workshop for activities like high-mountain hunting and tribal food tasting.

In recent years, tourists have been drawn to Luye for the Balloon Festival and red oolong tea. Taitung 2626 Market takes place at the Wuling Green Tunnel Bikeway on the second and fourth Saturdays of each month, where one can purchase organic vegetables, and toxin-free fruits. If you would like to find out why many people choose to relocate to the valley, it is recommended to visit The Family in the Valley and learn from the host family, who moved from city to Luye. Under the guidance of the hosts, you would collect home-grown ingredients and cook a meal from making fire, as experiencing the simple lifestyle of "half-farmer, half-X" for a day might trigger your imagination for a different kind of life. (by Jolin Lin)

在中央山脈與海岸山脈之間，縱谷平原狹長綿延，百年來是台灣各大族群爭相移居的豐饒之地。池上，由新武呂溪所沖積而成的肥沃平原，孕育出飽滿剔透的池上米；每年秋天登場的「秋收音樂祭」，以巍峨山脈為背景，金黃稻浪環繞全場，結合世界級表演，成為造訪池上最好的時刻。騎腳踏車探索池上是最剛好的速度，第一站先到「走走池上」咖啡廳獲得在地旅遊與年度活動資訊，晚上累了就回到「莊稼熟了」民宿，也推薦參加主人舉辦的季節農事體驗。

離池上不遠的海端鄉與延平鄉是布農族的世居地，過去小米為部落重要主食，但因種植不易，一度被稻米取代，直到近年族人開始積極復育，希望將「圍著小米作息」的傳統智慧教導給下一代。若對小米或布農族文化有興趣，可以造訪「蓋亞那工作坊 Kaiana」並品嚐滋味絕佳的小米飯，或到「烏尼囊多元文化工作坊」參加高山獵人與餐食體驗。

近年因「台灣國際熱氣球嘉年華」與香甜「紅烏龍」深受遊客喜愛的鹿野，每雙週六在武陵綠色隧道固定舉辦台東 2626 市集（facebook.com/2626market），可以採購放牧雞蛋、有機蔬菜與無毒水果等縱谷美好滋味。若想知道為何許多人選擇移居縱谷，推薦到「山谷裡的一家人」跟著由都市搬到鹿野的主人一家，採集自家栽種的食材並生火煮食，體驗一日半農半 X 的手作生活，想像不一樣的人生可能。（文 / 林苡秀）

ZHOUZHOU CHISHANG 走走池上

⌐ 台東縣池上鄉中山路99號 | facebook.com/zhouzhouTW
No. 99, Zhongshan Rd., Chishang Township, Taitung County
+886-986-367-216 | 13:30-17:30, 19:00-23:00 (CLosed on Saturdays)

UNINANG TALUHAN WORKSHOP 烏尼囊多元文化工作坊

⌐ 台東縣延平鄉泰平路82-2號 | www.facebook.com/uninang.taluhan
No. 82-2, Taiping Rd., Yanping Township, Taitung County
09:00-17:00 | +886-988-815-808

COASTLINE

海線特輯　讓人流連忘返的美麗海岸線

Credit：WSL 世界衝浪聯盟 /Matty Dunbar（臺東縣政提供）

SPECIAL FEATURE
TAITUNG
台東特輯
SPECIAL FEATURE

Taitung has the longest coastline in Taiwan, stretching 176 kilometers with lots of amazing and unique surfing points. Especially around Donghe, Jinzun, and Dulan, the flat coastal topography of sandy beaches mixed with pebbles provide safe surfing sites. Accompanying with the waves brought by the northeast monsoon in autumn and winter, Taitung has become an international surfing mecca and even been elected as competition venue by the World Surfing League (WSL). When visiting WaGaLiGong Surf Hostel Bar & Restaurant (facebook.com/WaGaLiGong) in Dulan, one may encounter surfers from Japan, America, Europe, and even South Africa, just like the united nations of surfing. For beginners, they can also take a surfing course at Yeah Surf House (facebook.com/yeahsurfhouse) in Donghe.

In addition to maritime sports, the gorgeous ocean and the placid pace of life that makes one forget worries have drawn numerous creatives here in search of inspiration. Xindong Sugar Refinery Culture Park in Dulan brings together artists' studios, performance spaces, bars, and select shops. On weekends, there are often music performances and markets of handmade items here, helping it grow into one of the important art and cultural hotspots in Taitung. The renowned Dulan tribe of Amis is also the hometown of Suming, a Golden Melody Award-winning singer. Since 2013, he and Dulan villagers have organized the Amis Music Festival in November (in two out of every three years), inviting musicians from various ethnic groups at home and abroad to Dulan, connecting Taiwan with the indigenous cultures around the world through music. No matter where you come from, you would feel like becoming part of the community as the festival embodies the dedication and passion the locals put into.

The railroad tickets during the music festival would be hard to get, so if you're interested in going, make sure to plan the trip ahead of time. (by Jolin Lin)

台東擁有全台灣最長的海岸線，從北到南綿延 176 公里，擁有許多得天獨厚的優異浪點。尤其在東河、金樽與都蘭一帶，有著由沙灘與鵝卵石組成的混和地形，地勢較為平穩安全，搭配秋冬東北季風吹拂帶來的浪勢，讓台東成為受世界衝浪聯盟 WSL（World Surfing League）認證的國際衝浪聖地。如果造訪都蘭的「哇軋力共」(facebook.com/WaGaLiGong)，常常可以看到來自日本、歐美甚至遠從南非來的浪人，宛如衝浪聯合國；若是對衝浪有興趣的初學者，也可以到東河的「野孩子衝浪社」(facebook.com/yeahsurfhouse) 參加教學課程。

除了海上運動外，台東讓人忘卻憂愁的大海與緩慢的生活步調，也吸引了許多文化創意工作者來此醞釀靈感，其中位於都蘭的「新東糖廠文化園區」，匯集了藝術家工作室、展演空間、酒吧與選品店等，週末也常有音樂表演與手作市集，是台東重要的藝文聚落之一。都蘭同時也是台灣知名的阿美族部落，金曲歌手 Suming 舒米恩的故鄉，他與族人自 2013 年起，每年 11 月舉辦「阿米斯音樂節」（辦兩屆休一屆），邀請來自國內外各族群部落代表來到都蘭，以音樂連結台灣與世界各地的原住民文化。在這裡，無論你來自哪個國家，都能在現場感受到部落的用心與熱情並融入其中。（文／林苙秀）

音樂節期間火車票一票難求，若有興趣參加，記得提早規劃以免向隅！

GOOD BUY HANDMADE ART CRAFTS STORE
都蘭好的擺手創藝術小店

台東縣東河鄉都蘭村61-1號（新東糖廠文化園區內）
No.61-1, Dulan Village, Donghe Township, Taitung County
+886-8-953-1702 | 10:00-17:00 (Closed on Mondays and Tuesdays)

TAIWAN OPEN OF SURFING
臺灣國際衝浪公開賽

www.taiwanopenofsurfing.org
facebook.com/taiwanopenofsurfin

A SEA LIKE NO OTHER

LANYU

離島特輯 —— 蘭嶼的海，與其他的方的海都不一樣

Sits off the southeast coast of Taiwan, Lanyu covers an area of 48 square kilometers. Administratively, the island belongs to Lanyu Township, Taitung County and can be reached by a 2.5-hour ferry ride from Taitung's Fugang Fishing Harbor. Lanyu is known for the unique culture of Tao people, who call their home "Pongso no Tao." As "Tao" means "people," "Pongso no Tao" means "Island of People." Among Taiwan's indigenous tribes, only the Tao have traditionally made their livings off the ocean and developed the culture around flying fish. Breathing with the ebbs and flows of the tides, Lanyu boasts its own rhythm of life.

Circling the island by scooter only takes two hours, while scenic beauty can be found everywhere on the road, highlighted by the blue ocean. Splendid under the sunshine and mysterious in the dark, the ocean expresses its changing mood through vigorous roars or gentle whispers. The trip to Lanyu would be worthwhile even just admiring the sea around the island. Also, welcoming the dawn at Tungching Bay, snorkeling or soaking in the water at Tungching Secret Spot, strolling and gazing at the sea at Green Green Grassland, or watching the sunset at Tiger Head Slope, are all worth a visit.

And of course, the island also offers delicious seafood. Lanyu Driftwood Restaurant in Yuren Village is especially recommended, from flying fish roe risotto to Yu-xian-yu-si (taro smoothie), are all mouth-watering delicacies that would make you want to visit Lanyu over and over again.

※ As the Tao people lead a life following traditional customs with certain taboos, visitors should look it up online and follow the rules. (by Wen Liu)

位於台灣東南方外海上的蘭嶼，全島面積約48 平方公里，行政區劃分在台東縣蘭嶼鄉，從台東富岡漁港搭船約 2.5 小時可以到達，因其獨特的原住民達悟族文化而著名。在達悟族語中，蘭嶼稱作「Pongso no Tao」，達悟族的「Tao」，在族語中是「人」的意思，「Pongso no Tao」就是「人的島」。達悟族是全台灣原住民中，唯一以漁業為生的族群，以飛魚為核心開展的文化，離不開海的蘭嶼，有著屬於自己的生活節奏。

騎機車環繞蘭嶼一圈，只需要 2 個小時，路上每一處風景都有大海——白日是燦爛奪目、大聲喧嘩的海，夜晚是深沉靜謐、碎碎細語的海，可以說光是能看到蘭嶼的海，這趟旅行就值得也不為過。而除了大片的海之外，像是可以看日出的「東清灣」、可以浮潛、泡水的「東清祕境」，適合散步、看海的「青青大草原」，或是觀賞日落的「虎頭坡」等，也都是值得造訪的景點。

蘭嶼島上連食物也離不開海，特別推薦漁人部落「蘭嶼漂流木餐廳」，無論是奶油飛魚卵燉飯，還是芋仙芋死（芋頭冰沙）都是美味到半夜想起會餓到哭的美食，啊，我真的可以去 100 次蘭嶼！

※ 達悟族仍依循傳統生活，有許多禁忌與注意事項，想體驗蘭嶼的海的朋友請務必於造訪前上網查詢並盡力遵守喔！（文／劉玟岑）

READ SEA BOOKSTORE 在海一方
Discover Lanyu at the island's first independent bookstore.
Appointments required
蘭嶼第一家獨立書店，在這裡看見更多蘭嶼（需預約）

⌈ 台東縣蘭嶼鄉紅頭村1號之8 | FB/IG: @readseadowawa
No. 1-8, Hongtou Village, Lanyu Township, Taitung County

BAIS CAFÉ 角落
A homey café hidden in Langdao Village
隱身朗島部落的溫馨咖啡店

⌈ 台東縣蘭嶼鄉朗島69-1號
No. 69-1, Langdao, Lanyu Township, Taitung County
13:00-18:00 (Closed on Mon. and Tue.)

GREEN ISLAND

離島特輯—— 從政治犯監獄到潛水勝地

edit : jphotos

SPECIAL FEATURE
TAITUNG
台東特輯
SPECIAL FEATURE

Green Island, the fourth-largest offshore island of Taiwan, was a place where political opponents of the regime were confined during the martial law period. The former prison camp, also known as Oasis Villa, has been transformed into the National Human Rights Museum—Green Island White Terror Memorial Park in 2002 and open to the public as an important portal to an understanding of Taiwan's history.

Moving beyond the somber past, Green Island now draws numerous tourists with diving and snorkeling, its natural beauty, and local delicacies. The gray peanut tofu is one of the most representative foods of the island. Simply dip it with soy sauce, one can truly taste its gritty texture and a slightly burnt fragrance. Fish rice dumpling is another delicious choice one shouldn't miss. Different from the pork rice dumpling wrapped in bamboo leaves of the island of Taiwan, Green Island's rice dumplings are stuffed with tuna fish and wrapped in shell ginger leaves. If you'd like to have a bite, visit Chunxia Eatery to taste these dishes.

Green Island is also one of the six diving hotspots in Taiwan. In the crystal clear blue ocean, divers can admire tropical fish and spectacular coral reefs. And if you're lucky, you may even dive with sea turtles and giant oceanic manta rays. In summer nights, one can also join the eco-friendly nighttime or intertidal zone tour organized by Caring for Green Island by Cutting Carbon Emissions (facebook.com/journeyvillage). Green Island even has one of the planet's only three underwater volcanic hot springs. At Zhaori Hot Springs, you may greet the sunrise in the morning, as well as enjoy soaking in hot pools while listening to the sound of waves and gazing into the starry sky at night. However, on Green Island surrounded by the sea, one can have a perfectly relaxing day by just sitting in a pavilion and reading a book over some coffee. (by Jolin Lin)

綠島,台灣的第四大離島,在戒嚴時期為羈押政治犯的囚禁地,曾為監獄的「綠洲山莊」在 2002 年轉型成「國家人權博物館—白色恐怖綠島紀念園區」對外開放,是認識台灣歷史非常重要的入口。

走過傷痛,綠島現在以潛水活動、自然生態與在地美食吸引許多遊客造訪。綠島的特色飲食,以「花生豆腐」最具代表性,灰色的花生豆腐擁有粗獷的顆粒感,吃來多了一股獨有的醇厚焦香,直接沾少許醬油膏食用,最能品嘗出火山岩地形孕育出的花生滋味。另外,「魚粽」也是不能錯過的選擇,有別於本島的肉粽以竹葉製作,魚粽以月桃葉製作,內餡也從豬肉換成鮪魚,月桃的清香搭配鮪魚的鮮美,意外的清爽美味,若想品嘗可到「春霞小吃部」試試。

綠島的海域是台灣六大潛點之一,寶石般透明的藍色海水中,可以觀賞熱帶魚與壯觀的珊瑚礁,幸運的話還能遇見海龜與鬼蝠魟。此外,島上還有許多特有種生物,夏夜可以預約「減碳愛綠島」(facebook.com/journeyvillage) 提供的生態友善夜遊與潮間帶導覽;綠島更擁有全世界唯三的海底火山溫泉,清晨可在「朝日溫泉」迎接日出,夜晚也能聽著陣陣海浪聲,邊賞星空邊泡湯,相當享受。不過在 360 度都看得到海的綠島,不用特地做什麼,只要帶一杯咖啡、選一個視野順眼的涼亭、配一本想看許久的書,就能度過完美的一天。(文 / 林苡秀)

MY TAITUNG TRIP 島嶼見學‧綠島層

Sign up for a variety of experiences in Green Island's culture, ecology, and marine life
來報名綠島文化、生態與海洋的各式體驗

⌐ www.mytaitungtrip.com/greenisland-experience-activity

SLOW ISLAND HOSTEL 緩島旅宿

Comfy accommodation at a convenient location, also offering customized travel advice
綠島舒適旅宿,位置方便,提供客製化行程諮詢

⌐ 台東縣綠島鄉南寮110-1號 | facebook.com/slowislandhostel
No. 110-1, Nanliao, Ludao Township, Taitung County

我們只是講話比較大聲，
沒有在生氣啦！

澎湖
PENGHU

WE REALLY AREN'T ANGRY,
WE JUST SPEAK A LITTLE
LOUDLY, THAT'S ALL.

—————— Yi-Lin Chen 陳亦琳

Photo credit : jphotos

Consisting of nearly a hundred islands, Penghu welcomed its population of overseas immigrants several thousand years ago. Life here has always been lived with close ties to the ocean. In order to survive the tough climate, residents of Penghu have developed an abundance of local wisdom. This includes temperature-regulating houses and caizhai, garden walls used to protect crops from winter-time winds, both of which are built with local coral stones called lao-gu shi. They also make stone weirs that use tidal fluctuations to trap fish. When speaking of winter preparations, they are masters of food preservation. With a fondness for fish-centered cuisine, they make an abundance of preserved fish and vegetables, which also demonstrates their renowned perseverance in the face of limited island resources.

Penghu was the first of Taiwan's offshore islands that I visited. At the time, I didn't realize how severe the Penghu sun could be, and was strolling around outside all day without sunglasses. As a result, my eyes became sunburned and it took me a week to recover. Even so, this was the first place where I learned about the connection between the environment and the food on my table, and where I first experienced ocean diving. The ocean has since captured my heart, and I've tried to find excuses to revisit Penghu and stay for a period of time every year. Eventually, I moved to Penghu and became a newcomer. You might think that the people here speak awfully loudly when you first arrive, but don't be afraid. If you stay a while, you will discover that it's because they are worried you can't hear them over the everlasting clamor of waves crashing in the background.

My favorite time of year in Penghu is between September and mid-October while the temperature is mild and there are less tourists around compared to summer vacation. Even guesthouse fares and flight tickets go on sale. Why not seize the opportunity and the deals, and come explore Penghu!

澎湖，由近百座小島集合而成，早期移民跨海來到這裡，生活與大海脫離不了關係，為了在艱困環境中生存，澎湖人發展出各式因地制宜的生活智慧，比如運用硓𥑮石搭建成冬暖夏涼的民宅、冬天用來擋風的「菜宅」，還有利用潮汐來捕魚的陷阱「石滬」；愛吃魚的澎湖人為了過冬也製作各式醃菜和魚乾，這些都是他們堅毅、不服輸的展現。

我第一個造訪的台灣離島，就是澎湖。當時不懂澎湖太陽的毒辣，沒戴太陽眼鏡就出海一整天，結果連眼球都曬傷，一個禮拜才復原。在這裡我第一次清楚知道餐桌上的食物是從哪裡來的，也體驗了生平第一次的潛水，自此便被這片海洋網羅，每年總要找理由回來住一段時間，甚至乾脆變成新移民。初來乍到的旅人會發現澎湖人講話好像特別大聲，但千萬別被嚇到，住久了就知道，在海邊嘛，不大聲點怕你聽不見啦。

我個人最喜歡 9 月到 10 月中旬的澎湖，那時溫度很舒服，少了暑假滿滿的遊客人潮，甚至民宿、機票也開始降價，有機會就趁這個最佳時機來認識澎湖吧！

By plane, it takes about 50 minutes to get to Penghu from Taipei. You can also choose to depart from Taichung or Kaohsiung. By boat, it takes between 1.5 and 4 hours to travel from Chiayi, Tainan or Kaohsiung. When in Penghu, it is recommended to get around by renting a scooter or car, or by taxi. Local taxis apply a flat rate ranging from NTD 100 per trip in the city area up to NTD 300 when traveling across the city and to other areas. Call in advance to make reservations. Taxi companies recommended by Penghu National Scenic Area：www.penghu-nsa.gov.tw/TravelGuide/Traffic/taxi.htm

由台北搭飛機前往澎湖約 50 分鐘（也可從中南部機場出發）；從嘉義、台南或高雄搭船約需 1.5－4 小時。島上交通建議租借汽車、摩托車或搭乘計程車。澎湖計程車需喊價，單趟約新台幣 100－300 元（市區內移動為 100 元），建議事先預約叫車。可上網查詢「澎湖國家風景區推薦計程車車行」。

RECOMMENDATIONS
推薦

▌▌ READING LIST 旅遊書籍

THE OFFSHORE ISLAND, AND ITS OFFSHORE ISLETS: PEOPLE AND HAPPENINGS IN PENGHU
《離島，以及離島的離島：那些澎湖的人與事》
Stories about people and happenings in Penghu written by a local female writer
由澎湖在地女兒書寫的菊島人與事
⌐ books.com.tw/products/0010813293

LET'S GO! MR. PLAY-AND-EAT'S FIRST DESTINATION: PENGHU ARCHIPELAGO
《出走吧!!玩食男 首發站：澎湖群島》
Manga book that takes you on a 5-day tour to discover Penghu's delicacies and culture
用漫畫帶你澎湖5日遊，輕鬆認識澎湖美食與文化！
⌐ books.com.tw/products/0010719449

▌▌ LOCAL PUBLICATIONS 在地刊物

PAPERPLANE: WANDERLUST OCEAN: PENGHU'S GOOD LIFE MOVEMENT
《紙飛機生活誌：海想流放：澎湖好好生活運動》
In-depth local editorial magazine exploring the people and their lives
澎湖人編輯的在地刊物，深入探訪島上的人物故事與生活
⌐ books.com.tw/products/0010801472

▌▌ GUIDED TOURS 導覽

PH SEA 沿著菊島旅行
Various short tours provided by an established Penghu travel agency, follow for the most up-to-date travel dates
老字號旅遊網站舉辦的澎湖小旅行，多條路線請追蹤網站洽詢最新出團日期
⌐ www.phsea.com.tw

▌▌ TRAVEL WEBSITES 旅遊網站

100 REASONS TO LIVE IN PENGHU
在澎湖生活的100種理由
Facebook page sharing local life and a collaboration with Design from Penghu called 100 Delicacies in Penghu
分享澎湖生活的臉書專頁，與「關於澎湖群島」合作了「澎湖百大飲食」圖文計畫
⌐ facebook.com/1594902223874122
Design from Penghu 關於澎湖群島 (Cute illustrations 插圖很可愛)
facebook.com/DesignFromPenghu

PENGHU.INFO 澎湖知識服務平台
Integrated knowledge system providing cultural, historic, religious and geographic information about Penghu
一個橫跨澎湖文化、歷史、宗教與地理的整合知識系統
⌐ penghu.info

▌▌ ANNUAL EVENTS 年度活動

PENGHU INTERNATIONAL FIREWORKS FESTIVAL (APR.-JUN.)
澎湖花火節（4月-6月）
Join the most popular event of the year and see the beautiful fireworks by the ocean
每年夏日澎湖最熱鬧的慶典，一起來海邊看美麗煙火
⌐ facebook.com/phfireworks

PENGHU ROCK FESTIVAL (SEP.)
命待！澎湖搖滾音樂節(9月)
Independent music festival held in autumn with market and beach cleanups
在秋天舉行，結合音樂、市集、淨灘的澎湖獨立音樂節
⌐ facebook.com/penghu.rockfestivel

A MAZU TEMPLE (MAGONG) 澎湖天后宮
Built in 1604, it's the oldest Matsu temple in Taiwan
1604年建立，台灣歷史最悠久的媽祖廟

⌐ 澎湖縣馬公市正義街1號
No. 1, Zhengyi St., Magong City, Penghu County
+886-6-927-2045
07:00-19:00

B DUXINGSHI VILLAGE CULTURE PARK 篤行十村
Deceased Taiwanese singer Chang Yu-sheng's childhood
home, now a veteran's village culture park with shops and
guesthouses
台灣歌手張雨生的老家，聚集小店與旅宿的眷村文化園區

⌐ 澎湖縣馬公市新復路2巷22號 | +886-6- 926-0412
No. 22, Ln. 2, Xinfu Rd., Magong City, Penghu County | 08:00-21:30

C ART STUDIO 風向空間
Multi-functioned space for art exhibitions, handicraft
workshops, educational programs, books and art classes
結合展覽、手作、教學、二手書、畫室的複合空間

⌐ 澎湖縣馬公市重慶街24-1號 | +886-932-008-486
No. 24-1, Chongqing St., Magong City, Penghu County
15:00-21:00 (Closed on Sundays)

D BIG WELL PENGHU 頂街工房
Established in the 1950s and originally called Xi He
Letterpress Workshop, Big Well Penghu is a good place to
shop for letterpress and postcards
來50年代創立的西河印刷廠找鉛字與質感明信片

⌐ 澎湖縣馬公市中央街37號 | +886-6-927-2045
No. 37, Zhongyang St., Magong City, Penghu County | 10:00-18:00

E GUIDING & TESTING FOR GOOD THINGS 植隱冊室
Plant-decorated bookstore doubles as a restaurant with
local publications
有植物與在地出版的餐廳複合式書店

⌐ 澎湖縣馬公市文光路131號 | 15:00-23:00 (Closed on Wednesdays)
No. 131, Wenguang Rd., Magong City, Penghu County
facebook.com/penghubookstore

F FISH SAYS 年年有鱻
A team promoting fish-eating education in Penghu. Visit
the bookstore or join a class!
推廣澎湖食魚教育的團隊，來逛書店或參加課程！

⌐ 澎湖縣馬公市臨海路4號 | fish-says.com
No. 4, Linhai Rd., Magong City, Penghu County
10:00-12:00, 13:30-18:30 (Closed on Mondays)

A ZHONG'S SHAOBING 鐘記燒餅

Clay oven rolls as soft as buns and topped with neritic squid or scallop sauce

如麵包般柔軟，淋上小卷或干貝醬的海味甕烤燒餅

⌂ 澎湖縣馬公市文康街37-1號 | +886-6-926-0700
No. 37-1, Wenkang St., Magong City, Penghu County
06:30-10:00

B MAMA YANG'S CHIVE DUMPLINGS 楊媽媽韭菜盒

Oil-free griddle-fried chive dumplings; Chiqian Deep-Fried Oyster Cake across the street is also a good choice

手工無油乾烙韭菜盒，對面的赤崁炸粿也好吃

⌂ 澎湖縣馬公市民權路89-1號 | +886-6-995-0079
No. 89-1, Minquan Rd., Magong City, Penghu County
13:15-20:00 (Closed on Sundays)

C SAN GE WINE-MARINATED FRIED CHICKEN 三哥酒釀雞排

Thick fried chicken fillets marinated with fermented sweet rice wine, usually sold out within 2 hours

來以酒醃製的厚實雞排，開店後通常2個小時內就會賣光

⌂ 澎湖縣馬公市中興路11號 | +886-6-926-9693
No. 11, Zhongxing Rd., Magong City, Penghu County | 14:30-20:00

D PENGHU 23.5 CACTUS SORBET

澎湖235掌上明珠 (仙人掌冰淇淋專賣)

First Penghu gelato shop to make tapioca balls from cactus

澎湖第一間把仙人掌做成珍珠的義式冰淇淋店

⌂ 澎湖縣馬公市治平路30號 | +886-6-927-2323 | 12:00-18:00
No. 30, Zhiping Rd., Magong City, Penghu County

E GILLY PRIMAVERA 及林春咖啡館

Located in a lush park by the beach, great for passing a tranquil afternoon

森林中的咖啡館，坐擁得天獨厚的沙灘與寧靜的午後

⌂ 澎湖縣湖西鄉林投村1-3號 | +886-6-992-3639
No. 1-3, Lintou, Huxi Township, Penghu County
10:00-19:00

F 1957 PARIS 巴里園冰菓室

First café to open in Penghu. Give the King Hadhramaut coffee topped with whiskey a try

澎湖最富歷史的咖啡店，試試看淋上威士忌的帝王咖啡

⌂ 澎湖縣馬公市民權路61號 | +886-6-926-2839
No. 61, Minquan Rd., Magong City, Penghu County
12:00-18:00

A ORIGEN BY MOLINO DE URDANIZ

A Spanish restaurant in Penghu created by the team behind the Michelin-starred Molino de Urdaniz

米其林一星渥達尼斯磨坊在澎湖打造的西班牙料理餐聽

澎湖縣湖西鄉林投26-9號 | FB: @origenbymolinodeurdaniz
No. 26-9, Lintou, Huxi Township, Penghu County
營業時間請洽臉書 For operating hours, please check Facebook

B PESCE BUONE 魚好。刺身專賣店

Sashimi heaven serving limited fresh sashimi meals made with local daily catch

生魚片天堂，每日以澎湖現撈漁獲製作限量刺身套餐

澎湖縣西嶼鄉二崁22之1號
No. 22-1, Erkan, Xiyu Township, Penghu County
11:30-17:00 | facebook.com/pesce.buone

C CAULIFLOWER OLD MEMORY RESTAURANT
花菜干人文懷舊餐館

Savor the authentic traditional fishing-village dishes on offer in this old house built with lao-gu shi

在硓𥑮石古厝裡，吃正港的老澎湖傳統漁村菜

澎湖縣馬公市新店路4-2號 | 11:00~14:00, 17:00~21:00
No.4-2, Xindian Rd., Magong City, Penghu County | +886-6-921-3695

D MERCATO PIZZA 瑪咖朵披薩

Turning local seafood into tasty Neapolitan pizza and American style deep-fried platter

運用在地食材製作出美味的拿坡里披薩與各式美式炸物

澎湖縣馬公市北辰街10號 | facebook.com/mercatopizza.tw
No. 10, Beichen St., Magong City, Penghu County
Mon.-Thur. 11:30-14:30, 17:00-20:30, Fri.-Sun. 10:00-14:30, 17:00-21:00

E 燒ZONE

A great spot for late-night bites in Penghu. Enjoy drinks with BBQ and fresh Penghu seafood

澎湖消夜好去處，來喝酒配燒烤和澎湖海鮮

澎湖縣馬公市海埔路89號 | instagram.com/grilled_zone
No. 89, Haipu Rd., Magong City, Penghu County
19:00-03:00 (Closed on Sundays)

F CHAO XI LU 朝昔廬客棧

Penghu's restaurant of old-fashioned cuisine, don't miss its signature clam rice (seashell rice dumpling) !

澎湖古早味餐廳，別錯過招牌菜色大蛤米(貝殼粽)！

澎湖縣馬公市宅腳嶼200號 | +886-6-921-0750
No. 200, Zhaijiaoyu, Magong City, Penghu County
11:00-14:00, 17:00-21:00 | facebook.com/ChaoXiLu

Photo credit：候鳥潮間帶民宿

A BEACON BEER TALKER 說酒人

Craft beer bar hidden down an alleyway. If you don't know where to begin, just ask the owner what to order

藏在巷子裡的精釀啤酒吧，不知道喝什麼問老闆就對了

⌂ 澎湖縣馬公市臨海路15-3號 | +886-933-833-394
No. 15-3, Linhai Rd., Magong City, Penghu County
19:00–00:00 | facebook.com/beaconbeertalker

B THE GARDEN TAPAS & BAR 菜宅裡的小酒館

Spanish and home-style fusion tapas bar perfect for a tipsy time

西班牙風格的家庭式小酒館，適合微醺

⌂ 澎湖縣馬公市109之2號 | facebook.com/ElynRichiePengHu
No. 109-2, Magong City, Penghu County
Fri. to Sat. 18:00-22:00

C BRUNCH+BACKPACKER 小島家

Hipsters' favorite place for brunch; Owner also runs a late-night snack shop called Xianshuihao

文青最愛的早午餐店，老闆還有一間消夜店「鹹水號」

⌂ 澎湖縣馬公市中山路8號 | +886-933-868-639
No. 8, Zhongshan Rd., Magong City, Penghu County
10:30-15:00 | facebook.com/lovePenghuIslands

D ENISHI RESORT VILLA 緣民宿

Fair-faced concrete building by the ocean, won ADA Awards for Emerging Architects in 2018

2018年ADA新銳建築獎，在海邊的清水模建築

⌂ 澎湖縣湖西鄉45之3號 | +886-6-921-5423
No. 45-3, Huxi Township, Penghu County
facebook.com/EnishiResortVilla

E FLOWER HOUSE 51 花羨花宅

Located in a 300-year-old Huazhai Community in Wangan Township, a cozy guesthouse with ingenious design

位於望安300多年的花宅社區中，充滿巧思的舒適民宿

⌂ 澎湖縣望安鄉花宅51號 | +886-989-218-859
No. 51, Huazhai, Wang'an Township, Penghu County
facebook.com/flowerhoues51

F MIGRATOR INTERTIDAL HOMESTAY 候鳥潮間帶民宿

Enjoy a private beach and join the host for a nighttime intertidal zone exploration!

擁有私人海灘，晚上跟著主人一起夜探潮間帶！

⌂ 澎湖縣白沙鄉城前村34-2號、34-3號
No. 34-2 & 34-3, Chengqian Village, Baisha Township, Penghu County
migrator.com.tw

OLD-FASHIONED AND MODERN LIFESTYLE BY THE SEA

新舊之間的討海生活

澎湖灣
Penghu Bay

馬公港
Magong Port

台灣海峽
Taiwan Strait

用手機掃描 QR code，存取推薦路線的 Google M
Scan the QR code to access this recommended route on Google M

1) **05:30** Visit The Third Fish Market in Magong City for lively fish auctions

2) **06:30** Have breakfast at the local fishermen's favorite, Penghu Harbor Noodles

3) **07:00** Visit Beichen Market and explore the locale-specific produce

4) **09:00** Sign up for Sea Walk's diving activities or Fenggui Elementary School's standup-paddleboarding and coral-branching activities

5) **12:30** Recharge yourself at the nearby beef noodle shops

6) **13:30** Visit the Nanliao Old Residences area for its classic coral stone walls

7) **14:30** Learn to make a traditional Lantern Festival snack at Pond Food Traditional Cuisine

8) **17:00** Go wave-chasing in Kuibishan or learn about marine debris issues at O2 Lab

9) **18:00** Enjoy a savory dinner at Longmen Seafood

10) **19:00** Join a night tour and observe the intertidal zone life

11) **22:00** If you still have energy, go have some beer at Grassroots & Fruit

---

1) **05:30** 到馬公「第三漁港魚市場」看熱鬧的漁市交易

2) **06:30** 吃正港討海人的早餐「澎湖漁港麵」

3) **07:00** 逛「北辰市場」尋找澎湖當地特產

4) **09:00** 到「海底漫步」參加潛水活動 或「風櫃國小」體驗划 SUP、植珊瑚

5) **12:30** 在附近的牛肉麵店吃午餐補充元氣

6) **13:30** 前往「南寮古厝」看經典的澎湖砝砧石牆老屋

7) **14:30** 在「澎福古棗味」學做元宵傳統小點「肪片龜」

8) **17:00** 去看「奎壁山摩西分海」或到 O2 Lab「海漂實驗室」認識海廢議題

9) **18:00** 晚餐就到「龍門海鮮」大嗑美食

10) **19:00** 參加夜間照海活動，看潮間帶生物

11) **22:00** 還有力氣就去「草根果子」喝酒吃消夜吧

此路線是行軍行程，深度慢遊請參考澎湖特輯！

This is an intensive itinerary. For itineraries that move at a slower pace please refer to our Special Feature.

05:30
THE THIRD FISH MARKET

1. 第三漁港魚市場

At 3:30 in the morning, fishing boats successively dock in the harbor, and offload their freshest catch of the day for auction. Vendors, wholesalers and restaurant owners gradually gather around, ready to bring back some of the finest seafood with them. If you are a curious food-lover, the fish market is a good place to see where the food on your table comes from. You can even seize the chance to consult some fishermen for more information about their boats and fishing methods. Be a conscious consumer and protect our oceans.

凌晨三點半起漁船們陸續回港，卸下當日最新鮮的漁獲，等待競標出售，批商、小販、店家們也在此聚集，準備帶回最優質的海鮮。饕客不如直接到現場看看食物從哪裡來，有興趣還可以進一步了解漁船類型和捕魚方式，透過有意識的選購，一起守護海洋未來。

06:30
PENGHU HARBOR NOODLES

2. 澎湖漁港麵

Located beside The First Harbor, Penghu Harbor Noodles is in the front row for the best sea view. With great portions and prices, their pork bone broth with rice noodles and/or wheat noodles is the local fishermen's go-to breakfast. Get a side dish of various sliced delicacies for a perfect sample of these local favorites.

位於第一漁港旁，海景第一排的漁港麵，是討海人們出海前的早餐，用大骨熬煮的湯頭，可以選擇搭配米粉、麵或是米粉麵（各加一半），分量多且價格划算，搭配自由選擇的黑白切，便是在地人的夢幻組合。

07:00
BEICHEN MARKET

3. 北辰市場

In Beichen Market, the biggest and oldest traditional market in Penghu, you can find vegetables grown by local grandmas, homemade preserves and fresh seafood right from the ocean. Fermented cabbage or oriental pickling melons make great gifts for those in the know! If you are interested in relieving the summer heat, Penghu's special summery teasane, hsiang-ju cha, and Penghu's sweet-yet-slightly-salty watermelon are your best bet. Not cool enough yet? Just take a walk to Yong Quan Popsicle Shop and get a fruity popsicle made with local watermelon and cactus!

北辰市場是澎湖最大且歷史悠久的傳統市場，在此隨處可見阿婆們自己種的菜、私房醃製物和剛上岸的新鮮漁獲。伴手禮帶點高麗菜酸或酸瓜，立即知道你內行的。想消暑可試試夏日消暑良品——澎湖青草茶「風茹茶」或橘紅果肉甜中帶點鹹的「嘉寶瓜」！還不夠涼爽？散步到「永泉冰品」，來枝鮮果冰棒，嚐嚐澎湖限定的嘉寶瓜和仙人掌口味！

09:00
SEA WALK

4. 海底漫步

No matter if you are a swimmer or not, as long as you like the ocean, come join one of Sea Walk's activities and explore the underwater world! Just put on your diving gear, and you will soon find yourself swimming with schools of fish. If you are a natural born adventurer, you could even jump into the ocean from a two-story-high boat. Standup paddleboarding and scuba diving experiences make for another worthwhile option, and cultivating young branching corals on plates in the ocean at Fenggui Elementary School is your chance to make a little contribution to the marine environment.

來一窺澎湖海底世界吧，無論會不會游泳，海底漫步都適合喜歡海洋的人參加，只要穿戴頭盔式潛水設備，就能緩緩下潛，親近魚群。膽子大一點的人還可以從兩層樓高的船上跳進大海。另外一種有趣的選擇，是到風櫃國小划著 SUP（立槳式衝浪板）搭配浮潛，將培育好的珊瑚分枝植栽置入海裡的珊瑚移植磚內生長，為海洋環境盡一份小小的心力。

12:30
BEEF NOODLES

5. 鎖港牛肉麵 與 山水牛肉麵

After the exciting Sea Walk activity, you'll certainly be starving. Head to either of the beef noodle restaurants nearby and recharge yourself! The closer Suogana Beef Noodles offers generous beef chunks, and neritic squid caught by the owner is available on occasion. Though slightly farther away, Shanshui Beef Noodles is the go-to place for locals. People love their hand-sliced noodles.

海底漫步完應該餓壞了，趕緊到附近兩家牛肉麵打牙祭吧。比較近的「鎖港牛肉麵」肉塊量毫不手軟，運氣好小菜還有老闆親自捕釣的水晶小管可選擇；稍遠的「山水牛肉麵」則是當地人的口袋名單，刀削麵條深受大家喜愛。

13:30
NANLIAO OLD RESIDENCES

6. 南寮古厝

After your luncheon feast, head to Huxi, Penghu's biggest agriculture township, and take a walk between the old residential houses and the rural scenery in Nanliao Village. You'll see Penghu's traditional old houses built with coral stones, basalt and red bricks and tiles, as well as some more diverse buildings like Xu Fan's Old Residence that is decorated with clay sculptures and ornamental Japanese tiles. Discover Penghu by exploring Nanliao village in the afternoon.

吃飽離開鎖港前往澎湖最大的農業鄉湖西鄉，在擁有樸實農村風景與舊時老宅的南寮村裡散步。這邊有以硓𥑮石、玄武岩塊與紅色磚瓦蓋成的澎湖傳統老屋群，也有融合泥塑工藝與日式花磚的多元建築如「許返古宅」。午後在此穿梭探險，發現澎湖。

14:30
POND FOOD TRADITIONAL CUISINE
7. 澎福古棗味

While still in Nanliao, buy some deep-fried sticky rice balls, called zhazao, at the famous, old Xu Xi Cake Shop. In Penghu, they are used only for weddings, but are also perfect as gifts. If you are interested in learning how to make Penghu's traditional snacks, sign up for the daily DIY class at Pond Food Traditional Cuisine, and make your own zhazao and zhipiangui, a sticky rice snack shaped like a turtle and is used as offerings for special festivals. Booking in advance and checking in 20 minutes prior to the class are required. (www.klook.com/zh-TW/activity/1094)

來南寮就到口碑老店「旭西餅舖」買名產「炸棗」當伴手禮吧！如果想更深入體驗如何製作，也可到「澎福古棗味」參加每日固定舉辦的 DIY 課程，學習製作有喜事才會發送的炸棗與節慶供品「肪片龜」，記得先上網站預約並於 20 分前報到。(www.klook.com/zh-TW/activity/1094)

17:00
KUIBISHAN

8a. 奎壁山摩西分海

Keep heading north to Kuibishan Geopark in Beiliao Village and watch the rare geographic phenomena known by the locals as "Moses parting the sea." In spring and summer, when the tides are low, you can see seawater fading off from both sides of the coast, revealing an S-shaped gravel path connecting Kuibishan and Chi Yu islet. Travelers can "cross the ocean" to Chi Yu like the story of Moses crossing the Red Sea in the Bible. Due to the fact that tidal fluctuations vary daily, don't forget to look up the calendar before you go. (penghu.info/Moses)

繼續往北前往北寮村，在奎壁山地質公園裡有著暱稱為「摩西分海」的地理奇景，每逢春、夏退潮時，海水往兩側慢慢退去，浮現出一條連接奎壁山與赤嶼的 S 形礫石步道，讓旅人可以如穿越大海般走到海中央的小島。由於每日漲退潮時間不定，去之前請先查詢潮汐時間，以免撲空！(penghu.info/Moses)

17:00
O2 LAB

8b. O2 Lab 海漂實驗室

If you cannot make it to the low water, I recommend you to visit O2 Lab and learn about marine debris issues instead. After moving to Penghu, the lab owner, who used to be a photographer, found out that there is a serious marine debris problem in Penghu and decided to start a series of beach cleanups. Furthermore, he makes installation artwork and daily items from marine debris, hoping to arouse people's attention to this important issue. The lab is only irregularly open to the public, so please make an appointment before visiting. (facebook.com/O2Lab)

若搭不上摩西分海的時間，建議直奔「O2 Lab 海漂實驗室」來一場與海廢的私密約會！原是攝影師實驗室主理人在移居澎湖後，發現這裡有嚴重的海漂垃圾問題，於是發起淨灘活動，更利用海廢製作成雜貨或是裝置藝術，希望喚起大家對海洋議題的重視。實驗室不定期開放，若要參觀請記得先預約。(facebook.com/O2Lab)

18:00
LONGMEN SEAFOOD
9. 龍門海鮮

Using fresh seafood selected daily, the menu can be customized according to number of guests and desired price. With reasonable prices and a feisty owner who dares to fight with you if you "misbehave," Longmen Seafood will definitely satisfy your stomach and mind with local delicacies, so long as you behave.

每日嚴選的新鮮海味,可依人數、價格客製化安排菜單,價錢公道不浮誇,充滿個性又有點淘氣(?)的老闆,遇到奧客還會直接開嗆,但如果你乖的話,絕對是吃好吃滿,獲得身心靈的大滿足。

19:00
INTERTIDAL ZONE NIGHT TOUR
10. 夜照潮間帶

Between high and low water, the intertidal zone with its unique and fascinating ecology is formed. The intertidal zone night tour is an activity you should not miss when traveling in Penghu. Wearing a headlight, you follow the instructor and look for cute sea slugs, starfish and other creatures along the coast. The activity takes about 3 hours, and includes a seafood meal! Departure times vary according to the changing period of the tide. Please sign up via their Facebook page. (facebook.com/452133078552088)

在海洋與陸地漲退潮的交界之處,便是有著獨特生態系統的潮間帶。來澎湖別錯過夜照潮間帶的活動,頭戴著大燈,跟著導覽老師一起尋找可愛的海兔、海星等海洋生物。活動約 3 小時,還包含一頓海味料理!報到時間依當日潮汐而定,請到粉絲專頁洽詢報名。(facebook.com/452133078552088)

22:00
GRASSROOTS & FRUIT
11. 草根果子

Grassroots & Fruit is a place where you can get rid of your worries and find a sense of belonging. Just talk to the owner Austin Huang about what you have in mind and he will happily recommend the perfect herbal tea, craft beer, or book for you, or even give you a spiritual healing therapy session just right for your mood that day.

澎湖版解憂雜貨店,新澎湖人的取暖歸屬地,跟老闆雞健聊聊心事吧,他會根據你的狀況幫你推薦今日適合的養身茶、精釀啤酒或是一本書,甚至是靈氣治療!搭配用十多種漢方草本中藥調製的滷味和母親的手作饅頭跟假日週六限定的家常飯,不知為何就舒服得賴著不想離開。

EXPLORE PENGHU

澎湖的離島要怎麼玩？下面是深度放空版

SPECIAL FEATURE
PENGHU
澎湖特輯
SPECIAL FEATURE

If you ask new residents what they like most about Penghu, their answers might not include the usual sightseeing spots that you can find in the travel guides, but rather some secret place that only the locals know about. Instead of checking in at several popular places, the most luxurious pleasure here is to look at the ocean from some quiet, relaxing corner. On the other hand, you might not feel satisfied with the local restaurant fare, but rather find yourself savoring some local lady's signature fishing-village dishes, or today's fresh catch just brought back by the fishermen. And so, if you ask me where to go to see the best Penghu scenery, or how to arrange a Penghu itinerary, my answer would be to go make friends with some locals! (It's best if they happen to visit the ocean a lot.)

Unwind your mind in the South Sea

The above suggestion might not be for you, so I'm going to propose some practical ideas, hoping to help you start planning your trip. My personal preference is Penghu's South Sea area where tourists are rare because of its delayed development, and where you can enjoy the beautiful underwater world. The South Sea area includes the well-known Wangan, Chimei and other small islets, and South Penghu Marine National Park that was established after the Blue Cave went viral. It consists of four main islands: Dongjiyu, Xijiyu, Donyupingyu, Xiyupingyu, as well as other islets. The historical buildings and natural landscapes in the park are all well-preserved. Moreover, the surrounding waters contain abundant coral reefs, and 28 species of fish only recently discovered in the area, making the park a popular headline in international news media and a world-famous diving spot.

如果問過移居澎湖的外地人，他們最喜歡澎湖哪裡，答案不會是旅遊書上的景點，而是只有在地人知道的祕境；最大的享受不是到哪裡打了多少卡，而是找一個無人安靜的角落，看著海發呆；真正的佳餚也不在餐廳裡，而是藏在民宅裡，像是船長剛下船帶回來的新鮮漁獲，或是在地阿姨的拿手漁村菜。

所以如果你問我到底要怎麼樣才能看到澎湖最在地的風景？到澎湖玩到底要怎麼安排行程？我會說：「去認識個澎湖人吧！」（最好是常跑海邊的。）

去澎湖南海放空吧

這樣講好像有點像是在說幹話，這裡提供一些具體建議，幫助大家開始規劃澎湖行程。我個人喜歡澎湖的南海，因為開發得晚，不僅遊客少，民風淳樸，海底也很豐沛精彩。南海大家比較常聽到的島有望安、七美，和一些周邊小島，以及因藍洞爆紅後而成立的「南方四島國家公園」，以東吉島、西吉島和東嶼坪、西嶼坪四個島為主，島上的歷史建物、自然景色都還保存得十分良好，周邊海域珊瑚礁覆蓋率極高，更找到28種澎湖從未發現的魚類新記錄種，一舉躍上國際媒體版面成為世界級潛點！

If you decide to visit the South Sea, you can take public boats that travel to Wangan and Chimei daily from the South Sea Visitor Center. There are also boats that travel to the four main South Sea islands every Monday, Wednesday and Friday. The boat schedule allows you to stay on one of the islands overnight, and enjoy the tranquility after most other tourists have headed back.

You can also book a dive in the ocean to appreciate the stunning coral reefs, or kayak to a deserted islet where you can play with wild goats and fantasize about owning the whole island.

If you are interested to hear some folk stories, you can try chatting with the fishermen at the harbors, or have some tea with them in front of a temple. The key is to be friendly and polite. You might just find yourself overwhelmed by their hospitality and following them out to the ocean on their fishing boats. If you'd prefer to avoid wandering around aimlessly and are keen to participate in some in-depth tours, here are my recommendations:

Under the water: Island 77

Ye Sheng-Hong is a young fellow who returned to his hometown and led a group of divers to draw the first diving map of the four main South Sea islands. He applied his previous fishing experience to his diving business, and constructed a professional certified diving boat that fits all divers' needs. Divers from more than 10 countries have followed his lead to explore the secluded beauty of South Penghu Marine National Park.

On the water: PH Sea: in-depth culture tour of the South Sea islands

Planned and led by an established Penghu travel website, this one and only in-depth guided tour focuses on the four main South Sea islands and other islets, allowing you to discover their beauty from a cultural perspective.

如果大家想去這些地方看看，可以至「南海遊客中心」搭乘公家船，每日都有船班前往望安、七美；每週一、三、五也有交通船到南方四島，可以配合船班時間在島上停留一兩晚，不用被制式行程追趕，獨享遊客散去後島嶼的寧靜。

在這裡可以下海浮潛，被珊瑚礁美景給深深震懾；或是划著獨木舟跳往周邊無人小島，在島上與羊兒玩你追我跑，幻想自己是島主。

如果想聽到更多在地故事，可以到港口跟船長們聊天，或是到廟口跟他們一起泡茶，只要親切有禮貌，通常在地人也會回以讓你無法招架的熱情，可能不小心就出海了！若不想漫無目的地遊走，想找一些深入在地的行程，在這裡我也推薦幾個：

水下：澎湖島澳七七潛水俱樂部

第一個帶領潛客，畫出南方四島海下的潛水地圖的返鄉青年——葉生弘，將過往討海的經驗轉為帶潛客深入海底，並打造專業、符合法規，且更貼近潛水客所需的潛水船，帶領超過 10 個國家以上的潛水員，探索澎湖南方四島國家公園的祕境。

水上：沿著菊島去旅行：南方四島人文深覽團

目前南方四島及周邊島嶼的唯一深度解說團，由在地深耕十多年的老牌旅遊網站獨家設計的行程，以人文角度帶領遊客深入認識南方四島之美。

Photo credit：高世澤

PH SEA: IN-DEPTH CULTURE TOUR OF THE SOUTH SEA ISLANDS
沿著菊島去旅行：南方四島人文深覽團

⌐ 澎湖縣馬公市惠民路36號
No. 36, Huimin Rd., Magong City, Penghu County
facebook.com/xianshuihao
+886-6-926-0302

ISLAND 77 澎湖島澳七七潛水俱樂部

⌐ 澎湖縣望安鄉將軍村111-1號
No. 111-1, Jiangjyun Village, Wang'an Township, Penghu County
09:00-20:00 | +886-6-990-2303
facebook.com/phisland77
www.island77.tw

RETURNING YOUNGSTERS

修復一條連結回海洋的路

Most children from offshore islands experience the fate of leaving their hometown for study or work when they grow up. Whenever they relocate back to their hometown, most local elders affix a negative label to them, as if "they must have failed to achieve anything in the big city." However, the following stories of these remarkable young people ought to gradually overturn such ingrained biases.

"When I first returned from mainland Taiwan, everyone in my family thought it was a bad idea. In particular, they couldn't accept the fact that a pretty young granddaughter like me would choose to repair stone weirs in Penghu," recalled Fu-Tzu Yang, the host of the Run Away From Island studio. Four years ago, when she started operating the studio with her partner Jerry Tseng, their first project was to make a general survey of Penghu's stone weirs. Following that, they went on to find the last remaining artisans, reviving and recording their stone-building techniques, simplifying the construction process, and transforming the labor-intensive work of weir repairation into an interesting experience that every citizen can take part in. Their aim was to reintroduce these century-old fish-trapping techniques to the public.

Born and raised in Penghu, Yuchen Hung joked about being someone who knew nothing about Penghu's traditional culture, totally disconnected from the surrounding ocean. Years ago, she visited Huazhai Community in Wangan Township for a school project and discovered Ye Cheng-Ren, a local elder who possessed some tools for making straw sandals. She suddenly realized that people in every household in Penghu used to wear straw sandals which they made with their own hands. The sandals were worn to the intertidal zone for foraging, which inspired her interest in learning about the marine environment and local plants, and further developed into a research project for the promotion of straw sandals called "iwwwi daobien," devoted to guiding kids and adults alike in making their own tidal sandals.

離島的孩子，總有離家遠行的命運，要不是讀書，就是為了工作，對老人家而言，年輕人回到島上，很容易被貼上「在城市裡混不下去」的負面標籤，但是以下這群人做的事，卻逐漸顛覆了這個刻板印象。

「剛從台灣回來的時候，家人很不諒解，覺得為什麼一個養得漂漂亮亮的小孫女，不去外面讀書，要跑去做『修石滬』這種粗工？」現為「離島出走工作室」負責人的楊馥慈說道。4 年來，她和夥伴曾宥輯，從澎湖石滬普查計畫開始，找回碩果僅存的匠師，重拾石砌技藝，記錄並簡化工序，將繁複辛苦的修復作業，轉化為每一個人都能親身參與的有趣體驗，試圖讓承載百年的捕魚智慧，重新被世人看見。

另外笑說自己是「澎湖俗」的洪瑪蓁，雖自小在澎湖長大，但對傳統文化一概不知，心中與海的距離非常遙遠。某次她因為學校計畫來到望安花宅，在葉成仁阿公的家中發現做草鞋的工具，才知道原來過去家家戶戶都是靠自己手作的草鞋，走入潮間帶採集，因而啟發對海洋知識與在地植物應用的好奇，讓她一頭栽入草鞋文化的研究與推廣，成立了「島編有潮事」，帶領男女老少打出一雙雙屬於自己的「潮鞋」。

Another returning youngster, Austin Huang, once discovered some seashells in his grandparents' fields, leading him to the realization that farmers in Penghu used to bring sand from the seaside to mix with existing soils in their fields in order to improve the quality of the soil. Penghu's soils are naturally lacking in certain nutrients required for growing vegetables, yet farming harvests have always been equally as important as fishing catch. In addition, due to the fact that the Penghu summer is scorching hot and northeast monsoons are severe in winter, the Penghu locals have had to develop unique ways of growing crops to survive. However, as the population ages over time, the once-important village fields are now mostly left uncultivated, even being replaced by concrete buildings, a fact which has been hard for Austin Huang to accept. Later, he decided to found the "Penghu Young Farmer" project, recruiting groups of young volunteers with the aim of bringing the farming traditions of Penghu back to life!

All three of these remarkable individuals expressed that what they do has not only helped them to reconnect with the culture of Penghu and regain a sense of belonging, but also to improve their family interactions. Fu-Tzu Yang said, "I used to have nothing to chat about with my grandparents, simply because we had so little in common in our daily lives. Now, I'm pursuing things that they are familiar with, and we have a lot to share with each other. I never understood why my grandpa would go to the ocean and come back all dirty, even for a measly catch. Now, I finally understand his love of the ocean!"

Taiwan is a country of islands. Somehow, we often forget that we are all children of the surrounding ocean, children of this piece of land. The slow decay of traditional life and culture are now transforming into a great way for tourists to experience nature through the creative projects of these remarkable youngsters. What they are trying to preserve is not just the culture, but a path to reconnect with the ocean.

STONE WEIR REPAIRING EXPERIENTIAL ACTIVITY
Available for 3 or more participants, repairing of stone weirs and with it, your relationship with the ocean

⌐ www.isle.travel | isle.travel.tw@gmail.com
Fee : NTD 750/person | Duration : 2.5 hours

STRAW SANDALS EXPERIENTIAL CLASS
Learn how to weave a pair of straw sandals traditionally worn by Penghu fisherfolks

⌐ facebook.com/daobien.iwwwi | Fee : NTD 400/person | Duration : 2 hours

FISHNET BAG WEAVING CLASS
Make a useful mesh bag from repurposed fishnet

⌐ facebook.com/daobien.iwwwi | Fee : NTD 600/person | Duration : 3 hours

BEND DOWN IN CAIZHAI
Learn about Penghu's unique caizhai culture through farming activities

⌐ facebook.com/penghuyoungfarmer | Fee : NTD 350/person | Duration : 2 hours

同為返鄉青年的黃士恩，偶然在外公外婆的田間發現貝殼，才知道原來澎湖的農田是靠著人工到海邊載海砂來混土，改善土壤後才得以種植。澎湖地理環境險惡，農耕的重要性並不亞於漁獵，加上夏季十分炎熱，冬季東北季風狂妄，逐漸發展出在地獨有的種植邏輯與智慧。但隨著人口老化，村中的農田逐一荒廢，甚至被鋪上水泥，蓋起房子，令他感到十分不捨，因而發起「彎腰青年｜澎湖農田復甦計畫」，帶領青年志工們組成協力隊，要把澎湖的傳統生活價值種回來！

以上這幾位青年不約而同地說，做這些事不僅幫助他們更認識澎湖文化，找到在地歸屬感，也修復了與家人之間的關係。馥慈說：「以前我不知道要跟阿公阿嬤聊什麼，因為沒有共通話題，可是現在我在做的事跟他們的生活是貼近的，因此有很多東西可以聊。以前不懂阿公為什麼要去海裡把自己弄得髒兮兮地回來，有時漁獲也沒有很好，但現在我終於理解他愛海的心情！」

台灣是一個海島國家，但我們卻時常忘了，我們都是被這片海、這片土地養大的孩子。逐漸式微的澎湖傳統生活模式，在青年們重新設計規劃下，轉化成遊客親近自然最好的方式。他們急欲保存的，並不只是文化，而是一條連結回海洋的路。

以下是深度認識澎湖的體驗活動推薦：

石滬修復體驗
3人成團，修復石滬，也修護與海洋的關係

⌐ FB：離島出走｜+886-978-881-955
費用：NTD 750/人｜體驗時長：2.5小時

小潮鞋編織體驗
學習如何編織澎湖討海人的傳統草鞋

⌐ FB：島編有潮事｜FB：@daobien.iwwwi
費用：NTD 400/人｜體驗時長：2小時

漁網編織袋
利用廢棄漁網改造成實用的網袋包

⌐ FB：島編有潮事｜FB：@daobien.iwwwi
費用：NTD 600/人｜體驗時長：3小時

菜宅裡彎腰
透過親身從事農事，了解澎湖獨有菜宅文化

⌐ FB：彎腰青年 penghuyoungfarmer
費用：NTD 350/人｜體驗時長：2小時

古蹟比便利商店多的文化島嶼

金門
KINMEN

CULTURAL ISLANDS WITH MORE HERITAGE BUILDINGS THAN CONVENIENCE STORES

Most people associate Kinmen with its wartime history, when the coastline was garrisoned with hundreds of thousands of soldiers who bore severe bombing attacks from China. Not until the government lifted martial law, relinquishing military control of Kinmen in 1992, did the islands open to visitors once again.

A few years ago, I had the privilege to stay at a friend's place in Big Kinmen, the main Kinmen island, during Chinese Year, relishing the simple life there. I could go to the garden when I felt like having some vegetables, or head out immediately the moment I felt like having an adventure. During those days, I saw the magnificent western-style buildings and old residential villages, learned Kinmen's Southeast Asian immigration history through cultural exhibitions, and heard the locals call me "you Taiwanese." Through that experience, I realized that, to some extent, Kinmen has a special presence exclusive from mainland Taiwan.

As another Kinmen friend of mine says, Kinmen is right beside Xiamen, China, but lies 200 kilometers away from mainland Taiwan. The parent body of Kinmen's culture could more likely be Fujian Province of China on the other side of the strait, yet, history had other ideas regarding Kinmen's destiny.

As former cross-strait military conflicts gradually transformed into indistinct cultural contradictions with Taiwan, the relationship between Kinmen and Taiwan has become a close but strange one. Even China and the Southeast have closer relationships with Kinmen. However, if you ask me, this obscure status turns out to be the most enchanting part of Kinmen. No matter where you are from, just make a toast with a glass of acclaimed Kinmen sorghum liquor, and you will discover the unique cultural scenes that are nowhere else to be found in Taiwan.

提起金門，許多人會想到其戰地歷史，這裡曾經駐守 10 萬大軍，承受中國猛烈的砲擊，直到 1992 年金門才解除軍事管制與戒嚴，重新開放觀光。

幾年前趁著新年假期叨擾了朋友在大金的家，過著想吃菜就去菜園拔，想探險就出門走走的悠哉生活。那些天在島上見到了華麗洋樓與古厝聚落，在展覽中閱讀了金門的南洋移民歷史，還有對話中時不時聽到的「你們台灣人」的稱呼，都讓我慢慢意識到金門在某種程度上，是獨立於台灣本島外的獨特所在。

如同另外一位金門朋友所說，緊挨著廈門的金門與台灣島隔著 200 公里，若不是因為歷史的捉弄，金門的文化母體其實是海另一端的福建。

曾經的軍事衝突轉化成了隱約的文化衝突，這裡與台灣似近又遠，甚至跟東南亞與中國有著更緊密的連結。然而這種曖昧狀態，反而是我認為金門最有趣迷人的地方。無論是哪個地方來的旅人，都來乾一杯遠近馳名的金門高粱吧。在這裡，能看見截然不同於台灣的人文風景。

TRANSPORTATION
交通

All domestic airports in Taiwan (including Penghu Airport) provide flights to and from Kinmen, with a flight time of about 50 minutes. Travel between Big Kinmen (the Kinmen main island) and Little Kinmen (the Lieyu island) is done by ferry. When traveling in each island, even though bus service is available, renting a scooter is advisable as it offers more mobility. Apart from that, guided taxi tours with suggested itineraries are also at your service.Guided Taxi Tours: kinmen.travel/zh-tw/information/taxi

台灣各國內機場均有航班往返金門，約 50 分左右抵達。大金、小金之間有固定船班，島上交通可搭乘公車。若要更方便移動，建議租借機車。另金門也有觀光計程車服務，可提供套裝行程與導覽解說。觀光計程車：kinmen.travel/zh-tw/information/taxi

RECOMMENDATIONS
推薦

◤◣ READING LIST 旅遊書籍

KINMEN LOCAL-M VILLAGE LIVE READER: MUSIC, CULTURE, VILLAGE, LIFE 《聚落求生指南》
Series publication of the 2017 Local-M Village Live music event, starter for exploring Kinmen and its villages
2017土豆音樂祭的周邊刊物，探索金門和聚落的入門讀本

⌐ facebook.com/villagelive/posts/590348974827250

HOLIDAYS IN THE OFFSHORE ISLANDS: FUN IN KINMEN AND MATSU
《放假去離島！：金門馬祖輕鬆玩》
Rare travel guide especially for Kinmen and Matsu offering travel tips and photographic reminders
少數專門介紹金門馬祖的旅遊書，並有旅行和攝影小提醒

⌐ books.com.tw/products/0010673775

◤◣ ANNUAL EVENTS 年度活動

KINMEN MARATHON (JANUARY-FEBRUARY)
金門馬拉松 (1月-2月)
Established in 2008, this sporting event is popular regardless of the cold winds
2008年起舉辦的熱門賽事，不畏寒風也要奔跑

⌐ www.sportsnet.org.tw (Signup starts in October)

KINMEN TUNNEL MUSIC FESTIVAL (OCTOBER)
金門坑道音樂節 (10月)
Enjoy music performances inside the wartime heritage site Zhaishan Tunnel. Don't forget to purchase your ticket while supplies last!
體驗在戰時遺跡「翟山坑道」欣賞音樂演出，記得搶票！

⌐ www.kmnp.gov.tw

◤◣ TRAVEL WEBSITES 旅遊網站

CLASSIC KINMEN TRAVEL 金門觀光旅遊
Official Kinmen travel website. Multiple language versions available
金門官方旅遊網站，有多國語言資訊

⌐ facebook.com/kinmentour | kinmen.travel

LOCAL KINMEN 好金門在地誌
Young local media outlet sharing the happenings in Kinmen via their Facebook page
年輕在地媒體，透過臉書分享金門大小事

⌐ facebook.com/LocalKinmen

◤◣ TOURIST SHUTTLES 觀光巴士

KINMEN TOURIST SHUTTLE ROUTES 台灣好行@金門
Offering four classic shuttle routes hosted by the Tourism Bureau
觀光局主辦的巴士服務，共有4條經典路線可選擇

⌐ kinmendiway.com

◤◣ LOCAL PUBLICATIONS 在地刊物

KINMEN LITERATURE 《金門文藝》
Literature quarterly established in 1973 fostering countless Kinmen writers
1973年創立的文學季刊，滋養無數金門文學創作者

⌐ ffacebook.com/KinmenLiterature

KINMEN STORY 《浯島城事》
Quality local publications from 2020-2022, available for online reading
2020-2022年出版的質感地方刊物，可線上閱讀

⌐ https://kinmen-story.tw/magazine

LIFESTYLE AND DESSERTS
風格店家與甜點

Photo credit：村復號

A VIVA VILLAGES GOODS 村復號

Kinmen specialty goods and souvenirs, along with local
tours and experiential activities
金門特色選物與伴手禮，還有在地導覽與體驗活動

⌐ 金門縣金城鎮民族路43號 | www.vivavillagesgoods.com
No. 43, Minzu Rd., Jincheng Township, Kinmen County
13:30-18:30 (Closed on Tue. and Wed.)

B WENG WENG BOOKSTORE 蓊蓊書店

Adorable bookstore beside the City God temple, also serves
drinks and cakes
城隍廟旁的可愛書店，提供飲品與甜點

⌐ 金門縣金城鎮光前路29巷2號 | +886-8-232-1882
No. 2, Ln. 29, Guangqian Rd., Jincheng Township, Kinmen County
12:000-20:30 (Closed from Mon. to Wed.) | FB: weng3weng3

C NI COFFEE STUDIO 膩珈琲

Relax and unwind in Dongsha, Kinmen, as you savor the
flavors of hand-poured coffee and homemade desserts
膩在東沙放空，細細品嚐手沖咖啡與手作甜點

⌐ 金門縣金城鎮東沙18號 | instagram.com/ni_coffee_studio
No. 18, Dongsha, Jincheng Township, Kinmen County
13:30-18:00 (Closed from Mon. to Wed.)

D HOPE 16 後浦十六藝文特區

16 shops including cultural stores and bars beside the
Chen Clan Ancestral Hall
陳氏宗祠旁16間店屋，有文創店家還有酒吧

⌐ 金門縣金城鎮莒光路112號
No. 112, Juguang Rd., Jincheng Township, Kinmen County
facebook.com/HOPE16.KM

E CARNIVAL ICE STORE 烈嶼嘉年華冰菓室

Vintage-style ice shop in Little Kinmen hosting frequent
community events
位於小金門的復古冰果室，常舉辦各式社區活動

⌐ 金門縣烈嶼鄉西口村西方社區19號 | +886-8-236-3126
No. 19, Xifang Community, Lieyu Township, Kinmen County
11:00-18:00

F QIEYI DESSERT 愜意甜點工作室

Operated by a young chef, enjoy desserts in this century-
old Minnan residential building
年輕主廚開設，在百年閩南古厝中享用甜點

⌐ 金門縣金沙鎮后浦頭60號 | +886-8-235-3585
No. 60, Houputou, Jinsha Township, Kinmen County
13:00-18:00 (Closed on Tuesdays)

Photo credit：島嶼披薩

A XIN-YUAN SEAFOOD RESTAURANT–HUXIA BRANCH
信源海產店 - 湖下店
A variety of curious Kinmen seafood specialties. Be brave and try some stir-fried peanut worms
各種金門新奇海產熱炒，鼓起勇氣試試炒沙蟲吧

📍 金門縣金寧鄉湖下村60號 | 10:00~14:00, 17:00~20:30 (Closed on Thur.)
No. 60, Huxia, Jinning Township, Kinmen County | +886-8-232-7743

B QUAN-MIN CREATIVE FRUIT CUISINE 湶民水果創意料理
Menuless cuisine made of seasonal fruit accompanied by unlimited fresh fruit juice
當季水果入菜的無菜單料理，還有新鮮果汁喝到飽

📍 金門縣金寧鄉伯玉路二段224巷8號 | +886-8-232-4489
No. 8, Aly. 224, Sec. 2, Boyu Rd., Jinning Township, Kinmen County
11:00~14:00, 17:30~20:00

C ISOLA PIZZA NAPOLETANA 島嶼披薩
Rare western-style bistro run by young Kinmen locals
在地青年開設，金門難得的西式料理小餐館

📍 金門縣金寧鄉埔邊13號2樓 | +886-8-232-0925
2F., No. 13, Pubian, Jinning Township, Kinmen County
11:30~14:00, 17:00~21:00 (Closed on Tuesdays)
www.facebook.com/mikesquiches

D VENT BAR 夢酒館
Cocktail bar established by later Generation Ys and offering Kinmen Kaoliang (sorghum) Weissbier
8年級生創立的調酒吧，還有金門精釀啤酒

📍 金門縣金城鎮莒光路110巷4號 | facebook.com/ventbarkm
No. 4, Aly. 110, Juguang Rd., Jincheng Township, Kinmen County
19:30~00:30 (Closed on Tuesdays)

E LIVE GUESTHOUSE 來福客棧
Music-themed guesthouse in an old residential building near Oucuo Beach
歐厝海灘附近的音樂主題古厝民宿

📍 金門縣金城鎮歐厝17號
No. 17, Oucuo, Jincheng Township, Kinmen County
facebook.com/Liveguesthouse

F DWELL IN QUEMOY 時苑 | 私宅
Sophisticated guesthouse with cats for companions. Booking an entire building to enjoy the privacy is recommended
有貓、有生活的質感民宿，建議包棟，自在做自己

📍 金門縣金城鎮歐厝66號 | facebook.com/dwellinquemoy
No. 66, Oucuo, Jincheng Township, Kinmen County

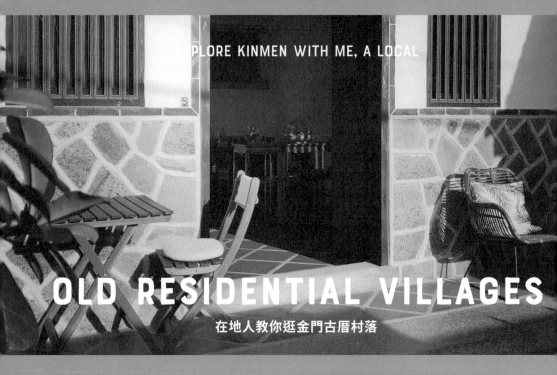

OLD RESIDENTIAL VILLAGES

在地人教你逛金門古厝村落

While many people recognize Kinmen as a former battlefield, few realize that it also preserves the most beautiful and well-maintained traditional Minnan villages in Taiwan. Among them, the spectacular western-style buildings are must-see highlights.

What have western-style buildings to do with opium?

The western-style buildings can be considered by-products of the Opium War which occurred in the mid-19th century. After the Opium War, the Qing government opened five harbors in China for the purpose of trading. Meanwhile, large numbers of people from Guangzhou moved to the United States to prospect for gold. On the other hand, groups of people from Kinmen, instead of working in Xiamen, chose to follow the overflow of population from rural China that migrated to British and French colonies in Southeast Asia. Kinmen residents called them Lofan (literally meaning to travel southward to foreign lands, referring to their journey to the South Sea).

Those Fanke (literally meaning people who travel to foreign lands) made a good income abroad, started to send money back and built mansions in Kinmen. In the beginning, they constructed traditional courtyard homes. In the early 20th century, due to the stylistic influence of colonial architecture, the western-style Fanzhaicuo (literally meaning foreigners' residence) started to appear. Some of them were multi-story Minnan courtyard homes, while others exhibited a Chinese-Western eclectic style. In this way, the migration caused by the Opium War unexpectedly contributed to the beautiful architectural scenery now visible in Kinmen.

很多人知道金門曾是戰地，卻未必知道金門擁有台灣最美麗、保存最完整的閩南傳統村落。其中，又以風華絕代的「洋樓」最是不能錯過的亮點。

洋樓竟跟鴉片有關係?!

洋樓可以說是鴉片戰爭的間接產物。19 世紀中鴉片戰爭後五口通商，大批華人從廣州前往美國淘金，與此同時大批金門人也隨著其他中國農村過剩人口，從廈門轉往東南亞的英法殖民地工作，這群人被金門人稱為「落番」（下南洋之意）。

許多在外地賺了錢的「番客」，紛紛把錢寄回金門起造大厝，最初蓋的還是傳統合院，20 世紀初期開始出現受殖民地建築風格影響的「番仔厝」，也就是洋樓。它們有的是疊高的閩南合院，有的則是完全中西合璧的設計。因鴉片戰爭而促成的人口流動，竟意外造成金門美麗的風景。

Villages comprised of more than western-style buildings

However, visiting the western-style buildings without exploring the surrounding village is like viewing individual trees while neglecting the forest. When you first arrive at a village, you might get lost in the winding alleys, but after learning its basic elements and spatial arrangement, you will find yourself easily cruising throughout the entire village without a worry in the world.

First of all, a village mainly consists of the ancestral halls of various family clans, ponds, residential buildings, and the surrounding fields, while some of them may contain an additional local temple.

As sacred spaces for ancestor worship, ancestral halls are often built with tall black walls and sparrow-tail-shaped ridges on the roof. Some ancestral halls like those in Qionglin Village are open to the public, while others only operate on important occasions like ceremonies, meetings, and banquets. Serving as core venues within village life, the importance of the ancestral halls of family clans is similar to the principal churches found in towns throughout Europe during the Middle Ages.

Second, the ponds, also known as the feng shui ponds, might seem superstitious, but they also served as practical tools for water storage, water provision, and fire fighting. As for the residential buildings, those with higher ridges, more ornaments, and greater land area usually represented the higher social status of the household due to outstanding achievements in the imperial examination system or the holding of reputable official positions. On the other hand, ordinary households consist of medium or small-sized buildings and have round, horse-saddle-shaped ends on both sides of the roof ridges. By grasping these essential architectural elements, you will be able to see the big picture as you survey a village.

If you are interested in comparing the differences between villages, besides the spatial arrangement, you can also pay attention to the details on old residential buildings, which include the wall structure of courtyard homes, couplets, and ornaments on exterior walls. Most Minnan buildings are built with local materials like red bricks, ornamental tiles, rocks, or granite slates. However, because of the varied natural resources each village can obtain, the Minnan buildings in different villages have diverse appearances, which demonstrates the adaptable and creative character of the Kinmen locals.

In recent years, the government has invested more resources in repairing old residential buildings and promoting revitalization projects for old spaces, resulting in an emerging trend of guesthouses, cafés, restaurants, dessert shops, gift shops, Chinese medicine shops, and even entrepreneur worksites, not to mention distinctive spaces operated by new immigrants and young locals returning from abroad. Seize the chance to talk to those shop owners and discover the magnificence hidden underneath Kinmen's stern wartime demeanor. (by Ting-Chi Wang)

村落，不只是洋樓

到了村落如果只造訪洋樓，就像見樹不見林，極為可惜。初到村落可能會在巷弄間暈頭轉向，但只要抓出村落的空間要素，就能突然開竅，放心在村落中自在穿梭。

首先，村落主要由宗祠（家廟）、埤塘、民居以及周圍田野組成，部分村落還有地方信仰的宮廟。

宗祠是供奉祖先的神聖空間，通常黑牆高聳，有著兩端尖翹的「燕尾式」屋脊。有的家廟開放自由進入（如瓊林村），有的則僅在重要祭典、會議或宴席時開啟使用，其重要性類似於中世紀歐洲城鎮裡的大教堂，是村落的核心。

再來，埤塘又叫「風水池」，看似迷信，在古代實則有著儲水、供水、滅火等實用功能。而民居中屋脊越翹、裝飾越豐富、腹地越大的，往往是官宦或功名及第人家；一般家庭則以兩端圓潤似馬鞍的「馬背式」屋脊和中小型建築為主。若能掌握以上幾個大重點，就已能稍微看出一個村落的輪廓與結構。

至於不同村落間的觀察比較，除了空間要素的配置外，還可以從古厝的細節著手，包括合院牆體、門聯和外牆裝飾等。閩南建築主要就地取材，同樣使用紅磚、花磚、石塊或花崗石板，卻因各村的自然資源不同而有不同的風貌，這也是金門人因地制宜、創新求突破的具體展現。

近年來政府投入資源修繕古厝，鼓勵空間活化，除了大量的古厝民宿外，還有咖啡茶館、餐廳、甜點店、紀念品賣店、中醫診所，甚至連青創基地也設在古厝裡，更不乏返鄉青年或金門新住民經營的特色空間。若有機會多和村落裡的老闆們聊聊天，看見隱藏在金門戰地形象下的多彩多姿！（文／王蓮頎）

Recommended villages 推薦村落：

Shanhou, Shuitou, and Zhushan villages.
山后、水頭、珠山

More information 更多資訊：

kinmen.travel/zh-tw/tag/detail/2/1?page=1

3-DAY EXPLORATION OF KINMEN

3 日探索金門

Photo credit : Jan

SPECIAL FEATURE

KINMEN
金門特輯

SPECIAL FEATURE

If you're heading to Kinmen, give yourself at least three days to fully immerse in its magic. This island blends military history with Minnan culture against a backdrop of lush landscapes and traditional villages. There's something enchanting about Kinmen that slows your pace and invites you to delve into its rich stories. Stroll through its streets and alleys, and let Kinmen reveal its unique character and rhythm to you!

Day 1: Exploring Old Streets and History

There are several flights from Taiwan to Kinmen, with arrival recommended around noon. Once settled in your accommodation, head to Jincheng Township to start exploring Kinmen, beginning in the lively Houpu Shopping District. To truly experience the local culture, try the golden, crispy savory rice cake and oyster fritter at Yong Kuan Savory Rice Cake Shop and Oyster Fritter's Home near Qiu Liang-Gung's Mother Chastity Arch.

As you wander through Kinmen's old streets, you'll find a charming blend of red-brick arcades, historical landmarks, and both century-old and modern shops. Don't miss the small alleys off the main roads. Visit historical sites like the nearly 200-year-old Tsun De Chinese Medicine Shop and pick up some signature white pepper or marinade packets as souvenirs. The Kinmen Military Headquarters of the Qing Dynasty and Wushui River Academy are worth exploring day or night. For a deeper dive, join the "Houpu Beautiful Town Tour" evening guided tour, starting daily at 19:30 from the Kinmen Military Headquarters (+886-82-371717), lasting about two hours.

若有機會來到金門，建議至少保留 3 天的時間，才能好好認識這座融合了戰地歷史與閩南文化，擁有豐富自然景觀和傳統聚落的島嶼，這裡獨特的人文地景有一種神奇的魔力，讓人不自覺地放慢腳步，想更認識這裡的故事。來隨意穿梭於大街小巷間吧，慢慢地感受專屬於金門的個性與步調！

第一日：老街漫遊與歷史探索

從台灣前往金門有多個航班可選，建議中午左右抵達。到旅宿安頓好行李後，就直接前往金城鎮，從最熱鬧的後浦商圈開始探索金門。想了解一個地方，就先從品嚐在地小吃開始吧！來邱良功母節孝坊附近的「永寬鹹粿店」和「蚵嗲之家」，試試炸得金黃酥脆的鹹粿與蚵嗲，感受金門獨特的滋味。

接著繼續走逛紅磚拱廊與歷史古蹟、百年老店和年輕店鋪融合並存的金門老街，除了主要街道外，也別錯過小巷弄。若想感受金門悠久的歷史，可以先造訪擁有近 200 年歷史的「存德中藥房」，別忘了帶包招牌白胡椒或滷包回去當伴手禮。同樣興建於清代的「清金門鎮總兵署」和「浯江書院」等古蹟，無論白天或夜晚都適合走走逛逛。若想更深入了解背後故事，推薦參加「後浦美麗小鎮之旅」夜間導覽（每日晚間 19:30 在總兵署報名，約 2 小時，洽詢專線 +886-82-371717）。

In recent years, many young locals in Kinmen have established unique stores, especially around the Houpu Shopping District. Notable among them is the independent bookstore "Weng Weng," hidden in the alleys near the City God Temple, and "Viva Villages Goods ," a select shop aimed at revitalizing the village, both of which are well worth a special visit. Kinmen nights are quiet and peaceful. If you're not ready for bed, head to the creatively repurposed "Hope 16 Arts District," where impromptu music performances liven up summer evenings. Within this cultural hub, "Vent Bar" and the nearby "Kinmen Night Owl," a gastropub open until late, are perfect spots to enjoy Kinmen's evening charm.

Day 2: Wartime Relics and Natural Beauty

On the second day, start early with breakfast at local favorites "Yongchun Cantonese Congee" and "He Ji Fried Dough Sticks." The smooth porridge and fluffy fried dough sticks offer a unique Kinmen flavor. Then drive to Lieyu, or Little Kinmen, dotted with wartime relics and bunkers, perfect for exploring. Don't miss "Carnival Ice Store" for ice cream with local taro and Leiyu pastry.

Around noon, head back near Kinmen Bridge for lunch at "La Même Histoire" or "Xinyuan Seafood Restaurant." After a short rest, spend the afternoon exploring north or south. To the north, visit the "Guningtou Battle Museum" and "Beishan Broadcasting Wall" among other wartime relics. To the south, "Shuitou Village" features the grand "Deyue Tower" mansion and "KOKI Quemoy," a stylish café in a former school building established by overseas Chinese. Whether heading north or south, you'll find stunning sunset views. The "Ci Lake Sunset Platform" in the north and the tidal island "Jiangong Islet" in the south, accessible by a pathway during low tide, both offer spectacular scenery.

Day 3: Leisurely Exploring the East

In the morning, visit "Qionglin Village" to see one of Kinmen's most famous Wind Lion Gods, the "Qionglin Wind Lion God." Then, head east to stroll through "Yangzhai Old Street" and "Shamei Old Street." The former, a filming location for the movie *Paradise in Service*, retains many retro 1960s scenes, while the latter is one of Kinmen's oldest market streets. Enjoy the sweet and savory "Min-style Shaobing" and visit "Qieyi Dessert," founded by the second generation of the traditional Changhe pastry brand, where both traditional and contemporary desserts are delightful.

Next, visit "Kinmen Kaoliang Liquor Inc." to learn about sorghum liquor brewing and pick up some souvenirs, or head to "Shishan (Mt. Lion) Howitzer Front" for a thrilling artillery drill demonstration. Finally, return to Jincheng Town to buy local specialties like Kinmen tribute candy (highly recommend "Tico Tribute Candy" mung bean cake, perfect with tea) and Kinmen kitchen knives, concluding your Kinmen trip perfectly.

近年來，許多金門在地青年創立了獨具風格的小店，尤其在後浦商圈一帶，如隱身於城隍廟巷內的獨立書店「薯薯」，和目標為「村落復興」的在地選品店「村復號」，都值得專程前往；金門夜晚寧靜平和，若還捨不得入睡，可以前往古蹟再生的創意聚落「後浦16藝文特區」，夏日晚上不定時有音樂演出。聚落內的「夢酒館」，與附近營業到深夜的「金門夜貓」餐酒館，也都是金門晚間的理想去處。

第二日：戰地遺跡與自然美景

第二天一早，趕緊到在地老店「永春廣東粥」和「和記油條」試試當地早餐，綿密的粥糜與蓬鬆Q軟的油條，口感風味皆與台灣不同，是必試的金門風味。接著開車前往被稱為小金門的「烈嶼」，沿途有不少戰地遺跡與碉堡，可隨意停下走逛。來到小金不可錯過「嘉年華冰菓室」，來碗冰品嚐當地特產芋頭與桶餅融合的美妙滋味。

中午左右可返回金門大橋附近的「舊書書坊」或「信源海產店」用餐。稍作休息後，下午可依喜好往北或往南探索。北邊有「古寧頭戰史館」和「北山播音牆」等戰時遺跡，南邊可至「水頭聚落」參觀華麗洋樓「得月樓」，以及由華僑成立的古岡學校改造而成的質感洋樓咖啡廳「百花」。無論往北或往南，都能好好欣賞金門美麗的夕陽風景。北邊有「慈湖落日觀海平台」，南邊則推薦潮汐小島「建功嶼」，退潮時可沿著石板道步行至小島上，風景絕美。

第三日：輕鬆探索東邊風景

上午推薦前往「瓊林部落」，欣賞金門最有名的風獅爺之一「瓊林風獅爺」。接著往東走逛「陽翟老街」和「沙美老街」，前者曾為電影《軍中樂園》拍攝地，保留許多為此搭建的60年代復古場景；後者則是金門最早期的市街之一。這裡推薦鹹甜都好吃的「閩式燒餅」與由金門傳統老字號長合食品二代創立的「愜意甜點工作室」，傳統糕餅與當代甜點同樣美味。

接著，可前往「金門酒廠」參觀，了解高粱酒的釀造過程，並選購一些伴手禮帶回家；或前往「獅山砲陣地」看砲操示範，也相當震撼。最後，返回金城鎮購買當地特產如金門貢糖（個人推薦「天工貢糖」的綠豆糕，配上一杯好茶立刻身心放鬆）和金門菜刀，為金門之旅畫上完美句點。

女神的故鄉

馬祖
MATSU

Photo credit : Hans Liu

THE HOMETOWN OF THE GODDESS
———— Cheng-Tao Lee 李政道

Named after the Chinese sea goddess Mazu, Matsu plays an important role in the origin of the Taiwanese belief in the goddess. Calling Matsu a "place" doesn't do it justice since it is in fact an archipelago consisting of 36 islets. Moreover, being 211 kilometers away from Taiwan, Matsu sometimes seems like an independent country.

Stories of Matsu are as exciting as the Japanese manga series *One Piece*. It was once a pirate base, a site under the control of the Japanese army after World War II, then an important fortified point during the Chinese Civil War, and did not open to visitors until 1994. Since the end of the Cold War between the KMT (the Kuomintang of China) and the Communist Party of China, nearly 300 military facilities have gradually transformed into coffee shops, artist villages, and other public venues.

When the southwesterly flow blows in spring and summer, the archipelago is embraced by mist. It's also the time of year when the world-famous natural phenomenon of the bioluminescent "Blue Tears" waves occurs. If you decide to make a trip to Matsu, this is a good time to come. You can imagine yourself as the young Pi in *Life of Pi*, sailing through glowing blue ocean waves. Come chase the waves around the remote islands of Matsu, and see the most mysterious, beautiful blue of your life.

Multilingual interpretation service is available for foreign visitors at Nangang Airport Visitor Center.

Janet Chen +886-836-26402 (Mandarin / English)

馬祖的名字來自於台灣航海女神「媽祖」,這裡是台灣女神信仰最重要的發源地。說馬祖是一個「地方」太過抽象,比較正確地說它是由36座大小島嶼組成的列島,距台灣本島211公里,像是另一個獨立的國度。

馬祖列島上的故事有如日本漫畫《航海王》一樣精采,它曾是海盜聚集之地、被日軍間接控制、也曾直接面對國共砲戰,成為軍事要地,直到1994年才開放對外觀光。冷戰過後島上近300個軍事據點(碉堡)也陸續開放,甚至部分讓民間單位申請進駐,活化改造成咖啡廳或藝術村等空間。

每年春夏時節西南氣流旺盛時,各島雲霧繚繞,正是聞名世界的自然奇景──「藍眼淚」的季節,如果要風塵僕僕來一趟馬祖,建議在此時拜訪,想像自己如同電影《少年Pi的奇幻漂流》裡的Pi一樣,在一片閃閃發光的藍中乘風破浪。來馬祖「追淚」吧,在遙遠的島嶼遇見此生最神祕絕美的藍。

外籍遊客若需要協助,以下單位可協助口譯:
南竿機場旅遊服務中心
Janet Chen:+886-836-26402(中、英)

TRANSPORTATION
交通

Both Taipei Songshan Airport and Taichung Airport offer flights to Matsu. Flights may be canceled in spring and summer due to weather conditions, causing the locals to joke that traveling to Matsu is actually a Guam tour (Guam in Mandarin has the same pronunciation as "closed island"). Take Taima Star or Tai Ma ferries, requiring eight to nine hours, to avoid the unpredictable inconvenience of a flight cancelation. When traveling on the islands, scooter rental and taxi service are available. When traveling between islands, ferry tickets are provided at Fuao Harbor on Nangan island and Baisha Harbor on Beigan island. Check out Matsu eTravel for information about flight and ferry schedules: ematsu.com (APP version is also available) Booking ferry tickets: shinhwa.com.tw or call +886-2-2424-6868. Taxi service: ematsu.com/traffic/page_taxi

松山、台中均有飛機飛往馬祖，需注意春夏時節停飛率極高，當地人笑稱這是「關島遊」。若擔心誤點可改搭「臺馬之星」或「臺馬輪」船班進出馬祖，約 8-9 小時抵達。島內移動可租機車或搭計程車。跳島旅行可在南竿福澳港或北竿白沙港購票。船班與航班時間可參考「馬祖 e 點通」(ematsu.com)

船票預定：shinhwa.com.tw

計程車：ematsu.com/traffic/page_taxi

RECOMMENDATIONS
推薦

⚑ READING LIST 旅遊書籍

HAND-DRAWN TRIPS IN MATSU 《馬祖手繪行旅》
Travel book with abundant illustrations by an artist-in-residence on the island
由插畫家在島上駐村繪製的馬祖圖文旅遊書

⌐ books.com.tw/products/0010692922

GOOD DONGJU: YELLOW OF WINE, RED OF LEES, AND GREEN OF FARMLANDS
《好東島-酒黃·糟紅·田綠》
Book about the women on Dongju island and their food culture (good content, illustrations, and design!)
馬祖東莒島的女人飲食地方志 (無論內容、插畫和設計都很好！)

⌐ ducawu.wixsite.com/gooddj

A NON-TRAVEL GUIDE OF MATSU FOR TAIWANESE (WEB ARTICLE)
給台灣人的「馬祖非旅遊指南」(網路文章)
Observations of Matsu by an artist-in-residence written for *Fountain* magazine
馬祖駐村創作者陳泳瀚為刊物《新活水》撰寫的馬祖觀察系列文章

⌐ www.fountain.org.tw/issue/matsu

⚑ TOURIST SHUTTLE 觀光巴士

MATSU TOURIST SHUTTLE ROUTES 台灣好行@馬祖
Shuttle routes hosted by the Tourism Bureau. Sign up online, two people or more required
觀光局主辦的觀光巴士，需線上報名，2人成行

⌐ matsu-trip.tw

⚑ TRAVEL WEBSITES 旅遊網站

MATSU NATIONAL SCENIC AREA 馬祖國家風景區
Official Matsu travel website. English and Japanese information available
馬祖官方旅遊網站，有英、日語資訊

⌐ matsu-nsa.gov.tw

MATSU YAHO 馬祖YAHO
Yaho means "really good" in the Mindong dialect. Sharing the happenings in Matsu with decent pictures
閩東話「馬祖很好」的意思，以美麗照片分享馬祖大小事

⌐ facebook.com/matsutrw

⚑ ANNUAL EVENTS 年度活動

MATSU BIENNIAL (FALL) 馬祖國際藝術島 (秋天)
Matsu's most significant art event, and Taiwan's first island-hopping art experience
馬祖最重要的藝術盛事，台灣第一個跳島藝術體驗

⌐ matsubiennial.tw

THE BLUE TEARS (MAR.-SEP.) 藍眼淚 (3月-9月)
World-class scenery, visible between March and September
國際級的自然美景，3 月到 9 月為觀賞期

⌐ Tips for planning available on Matsu Info Site : reurl.cc/Zm9Nl
⌐ 馬祖資訊網追淚攻略：reurl.cc/Zm9Nl

LANTERN CELEBRATION CEREMONY (LUNAR JANUARY)
元宵擺暝文化祭 (農曆正月)
Biggest folk event in Matsu lasting from dusk to midnight with lively deity-welcoming parade
馬祖最盛大的民俗祭典，期間從傍晚到深夜都有擺暝、迎神遶境等活動，相當熱鬧！

⌐ Video 影片：reurl.cc/WnROe

Photo credit：好食人家

A JING-WO FOOD SHOP 鏡沃小吃部

One of the best Matsu old wine thin noodle shops in Beigan, sometimes closes on an unfixed schedule

號稱北竿最好吃的老酒麵線，偶爾會不開門營業

連江縣北竿鄉芹壁村75號 | +886-8-365-5558
No. 75, Qinbi Vil., Beigan Township, Lienchiang County
10:00–13:30, 16:00–18:30

B XIA-LIAO DINING HALL 蝦寮食堂

Stir-fry specialty restaurant in a traditional building. The only place offering draft beer in Matsu

在馬祖傳統建築內的熱炒餐廳，有馬祖唯一的生啤酒

連江縣南竿鄉復興村136之1號 | +886-8-362-3452
No. 136-1, Fuxing Vil., Nangan Township, Lienchiang County
11:30–13:00, 17:00–20:00 (Closed on Tuesdyas)

C A-MEI'S SHOP 阿妹的店

Must-try authentic Matsu flavors including Ding Bien Hu, fish balls, and Yan dumplings

一定要來吃的鼎邊糊，有魚丸、燕餃，還有馬祖人的情感

連江縣南竿鄉介壽村(獅子市場2樓右側) | +886-8-362-6375
Jieshou Vil., Nangan Township, Lienchiang County (on the right side of the 2F in Lion Market) | 05:30–12:00

D LIN YIHE FACTORY 林義和工坊

Old wine DIY classes available. Booking in advance is advisable

可體驗老酒 DIY 的課程，建議提前預約

連江縣南竿鄉四維村72號 | 11:00-14:00, 17:00-20:00
No. 72, Siwei Vil., Nangan Township, Lienchiang County
+886-8-362-2455 (call for reservations three days prior)

E DONGYIN MULLETROE 西尾半島物產店

Enjoy curry and unique Matsu flavors at the western tip of the island.

在島嶼的西端尾巴享用咖喱飯與獨特馬祖風味

連江縣南竿鄉四維村21號 | FB: XIWEIPENINSULA
No. 21, Siwei Vil., Nangan Township, Lienchiang County
11:30-20:00 (Closed on Tue. and Wed.)

F HAOSHIH HOUSE 好食人家.HOUSE

Hotel-chef-level menuless restaurant

飯店主廚水準的無菜單料理餐廳

連江縣南竿鄉清水村104號 | +886-8-362-5929
No. 104, Qingshui Vil., Nangan Township, Lienchiang County
18:00-21:00

CAFÉS AND ACCOMMODATIONS
咖啡店與住宿

Photo credit：鹹味島合作社

A THORN BIRD COFFEE 刺鳥咖啡獨立書店
First independent bookstore/café to open on the island, operated by the former director of the Cultural Affairs Bureau of Lienchiang County
由連江縣前文化局長經營，島上第一間獨立書店與咖啡店

⌂ 連江縣南竿鄉復興村222號 | facebook.com/thornbirdcoffee
No. 222, Fuxing Vil, Nangan TWP., Lienchiang CTY | 10:00–18:00

B CAFÉ NANMON 南萌咖啡館
Nanmon means "silly" in the Matsu dialect. A place with cats and cocktails where it is easy to make friends
南萌，是馬祖話傻呼呼的意思。有貓咪、調酒、很好交朋友的地方 | 13:00–18:00 (Closed from Mon. to Thur.)

⌂ 連江縣南竿鄉仁愛村69號 | facebook.com/CafeNanmon
No.69, Ren'ai Vil, Nangan Township, Lienchiang County

C QINWO BAKERY 芹沃咖啡烘焙館
Café opened by the famous baker Zeng Mei-Zi who learned her craft in Japan
留日烘焙名人曾美子老師在馬祖開設的咖啡館

⌂ 連江縣北竿鄉芹壁村53-1號 | facebook.com/QinWoBakery
No. 53-1, Qinbi Vil., Beigan Township, Lienchiang County
10:00–14:00, 15:00–18:30 (Closed on Wednesdays)

D SALTY ISLAND STUDIO 鹹味島合作社
An independent coffee shop and local arts and cultural hub that also creates the Dongyin tourism website
是咖啡館也是在地藝文交流中心，更製作東引觀光網站

⌂ 連江縣東引鄉樂華村4號 | facebook.com/saltyislandstudio
No. 4, Lehua Vil., Dongyin Township, Lienchiang County
14:00–22:00 (Closed on Tuesdays)

E DAYSPRING.日光春和 (日光海岸)
Aesthetics of fair-faced concrete architecture infused with Matsu landscapes
將清水模的建築美學融入馬祖地景

⌂ 連江縣南竿鄉仁愛村1-1號 | +886-8-362-6666
No. 1-1, Ren'ai Vil., Nangan Township, Lienchiang County
facebook.com/Dayspring.Matsu

F CHINBE D.S HOUSE B&B 芹壁德順號民宿
Simple, clean B&B in an old house
簡單乾淨的芹壁老屋民宿

⌂ 連江縣北竿鄉芹壁村31號
No. 31, Qinbi Vil., Beigan Township, Lienchiang County
facebook.com/Chinbe.DShouse

ARCHITECTURE

馬祖傳統建築與廟宇——在地人帶你看 3 個重點！

SPECIAL FEATURE

MATSU
馬祖特輯

SPECIAL FEATURE

Matsu stone houses: Matsu residents have always lived with close ties to the ocean, mostly clustering around natural marinas where boat docking is accessible. In early times, they built simple sheds of wood and grass for temporary housing. Later, they used local granite to build stronger stone houses with tile roofs which, over time, formed into villages. The roofing tiles used on Matsu stone houses are held down with rocks to prevent them from blowing away in strong winds. In looking at the stone walls, you will find that brickwork techniques such as the stretcher bond, the herringbone bond, and the mixed bond have alternatingly been used in their construction.

Military facilities: As the frontline of resistance against China during the Cold War, Matsu endured four battles leaving over 300 military structures along the coastline including tunnels, strongholds, and air defense refuge facilities, and making Matsu the island with the highest density of tunnels in the world. Currently, Taiwan and China have a fairly peaceful relationship (even though China never ceases to threaten war with Taiwan)`, and the military facilities therefore have been opened to the public for alternative purposes, such as guesthouses and cultural spaces. Some strongholds were constructed with complex winding underground tunnels spreading from hill to coast like ant colonies.

Fonghoushan walls: There are more than 60 temples in Matsu. The most distinctive feature of the temples here are the Fonghoushan walls, the firewalls that were intentionally built higher than the roofs. Fong can be written in Chinese either as the character meaning stop（封）or that meaning wind（風）. Hou（火）means fire and shan（山）means mountain. The name comes from the mountain-character-shaped profile of such walls, and the function of stopping fire and wind. Another notable feature of Matsu is the temple murals. Due to wartime military restrictions, temples here were constructed, painted, and repaired through the teamwork of the army and the local residents. The murals might not be so detailed or skillful as those seen in mainland Taiwan, but those in Matsu carry a colorful, rough, comic- or graffiti-like texture, which has become a treasured part of the unique wartime heritage.

馬祖石屋

馬祖人靠海維生，人口多聚集在船隻容易停泊的天然澳口周圍，早期人們以草木搭建簡單房舍短暫居住，後來利用島上盛產的花崗岩石材蓋起了一間間更為堅固、石牆瓦頂的民居，漸漸地形成聚落。馬祖石屋的屋頂為防強風皆用磚石壓住瓦片，石牆的砌法則有工字砌、人字砌還有亂石砌等變化。到馬祖後建議前往聚落的制高點，欣賞石屋群的特別風景。

軍事據點

在國民黨與中國共產黨冷戰時期，馬祖列島成為福建沿海對抗中國的前線，也曾發生過 4 次戰役，因此海景第一排多為軍事建築，像是坑道、碉堡與防空避難等設施，目前估計有 300 多座，是世界上坑道最密集的島嶼。目前因兩岸趨於和平（但中國仍不放棄武力威脅台灣），陸續開放民間營運，發展為民宿或藝文空間。到了馬祖記得一定要到坑道或碉堡走走，有的碉堡內有著如螞蟻窩一樣的地下坑道，從山坡綿延而下直到海岸，沿途充滿驚奇。

風火山牆

馬祖共有 60 多座大小廟宇，其最大的建築特色為「封火山牆（風乃轉字）」，因建築體的左右側像著中文「山」的古字而得名，而高過屋頂的牆頭能夠防風、防火，因此稱為封（風）火。馬祖廟宇另外一個有趣的地方是充滿野趣的壁畫，馬祖因為戰時進行嚴格管制，廟宇新建、修復與上色等多由島民與駐軍共創而成，風格不若台灣本島廟宇精細，但在用色上更為多采多姿，產生接近漫畫、塗鴉的粗獷美感，是馬祖特殊歷史下的珍貴產物。

SPOTLIGHT ON THE COMMUNITY, ARTS, AND CULTURAL SCENES IN MATSU

CULTURAL SCENES

馬祖社區、藝文現場直擊

SPECIAL FEATURE
MATSU
馬祖特輯
SPECIAL FEATURE

After the dismissal of the army and the lifting of martial law, community builders have collaborated with local culture and history workers, devoting themselves to converting the deserted military facilities into coffee shops, bookstores, guesthouses, military heritage museums, and so on. Moreover, the once-decaying Mindong-style villages have now been repaired and are on the path to re-defining themselves. The following are two worth-exploring community and arts projects, presenting you with ever-changing archipelago scenes.

Self-empowered community building: Good Matsu

Hosted by the Department of Economic Development of Lienchiang County, Good Matsu is a community worker coaching program. Aimed at making the islands better, local communities and teams are encouraged to propose space revitalization or other creative plans through annual open calls. Funds and related resources are provided for those who are approved to implement their ideas. Successful examples include edible gardens transformed from unused corners and space sharing projects, just to name a few. Related events are held on an unfixed schedule which include inviting foreign lecturers to Matsu to share their community-building experiences. (facebook.com/goodmatsu)

Exchange for life in Matsu: Dapu Plus

After being assigned as a cultural heritage village by the Bureau of Cultural Heritage of the Ministry of Culture, the Dapu village on Dongju island has received support from the government to repair its old houses. Furthermore, through community artist-in-residence and chef-in-residence programs organized by the government, some former residents eventually moved back to settle here, bringing new life into old houses. Numerous professionals and adventurers visit Dapu every year like migratory birds, gradually forming a community-building underground brand (facebook.com/dapuplus). If you are willing to rough it, are able to arrange more than 10 days off, enjoy cooking, dining, and participating in community events with groups of people, come to Dapu and experience a different way of life. (by Yung-Han Chen)

近幾年，許多荒廢軍事據點被改造成咖啡店、書店、民宿、軍事遺產博物館等空間；一度凋敝的閩東式建築聚落，則在修繕完畢後，重新定義自己的存在價值。以下介紹兩個值得認識的社區與藝文計畫，看見正在轉變中的列島風景。

自己的社區自己經營——島上好

「島上好」是由連江縣政府產業發展處主辦的社區規劃師輔導計畫，每年透過徵選，讓島上社區及團隊提出空間改造或其他創意計畫，通過的提案將獲得相關資源與補助，實現理想中的內容，一起讓島上更好！過去「島上好」有將社區畸零地改造成共享空間的成功案例，也不定期舉辦相關活動，邀請國內外講者到馬祖，與大家分享地方創生的相關經驗。（facebook.com/goodmatsu）

我在馬祖「以 X 換生活」——大浦 Plus+

位於東莒島上的大浦聚落被指定為文化資產保存聚落後，由官方修繕老屋，徵求團隊辦理藝術家進駐、主廚駐村等社區活動後，漸漸吸引居民回流，老屋重獲新生。

眾多專業工作者和換生活體驗者，如同候鳥般年年過境大浦聚落，逐漸建立起一個小眾的社區營造地下品牌。愛之者迷戀小島的自然風光和傳統樣貌、念念不忘於換生活期間的單純人際關係，即便帶著曬痕和蚊子咬疤離開，這群人多年後仍然透過社群媒體等媒介，持續關心島上發生的大小事件，讓大浦成了一處外來旅客與本地居民相互刺激的風土交流平台。（facebook.com/dapuplus）

如果不排斥撥出 10 天以上的時間，每天與一群人共同煮食、參與社區活動，歡迎來申請大浦換生活。戲仿海明威的名言——如果你有幸待過大浦，未來不管身在何處，大浦將永遠跟隨著你。（文／陳泳翰）

YOU MAY JUST CRY IF YOU MISS THE BLUE TEARS

BLUE TEARS

沒追到會流眼淚的藍眼淚

SPECIAL FEATURE
MATSU
馬祖特輯
SPECIAL FEATURE

The dreamlike blue color that glows on the surface of the seas around Matsu in spring and summer is rarely seen anywhere in the world. It has a beautiful name: the Blue Tears. People who visit Matsu especially for the experience of the Blue Tears are called "tear chasers." Blue Tears is actually bioluminescence emitted by Noctiluca scintillans, a kind of marine plankton. While observing Blue Tears first-hand requires an element of luck, for many years, a large number of tear-chasing forerunners and specialists have accumulated a wealth of in-the-field experience which I will now share with everyone.

Tear chasing times:

The approximate time period when the Matsu Blue Tears phenomenon occurs begins in March and continues until September each year. Many people agree that the best time to view the phenomenon is from May to June, while some locals maintain that the Blue Tears are in full bloom during July and August. It is worth noting, though, that heavy fog around the time of the Dragon Boat Festival causes frequent groundings of commercial flight, and summer holidays are the peak travel season. As such, September may well be the most comfortable choice for a tear-chasing flight.

每年春夏之際在馬祖海面上閃爍的夢幻藍光，是世界少有的風景，它有個美麗的名字「藍眼淚」，而專程為藍眼淚而來的人們，則被稱為「追淚」團。藍眼淚其實是夜光蟲所發出的生物光，雖然要看到藍眼淚需要一點緣分與運氣，不過多年來已有許多追淚前輩與在地專家們累積了許多實戰經驗，在此與大家分享。

追淚時間：

馬祖藍眼淚的淚期，大約從 3 月開始延續到 9 月，有人說最佳觀賞時機是 5、6 月，但也有當地人認為 7、8 月才是藍眼淚爆發期，不過由於端午節前後容易碰到濃霧停飛，暑假又正值旅遊旺季，能舒服搭飛機前往的 9 月也是不錯的選擇。

Regarding accommodations:

During tear-chasing peak season, it is advisable to seek accommodations in a hostel. You can exchange information with the people you meet around because eight or nine out of ten camera-toting travelers will be there to chase the Blue Tears. Furthermore, various accommodations owners purportedly have a chat group on the LINE app exclusively for sharing information about the status of Blue Tears around each of the various islands, making it convenient for travelers, upon checking in, to discern exactly which island (s) currently have the greatest Blue Tears blooms. I strongly suggest that you check with the owner/operator of your guesthouse for the most up-to-date Blue Tears information.

Photography tips:

1. Camera equipment must have manual shutter settings which allow shutter to be held open at length

2. A sufficiently stable camera stand is required

3. Wide angle or telephoto lense is recommended, with the largest aperture possible (recommended settings, to be adjusted according to circumstances: ISO value 1600 to 6400, aperture focal ratio 2.8 to 4, shutter exposure 15 to 30 seconds, color temperature approximately 2500 to 3500K)

Recommended observation and photography spots:

For first-time tear chasers, it is recommended to go to the Beihai Tunnel as the odds are very good that Blue Tears will be visible from this vantage point. If you choose an outdoor observation spot such as along the coast or at a military stronghold, street lamps are rare to non-existent, making them ideal for photography. Also, remember to avoid the moonlight, especially during a full moon. Good luck, tear chasers!

Beaches:

Tanghoudao Beach on Beigan island
Fuzheng Beach on Dongju island
Kunqiu Beach on Xiju island

Harbors:

Fuao Harbor on Nangan island
Meng'ao Harbor on Dingju island

High points along the coasts:

Dahan Stronghold on Nangan island
Caipuao on Xiju island
Mysterious Little Bay on Dongju island

關於住宿：

追淚的高峰時間可選擇入住背包客棧，看到其他帶攝影機來的旅客，十之八九也是來追淚的旅人，可以互相交換資訊。另外據說民宿業者有個 LINE 群，在追淚期間像是情報中心一樣交換各島淚況，方便知道當天「藍眼淚大爆發」的島，提供給入住旅客，建議大家多與民宿老闆詢問最新淚況。

關於攝影：

1. 相機需能調整手動快門，可長時間曝光

2. 穩定度夠高的腳架

3. 鏡頭建議使用廣角或是望遠鏡頭，光圈越大越好（建議數值，ISO:1600-6400，光圈：2.8-4，曝光時間 15-30 秒，適情況調整，色溫約 2500-3500K）

建議觀賞與拍攝點：

初次追淚的人，建議到賞淚機率極高的「北海坑道」。若到戶外景點如海岸邊、軍事據點等，幾乎都沒有路燈，相當適合拍攝。另外記得避開月光，尤其滿月時間。祝大家追淚成功！

沙灘：

北竿塘后道沙灘
東莒福正沙灘
西莒坤坵沙灘

港邊：

南竿福澳港
東莒猛澳碼頭

海岸高處：

南竿大漢據點
西莒菜埔澳
東莒神祕小海灣

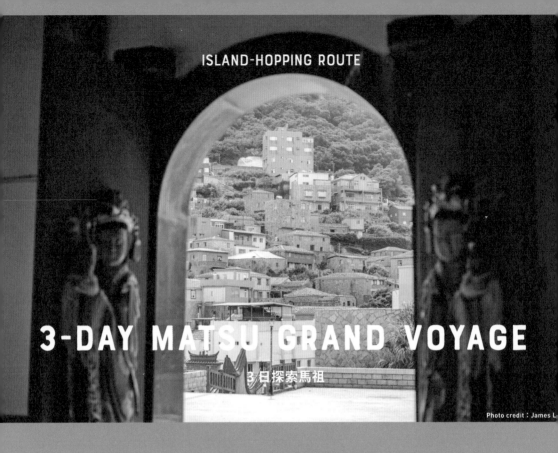

3-DAY MATSU GRAND VOYAGE

3 日探索馬祖

Photo credit：James L.

Matsu, an archipelago about 200 kilometers from Taiwan's main island, blends rich cultural history with pure natural beauty. Once a pirate haven and a battleground during the Chinese Civil War, Matsu is now the best place to witness the magical Blue Tears phenomenon in spring and summer, reminiscent of the romantic scenes from *Life of Pi*. Here is a carefully planned three-day island-hopping tour that will allow you to immerse yourself in the daily life of Matsu. Best of luck in experiencing the most stunning blue of your life.

Day 1: The History and Charm of Nangan

Depart from Keelung in the evening and take an overnight ferry to Matsu, arriving in the morning. Upon arrival, head to "A-Mei's Shop" in the Lion Market to enjoy a local breakfast of seafood soup-based Ding Bian Hu, pumpkin rice noodles, and Dumplings, experiencing the warmth of Matsu's hospitality. To understand Matsu's history and culture, including the migration from Fujian in the Qing Dynasty, the Japanese rule, the Cold War period, and modern life, start by praying for a safe journey with Matsu's guardian deity, Mazu. Visit the "Matsu Temple," which houses Mazu's sacred relics and tomb. Then, hike up to the giant Mazu statue for a panoramic sea view.

馬祖，這片距離台灣本島約 200 公里的島嶼群落，融合了豐富的人文歷史與純粹的自然美景。這裡曾是海盜的樂園，也曾面對國共砲戰，春夏更是藍眼淚奇景的最佳觀賞地，宛如《少年 Pi 的奇幻漂流》中的浪漫場景。以下是精心規劃的 3 天跳島之旅，讓你深入體驗馬祖的日常生活，祝你幸運，遇見此生絕美的藍。

Day 1：南竿風情

晚上從基隆出發，乘坐夜航船，早晨抵達馬祖。到港後，在獅子市場的「阿妹的店」享用海味湯底鼎邊糊、南瓜米粉及燕餃，感受馬祖人的情感。想了解馬祖的歷史與風土民情，包括清朝閩東移居、日治時代、冷戰時期及現代生活，就先從跟馬祖守護神媽祖祈求旅途平安開始吧！「馬祖境天后宮」有媽祖靈穴與衣冠塚，接著爬山前往媽祖巨神像俯瞰海景。

After descending, head to Magang Street to buy Jiguang buns for a quick energy boost. Then, take a leisurely stroll through the alleys of Jingsha Village, Nangan's largest fishing village, to soak in the historical atmosphere from the wartime period. Jingsha is famous for its spring water-brewed wine, for lunch, try the old wine noodles and red yeast dishes. In the afternoon, visit "Thorn Bird Coffee," founded by a former cultural director, to enjoy a no-menu meal and stunning views. Relax with a book, gaze at the sea, and sip your coffee.

Day 2: Exploring Dongju

Matsu's mornings are especially pleasant. Start the day with a walk through Renai Village, tasting the egg buns from Fuxing Buns. The western side of Tiebao has minimal light pollution, making it an excellent spot for observing the Blue Tears phenomenon. To learn about Matsu's modern history, including the impacts of the Cold War, "Shengli (Victory) Fort" serves as an ideal point of interest.

Catch the 11:00 AM ferry from Fuao Harbor to Dongju, with the journey taking about an hour. In Daping Village, grab a giant chicken cutlet from "Maple Snacks" or "Huamei Chicken Cutlet" to get a taste of military life. Dongju, once dwindling due to the decline in fishing, has been revitalized by the art residency program. Visit the "Dongquan Lighthouse" and admire the beautiful white windbreak walls.

In the evening, return to Nangan before transferring to Beigan to savor the famous local aged liquor noodles. For a late-night meal, head to Zhongyu Original Taste in Tangqi Village where you can enjoy barbecue, hot pot, and fried foods paired with various types of liquor, including the locally favored Dongyong sorghum liquor, often enjoyed until midnight.

Day 3: Exploring Beigan

Start your morning by admiring the scenery of Qinbi Mountain and experiencing the charm of traditional stone houses. Wander the Qinbi Trail to overlook the entire hill town. Bread enthusiasts shouldn't miss "Qinwo Bakery," where you can enjoy bread made by the renowned teacher Zeng Meizi.

Next, take a boat to Daqiu Island to watch the Sika deer. Upon returning to Qiaozi Village, grab a "Chongdi Cake" to satisfy your hunger before visiting Banli Beach and the smallest Mazu temple in Taiwan.

Then, board a ferry to Nangan to explore the "Beihai Tunnel," a tunnel carved into granite extending 640 meters with a waterway inside. During the Blue Tears season, the tunnel offers rowing tours to observe this natural phenomenon. In the evening, dine at "Xia-Liao Dining Hall" in Niu Jiao Village, the only place on the island that serves draft beer. Enjoy Matsu's village delicacies like clams, fried fish, and red yeast rice, paired with draft beer to end your night fully satisfied before heading home the next morning! (by Cheng-Tao Lee)

下山後，到馬港街上買繼光餅補充體力。接著漫步南竿第一大漁村「津沙聚落」的巷弄，感受抗戰期間的歷史氛圍。津沙以泉水釀酒聞名，午餐推薦老酒麵線與紅糖料理。下午可前往由前文化局長創立的「刺鳥咖啡」，享受無菜單料理與美景、一邊看書、一邊看海、一邊喝咖啡。

Day 2：探索東莒

馬祖的早晨特別舒服，早起可在仁愛村散步，品嚐「福興包子」的蛋餅。西邊的「鐵堡」光害極低，是觀賞藍眼淚的好地方。想了解馬祖的近代歷史，包括冷戰時期的影響，「勝利堡」是最佳據點。

在福澳港搭乘 11:00 的船班前往東莒，航程約 1 小時。到大坪村「楓樹林小吃」或「華美雞排」享用巨大雞排，感受軍人生活。東莒曾因漁業蕭條而人口外流，現已因藝術駐村計畫而重生。參觀「東犬燈塔」，欣賞白色防風牆的美景。

傍晚返回南竿，轉船前往北竿，享用當地有名的老酒麵線。消夜可在塘岐村的「忠漁原味」可以享用炭烤、火鍋、炸物等消夜，搭配各種酒類，尤其推薦本地的東湧高粱，喝到半夜 12 點也是常事。

Day 3：探索北竿

早晨欣賞芹壁山的風景，感受傳統石屋的魅力。漫步芹壁步道，俯瞰整個山城。麵包愛好者不可錯過「芹沃咖啡烘焙館」，品嚐曾美子老師的麵包。

接著搭船前往大坵島，觀賞梅花鹿。回到橋仔村後，買個「虫弟餅」止飢，再參觀阪里沙灘與全台灣最小的媽祖廟。

接著搭船前往南竿，探索「北海坑道」。這座坑道深入花崗岩，內有 640 公尺長的水道。在藍眼淚季節，坑道提供搖櫓觀淚行程。晚上前往牛角聚落的「蝦寮食堂」享用晚餐，這裡是全島唯一有生啤酒的店家。品嚐馬祖漁村的美食，如淡菜、煎魚、紅糖炒飯，搭配生啤酒，吃飽飽喝飽飽，明天早上就要回家囉！（文／李政道）

PRODUCTION TEAM
製作團隊

要用一本書完整介紹全台灣實屬不易，本書依賴許多在地專家與友人的協助才得以完成，
以下是團隊成員簡介，再次衷心感謝他們的強力支援。

It's not an easy task to deliver a comprehensive introduction to Taiwan in one book. Thanks to all the friends and knowledgeable locals who contributed to this project. The completion of this guide was possible only because of them. The following is a brief introduction of our team. Again, I offer my sincere thanks for their unwavering support.

編輯團隊 Editing

作者、主編：郭佩怜 | Author, Editor in chief: Pei-Ling Guo

台中人，現居台北，目前從事編輯、企劃與廣告製片，希望透過《台北挑剔指南》與《台灣挑剔指南》讓更多人認識台灣。

Born in Taichung and currently based in Taipei. Working as an editor, marketing planner, and TVC producer. Hoping more people can come to know about Taiwan through *Good Eye City Guide: Taipei* and *Good Eye City Guide: Taiwan*.

副主編：黃筱涵 | Deputy Editor in chief: Hsiao-Han Huang

小時想當作家，長大成為編輯。做著理性的事，承載感性的靈魂。始終以文字作為一種生命形式。

Had a dream to become a writer when little, now working as an editor. Burdened with a sensible soul and a rational manner. Words have always been my way of life.

校對：簡淑媛 | Proofreader: Shu-Yuan Chien

10 年以上資深編輯，但更樂於接抓別人錯的校對家。喜歡登山運動的中年宅女，上台北如進城，仰賴網路及快遞自由接稿。

Senior editor for over 10 years, but prefer proofreading projects where I can pick out other people's mistakes. As a middle-aged homebody who likes to get my exercise hiking in the mountains, visiting Taipei always feels like a journey to the big city. Freelance worker with a dependence upon the internet and express delivery.

編輯助理 Assistant Editors

- 鐘嘉瑜 Zhong Jia-Yu

1996 年的天蠍座。畢業於淡江大學中文系，曾任時報出版社實習生。

A Scorpio born in 1996 and a graduate of the Department of Chinese Literature at Tamkang University. Worked as an intern at China Times Publishing Company.

- 翁于庭 Yu-Ting Weng

自由影像 / 文字工作者。經營個人 IG 專頁 Portable Romance，持續書寫短小而利於攜帶閱讀的旅行見聞與愛情故事。

Freelance art director and writer who keeps writing traveling experience and love stories that are short and easy to read. Instagram page "Portable Romance" (location_stories).

- 潘彥捷 Benedict Pan

有信仰的人，對各種美的事物感到好奇。想窮極一生造訪世界上各個角落，探索眾人的日常。

A person of faith, who's curious about beautiful things. Wants to spend the entire life visiting every corner of the world and exploring people's daily lives.

- 周鈺珊 Yu-Shan, Chou

寫字的人。曾參與新文化運動紀念館《掛號二》製作、2019 台北市觀傳局旅遊手冊、報導者〈愛最大，同婚上路〉故事採寫。

A writer. Worked on Taiwan New Cultural Movement Memorial Museum's publication *Call For New Vol.2*, 2019 travel brochure of Taipei City Government's Department of Information and Tourism, and The Reporter's "Same-Sex Marriage Story."

翻譯團隊 Translation

Bacon Translations

翻譯工作室（中英翻譯），譯者季芮彤，編輯 Adam Blackbourn

Translation studio (Chinese to English and vice versa) consisting of translator Jacqueline Ruei Chi and editor Adam Blackbourn.

陳敬淳 Chin-Chun (Kate) Chen

國立台北大學應用外語系畢業，曾任藝術專案及出版社編輯。現居加拿大，擔任翻譯及編輯工作者。

Graduate of the Department of Foreign Languages and Applied Linguistics of National Taipei University. Former art project coordinator and book editor. Currently working as a freelance translator and editor based in Ontario, Canada.

mushroomkate@gmail.com

莊森 Neil Swanson

16 年在台翻譯和教學經驗，並取得國立台灣師範大學華語文教學學位。近年搬回加拿大享受湖與森林的懷抱。

Worked as a translator, interpreter, and instructor in Taiwan for 16 years. Earned a Bachelor from the Department of Chinese as a Second Language of National Taiwan Normal University. Currently based in Ontario, Canada.

swanson.neil@gmail.com

李育萱 Yu-Hsuan Lee, Markku Väisänen

用各種可行的方式，串連世界。

We are the Bridge Builder! (facebook.com/wearebridgebuilder)

陳子萱 Emily Tzu-Hsuan Chen

曾於雲門舞集與國藝會擔任藝術行政，現為自由文字工作者，從事文案寫作與翻譯。

Formerly an arts administrator worked with Cloud Gate Dance Theater Company and National Culture and Arts Foundation, now working as a freelance writer and translator.

tzuhsuanchen@gmail.com

設計團隊 Design

封面設計、內頁設計：平面室 | Graphic Design: graphic room

平面室集結經驗豐富、風格不同的設計師，以各種排列組合進行團隊設計合作，以滿足多樣化的客戶需求。

Pairing experienced in-house designers with different styles for project collaborations that satisfy various clients' needs.

info@graphicroom.co

插畫：陳宛昀 | Illustration: Wan-Yun Chen

插畫家，和家人、四隻貓及一隻狗生活在熱情高雄。

Illustrator living with family, four cats, and a dog in cordial Kaohsiung City.

WebApp: 黃欣迪 Dean Huang

半路出家的網站工程師。熱愛籃球和旅遊！

Self-taught web engineer who loves traveling and whose favorite sport is basketball!

排版（中部、南部）：黃雅藍 | Layout (Central and Southern Taiwan): Ya-Lan Huang

在排版公司工作 12 年後自行創業。感謝時報出版長期合作，與許多編輯同仁共創書籍製程，完成精美成品！

Self-employed after 12 years of in-house experience in a layout company. Thanks to a long-term partnership with China Times Publishing Co., I've had the pleasure to complete a number of fascinating books with many editor friends!

Line：yalan813

攝影團隊 Photography

Cat and Mouse Productions

影視創作公司，致力提供全球影視人才交流與全球影視製作服務，以充滿活力的創意與精準的專業執行，為全球客戶打造訂製專屬影像作品，合作客戶有 Google、Riot Games、Netflix、LVMH、New York Times 等國際品牌。(攝影師 - Ivan Hsu)

Video production company devoted to exchange between video professionals and to video production services around the globe. Execution characterized by vibrant creativity and precision, we customize our exclusive video projects for each client. Clients include Google, Riot Games, Netflix, LVMH, New York Times, and more. (Photographer - Ivan Hsu)

文字團隊 Content Contributors

北台灣 Northern Taiwan

基隆、花蓮：高韻涵 | Keelung and Hualien: Yun-Han Kao

來自基隆，在乎日常生活感，熱愛原住民文化，時常藏匿於東部山海的各個角落；蘭嶼得瓦拉甜點餐車共同創辦人，目前為藝術領域自由工作者。

Born in Keelung. Attentive to the quality of quotidian life and passionate about indigenous culture, often hiding in the mountains or by the sea in eastern Taiwan. Co-founder of the Terwara pastry truck. Currently working as a freelance artist.

基隆（特輯 p.32）：何昱泓 | Keelung (Special Feature p.32): Imobert Ho

故事 Storystudio 社群經理，俗稱故事小編。2012 創立冷知識平台每日一冷，興趣是和讀者吵架。

Social Media Manager for Storystudio, a.k.a. Gushi Xiaobian. Founded FB page Daily Trivia in 2012. Arguing with readers is his greatest interest.

新竹（路線與特輯）：見域工作室 | Hsinchu (Route and Special Feature): Citilens Studio

常駐於新竹舊城街區。獨立發行《貢丸湯》雜誌，經營「域室 CitiSelect」城市選物空間，以不同主題發展新竹的文化載體。

Based in the old-town area of Hsinchu. Publishing independent magazine *Pork Ball Soup* (literally means pork ball soup) and operating CitiSelect select shop, expanding the cultural reach of Hsinchu through differing topics.

facebook.com/CitiLens

桃園（特輯）：楊孟珣 | Taoyuan (Special Feature): Vivian Yang

英國倫敦大學國王學院文化、媒體與創意產業碩士，曾任《The Big Issue Taiwan 大誌雜誌》編輯，熱愛文字與旅行。

Graduated from King's College London with a master's degree in Culture, Media and Creative Industries. Former editor of *The Big Issue Taiwan* who loves writing and traveling.

中台灣 Central Taiwan

苗栗（簡介與特輯）：黃宣庭 | Miaoli (Introduction and Special Feature): Ting-Huang Hsuan

嗨我是宣庭也是小八，專注在生態建築與工藝設計上，喜歡各種材質實驗。來自南庄山上，熱愛山與海，相信一切源頭始於自然。

Hi, I'm Hsuan Ting Huang from the Nanzhuang Township of Miaoli. People also call me Hachi. Focused on environmental architecture and industrial design, enjoy experimenting with different materials. I love the mountains and the sea, and believe nature is the origin of everything.

台中（路線企劃）：張喬茵 | Taichung (Route)- Chiao-Yin Chang

2011 年回到喜歡的城市 - 台中，開始旅人之森，重新認識這個地方也提供旅人們體驗這個城市的另一種方式。

Relocating to my beloved city of Taichung in 2011, started operating Ryokoushanmori guesthouse to rediscover the city and offer travelers the chance to experience it from a different perspective.

facebook.com/ryokoushanomori

台中（特輯 p.30）：薑薑 | Taichung (Special Feature p.30): Giang Giang

台中大甲人，台灣獨立樂團拍謝少年貝斯手，喜歡熱炒與啤酒，深信只要有音樂與美食，日子不會太糟。

From Dajia District of Taichung City, bass player of the Taiwanese indie band Sorry Youth with an appetite for quick stir-fry and beer, I deeply believe that so long as there is music and good food, every day is a good day.

彰化：張翰豪 | Chunghua: Han-Hao Chang

文學研究出身，避免思考迴路封閉，離開學院後做過畫廊、媒體行銷與廣告專案經理。現在則是白天上菜市場，晚上賣燒烤。

Studied literature. In order to encourage thinking outside the box, after leaving academia, worked in a gallery, in media marketing, and as an advertisement project manager. Now visiting traditional markets during the day and selling grilled food at night.

雲林（南投、宜蘭、新北平溪特輯）：李佳芳 | Yunlin (Nantou, Yilan and Special feature of New Taipei City): Chia-Fang Li

主持 ESPRES:SO 如此表達工作室。長年從事編輯寫手工作，雜誌網媒的隱形協力俠，喜歡鑽進台灣鄉下找題目。

Hosting ESPRES:SO studio. Long-time editor and writer, invisible helping hand for multiple magazines and online media organizations, enjoying visiting the Taiwanese countryside to discover new topics.

南台灣 Southern Taiwan

嘉義：孫育晴 | Chiayi: Joanna Sun

來自台北永和，現任嘉義文化創意產業園區執行長。因為工作關係成為嘉義異鄉人，遊走於生活／旅行／工作間，感受嘉義特有的溫潤及活力。

From Yonghe District of New Taipei City. CEO of G9 Creative Park in Chiayi. Moved to Chiayi for work, now an outsider experiencing the uniquely warm vibe of Chiayi through life, travel, and work.

嘉義異鄉人 facebook.com/outsiderinchiayi

台南：黃蓉 | Tainan: Jung Huang

行銷企劃，黃藥師的女兒。生於台北，但上輩子應該是台南人。工作差旅台南 3 年，最喜歡這座古城的生活優雅。

Marketing planner. Pharmacist's daughter. Born in Taipei, but likely a Tainan local in a past life. Traveling to Tainan for work for the past three years, loving the elegant life of this old town.

高雄 Kaohsiung | Trista and Nato

高雄人，喜歡旅行、世界。2010 年回鄉創立「chez kiki hostel」和「去去高雄」。目前以「旅人與高雄的橋梁」為目標，在美麗島經營著「鶴宮寓」和「毊時間」。

Kaohsiung locals who enjoy traveling and love the Earth. Returned to Kaohsiung in 2010 to found "chez kiki" hostel and "chill chill Kaohsiung project." Current goal is to be a bridge between travelers and the city of Kaohsiung, operating the "hók house" guesthouse and the multi-function space "goöod time" near Formosa Boulevard Metro Station.

facebook.com/hokhouse.tw

屏東：黃銘彰 | Pingtung: Ming-Chang Huang

自由編輯／文字工作者。畢業於台灣大學法律學系，曾任《The Big Issue Taiwan 大誌》主編。編有《本地 The Place 03：屏東》、《在路上 On the Road：龍潭、關西、橫山、竹東、北埔、峨眉、獅潭、大湖、東勢》。

合作請洽：brian.mingzhanghuang@gmail.com

Freelance editor and writer. Graduated from the College of Law of National Taiwan University. Former editor in chief of The Big Issue Taiwan. Other editorial works include The Place 03: Pingtung and On the Road: Longtan, Guanxi, Hengshan, Zhudong, Beipu, Emei, Shitan, Dahu, and Dongshi.

For collaboration, please contact ——
brian.mingzhanghuang@gmail.com

東台灣 Eastern Taiwan
———

台東：劉玟苓 | Taitung: Wen Liu

自由工作者，曾創辦《台味誌》，參與企劃多本刊物。人生目標是持續挖掘台灣的好讓更多人知道。

合作請洽：Wenlingliu.wen@gmail.com

Freelancer. Co-founder of the *Tai-Way* magazine, participated in the planning of multiple magazines. Life goal: to continue discovering the wonder of Taiwan and helping to spread the word. For collaboration, please contact Wenlingliu.wen@gmail.com

花蓮、台東（特輯）：林苡秀 | Hualien, Taitung (Special Feature): Jolin Lin

歷經廣告、新創與自僱者職涯，目前人生的主要元素：芳療、策展、行銷與文字。情緒權威投射者，歡迎充滿創意與愛的邀請。

合作請洽：welcometoworld1111@gmail.com

Worked through a career in advertising, entrepreneurship, and self-employment. Current major elements of her life include aromatherapy, exhibition curating, marketing and writing. A Projector of Emotional Authority who welcomes creative and loving invitations. For collaboration, please contact welcometoworld1111@gmail.com

旅遊基本資訊 Basic information
———

科技：邱懷萱 | Technology: Elisa Chiu

Anchor Taiwan 創辦人兼執行長，從華爾街世界回家的女性投資人，致力於科技與文化的「新創外交」。

Founder and cultural alchemist at Anchor Taiwan. Wall Street refugee turned entrepreneur and ecosystem builder. A Dancing Soul.

文學：陳育律 | Literature: Hank Chen

在台北讀政治，在東京學新聞，在倫敦做文化研究。以字為業，從事寫作、翻譯及編劇，曾獲文學獎若干。

Studied politics in Taiwan, journalism in Tokyo, and culture in London. Producing words as a career, working on projects including creative writing, translating, and screenwriting. Winner of multiple literature awards.

離島 Offshore islands

澎湖：陳亦琳 | Penghu: Yi-Lin Chen

台灣深度旅行團隊「歐北來」共同創辦人，一起出版《人生至少歐北來一次，這個島嶼教我的事》，喜歡把美好的人事物湊在一起讓他們發光。

Co-founder of OBL Taiwan, an in-depth guided tour group. Co-writer of *Mess up once in Your Lifetime: Things That This Island Had Taught Me*. Enjoy connecting wonderful people and things and making them shine together.

金門（企劃協力與特輯）：王廷頎 | Kinmen (Planning Assistance and Special Feature): Ting-Chi Wang

戒嚴後期出生的金門人，英美文學和博物館學背景，旅美數年後返鄉成立「敬土豆文化工作室」重新認識自己的家鄉。

Born in Kinmen during the later martial laws period. Studied English literature and museology. Returned to Kinmen and founded the Local Methodology cultural studio after living in the United States for several years.

馬祖（企劃協力與特輯）：李政道 | Matsu (Planning and Special Feature): Cheng-Tao Lee

創辦西城 Taipei West Town，態度偏執的詮釋隱身台北巷弄的老味道。希望讀者迷途都會閒之餘，如內行人般走進台北日常。

Founder of Taipei West Town, an online magazine with a meticulous attitude towards interpreting the old souls hidden down the alleyways of Taipei, hoping to bring readers along on a walk through the everyday scenes of Taipei whilst getting lost in the metropolis.

Google search：西城 Taipei West Town | FB：Chengtao Lee

馬祖（特輯）：陳泳翰 | Matsu (Special Feature): Yung-Han Chen

跨領域寫作者，對產業史和離島兩個主題沒有抵抗力，有時會在社區辦點活動，交到的朋友比賺到的錢還要多。

Cross-discipline writer. Cannot resist topics related to Taiwan's industrial history and offshore islands. Sporadically hosting community events and making more friends than money.

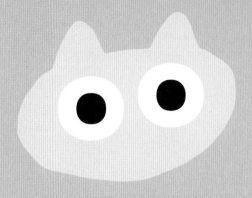

GOOD EYE 台灣挑剔指南：第一本讓世界認識台灣的中英文風格
旅遊書 = GOOD EYE CITY guide: Taiwan / 郭佩怜 等著.
-- 二版 . -- 臺北市：時報文化出版企業股份有限公司, 2024.06
328 面；16.5×23 公分 . --（Hello Design 叢書；HD00081）中英對照
ISBN 978-626-396-420-4（平裝）

1.CST: 旅遊 2.CST: 旅遊地圖 3.CST: 臺灣

733.6   113008095

Hello Design 叢書 HD00081

GOOD EYE CITY Guide: Taiwan
GOOD EYE 台灣挑剔指南—————第一本讓世界認識台灣的中英文風格旅遊書

作　　者—郭佩怜 等著
副 主 編—黃筱涵
校　　對—簡淑媛、Bethany Knox Hewson
翻　　譯—培根翻譯、陳敬淳、Neil Swanson、李育萱、Markku Väisänen、陳子萱
插　　畫—陳宛昀
美術設計—平面室 graphic room
Web App—邱慕安、黃欣迪
行銷企劃—鄭家謙
副總編輯—王建偉
董 事 長—趙政岷
出 版 者—時報文化出版企業股份有限公司
　　　　　108019 台北市和平西路三段 240 號 4 樓
　　　　　發行專線—(02) 2306-6842
　　　　　讀者服務專線—0800-231-705 · (02) 2304-7103
　　　　　讀者服務傳真—(02) 2304-6858
　　　　　郵撥—19344724 時報文化出版公司
　　　　　信箱—10899 臺北市華江橋郵局第 99 信箱
　　　　　時報悅讀網—http://www.readingtimes.com.tw
法律顧問—理律法律事務所　陳長文律師、李念祖律師
印　　刷—和楹印刷有限公司
初版一刷—2020 年 02 月 28 日
二版一刷—2024 年 06 月 21 日
定　　價—新台幣 599 元
版權所有　翻印必究（缺頁或破損的書，請寄回更換）
ISBN 978-626-396-420-4
Printed in Taiwan

本書作者獲文化部 107 年度「文化創意產業補助計畫」補助製作部分內容，委託時報文化出版印刷發行。
特別感謝各店家、空間或文化事業及單位提供照片與協助，讓本書得以順利完成。

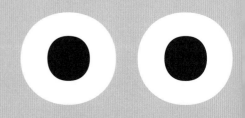